Personality Assessment via Questionnaires

Current Issues in Theory and Measurement

Edited by

A. Angleitner J. S. Wiggins

With 26 Figures and 47 Tables

Springer-Verlag
Berlin Heidelberg New York Tokyo

Professor Dr. ALOIS ANGLEITNER
Department of Psychology, University of Bielefeld
Universitätsstraße, D-4800 Bielefeld 1

Professor Dr. JERRY S. WIGGINS
Department of Psychology, University of British Columbia
2075 Wesbrook Mall, Vancouver, B.C., Canada V6T 1W5

Library of Congress Cataloging in Publication Data. Main entry under title: Personality assessment via questionnaires. Bibliography: p. Includes indexes. 1. Personality questionnaires. 2. Personality assessment. I. Angleitner, A. (Alois) II. Wiggins, Jerry S. BF698.8.P48P47 1985 155.2'83 85-20791
ISBN-13: 978-3-642-70753-7 **e-ISBN-13: 978-3-642-70751-3**
DOI: 10.1007/ 978-3-642-70751-3

Softcover reprint of the hardcover 1st edition 1986

Typesetting: Brühlsche Universitätsdruckerei, Giessen
2126/3130-543210

Table of Contents

List of Contributors

AMELANG, MANFRED, Prof. Dr., Institute of Psychology, University of Heidelberg, Hauptstr. 47–51, D-6900 Heidelberg

ANGLEITNER, ALOIS, Prof. Dr., Department of Psychology, University of Bielefeld, Universitätsstraße, D-4800 Bielefeld 1

BORKENAU, PETER, Dr., Department of Psychology, University of Bielefeld, Universitätsstraße, D-4800 Bielefeld 1

BURISCH, MATTHIAS, Dr., Institute of Psychology, University of Hamburg, von-Melle-Park 5, D-2000 Hamburg 13

DOMMEL, NORBERT, Dipl.-Psych., University of the Federal Armed Forces Hamburg, Holstenweg 85, D-2000 Hamburg 70

FISKE, DONALD W., Prof. Dr., Department of Behavioral Sciences, University of Chicago, 5848 South University Avenue, Chicago, IL 60637, USA

HELFRICH, HEDE, Dr., Institute of Psychology, University of Regensburg, Universitätsstr. 31, D-8400 Regensburg

HOFSTEE, WILLEM K. B., Prof. Dr., Institute of Personality Psychology, University of Groningen, Grote Markt 31–32, NL-9712 HV Groningen

JACKSON, DOUGLAS N., Prof. Dr., Department of Psychology, University of Western Ontario, London, Ontario, Canada N6A 5C2

JOHN, OLIVER P., Dipl.-Psych., Department of Psychology, University of Oregon, Eugene, OR 97403, USA

KASTNER, MICHAEL, Prof. Dr. Dr., University of the Armed Forces Munich, Werner-Heisenberg-Weg 39, D-8014 Neubiberg

LÖHR, FRANZ-JOSEF, Dipl.-Psych., Department of Psychology, University of Bielefeld, Universitätsstraße, D-4800 Bielefeld

PAULHUS, DELROY L., Prof. Dr., Department of Psychology, University of British Columbia, 2075 Wesbrook Mall, Vancouver, B.C., Canada V6T 1W5

RUDINGER, GEORG, Prof. Dr., Insitute of Psychology, University of Bonn, Römerstr. 164, D-5300 Bonn 1

SCHWARZER, RALF, Prof. Dr., Department of Psychology, FB 12 Free University of Berlin, Habelschwerdter Allee 45, D-1000 Berlin 33

SMID, NICO G., Dr., Institute of Personality Psychology, University of Groningen, Grote Markt 31–32, NL-9712 HV Groningen

WIGGINS, JERRY S., Prof. Dr., Department of Psychology, University of British Columbia, 2075 Wesbrook Mall, Vancouver, B.C., Canada V6T 1W5

Introduction

Alois Angleitner and Jerry S. Wiggins

The personality questionnaire has been with us for more than 60 years. It has been, and still is, the most popular method of personality assessment and it no doubt will continue to be so. The method has been sharply criticized since its inception (e.g., Allport, 1921; Watson, 1933; Ellis, 1946; Janke, 1973), and this criticism is also likely to continue. The long-standing indifference of test constructors to criticisms of their craft is brought home by noting the similarities between objections raised many years ago and those that are offered today (Gynther & Green, 1982). Within this context, one might well ask why a book on personality questionnaires should appear at this time.

Despite the centrality of the personality questionnaire to personality assessment, there are, to our knowledge, no recent books on the general topic of personality questionnaires. There are of course books on specific instruments (e.g., Dahlstrom, Welsh & Dahlstrom, 1972, 1975), books on interpretation of specific instruments (e.g., Comrey, 1980), and books on specific issues such as response styles (e.g., Block, 1965). Although not specifically focused on personality questionnaires, Bass and Berg's (1959) *Objective Approaches to Personality Assessment* dealt with a number of issues that are central to questionnaires. As such, the Bass and Berg volume may be appropriately compared with the present one to allow an appreciation of what we consider to be the substantial advances in theory and measurement that have accrued in the last quarter century.

Personality questionnaires are widely used in applied settings to make critically important decisions about human lives, and consequently their proper and ethical use are topics of grave concern. However, the present volume is *not* a "how to do it" or a "whether or not to do it" book. Instead it is a selective treatment of a number of theoretical and methodological issues that have arisen in the context of the construction and evaluation of personality questionnaires over a period of more than half a century. Although these issues are wide ranging and implicate spheres of inquiry well outside the questionnaire domain, we feel they are best understood within the context of their origin. The MMPI is a case in point. Quite aside from its diagnostic utility, or lack of same, the MMPI has been associated in one way or another with most of the contentious theoretical and methodological issues in personality psychometrics during the last 3 decades. To consider these issues independently of their origins is to ignore the often subtle contexts in which they arose.

Realizing a need for a contemporary appraisal of the state of the art of personality questionnaire construction and evaluation, the first author assembled a group of theorists, psychometricians, test constructors, linguists, and personality psychologists and suggested that they relate their own specialized work to issues involving personality questionnaires. The medium for this exchange was the Bielefeld Symposium on Personality Questionnaires held at the Center for Interdisciplinary Research of the University of Bielefeld in June, 1982. The authors who contributed to the present book represent diverse specializations and geographical locations (Canada, Germany, The Netherlands, and the United States). Although many of the authors appear committed to a nomothetic-psychometric-trait approach to personality assessment, there is nevertheless a diversity of opinion regarding the ultimate worth of personality questionnaires. Among the authors are the most prolific constructor of contemporary personality questionnaires (D. N. Jackson) and the most outspoken critic of self-report methods in personality assessment (D. W. Fiske). The contents of this volume may be summarized as responses to nine basic questions that must be answered before personality questionnaires can be properly constructed and evaluated:

- What is measured by personality questionnaires?
- How useful is the concept of "trait" for organizing and focusing measurement operations?
- What kinds of items should be generated for scale construction purposes?
- How should we formulate the process of responding to a personality questionnaire item?
- What kinds of factors influence subjects' comprehension of questionnaire items?
- How should items be combined to yield a total score for each subject?
- What strategy of scale construction should be applied in developing multiscale batteries?
- When and how should we attempt to control for social desirability response tendencies in assessment via personality questionnaires?
- How does one assess, with precision, the convergent and discriminant validity of personality scales?

On one level, these questions resemble those that might appear on a final examination in an undergraduate course in tests and measurements – and indeed they would be quite appropriate for such an examination. In reading the chapters that follow, the reader may be struck by the complexity of answers to what are surely very basic and not very complex questions. The reader may also recognize that most of these questions are very old ones that have not been given a satisfactory answer to date. In our opinion, the present contributors' responses to these questions provide a representative picture of current thought regarding basic issues surrounding the construction and evaluation of personality questionnaires.

The chapters in the present volume have been grouped according to somewhat more global issues: (I) The Trait Concept and Personality Questionnaires; (II) Item Generation and Scale Construction; (III) Models of Item Responding and Self-Presentation; and (IV) Problems of Convergent and Discriminant Validation. Although the variation within these sections is not as wide as that between sections, there may be less of a "main effect" than the reader anticipates. As is true of any well-developed discipline, the concepts and methods of personality assessment are intricately interrelated. Nevertheless, there is a certain logic to the grouping of chapters and to the order in which they appear. The order of the sections reflects the steps involved in test construction and the issues that must be faced at each step. In addition, the chapters are roughly ordered from the more general to the more specific. Nevertheless, the chapters are sufficiently self-contained to accommodate any pattern of browsing.

References

Allport, G.W. (1921). Personality and character. *Psychological Bulletin, 18*, 441–455.

Bass, B.M., & Berg, I.A. (Eds.). (1959). *Objective approaches to personality assessment*. Princeton: Van Nostrand.

Block, J. (1965). *The challenge of response sets*. New York: Appleton-Century-Crofts.

Comrey, A.L. (1980). *Handbook of interpretation for the Comrey Personality Scales*. San Diego: EdITS.

Dahlstrom, W.G., Welsh, G.S. & Dahlstrom, L.E. (1972). *An MMPI handbook. Vol. 1: Clinical interpretation* (rev. ed.) Minneapolis, University of Minnesota Press.

Dahlstrom, W.G., Welsh, G.S. & Dahlstrom, L.E. (1975). *An MMPI handbook. Vol. 2: Research applications* (rev. ed.). Minneapolis, University of Minnesota Press.

Ellis, A. (1946). The validity of personality questionnaires. *Psychological Bulletin, 43*, 385–440.

Gynther, M.D., & Green, S.B. (1982). Methodological problems in research with self-report inventories. In Kendall, P.C., & Butcher, J.N. (Eds.), *A handbook of research methods in clinical psychology* (pp. 355–386). New York: Wiley.

Janke, W. (1973). Über die Konstruktion von Fragebögen. Bericht über ein Symposium: Das Dilemma von Persönlichkeitsfragebögen. In Reinert, G. (Ed.), *Bericht über den 27. Kongreß der Deutschen Gesellschaft für Psychologie in Kiel 1970* (pp. 41–48). Göttingen: Hogrefe.

Watson, G.B. (1933). New steps in personality measurement. *Character and Personality, 2*, 66–73.

I. The Trait Concept and Personality Questionnaires

The Trait Concept: Current Theoretical Considerations, Empirical Facts, and Implications for Personality Inventory Construction *

MANFRED AMELANG and PETER BORKENAU

The book *Personality and Assessment* by Walter Mischel (1968) was very influential in the development of personality research. Whereas several authors had previously studied the situational specificity of behavior and the interaction of persons and situations (e.g., Byrne, 1964; Endler, Hunt, & Rosenstein, 1962; Helson, Blake, Mouton, & Olmstead, 1956), it was Mischel (1968) who most vehemently attacked the fundamental idea of the trait concept on which traditional differential psychology is based. He stated that "while trait theory predicts behavioral consistency, it is behavioral inconsistency that is typically observed" (Mischel, 1968). In his opinion, the consistency of individual behavior assumed by lay persons is illusory; our concepts are biased in this respect. This view seems to be supported by the literature on implicit personality theory (IPT) and the systematic distortion found in correlations between trait measures (D'Andrade, 1974; Schneider, 1973; Shweder, 1975, 1982). Mischel (1968), however, did not only criticize trait theories about personality structure. He stated that the many studies performed and scales constructed so far had produced validity coefficients of only about $r = .30$ – so-called "personality coefficients" – which are undoubtedly significant for large samples of subjects but useless for the prediction of individual behavior. Accordingly, the basis for trait-based psychodiagnostics also seemed to be impaired.

In response to these arguments, crisis management was instituted to reject the systematic distortion hypothesis and to overcome the magic .30 threshold. *First,* a stream of research efforts was directed at demonstrating the cross-situational consistency of personality. *Second,* some authors tried to identify subgroups of people whose behavior could be accurately predicted on the basis of their trait scores. *Third,* some efforts were made to specify situations in which the behavior of persons appeared to be largely determined by their personality. *Some* research was directed at working out criteria that would be appropriate for identification of trait-based differences in behavior. *Finally,* some authors implemented research directed at improvement of the instruments and procedures used to assess personality variables.

In this chapter, we will summarize the findings produced by these five lines of research and discuss their implications for personality inventory construction.

---

* The studies reported were supported by grants from the Deutsche Forschungsgemeinschaft to Manfred Amelang (Az. Am 37/5 and Am 37/7-1).

Implicit Personality Theory and the Semantic Bias Position

Usually, personality traits are identified neither with single behavioral acts nor with the aggregation of all observable behavior. Actually, different behavioral acts observed across time and situations are combined into categories, which may be said to differ in their level of inclusiveness (Hampson, 1982). In an attempt to account for the empirical covariations among single behavioral acts within the categories, traits are inferred as theoretical constructs. In principle, a trait is a disposition to act in a certain way and the covariations between pertinent behavioral acts may be said to indicate the trait. The assumption of traits helps to attain the goal of parsimony in scientific descriptions. Frequently, this assumption substantially reduces the network of relationships between multiple independent and multiple dependent variables (Eysenck & Eysenck, 1980). Moreover, predictions may be more precise and experimental error can be reduced if trait variables are incorporated into the analyses as predictors, moderators, or covariants.

Usually, the view is adopted that single behavioral acts cluster together within a trait category due to individual differences in trait dispositions. Therefore, to establish these dispositions empirically, covariations among observed acts are frequently factor analyzed. The resulting factor patterns are of a purely descriptive nature. If the factors are interpreted as basic dimensions underlying behavior and are given a label, however, connotations are implied that exceed a mere description of the factor-loading matrix (Pawlik, 1973). Moreover, whereas the theory is about covariations among behaviors, the empirical studies are usually based on ratings or questionnaires. The use of ratings based on the memories of subjects or their significant others is usually due to considerations of economy. It is thereby (often implicitly) assumed that subjects give valid descriptions of their own or their acquaintances' behavior.

Covariations among traits and factors derived from them are not only observed if individuals are rated by themselves or their relatives or acquaintances. For example, Passini and Norman (1966) found very similar patterns of correlation when the subjects were rated by strangers. Moreover, when instructed accordingly, subjects expressed hypotheses and beliefs concerning the relationships among traits and among aspects of trait-relevant behavior which were largely in agreement with the results established when real ratees were assessed (Mulaik, 1964). This network of beliefs is commonly referred to as 'Implicit Personality Theory' (IPT), despite some criticism of this term by Wiggins (1973). There is no doubt that IPT plays an important role in shaping our trait attributions about others.

There is some controversy, however, as to whether IPT is acquired on the grounds of observation and experience, and whether it provides an accurate reflection of the real structure of personality with its trait and behavior interrelations. Alternatively, it has been suggested, mainly by Shweder (1982) and D'Andrade (1974), that IPT is due to the semantic similarity structure of the trait-descriptive terms. To investigate the correspondence between IPT and reality, questionnaire items are frequently presented in pairs to subjects who are asked to estimate the probability of endorsement of item B if item A was endorsed. The resulting conditional probabilities are correlated with the empirical co-occurrences for the same item pairs found in a different subject sample. This procedure showed significant agreement in most studies (e.g., Lay, Burron, & Jackson, 1973; Lay & Jackson, 1969; Mirels, 1982a; Stricker, Jacobs, & Kogan, 1976). Mirels (1976), however, reported discrepant results.

While some aspects of measurement and statistical analysis are still a matter of controversy (Jackson, Chan, & Stricker, 1979; Jackson & Stricker, 1982; Mirels, 1982b; Tzeng, 1982; Tzeng & Tzeng, 1982), definite standpoints are taken about the origin of IPT. According to Lay and Jackson (1969) the agreement of IPT with trait co-occurrences "implies that the judge bases his inferential judgement to a great extent upon the relationship among personality traits as he observed them in others" (p. 19). Similarly, Stricker et al. (1974, p. 204) speculate that "the lay theories' communality and validity suggest that the theories reflect people's common exposure to information about the joint occurrence of personality traits rather than their own indiosyncratic inner states." These statements imply the assumption that subjects are sensitive to the actual relationships among traits.

In contrast to these hypotheses, Mirels (1982a, b) refers to the "illusory nature of IPT" and of "inferential illusions." His criticism is based on experiments in which the probability estimates of an endorsement of item A given the endorsement of item B were compared with the conditional probabilities of an endorsement of item B, if item A had been endorsed. Despite the high empirical discrepancies found for some item combinations, the subjects estimated the respective conditional probabilities to be quite similar. "This similarity of estimates very strongly argues that coendorsement judgements are biased, at least in considerable part, by factors other than observed empirical covariation" (Mirels, 1982a, p. 218).

One possible factor could be the semantic similarity relations among trait words. Thus, Shweder (1975, 1977a, 1982) and D'Andrade (1974) performed and reanalyzed some empirical studies to investigate these relationships. The behavior of the subjects was assessed using online as well as memory-based ratings. Moreover, the semantic similarity among the words used was measured via pairwise judgements. For that purpose, scales were used ranging from "identical in meaning" to "completely different in meaning." Usually, the behavior recorded online[1] revealed quite a different pattern of intercorrelations than the internal structure of the memory-based ratings. The pattern of intercorrelations among the rating scales, however, showed a "high correspondence" to the semantic similarity structure of the trait-descriptive terms. Especially illuminating were those cases where the semantic similarity of the trait words contradicted the correlational structure of the online-recorded behaviors. For those cases it was possible to demonstrate that the intercorrelations of the memory-based ratings were much more similar to the semantic similarity structure than the "real behavior structure" (Shweder, 1975).

Shweder and D'Andrade (1980) suggested a 'Systematic Distortion Hypothesis' (SDH) to explain these findings: The internal structure of memory-based judgements is biased towards the semantic similarity structure of the trait words. "Correlations between categories in memory-based ratings reflect the degree to which the categories are similar in meaning rather than reflecting the relationships found in immediately scored behavior" (Shweder & D'Andrade, 1980, p. 47). According to this extreme position "the evidence for the existence of covarying, multibehavior personality traits ... remains dubious" (Shweder & D'Andrade, 1979, p. 1075). "The correlational structure of rated behavior does not parallel the correlational structure of actual behavior" (Shweder, 1982, p. 70).

Rowe (1982), however, reports results that contradict this extreme position, which were obtained in 55 monozygotic twin pairs given 12 items. Not only conventional correlations were computed among different traits for the same person, but also cross-correlations (e.g., trait 1 for twin A with trait 2 for twin B, the two twins belonging to the same pair). His hypothesis was that the cross-correlations would be largely uninfluenced by IPT, since the correlated variables stem from different individuals. The internal structure and the pattern of factor loadings was quite similar for the two solutions, and thus, the major prediction that personality structure does not primarily reflect semantic associativity was supported. Rowe (1982) concluded that: "there may be some degree of bias inherent in 'implicit' personality structure, although it does not seem to greatly distort personality structure" (p. 1072).

Why do the results reported by Shweder and D'Andrade (1980) diverge to such a degree from the findings reported by Rowe (1982)? There are numerous differences between the studies, but the most important discrepancy may be that in the studies referred to by Shweder and D'Andrade the observers were instructed to classify behavior to only one class. Some of the categories provided, however, were very similar, e.g., "disagrees" and "shows antagonism." Retrospective ratings for these categories are highly intercorrelated; D'Andrade (1974) reports a correlation of $r = .75$. This may be due to the condition that many behaviors regarded as indicating one of the two equivalent classes of behaviors are usually seen as indicating the other one also. Thus, the high intercorrelation of the retrospective ratings may result from an implicit overlap of the two behavior categories. The intercorrelation of online-recorded behaviors, however, is low, at $r = .13$ (D'Andrade, 1974). The discrepancy between these two coefficients may indicate that the intercorrelation between the retrospective ratings stems mainly from a covariation of the diagnosticities or prototypicalities of the observed acts with regard to the two behavior classes. The intercorrelation of act frequencies, however, where observers *must* assign a behavior to only one category, may be quite unimportant for the intercorrelation of retrospective ratings.

Rowe (1982), however, administered questionnaires to his twin-subjects containing such items as "I make friends very quickly" and "I am very sociable." There may be many behaviors that foster the endorsement of *both* items and, if extraversion is inherited to a considerable degree (Hewitt, 1984), high cross-correlations may be expected on these grounds. Thus, it may be that "systematic overlap" rather than "systematic distortion" is responsible for the relationships referred to by Shweder and D'Andrade (1980). Borkenau is currently pursuing this hypothesis, and his first results (Borkenau & Angleitner, 1985) are encouraging: Using 500 verbally described acts that had to be rated for their prototypicality with regard to each of five trait categories, it was found that the prototypicality ratings were increasingly closely correlated over acts as two trait-descriptive terms became closer in meaning. The respective rank correlations were $r_s = .90$ for male and $r_s = .72$ for female actors (cf. Buss & Craik, 1980, for the procedure used to obtain prototypicality ratings).

Results on the *validity* of trait ratings also contradict the position that systematic distortion plays a large part in personality ratings. Thus, Passini and Norman (1966) found the factor structure of self-reports to be quite similar to that of ratings by strangers. This result is compatible with the SDH. The level f correlation of self-ratings with parallel ratings given by complete strangers, however, was considerably below the level of correlation among self-ratings and ratings by acquaintances. Thus, it is unlikely that the ratings given by acquaintances are uninfluenced by the ratees' behavior. The significant validities of most personality inventories when assessed against external criteria, and also the agreement of independent raters who all know the rated person, contradict the assumption that observed behavior is unimportant for memory-based ratings (Norman & Goldberg, 1966). In contradiction to this position, McCrae (1982) has argued that "measures that share the same method of observation are subject to the same biases, and the validity coefficients reported represent shared error rather than shared true variance" (p. 294). Intercorrelations of self-ratings, it is maintained, mirror common variance due to defensiveness, extreme responding, or acquiescence, and interrater agreement only reveals common stereotypes which all judges share to a high degree.

These arguments, however, ignore the pattern of covariations between self-reports and peer reports. These correlations seem to be especially high if rater and ratee know each other very well (Norman & Goldberg, 1966). For example, McCrae (1982) administered the Eysenck Personality Inventory to male and female subjects ($n = 261$) and correlated the resulting scores with trait ratings made by the subjects' spouses, finding correlations of $r = .53$ for extraversion and $r = .49$ for neuroticism. Moreover, a multitrait-multimethod analysis revealed some evidence of discriminant validity. These coefficients are of a similar size as those found after aggregating the ratings of several peers (e.g., Amelang & Borkenau, 1982; Burisch, 1978). The higher coefficients reported by McCrae (1982) may reveal a higher degree of mutual knowledge and thus a reduced arbitrariness in the trait ratings.

Self-reports reveal substantial correlations not only with ratings by significant others, but also with self-reported behavior (Buss & Craik, 1980, 1981; Fishbein & Ajzen, 1974; Jaccard, 1974) and online-recorded behaviors (Aries, Gold, & Weigel, 1983; McGowan & Gormly, 1976; Weigel & Newman, 1976) if aggregated behavioral measures are incorporated into the analysis. It is not clear how these results could be explained by IPT or SDH.

The article published by Shweder in 1975 had the provocative title: "How Relevant is an Individual Difference Theory of Personality?" The evidence reviewed here reveals that an individual difference theory of personality is still needed. This does not imply, however, that the systematic distortion hypothesis is completely false. Many studies have demonstrated the influence of IPT (see Schneider, 1973, for a review), and the distortion hypothesis outlined by Shweder (1982) has also found some empirical support (Berman & Kenny, 1976). Thus, personality ratings seem to reflect true behavioral variance to some degree, although their internal structure may be biased toward the semantic similarity structure of trait words.

Implications for Personality Inventory Construction

If semantic similarity structures systematically distort memory-based ratings of observed behavior, some strategies for the construction of personality inventories are tenuous. This is especially true with regard to the expectations of personality researchers who use factor analysis to discover the basic dimensions of personality. The difficulty arises from the fact that the data base consists almost exclusively of questionnaire or rating data which are subject to systematic distortion processes. Thus, the resulting factors could better be interpreted as dimensions of person perception. The most prominent researchers (e.g., Cattell, Eysenck, Guilford), however, accept them as basic personality dimensions and thus equate the structure of the ratings with the structure of the real world. This procedure would only be justifiable if it had been demonstrated that the factors emerging from questionnaire and rating data are identical with those derived from online-recorded behaviors. This, however, does not seem to be the case (Block, 1977).

Thus, in the context of personality inventory construction, the problem as to which traits shall be assessed needs careful consideration. Research efforts within the following realms might become fruitful in this respect:

1. Attempts should be made to refine a psychological taxonomy of trait-descriptive terms (Goldberg, 1981; John, Goldberg, Angleitner, 1984; Wiggins, 1979). These endeavors seem to be promising insofar as the trait-descriptive terms occurring in natural language are arranged into a system, thus providing a starting point for questionnaire construction. If the taxonomy is founded exclusively on memory-based ratings or on the semantic similarity structures inherent in the language, problems similar to those encountered in factor-analytic personality research arise. If the classes are distinguished on psychological rather than purely semantic grounds (Wiggins, 1979), their usefulness must be demonstrated within the domain of objectively recorded behavior.

2. Efforts should be made to develop coding schemes which yield more objective assessments of behavior than memory-based ratings and which also capture the gist of a person's actions. Whereas memory-based ratings seem to be

prone to distortion (Shweder, 1982), unaggregated molecular behavior counts seem to underestimate the consistency of personal behavior (Alker, 1972). The concept of traits as dispositions does not require that relevant observable behaviors be present in every situation, but only on a longitudinal and cross-sectional average (Herrmann, 1973). Moreover, quite different behavioral acts may lead to the attainment of the same goal (Alker, 1972; Bowers, 1973; Lewis, 1967; Magnusson, 1980). If the units of observation are chosen too atomistically, the gist of a person's actions may not be comprehended. A meaningful compromise may be to provide a sample of standardized situations for all ratees and to ask several independent judges to immediately rate their trait positions. The online records of behaviors analyzed by Shweder and D'Andrade are at about this level of abstraction.

3. Paunonen and Jackson (1979) report their endeavor to develop graphic, nonverbal stimulus and response materials in order to "unconfound the use of verbal materials in designating traits from the trait descriptions" (p. 1646). Their subjects were provided with either verbal or graphic, cartoon-like, descriptions of hypothetical characters. Responses also had to be given on verbal and nonverbal materials. The resulting personality descriptions and their factor structures were quite similar regardless of the type of stimulus and response materials used, although some statistically significant differences were observed. The authors conclude "that verbal information is neither necessary nor sufficient to account for major findings regarding the structure of perceived personality relationships" (Paunonen & Jackson, 1979, p. 1658). The authors distinguish between two sorts of cognitive processes, one verbal and the other involving imagery. In the context of our discussion, however, the question arises as to whether the postulated imagery processes are not susceptible to systematic distortion processes which could result from influences of conceptual similarity. A lot of research still needs to be done before we can be sure that nonverbal test materials are superior to the traditional verbal ones.

Restricting Trait Theory to Subgroups of People, Variables, and Situations

The Search for Cross-Situationally Consistent Subjects

In his book *Personality and Assessment,* Mischel (1968) pointed out the strong impact of experimental manipulations on behavior frequently established in the laboratories of experimental psychologists. Mischel argued that these results contradict basic premises of trait psychology. In a rejoinder, Alker (1972) emphasized that experimental studies and personality research usually rely upon different subject samples. Whereas experimental research almost exclusively uses college students as subjects, a great deal of personality research stems from clinical psychologists and psychiatrists who have studied disturbed samples. Alker (1972) claimed that the latter were often rigid and less susceptible to situational variations, and that people differed in their responsiveness to situational features. Thus, some groups ignore situational differences and "exhibit the rigid generalization across situations that Mischel regards as an acceptable instance of convergent validity of a trait concept" (Alker, 1972, p. 14), whereas others are more responsive to the cognitive features of particular tasks and exhibit "a purposively organized, reason-determined choice of different responses as the situation warrants" (Alker, 1972, p. 14).

Alker's arguments implicitly assume a continuous variable of cross-situational variability in behavior. This implies that at the one pole of this dimension there will be individuals who are cross-situationally consistent, whereas individuals at the other pole will exhibit cross-situationally inconsistent or situation-specific behaviors. The predictability of behavior on the basis of conventional personality questionnaires should be better for the former subjects.

Methods of identifying trait-consistent persons have been suggested (Campus, 1974). Snyder (1974, 1979), for example, developed his Self-Monitoring Scale. The behavior of subjects scoring low on this scale is assumed to be less highly situation-specific than that of high-scoring self-monitors (Snyder & Monson, 1975); their behavior will presumably be much more in accordance with their attitudes, whereas subjects scoring high on the scale will show little correspondence between their attitudes and their behavior (Snyder & Tanke, 1976).

A very influential study was performed by Bem and Allen (1974). They devised a direct procedure for identifying situation-specific subjects by asking (with regard to friedliness): "How much do you vary from one situation to another in how friendly and outgoing you are?" Analogous questions were formulated for conscientiousness, assertiveness, honesty, and sensitivity; subjects responded on seven-point rating scales. Bem and Allen (1974) indeed found higher intercorrelations among various trait measures for those subjects who had rated themselves as being cross-situationally consistent with regard to friendliness. Similar results were later reported by Buse (1980), Cheek (1982), Zanna, Olson, and Fazio (1980), Kenrick and Stringfield (1980), and Mischel and Peake (1982).

In an empirical study (see Amelang & Borkenau, 1981), we tried to replicate these findings. We also examined whether self-reported variability ratings for different traits covary substantially, since if this were found to be so cross-situational consistency could be conceptualized as a trait in itself.

We obtained data for a sample of 108 students in introductory psychology classes at the University of Heidelberg. A German version of the Cross Situation Behavior Survey (CSBS) devised by Bem and Allen (1974) was administered to each subject. This questionnaire asks for the subjects' actions in specified situations with regard to five trait dimensions, namely friendliness, conscientiousness, assertiveness, honesty, and sensitivity. Moreover, we asked our subjects to give global self-ratings for these five traits and for additional dimensions (i.e., venturesomeness, aggressiveness, depressiveness, and autonomic lability). Three peers or relatives provided the same set of ratings for each subject. These ratings were used as external criteria to assess the validity of subjects' self-reports.

To replicate Bem and Allen's (1974) central findings, we dichotomized our subject sample according to the responses to the variability items. Subjects below the median were designated cross-situationally consistent and those above the median, cross-situationally variable or inconsistent. These classifications were carried out separately for each of the five traits. Subsequently, the subjects' CSBS scores were correlated separately for consistent and inconsistent subjects with the sum of the three peer ratings for each trait. For none of the traits did the difference between the two correlation coefficients reach the level of statistical significance. Moreover, the direction of the differences varied unsystematically across the five trait dimensions. Quite similar results were obtained when, instead of self-rated variability being used as the moderator variable, the subjects' intraindividual variances across the items of the particular CSBS scale were used as moderators. Thus, with our peer rating criterion it was not possible to replicate the results reported by Bem and Allen (1974). Their approach, being of ingenious simplicity, was also unsuccessful for additional dimensions not studied before (Borkenau, 1981). Similar insignificant results have also been reported by Chaplin and Goldberg (1984).

We have not yet addressed the question as to whether the situational specificity of behavior can be understood as an individual disposition that is general across traits. According to the positions taken by Alker (1972), Campus (1974), and Snyder (1974, 1979), such a general disposition should be expected. Substantial correlations among the consistency indices for different traits would support this view. A combined measure of cross-situational consistency would then be more reliable and more appropriate and might, therefore, produce more pronounced moderator effects.

To investigate this hypothesis, the correlations between the intraindividual variances calculated for the five single CSBS scales were computed. The resulting coefficients were all positive and substantial ($\bar{r} = .48$). The correlation matrix was factor analyzed and a clear "g" factor of cross-situational variability could be identified. In view of the high correlation between the g factor score and the raw sum of the five intraindividual variances ($r = .99$), we used the raw sum for further analyses, for reasons of simplicity. The behavior of subjects with values below the median were designated trait-like and that of those with values above the median, trait-free. To study the moderator effect of the aggregated measure, correlations between self- and peer ratings were calculated for six traits. These were done separately for our cross-situationally consistent and inconsistent subjects. The resulting coefficients are listed in Table 1.

As can be seen from Table 1, the direction of all the differences favors our hypothesis; the difference reaches statistical significance in three of six cases. Moreover, the aggregated measure of trait consistency also has a moderator effect for those dimensions not considered by the CSBS scales (depressiveness and autonomic lability). (Honesty and sensitivity were excluded from our analyses due to low interrater agreement.) Further analyses revealed that the

Table 1. Correlations among self- and peer ratings for subjects scoring low or high on a global measure of cross-situational variability

Dimension	Groups of subjects ($n=54$)		Probability of identical population correlations
	Unvarying consistent	Varying inconsistent	
Gregariousness	0.74	0.50	$P<0.05$
Venturesomeness	0.36	0.29	$P>0.05$
Aggressiveness	0.54	0.39	$P>0.05$
Depressiveness	0.62	0.30	$P<0.05$
Autonomic lability	0.53	0.40	$P>0.05$
Conscientiousness	0.60	0.35	$P<0.05$

variances of the correlated measures did not differ significantly between the two groups of subjects. Thus far, it can be stated that cross-situational consistency may be a "trait" itself. Additionally, the validity coefficients calculated for the subjects with trait-like behavior are substantially higher than the magic .30 threshold.

These results, however, are quite specific in one respect: The differences between the trait-consistent and -inconsistent behavior groups turned out to be insignificant when the raw sum of individual responses to the items "How much do you vary from one situation to another ...?" was tested for its moderator function, even though the single variability items were substantially intercorrelated ($\bar{r}=.35$). Some other problems have been discussed by Amelang and Borkenau (1984 a) and are only mentioned briefly here:

1. A multitrait-multimethod analysis of the indices indicating cross-situational variability reveals a strong method component. Scores established by the same method (e.g., self-rated variability) but referring to different traits correlate substantially, as has already been mentioned. In contrast, indices established by different methods but referring to the same trait show correlations that are not significantly different from zero (Borkenau, 1981). The same pattern of results was obtained by Chaplin and Goldberg (1984).

2. The stability of self-rated variability, measured at 6-month intervals, turned out not to be significantly different from zero (Borkenau, 1981).

3. Usually, a negative correlation between self-rated variability and the extremity of the subjects' position on the global trait scale can be observed not only if extremity is defined as a deviation of the subjects' position from the neutral point of the scale (Rushton, Jackson, & Paunonen, 1981; Stones & Burt, 1978), but also if extremity is taken as the deviation of the subjects' score from the sample mean (Borkenau, 1981). Thus, the subgroup of low-variability subjects tends to have higher interindividual variances, a fact which confounds possible moderator effects. For the data reported in Table 1, however, no such relations could be observed.

Despite the plausibility of Bem and Allen's (1974) approach, their indices of cross-situational consistency are subject to severe methodological problems. Therefore, it might be preferable to look for other moderator variables if we want to retain the conviction that the traditional trait model is appropriate for at least some people. Some alternatives are discussed below.

The Search for Subjects Who Can be Described by Particular Traits

Some failures to verify the Bem and Allen hypothesis empirically may stem from their identification of situational variability with trait consistency. However, in the course of the interactionism debate, Golding (1975) and Olweus (1977) have argued that situational variability is completely compatible with trait consistency as long as the *rank order* of individuals does not change from one situation to another. Whereas some types of situational variability correspond with the ascription of a trait, others do not. This has been illustrated by Bem and Allen (1974) with regard to friendliness. Therefore, a question worded "How much do you vary from one situation to another in how friendly and outgoing you are?" seems to be inadequate for distinguishing trait-consistent from -inconsistent subjects. Furthermore, subjects may be inconsistent because their *behavioral* equivalences do not match the equivalence class of behaviors implied by that trait. For example, "friendliness" implies not only being agreeable but also being outgoing to some degree. A person who is agreeable and introverted may therefore be inconsistent with regard to friendliness although she does not vary in this respect from one situation to another. A question that only emphasizes *cross-situational* variability may therefore fail to identify the subjects consistent with regard to the trait under study.

Trait consistency seems to be a completely different concept from situational variability, and it seems to be closely related to trait appropriateness or trait relevance. Therefore, we assume that a better strategy would be to ask subjects how appropriate they think a trait is for characterizing their personality. Moreover, a further promising approach might be to let subjects themselves generate the trait words they think describe them best. Both strategies were pursued in a study by Borkenau and Amelang (1985). The subjects were 389 German adults who first provided global self-ratings of 45 trait dimensions which had been proposed as superordinate categories in a taxonomy of trait-descriptive terms by Layman and McDonald (see Turner & Gilliland, 1979). Subsequently, the subjects rated the extent to which these dimensions were appropriate for describing their personality. Finally, they listed six to ten trait words which they thought characterized them. The average of three peer ratings obtained in the same way was used as the criterion. Since the subgroup of trait-relevant subjects was expected to have higher standard deviations of their global trait scores, we computed not only correlations between self- and peer reports but also (nonstandardized) regression coefficients and standard errors of estimation for the criterion variable, the last two statistics being in-

Table 2. Moderator function of self-rated trait appropriateness

	Trait-relevant subjects	Trait-irrelevant subjects	Result of a sign test
Correlation higher	37 traits	8 traits	$P < 0.001$
Regression higher	35 traits	10 traits	$P < 0.01$
Residual variance higher	20 traits	25 traits	$P > 0.05$

dependent of trait variance. In these regression analyses, the self-ratings were used as predictors and the average peer ratings as criteria.

To test the moderator function of self-rated trait appropriateness, the total sample was divided at the median into two subgroups separately for each trait, one comprising the trait-irrelevant and the other one the trait-relevant persons. Separate correlation and regression analyses were then conducted for the two subsamples on each of the 45-trait dimensions. The results are summarized in Table 2.

On all three statistics, predictability was superior for the trait-relevant subjects. This difference reached the level of statistical significance for the correlation and regression coefficients, whereas the residual variances showed a tendency in the expected direction but fell short of being significant. Thus, there is some evidence that there is higher agreement among self- and peer ratings for those people who view the trait dimension as more appropriate for describing their personality.

To test the hypothesis that superior validities can be obtained for trait words which subjects generate themselves, the trait-descriptive terms listed by the subjects were assigned by two independent raters to 1 of the 45 dimensions mentioned above. For 98% of all trait words generated, the two judges made identical assignments. If both judges agreed that at least one trait word should be assigned to a specific one of the 45 categories, the dimension was assumed to be suitable for describing the subject's personality. For each of the 45 dimensions, the validity calculated for that subsample of subjects was then compared with the validity of the group of persons who had listed no trait-descriptive term pertinent to the category. Once again, not only correlation coefficients but also regression slopes and residual variances were compared. The results are given in Table 3.

All differences in Table 3 are in the expected direction and reach the level of statistical significance. Moreover, an inspection of the single correlations which are not presented here reveals that in the trait-irrelevant subject group the highest coefficient is $r = .50$, whereas in the trait-relevant group 13 single correlations break this barrier and the highest coefficient is .81. Thus, the hypothesis of higher interrater agreement for trait-relevant subjects was also confirmed when subjects were identified by our adjective generation criterion.

The consequences for questionnaire construction are straightforward: When subjects are given an inventory, items asking about the appropriateness

Table 3. Predictability depending on the listing of trait-descriptive terms classified to a category

	Pertinent attribute generated	No pertinent attribute generated	Result of a sign test
Correlations higher	35 traits	10 traits	$P<0.01$
Regression higher	32 traits	13 traits	$P<0.01$
Residual variance higher	15 traits	30 traits	$P<0.05$

of several trait dimensions as descriptors of their personality should be incorporated. Moreover, subjects should be asked which traits *they* would use to describe themselves.

The Search for Subjects Whose Trait Positions Are Observable

Kenrick and Stringfield (1980) suggested using self-rated trait observability as a moderator. They argued that substantial agreement between self- and peer ratings could be expected only when subjects' trait positions can be observed by others. This, they thought, was especially true for such trait dimensions as emotionality, which may be kept essentially "private" by *some* people whereas others may be less inclined to monitor their emotional behavior.

Kenrick and Stringfield (1980) asked their subjects with regard to 16 traits: "How publicly observable is your behavior on the ... dimension?" The dimensions chosen were the 16 incorporated into Cattell's Sixteen Personality Factors Questionnaire. The authors report a somewhat superior predictability for those subjects who described themselves as being more observable on a trait. Their results are difficult to interpret, however, because they report only correlations and no standard deviations of their predictor and criterion measures. The same criticism pertains to a similar study by Cheek (1982). Thus, it may well be that the subjects who were easier to observe were those with more extreme trait scores, and the reported differences in validity may be entirely due to this confounding. Another problem not solved by the Kenrick and Stringfield analysis is whether observability should be regarded as trait-specific (i.e., people conceal their real character only for certain traits) or whether people differ in their global tendency to express their "true" personality, feelings, and attitudes. The latter view would be in accordance with Snyder's theory on interindividual differences in self-monitoring (Snyder, 1974, 1979).

To investigate these questions, we extended our study (described in the previous section) by asking our 389 subjects how observable they were on each of the 45 trait dimensions. The sample was then divided at the median according to self-rated observability for each trait. Once again, not only self-peer correlations but also regression coefficients and standard errors of estimation of the criterion variable were computed. Self-ratings were used as predictors and

Table 4. Moderator function of self-rated trait observability

	Observable subjects	Unobservable subjects	Result of a sign test
Correlation higher	42 traits	3 traits	$P<0.001$
Regression higher	41 traits	4 traits	$P<0.001$
Residual variance higher	22 traits	23 traits	$P>0.05$

the averages of three peer ratings were used as criteria. The results of these analyses are summarized in Table 4.

Table 4 shows clearly higher validities for the observable subjects, for both self-peer correlations and regression slopes. This conclusion is also supported by the median correlation and regression coefficients for the unobservable and observable subjects. The mean correlations are .20 and .41, respectively, the median regression coefficients being .16 and .26. Thus, in keeping with our hypotheses, observable subjects can be more precisely predicted on the peer rating criterion than unobservable ones. Not only the differences in correlations but also those in regression slopes are in the expected direction.

For testing the hypothesis that a subject's observability may be understood as a global disposition not restricted to only one or a few trait dimensions, the 45 observability self-ratings were intercorrelated, revealing a mean correlation of .11. Although not impressive, this average correlation is approximately the same as the mean interitem correlation of frequently used personality scales (e.g., the EPI Extraversion Scale; Eysenck & Eysenck, 1964). The correlation matrix was factor analyzed, and a high correlation ($r=.99$) found between the factor score for the unrotated first principal axis and the sum of the 45 observability ratings. Therefore, the 389 subjects were divided at the median for this sum score: Subjects scoring above the median were regarded as globally observable, whereas those below the median were defined as globally unobservable. It was expected that observable subjects would reveal a higher self-peer correlation and a steeper regression slope. The results of our analyses are in agreement with this hypothesis: The median correlations are .26 (unobservables) and .36 (observables). The sign test for the correlation differences is highly significant, the observable group showing higher validities for 34 dimensions. The median regression coefficients are .18 (unobservables) and .26 (observables), and the sign test applied to the regression differences also gives a significant result. Here, the observables surpass the unobservables for 31 traits. The moderator effect of global observability, however, seems to be less pronounced than that of the trait-specific observability moderators summarized in Table 4. Thus, our data show a bandwidth fidelity dilemma (Cronbach & Gleser, 1965) for the choice of the moderator variable.

This bandwidth fidelity dilemma arises in spite of an expected higher reliability of the global observability score compared with the trait-specific ones, which are usually quite unreliable. The same argument pertains to trait-specific variability and trait appropriateness scores. Amelang, Kobelt, and Frasch (1985) found mean reliability coefficients ranging from .07 to .36, where rater agreement was less pronounced than temporal stability. Burke, Kraut, and Dworkin (1984) report mean internal consistency coefficients for measures of cross-situational consistency of about .22. Thus, the usually significant but not very impressive moderator effects might be considerably more pronounced if more reliable moderator variables were established and used in the analyses.

Some conclusions can be drawn concerning the construction of questionnaires: Substantial correspondence between the self-rated trait position and the ratings by others can only be expected if the person being assessed is observable with regard to the trait. Therefore, if the criterion is the subjects' position on a rating scale, these relationships must be considered in the process of questionnaire validation. In any case, it may be helpful to incorporate some "observability items" into the questionnaire which could be used as moderating variables.

Social Desirability as a Moderating Variable

In a theoretical paper, Bem (1972) argued that defensiveness as measured by Need for Approval or Social Desirability (SD) scales should be an effective moderating variable allowing division of the world into useful equivalence classes. As several empirical findings seem to suggest, for individuals with a high need for approval "'socially desirable responses' form an equivalence class of behaviors and 'interpersonally evaluative settings' form an equivalence class of situations. For non-defensive individuals, however, these responses and situations may have nothing in common and hence their behavior cannot be predicted from one of these situations to the other" (Bem, 1972, p. 21–22).

Therefore, defensiveness can provide one important answer to the question of what kinds of people might display cross-situational consistency across socially evaluative settings. Because the defensive individuals appear to monitor their behavior to maintain particular self-presentations, they may be unwilling or motivationally unable to alter their behavior to take advantage of shifting situational contingencies *beyond* social approval. Accordingly, they will display cross-situational consistency. This general idea, suggested by Bem (1972), has been tested in several studies, which we have described in more detail elsewhere (Amelang & Borkenau, 1984b). We confirmed Bem's theoretical statements by showing that

1. Subjects scoring high on a social desirability (SD) scale exhibited a higher retest reliability for extraversion and neuroticism scores compared to subjects scoring low on SD.
2. Subjects with high scores on a lie scale constructed according to the principles used by Marlowe and Crowne revealed a higher cross-situational consistency than the nondefensive ones for those items of the CSBS published by Bem and Allen (1974) that had been rated as high on social desirability.

Bem (1972) argues further that only those overt behaviors can be monitored which are under the actor's functional control. "Expressive behaviors, projective behaviors, and physiological responses probably escape the monitoring process. Accordingly, even when more monitorable behaviors are being suppressed, these 'covert' indices may still occur. This suggests that within a single situation, the defensive individual may show *inconsistency across* those *response modes* which are differentially subject to monitoring. In contrast, the nondefensive individual will show consistency across response modes" (Bem, 1972, p. 32).

Corresponding to Bem's (1972) predictions we found that subjects scoring high on SD showed less agreement among questionnaire scores and pertinent physiological reactions and trait ratings by significant others.

These results indicate that meaningful equivalence classes of situations and responses can be identified following Bem's (1972) theoretical considerations. Moreover, the prediction of behavior via questionnaires can be improved by including lie scales in the inventories. Subjects scoring high on these scales can be expected to show a lower degree of *cross-modal* consistency, therefore making their self-reports nonvalid predictors.

Searching for Subgroups of Situations in Which Behavior can be Predicted from Trait Measures

Ambiguity and Constraint of Situations

Experimental research seems to have lent little support to the trait position (Mischel, 1968). One reason for this finding may be that the situations realized in psychological experiments are not a random sample of all situations occurring in real life. The prevailing experimental situations are established to demonstrate how behavior is influenced by situational variations. Therefore, experimenters tend to select treatments assumed to affect the subjects' behavior to a significant extent. Usually, treatments are selected which have been shown by theories already subscribed to, pretests, or experience to produce a high amount of treatment variance and a low degree of interindividual "error" variance, because this combination is optimal for detecting significant treatment effects. Thus, the selection of treatments is biased in that effects due to individual differences are systematically underestimated and situational factors are systematically overestimated. In psychological experiments, situations are often structured in such a way that traits cannot be used as predictors.

Thus, we are confronted not only with the problem of identifying those persons whose behavior can be predicted from their trait scores, but also with the difficulty of identifying situations in which "individual differences make a difference" (Mischel, 1977, p. 346). As an illustration, Mischel (1977) quotes specific situational settings in which behavior is constrained by social norms to such a degree that interindividual differences are almost nonexistent. For example, if the traffic lights are red, a stimulus indicates unambiguously to all drivers that they should stop, and (it is to be hoped) all do so regardless of their trait scores.

Price and Bouffard (1974) have given some examples of situations where less formal norms restrict the range of permissible behaviors. Many behaviors which people may engage in privately would be unacceptable in church or at the theater. Smaller interindividual differences can therefore be expected within these last environments. Nevertheless, situations which are especially weakly and ambiguously structured do exist. These settings are more likely to have different psychological meanings for different people. Consequently, a substantial amount of interindividual variance of behavior can be expected in such situations, and the knowledge of people's trait positions should then be very helpful for predicting their behavior.

Similar remarks have been made by many other authors. For example, Stagner (1977) reviewed papers presented by Bandura, Mischel, Hunt and other critics of trait theory, and concluded that "situational pressure often overrules any inner-determined tendency toward action guided by a generalized trait" (p. 193). Snyder (1979) also takes the position that "it may be possible to specify when situational and dispositional information is particularly relevant to the individual actor" (p. 133). Moreover, he describes "low-monitoring environments" in which behavior can be predicted from knowledge of personal dispositions, attitudes, and affective states.

A different approach to the problem stems from Wicklund and his group, who experimentally induced self-awareness by confronting each subject with his or her mirror image (Hormuth, 1982; Pryor, Gibbons, Wicklund, Fazio, & Hood, 1977). It may be assumed that the influence of situational and interfering factors was suppressed by this procedure, since the subjects' behavior was more predictable from trait scores in the "mirror condition."

Monson, Hesley, and Chernik (1982) investigated the effects of situational pressure directly. They experimentally constructed three situations, two of them characterized by a high amount of situational pressure to behave in an extraverted (situation 1) or introverted (situation 2) manner. The third situation was neutral in this respect. Subjects' pretested extraversion scores were then correlated with their talkativeness as rated by independent judges. For the subject groups observed under the two conditions of situational constraint, the resulting correlations were insignificant ($r = .10$ in situation 1, and $r = .38$ in situation 2). When the situation was ambiguous, however, the correlation was significant and substantial ($r = .56$). One reason for this moderating effect of situational pressure is that the variance of behavior was considerably higher in situation 3 than in situations 1 and 2. This result is in full agreement with the hypothesis that it is only under specific circumstances that interindividual differences make a difference.

In a second experiment, in which self-reports were the only dependent variables, Monson et al. (1982) constructed three degrees of situational pressure. The results reported indicate that the higher the situational constraint the lower the predictability of behavior from trait scores. Thus, it appears that recourse to trait variables is useful only for those classes of situations which allow different interpretations of the stimulus conditions and some freedom of choice with regard to several likely behaviors.

The studies conducted by situationists and interactionists on the relative influences of persons and situations are thus deficient in two respects. First, the strategy of randomly assigning subjects to different treatments neglects the principle of ecological validity (Pawlik, 1979; Stagner, 1977; Wachtel, 1973), because the probability that all subjects can be found in a specific situation is assumed to be equal. It is, however, plausible and has been demonstrated that people actively seek out situations which fit their trait or need structure (Argyle, 1977; Diener, Larsen, & Emmons, 1984; Gormly, 1983; Snyder & Gangestad, 1982; Stern, 1970). If the situations selected for study are characterized by strong situational pressure, and if the systematic selection of situations dependent upon trait variables is neglected, no confirmation of the trait position can be expected, since the experimental design is biased against trait theory.

Some implications for the validation and application of questionnaires are apparent: It is desirable that personality inventories be validated, using behaviors recorded online as one of the criteria. The situations and behaviors selected should be structured in such a way that substantial individual differences in behavior can be expected a priori. Otherwise, the validation procedure is pointless. Moreover, personality questionnaires can be useful tools for predicting behavior only when several ways of perceiving situations and several behaviors are plausible. When individual differences make no difference no benefit should be expected from the application of trait scores.

Single-Act vs Multiple-Act Criteria

Analyzing the complex empirical relationships between personality traits and behavior, Block (1977) has made a distinction among three types of data relevant for personality research: observer ratings (R data), self-ratings (S data), and objective measurement procedures, which are most often used in laboratory work (T data). According to Block, R and S data reveal a substantial amount of intraindividual consistency and thus confirm the trait position, provided that the measuring instruments are developed and applied in a way that satisfies scientific standards. When T data are used, however, the predictability of behavior is substantially lower. Thus, Block suggests an investigation to find what inadequacies in the T data could be responsible for their lack of predictability. It seems inappropriate to question the trait position in general.

One reason why T data may not provide much evidence for traits is that they are seldom based on multiple observations of behavior or multiple pieces of information, whereas R and S data usually are. Indeed, many studies cited by Mischel (1968) as providing evidence against the trait position rely on simple information of the "one way or the other" type: within a crucial experimental or field situation, the a priori defined behavior did appear (a hint at personal consistency) or it did not appear. The latter case is usually explained by inconsistency of the personality. According to the definitions by Fishbein and Ajzen (1974), such a dichotomous criterion is the most radical definition of personal consistency, and is inadequate in several ways. First, the units of observation in experiments are usually very short, giving some of the subjects no opportunity to exhibit the behavior regarded as crucial by the experimenter. Moreover, not all persons choose the same operationally defined behavior, although they may all manifest the same trait. Thus, for example, aggression may be expressed by ignoring somebody, staring at him in a hostile way, making ironic comments, scolding him, beating him, or even killing him. All these obviously different behaviors may be regarded as indicating an aggressive disposition.

These relationships are addressed in a second, less restrictive definition of consistency. It is argued that several different behaviors can be assumed to be manifestations of the same trait if all the responses can be categorized as falling on the same side of the trait dimension. A still more general and "weak" definition recognizes degrees or levels of a trait and therefore conceptualizes consistency as a relatively constant level or amount of trait-relevant behavior.

This definition allows that individuals may sometimes even exhibit behaviors usually not associated with the trait in question. Thus, a person who scores comparatively high on a scale of aggressiveness should not be expected to be aggressive in every instance. Generally, trait theories have proposed that the measurement of behavior should be aggregated across occasions, trait-relevant behaviors, and the intensity, frequency, and duration of these behaviors, and that the correlations between trait scores and pertinent behaviors will then increase.

As far as R data and S data are concerned, the human judges seem to perform some kind of data aggregation. With regard to T data, efforts to construct multiple-act criteria (MAC) have become prominent within the last decade. The magnitude of the validity coefficients has been substantially increased by application of these criteria. Thus, Jaccard (1974) reports correlations between a conventional dominance scale and single dominant acts of about .20. When the single dominant acts were combined into a multiple-act criterion, however, the validity coefficient was raised to .60. Comparable results are reported by McGowan and Gormly (1976) for the trait "energetic behavior" and by Gifford (1982) for the construct "affiliativeness." Gifford reports that a trait measure of affiliativeness predicts a single-act criterion worst ($r = .25$), a repeated measure of a single act somewhat better ($r = .40$), and a multiple-act criterion best ($r = .55$).

Epstein (1979) presented results demonstrating that increasing the reliability of the correlated measures by averaging over occasions raises the intercorrelations of objective events. He argued further that most single items of behavior do not only have a high component of error of measurement but also a narrow range of generality and that low correlations between self-ratings and pertinent behaviors may result from both conditions. The results presented by

Gifford (1982) indicate that the "generality problem" is in fact the more important one, as they reveal a superiority of multiple-act criteria over repeated measurement of the same behavioral act.

Moskowitz (1982) starts from Block's (1977) and Magnusson and Endler's (1977) distinction between the concept of coherence (i.e., the referents of personality constructs tend to be only weakly intercorrelated) and the problem of consistency (i.e., measures of the constructs obtained in different situations are often found to be weakly related to one another). Furthermore, he proposes that "constructs can be analyzed according to the range of referents sampled and the range of situations sampled" (Moskowitz, 1982, p. 755). Both sampling procedures, he says, have implications for the kind and accuracy of the predictions made from that construct: "Broad constructs will have the advantage of predicting diverse behaviors at modest levels of accuracy, whereas the narrow construct will predict with high accuracy within a limited range and very poorly outside that range" (p. 755). The main hypothesis of his study was that if personality constructs are assessed by sampling multiple referents of the construct in multiple situations, both coherence and cross-situational consistency should emerge. Moskowitz (1982) found that increasing the number of observations or repeating the measurement increased the stability over time. Multiple-referent sampling raised the indices of coherence, whereas multiple-situation sampling increased cross-situational consistency. For the construct dominance Moskowitz (1982) reports coefficients of cross-situational consistency of about .60 – a result that is "inconsistent with the current vogue for denigrating personality constructs that are not cognitive" (p. 766).

The implications of these findings for personality research and questionnaire construction are obvious. If individual differences concerning global constructs are to be assessed it is necessary to obtain measurements relying on comparatively broad samples of behaviors, settings, and occasions. Thus, the items on "broad" trait scales should comprise a wide diversity of behavioral referents, multiple situations, and multiple occasions. It seems that people do something like this when they provide global personality ratings on such items as "In general, how friendly are you?" When answering questions like this, the subjects seem to think of a wide variety of behavioral referents of friendliness and of several situations in which the trait-relevant behaviors have been exhibited. From this they arrive at a judgement of the average trait position. Surprisingly, these global one-item personality ratings show validity coefficients that reach or even surpass the accuracy of predictions from multifactor inventories or projective test devices, as has recently been demonstrated again by Shrauger and Osberg (1981) and by Burisch (1984). This result may be explained by the assumption that in responding to global trait ratings the subjects use an extremely broad referent and situation sampling. Moreover, they seem to weigh particular prototypic behaviors and settings more heavily, as Mischel and Peake (1982) and Buss and Craik (1980) have demonstrated.

Technical Refinements on Questionnaires

In a discussion of the merits of personality and ability tests, Fiske and Butler (1963) have taken the position that the superiority of ability and achievement tests over personality questionnaires results from several differences between the measuring devices. The items on achievement tests are usually unambiguous, whereas questionnaire items are frequently ambiguously worded. Moreover, ability items have an unequivocally correct solution, whereas questionnaire items do not. The most important difference, according to Fiske and Butler (1963), lies in the instructions. Whereas subjects filling out achievement tests are instructed to show the maximal achievement possible, persons filling out questionnaires are told to be honest and report their typical behavior. Thus, when subjects' ability test scores are compared the comparison involves their *maximal* possible performance, whereas as far as questionnaire scores are concerned, self-reported *typical* performances are being compared.

Willerman, Turner, and Peterson (1976) accepted this distinction and constructed maximal performance paper and pencil tests of personality in which the subjects were instructed to describe their highest degree of annoyance. The results of this maximal performance test were then compared with a typical performance test, using maximal and typical performance behaviors observed in a laboratory as criteria. The correlation of the self-reported maximal expression of anger with the expression of anger observed under "typical" instructions in the laboratory, and with the expression of anger observed under "maximal" instructions was calculated, giving coefficients of .48 and .59, respectively. The corresponding correlation coefficients for a conventional questionnaire instruction amounted to .32 and −.03, respectively. In a more recent study (Turner, 1978), self-reported maximal dominance outpredicted the self-reported typical dominance for both typical and maximal expressions of dominance observed in the laboratory. Results on trait elation reported by Willerman et al. (1976), however, are less favorable to the maximal performance format. In addition, it can be argued that maximal performance instructions reduce the ambiguity of the situation, and interindividual differences should therefore become less important. Thus, it seems premature to recommend maximal performance instructions for routine use.

Another approach is directed to the improvement of the wording of questionnaire items and other item characteristics. In this context, some studies have investigated the relationship among several item characteristics and item reliability and validity. Tränkle (1982), referring to studies by Flesch (1948), Dickes and Steiwer (1977), and Farr, Jenkins, and Paterson (1951), calculated difficulty scores for the items in the short version of the Freiburger Persönlichkeits-Inventar (Fahrenberg & Selg, 1974), a personality inventory which is very popular in Germany. The indices investigated by Tränkle (1982) were (a) the average number of words per sentence; (b) the average number of letters per word; (c) the number of syllables per 100 words; and (d) the percentage of one-syllable words. Tränkle (1982) found a correlation between some aspects of the item wording and the retest reliability of item endorsement after a time interval of 4–6 weeks. The correlation coefficients were .25 for percentage of one-syllable words, and −.40 for the average number of words per sentence, the coefficients being based on a sample of 192 subjects. Currently, Tränkle and Amelang are investigating the influence of item characteristics on validity.

Löhr (1977) and Keren (1979) instructed 230 psychology students to rate a large pool of questionnaire items on intelligibility, ambiguity, self-reference, and social desirability. Later, M. Amelang and F. J. Löhr (1983, unpublished manuscript)[2] investigated whether these item characteristics were systematically related to item validity. To do this, validity coefficients were calculated separately for various item subgroups, using data collected by Amelang and Borkenau (1982) which consisted of self-reports and trait ratings by significant others. It was found that the following groups of items showed higher average validities:

- Socially evaluated items with extreme social desirability values compared with questions with evaluatively neutral content
- Comprehensible items compared with less comprehensible ones;
- Clear items compared with ambiguous items;
- Items referring to the self compared with questions not referring to the self.

Although not completely consistent, these findings emerged in both extraversion and neuroticism items. However, the effect was mainly due to differences in the items' standard deviations. That is, the dichotomous items which were socially evaluated, comprehensive, unambiguous, or referred to the subject's personality had difficulty levels of about .5, whereas the other questions revealed less balanced endorsement patterns.

Thus, some item characteristics can be identified that distinguish "good" items from "bad" items. If only good items were incorporated into the analysis prediction could be improved. Thus, improvement of the questionnaire item itself seems to be one more way to raise the validity of personality questionnaires and to break the ominous .30 barrier (Mischel, 1968).

Summary

From a review of the recent literature on the consistency of personality and the predictive validity of self-report measures it can be concluded that traits are alive and well. On the other hand, it has clearly been demonstrated that no questionnaire can be expected to predict specific pertinent behaviors for all persons in all situations. Under favorable conditions, however, quite satisfactory validity coefficients can be obtained. What are these conditions?

A number of studies show that questionnaires or global self-ratings are capable of predicting multiple-act criteria quite well, but they are poor predictors of narrowly defined behaviors. This seems more to be a question of the generality of the criterion than of its reliability (of course, validity is highest when both conditions are met). Moreover, the obvious hypothesis that validity coefficients are superior if there are perceptible interindividual differences in behavior has been empirically supported. This seems to be the prevailing condition if the situation is ambiguously structured with regard to social norms. Otherwise, individual differences will have no impact. These relationships should be considered if self-report data are validated or a decision is made dependent upon personality scores.

Another topic is the superior predictability in some people. The moderating variable approach is viable if the moderators are chosen on a priori grounds. Social desirability as measured by the Crowne and Marlowe scale seems to be a promising moderator of this kind. Others have been shown also to be effective within peer rating studies, namely trait relevance and trait observability. Thus, it seems useful for questionnaires to incorporate lie scales and items asking for the relevance and observability of the traits under study, to identify those subjects for whom one can make more confident predictions. On the other hand, more data should be available on the effectiveness of these moderators, using online recorded behaviors as validity criteria.

The currently most serious challenge to questionnaire construction seems to be Shweder and D'Andrade's systematic distortion hypothesis: If the internal structure of memory-based trait ratings is biased towards the semantic similarity structure of the nouns and adjectives used, a new search has to be started for basic dimensions of personality. Numerous factor-analytic studies using self- or peer reports would then have basic dimensions of *person perception* instead of *personality*. However, the results reported by Shweder and D'Andrade (1980) may be due more to the neglect of systematic overlap between trait categories than to the systematic distortion of memory-based ratings. Moreover, some proposals have been made in this paper as to how systematic distortions might be diminished: nonverbal trait inferences; better control of the observational basis of trait ratings; and development of a psychological taxonomy of trait-descriptive terms. A great deal of research is still needed on these topics, however, and it must be emphasized that substantial validity coefficients of self-reports can be attained in spite of some empirical support for the systematic distortion hypothesis.

Finally, some improvement might arise from better formulation of the single items constituting a personality scale. Systematic differences seem to exist between reliable and valid items compared with unreliable and invalid ones. If this research is continued it may be possible to predict on a priori grounds which items will have greater validity in the empirical analyses and, with combined application of all the strategies suggested in this article, we may be able to predict most of the people most of the time.

Acknowledgements. The authors are indebted to Lewis R. Goldberg and Oliver P. John for their helpful comments on an earlier draft of this paper.

Notes

1 Shweder (1975, 1982), D'Andrade (1974), and Shweder and D'Andrade (1980) declare that they compared the internal structure within the semantic similarity of trait-descriptive terms and within memory-based ratings to the covariations within on-line recorded *behaviors*. Actually, molecular behavior counts took place in none of the studies mentioned. The records made online were ratings involving a great deal of inferential reasoning and made by observers immediately after viewing the behavior sequences. Thus, it would be more precise to use the term 'online ratings.'

2 The title of this paper is: „Formale und inhaltliche Gesichtspunkte der Item-Formulierung (Soziale Erwünschtheit, Verständlichkeit und Abstraktheit) als Einflußfaktoren der Validität".

References

Alker, H.A. (1972). Is personality situationally specific or intrapsychically consistent? *Journal of Personality, 40*, 1–16.

Amelang, M., & Borkenau, P. (1981). Vorhersagen für einige Personen und viele Merkmale. Oder: Konsistenz über Merkmale und Kontextbedingungen als Eigenschaft. In Michaelis, W. (Ed.), *Bericht über den 32. Kongreß der Deutschen Gesellschaft für Psychologie in Zürich, 1980* (Vol. 2). Göttingen: Hogrefe.

Amelang, M., & Borkenau, P. (1982). Über die faktorielle Struktur und externe Validität einiger Fragebogen-Skalen zur Erfassung von Dimensionen der Extraversion und emotionalen Stabilität. *Zeitschrift für Differentielle und Diagnostische Psychologie, 3*, 119–146.

Amelang, M., & Borkenau, P. (1984a). Versuche einer Differenzierung des Eigenschaftskonzepts: Aspekte intraindividueller Variabilität und differentieller Vorhersagbarkeit. In Amelang, M., & Ahrens, H.J. (Eds.), *Brennpunkte der Persönlichkeitsforschung*. Göttingen: Hogrefe.

Amelang, M., & Borkenau, P. (1984b). Constructing cross-situational consistency in behavior: Some tests on Bem's thoughts on social desirability as a moderator variable. In Bonarius, H., van Heck, G., & Smid, N. (Eds.), *Personality psychology in Europe: Theoretical and empirical developments*. Lisse: Swets & Zeitlinger.

Amelang, M., & Löhr, F.J. (1983). *Formale und inhaltliche Gesichtspunkte der Item-Formulierung (Soziale Erwünschtheit, Verständlichkeit und Abstraktheit) als Einflußfaktoren der Validität* (Unpublished manuscript).

Amelang, M., Kobelt, C., & Frasch, A. (1985). Auf der Suche nach Personen mit Eigenschaften: Untersuchungen zur Restriktion des Eigenschaftsmodells auf Untergruppen von Personen, Verhaltensweisen und Situationen. In Albert, D. (Ed.), *Bericht über den 34. Kongreß der Deutschen Gesellschaft für Psychologie in Wien, 1984* (Vol. 1). Göttingen: Hogrefe.

Argyle, M. (1977). Predicted and generated rules model of P × S interaction. In Magnusson, D., & Endler, N.S. (Eds.), *Personality at the cross-roads: Current issues in interactional psychology*. Hillsdale: Erlbaum.

Aries, E.J., Gold, C., & Weigel, R.H. (1983). Dispositional and situational influences on dominance behavior in small groups. *Journal of Personality and Social Psychology, 44*, 779–786.

Bem, D.J. (1972). Constructing cross-situational consistency in behavior: Some thoughts on Alker's critique of Mischel. *Journal of Personality, 40*, 17–26.

Bem, D.J., & Allen, A. (1974). On predicting some of the people some of the time: The search for cross-situational consistencies in behavior. *Psychological Review, 81*, 506–520.

Berman, J.S., & Kenny, D.A. (1976). Correlational bias in observer ratings. *Journal of Personality and Social Psychology, 34*, 263–273.

Block, J. (1977). Advancing the psychology of personality: Paradigmatic shift or improving the quality of research. In Magnusson, D., & Endler, N.S. (Eds.), *Personality at the cross-roads: Current issues in interactional psychology*. Hillsdale: Erlbaum.

Borkenau, P. (1981). *Intraindividuelle Variabilität und differentielle Vorhersagbarkeit*. Unpublished doctoral dissertation, University of Heidelberg.
Borkenau, P., & Amelang, M. (1985). Individuelle Angemessenheit von Eigenschaftskonstrukten als Moderatorvariable für die Übereinstimmung zwischen Selbst- und Bekanntenratings. *Diagnostica, 31*, 105–118.
Borkenau, P., & Angleitner, A. (1985). Systematische Verzerrungen in der Beurteilung von Personen: Faktum oder Fiktion? In Albert, D. (Ed.), *Bericht über den 34. Kongreß der Deutschen Gesellschaft für Psychologie in Wien* 1984 (Vol. 1). Göttingen: Hogrefe.
Bowers, K.S. (1973).Situationism in psychology: An analysis and a critique. *Psychological Review, 80*, 307–330.
Burisch, M. (1978). Construction strategies for multi-scale personality inventories. *Applied Psychological Measurement, 2*, 97–111.
Burisch, M. (1984). Approaches to personality inventory construction: A comparison of merits. *American Psychologist, 39*, 214–227.
Burke, P.A., Kraut, R.E., & Dworkin, R.H. (1984). Traits, consistency, and self-schemata: What do our methods measure? *Journal of Personality and Social Psychology, 47*, 568–579.
Buse, L. (1980). Intraindividuelle Merkmalsvariation und Validität eines Extraversionsfragebogens. Eine Untersuchung zur Gültigkeit des Eigenschaftsbegriffs. *Zeitschrift für Differentielle und Diagnostische Psychologie, 1*, 35–42.
Buss, D.M., & Craik, K.H. (1980). The frequency concept of disposition: Dominance and prototypically dominant acts. *Journal of Personality, 48*, 379–392.
Buss, D.M., & Craik, K.H. (1981). The act frequency analysis of interpersonal dispositions: Aloofness, gregariousness, dominance and submissiveness. *Journal of Personality, 49*, 175–192.
Byrne, D. (1964). Repression-sensitization as a dimension of personality. *Progress in Experimental Personality Research, 1*.
Campus, N. (1974). Transsituational consistency as a dimension of personality. *Journal of Personality and Social Psychology, 29*, 593–600.
Chaplin, W.F., & Goldberg, L.R. (1984). A failure to replicate the Bem & Allen study of individual differences in cross-situational consistency. *Journal of Personality and Social Psychology, 47*, 1074–1090.
Cheek, J.M. (1982). Aggregation, moderator variables, and the validity of personality tests: A peer rating study. *Journal of Personality and Social Psychology, 43*, 1254–1269.
Cronbach, L.J., & Gleser, G.C. (1965). *Psychological tests and personnel decisions*. Urbana: University of Illinois Press.
D'Andrade, R.G. (1974). Memory and the assessment of behavior. In Blalock, H. (Ed.), *Measurement in the social sciences*. Chicago: Aldine.
Dickes, P., & Steiwer, L. (1977). Ausarbeitung von Lesbarkeitsformeln für die deutsche Sprache. *Zeitschrift für Entwicklungspsychologie und Pädagogische Psychologie, 9*, 20–28.
Diener, E., Larsen, R.J., & Emmons, R.A. (1984). Person x situation interactions: Choice of situations and congruence response models. *Journal of Personality and Social Psychology, 47*, 580–592.
Endler, N.S., Hunt, J.McV., & Rosenstein, A.J. (1962). An S-R-inventory of anxiousness. *Psychological Monographs, 76*, (No. 17).
Epstein, S. (1979). The stability of behavior: On predicting most of the people much of the time. *Journal of Personality and Social Psychology, 37*, 1097–1126.
Eysenck, H.J., & Eysenck, S.B.G. (1964). *Manual of the Eysenck Personality Inventory*. London: University of London Press.
Eysenck, M., & Eysenck, H.J. (1980). Mischel and the concept of personality. *British Journal of Psychology, 71*, 191–204.
Fahrenberg, J., & Selg, H. (1974). *Das Freiburger Persönlichkeitsinventar FPI* (2nd ed.). Göttingen: Hogrefe.
Farr, J.N., Jenkins, J.J., & Paterson, D.G. (1951). Simplification of Flesch's reading ease formular. *Journal of Applied Psychology, 35*, 333–337.

Fishbein, M., & Ajzen, I. (1974). Attitudes towards objects as predictors of single and multiple behavioral criteria. *Psychological Review, 81*, 59–74.
Fiske, D.W., & Butler, J.M. (1963). The experimental conditions for measuring individual differences. *Educational and Psychological Measurement, 23*, 249–266.
Flesch, R. (1948). A new readability yardstick. *Journal of Applied Psychology, 32*, 321-323.
Gifford, R. (1982). Affiliativeness: A trait-measure in relation to single-act and multi-act behavior criteria. *Journal of Research in Personality, 16*, 128–134.
Goldberg, L.R. (1981). Developing a taxonomy of trait-descriptive terms. In Fiske, D. (Ed.), *New directions for methodology of social and behavioral science: Problems with language imprecision* (No. 9). San Francisco: Jossey-Bass.
Golding, S.L. (1975). Flies in the ointment: Methodological problems in the analysis of the percentage of variance due to person and situation. *Psychological Bulletin, 82*, 278–288.
Gormly, J. (1983). Predicting behavior from personality trait-scores. *Personality and Social Psychology Bulletin, 9*, 267–270.
Hampson, S.E. (1982). Person memory: A semantic category model of personality traits. *British Journal of Psychology, 73*, 1–11.
Helson, H., Blake, E.E., Mouton, J.S., & Olmstead, J.A. (1956). Attitudes as adjustments to stimulus, background, and residual factors. *Journal of Abnormal and Social Psychology, 52*, 314–322.
Herrmann, T. (1973). *Persönlichkeitsmerkmale*. Stuttgart: Kohlhammer.
Hewitt, J.K. (1984). Normal components of personality variation. *Journal of Personality and Social Psychology, 47*, 671–675.
Hormuth, S.E. (1982). Self-focused attention and the adherence to personal standards. In Kosakowsky, A., & Obuchowski, K. (Eds.), *Progress in psychology of personality*. Berlin: VEB Deutscher Verlag der Wissenschaften.
Jaccard, J.J. (1974). Predicting social behavior from personality traits. *Journal of Research in Personality, 7*, 358–367.
Jackson, D.N., & Stricker, L.J. (1982). Is implicit personality theory illusory? Armchair criticism vs. replicated empirical research. *Journal of Personality, 50*, 240–244.
Jackson, D.N., Chan, D.W., & Stricker, L.J. (1979). Implicit personality theory: Is it illusory? *Journal of Personality, 47*, 1–10.
John, O.P., Goldberg, L.R., & Angleitner, A. (1984). Better than the alphabet: Taxonomies of personality descriptive terms in Englisch, Dutch, and German. In Bonarius, H.M., van Heck, G., & Smid, N. (Eds.), *Personality psychology in Europe: Theoretical annd empirical developments*. Lisse: Swets & Zeitlinger.
Kenrick, D.T., & Stringfield, D.O. (1980). Personality traits and the eye of the beholder: Crossing some traditional philosophical bounderies in the search for consistency in all of the people. *Psychological Review, 87*, 88–104.
Keren, A. (1979). *Inhaltlich-semantische Analyse der Items aus fünf deutschsprachigen Persönlichkeitsfragebogen*. Bonn: Diplomarbeit, Psychologisches Institut Bonn.
Lay, C.H., & Jackson, D.N. (1969). Analysis of the generality of trait inferential relationships. *Journal of Personality and Social Psychology, 12*, 12–21.
Lay, C.H., Burron, B.F., & Jackson, D.N. (1973). Base rates and information value in impression formation. *Journal of Personality and Social Psychology, 28*, 390–395.
Lewis, M. (1967). The meaning of a response, or why researchers in infant-behavior should be oriental metaphysicians. *Merrill Palmer Quarterly, 13*, 7–18.
Löhr, F.J. (1977). *Formale und inhaltliche Merkmale von Fragebogenitems – zum Einfluß von Itemeigenschaften auf den Beantwortungsprozeß bei deutschen Persönlichkeitsfragebogen* (Vols. 1, 2). Bonn: Master's thesis.
Magnusson, D. (1980). Personality in an interactional paradigm of research. *Zeitschrift für Differentielle und Diagnostische Psychologie, 1*, 17–34.
Magnusson, D., & Endler, N.S. (1977). Interactional psychology: Present status and future prospects. In Magnusson, D. & Endler, N.S. (Eds.), *Personality at the cross-roads: Current issues in interactional psychology*. Hillsdale: Erlbaum.

McCrae, R.R. (1982). Consensual validation of personality traits: Evidence from self-reports and ratings. *Journal of Personality and Social Psychology, 43*, 293–303.
McGowan, J., & Gormly, J. (1976). Validation of personality traits: A multicriteria approach. *Journal of Personality and Social Psychology, 34*, 791–795.
Mirels, H.L. (1976). Implicit personality theory and inferential illusions. *Journal of Personality, 44*, 467–487.
Mirels, H.L. (1982a). The illusory nature of implicit personality theory. Logical and empirical considerations. *Journal of Personality, 50*, 203–222.
Mirels, H.L. (1982b). Tenacious inferential illusions: Experimental facts vs. critical fancy. *Journal of Personality, 50*, 245–250.
Mischel, W. (1968). *Personality and assessment*. New York: Wiley.
Mischel, W. (1977). The interaction of persons and situation. In Magnusson, D., & Endler, N.S. (Eds.), *Personality at the cross-roads: Current issues in interactional psychology*. Hillsdale: Erlbaum.
Mischel, W., & Peake, P.K. (1982). Beyond déjà vu in the search for cross-situational consistency. *Psychological Review, 89*, 730–755.
Monson, T.C., Hesley, J.W., & Chernick, L. (1982). Specifying when personality traits can and cannot predict behavior: An alternative to abandoning the attempt to predict single-act criteria. *Journal of Personality and Social Psychology, 43*, 385–399.
Moskowitz, D.S. (1982). Coherence and cross-situational generality in personality: A new analysis of old problems. *Journal of Personality and Social Psychology, 43*, 754–768.
Mulaik, S.A. (1964). Are personality factors raters' conceptual factors? *Journal of Consulting Psychology, 28*, 506–511.
Norman, W.T., & Goldberg, L.R. (1966). Raters, ratees and randomness in personality structure. *Journal of Personality and Social Psychology, 4*, 681–691.
Olweus, D.A. (1977). A critical analysis of the "modern" interactionist position. In Magnusson, D., & Endler, N.S. (Eds.), *Personality at the cross-roads: Current issues in interactional psychology*. Hillsdale: Erlbaum.
Passini, F.T., & Norman, W.T. (1966). A universal conception of personality structure? *Journal of Personality and Social Psychology, 4*, 44–49.
Paunonen, S.V., & Jackson, D.N. (1979). Nonverbal trait inference. *Journal of Personality and Social Psychology, 37*, 1645–1659.
Pawlik, K. (1973). Right answers to the wrong questions? A reexamination of factor analytic personality research and its contribution to personality theory. In Royce, J.R. (Ed.), *Multivariate analysis and psychological theory*. London: Academic.
Pawlik, K. (1979). Der „Interaktionismus" aus verhaltenswissenschaftlicher Sicht. In Eckensberger, H. (Ed.), *Bericht uber den 31. Kongreß der Deutschen Gesellschaft für Psychologie in Mannheim, 1978*, (Vol. 1). Göttingen: Hogrefe.
Price, R.H., & Bouffard, D.L. (1974). Behavioral appropriateness and situational constraint as dimensions of social behavior. *Journal of Personality and Social Psychology, 30*, 579–586.
Pryor, J.B., Gibbons, F.X., Wicklund, R.A., Fazio, R.H., & Hood, R. (1977). Self-focussed attention and self-report validity. *Journal of Personality, 45*, 513–527.
Rowe, D.C. (1982). Monozygotic twin cross-correlations as a validation of personality structure: A test of the semantic bias hypothesis. *Journal of Personality and Social Psychology, 43*, 1072–1079.
Rushton, J.P., Jackson, D.N., & Paunonen, S.V. (1981). Personality: Nomothetic or idiographic? A response to Kenrick & Stringfield. *Psychological Review, 88*, 582–589.
Schneider, D.J. (1973). Implicit personality theory: A review. *Psychological Bulletin, 79*, 294–309.
Shrauger, J.S., & Osberg, T.M. (1981). The relative accuracy of self-prediction and judgements by others in psychological assessment. *Psychological Bulletin, 90*, 322–351.
Shweder, R.A. (1975). How relevant is an individual difference theory of personality? *Journal of Personality, 43*, 455–484.
Shweder, R.A. (1977a). Illusory correlation and the MMPI controversy (Commentaries by J. Block and A. Edwards). *Journal of Consulting and Clinical Psychology, 49*, 917–924.

Shweder, R.A. (1977b). Illusory correlation and the MMPI controversy: Author's reply to some of the allusions and illusions in Block's and Edward's commentaries. *Journal of Consulting and Clinical Psychology, 45*, 936–940.

Shweder, R.A. (1982). Fact and artifact in trait-perception: The systematic distortion hypothesis. *Progress in Experimental Personality Research, 11*, 65–100.

Shweder, R.A., & D'Andrade, R.G. (1979). Accurate reflection or systematic distortion? A reply to Block, Weiss, and Thorne. *Journal of Personality and Social Psychology, 37*, 1075–1084

Shweder, R.A., & D'Andrade, R.G. (1980). The systematic distortion hypothesis. In Shweder, R.A. (Ed.). *Fallible judgement in behavioral research.* New directions for methodology of social and behavioral science (Vol. 4). San Francisco: Jossey-Bass. *Journal of Personality and Social Psychology, 37*, 1075–1084.

Snyder, M. (1974). Self-monitoring of expressive behavior. *Journal of Personality and Social Psychology, 30*, 526–537.

Snyder, M. (1979). Self-monitoring processes. *Advances in Experimental Social Psychology, 12*, 85–128.

Snyder, M., & Gangestad, S. (1982). Choosing social situations: Two investigations of self-monitoring processes. *Journal of Personality and Social Psychology, 43*, 123–135.

Snyder, M., & Monson, T.C. (1975). Persons, situations, and the control of social behavior. *Journal of Personality and Social Psychology, 32*, 637–644.

Snyder, M., & Tanke, E.D. (1976). Behavior and attitude: Some people are more consistent than others. *Journal of Personality, 44*, 501–517.

Stagner, R. (1977). On the reality and relevance of traits. *The Journal of General Psychology, 96*, 185–207.

Stern, G.G. (1970). *People in context: Measuring person-environment congruence in education and industry.* New York: Wiley.

Stones, M.J., & Burt, D. (1978). Quasi-statistical inference in rating behavior. *Journal of Research in Personality, 12*, 381–389.

Stricker, L.J., Jacobs, P.I., & Kogan, N. (1974). Trait interrelations and implicit personality theories and questionnaire data. *Journal of Personality and Social Psychology, 30*, 198–207

Tränkle, U. (1982). Über Zusammenhänge zwischen der sprachlichen Schwierigkeit von Fragebogen-Items, teststatistischen Gütekriterien und Beantwortungsverhalten. *Diagnostica, 28*, 289–306.

Turner, R.G. (1978). Consistency, self-consciousness, and the predictive validity of typical and maximal personality measures. *Journal of Research in Personality. 12*, 117–132.

Turner, R.G., & Gilliland, L. (1979). The comparative relevance and predictive validity of subject generated trait descriptions. *Journal of Personality, 47*, 230–244.

Tzeng, O.C.S. (1982). The artificial dispute over implicit personality theory: An answer to Jackson, Stricker, and Mirels. *Journal of Personality, 50*, 251–260.

Tzeng, O.C.S., & Tzeng, C.-H. (1982). Implicit personality theory: Myth or fact? An illustration of how empirical research can miss. *Journal of Personality, 50*, 223–239.

Wachtel, P.L. (1973). Psychodynamics, behavior therapy and the implacable experimenter: An inquiry into the consistency of personality. *Journal of Psychology, 82*, 324–334.

Weigel, R.H., & Newman, L.S. (1976). Increasing attitude-behavior correspondence by broadening the scope of the behavioral measure. *Journal of Personality and Social Psychology, 33*, 793–802.

Wiggins, J.S. (1973). *Personality and prediction. Principles of personality assessment.* Reading: Addison-Wesley.

Wiggins, J.S. (1979). Psychological taxonomy of trait descriptive terms: The interpersonal domain. *Journal of Personality and Social Psychology, 37*, 395–412.

Willerman, L., Turner, R.P., & Peterson, M. (1976). A comparison of the predictive validity of typical and maximal personality measures. *Journal of Research in Personality, 10*, 482–492.

Zanna, M.P., Olson, J.M., & Fazio, R.H. (1980). Attitude-behavior consistency – An individual difference perspective. *Journal of Personality and Social Psychology, 38*, 432–440.

The Trait Concept and the Personality Questionnaire *

Donald W. Fiske

This paper considers the concept of trait as a natural category from everyday usage and the reasons why self-report questionnaires have been used to measure traits. It argues that such questionnaires cannot be used in scientific work as operational definitions of traits. Discussing possible new directions for research in this domain, it makes two main points: (a) Questionnaires can be useful instruments for applied purposes when they have been designed and validated for the particular application, and when there is empirical evidence to support their use they can be of some value; (b) the use of questionnaires for scientific work, however, requires us to have a better theory of these instruments and of the processes involved in their administration and in the subjects' selection of their answers. Just as measurement helps us develop substantive theory, so we must have the relevant substantive theory to enable us to understand our measuring operations and to develop the rationale for their use.

The Trait Concept

The concept of trait was developed by psychologists from the ways people describe other people in everyday life. As Goldberg (1981) has said, people find words to talk about the differences they encounter in their daily interactions with others. Most of the constructs specified by personality theorists have been taken from the same source and then refined to some degree. Traits are "natural categories" (Mervis & Rosch, 1981; Wiggins, 1980). They are labels for fuzzy sets, for categories of behaviors with vague boundaries, with multiple alternative criteria, and with some instances more prototypic, more nearly pure types than others (Buss & Craik, 1980). Further analyses of the trait concept and its origins can be found in Fiske (1978) and in Nisbett (1980).

Given the nature of trait concepts, it is obvious that they cannot be fruitful scientific concepts. They are poor components for scientific theories. (The more advanced sciences abandoned lay concepts long ago.) A good scientific concept must be well specified and have a well-restricted meaning. At the least, the disposition embodied in a trait concept should be defined as a reaction in a stated context or situation. The quality or type of response should vary only in intensity or in frequency of occurrence, along a homogeneous dimension.

* This paper has profited from comments on the earlier version presented at the Bielefeld Symposium, especially those of Jerry Wiggins.

A good scientific construct should be embedded in a nomological net, a set of theoretical propositions stating relationships between that construct and others. The goal of science is to develop theory postulating constructs and their interrelationships, theory that is supported by empirical laws. We validate our constructs by determining whether the propositions involving them are supported empirically. That is, we seek to establish firm empirical relationships corresponding to those in the nomological net. We have had great difficulty in identifying any such empirical laws in the personality area, especially because empirical relationships vary with the instruments used, different questionnaires purporting to measure the same constructs often yielding disparate results (e.g., Fiske, 1973).

We must of course be prepared to modify our conceptual formulations when empirical facts require this. We must expect that some of the propositions involving a construct and giving it meaning will not be supported in empirical investigations. When that happens, the construct must be modified (or even dropped entirely). In this sense, a construct must be open to change. But such reasoning does not support the loose assertion that our constructs should be open in the sense of lacking explicit delineation. If a construct is vaguely defined, it is slippery and can never be proved inadequate by empirical testing. Because personality traits are poorly specified they have managed to survive, even though decades of research on them have generated mostly equivocal evidence for them.

Although traits originated in descriptions of other people, psychological research uses such descriptions less than self-reports. There are many limitations to descriptions made by other people. They often vary with the degree of acquaintance between the rater and the person rated; in contrast, everybody has an equal opportunity to know about their own behavior. Descriptions by others also vary with the raters' perspectives and opportunities to observe the subject: superiors, inferiors, coworkers, social friends, and intimates may see different behaviors and may also interpret similar behaviors in different ways. Self-reports are responses made in a standardized situation. (In choosing responses, however, a subject may have particular situations in mind and this information is typically not available to the researcher.) Finally, it is much more economical to obtain self-reports instead of going to the trouble of locating several other persons to describe the subject for us. Thus, the observation of Coleman (1969) about sociology applies here: "... most research techniques which analyze behavioral data take a shortcut in data-collection, and base their methods on individuals' *reports* of their own behavior and, less frequently, on those of others" (p. 109).

So, even when we are really interested in how other people see our subjects, we may use self-reports to estimate such descriptions. In so doing, we conveniently overlook the fact that scores from self-report instruments do not agree closely with ratings by others (the correlation coefficients may reach .50, although values around .35 are more common). At times, however, we do use ratings by others to evaluate the adequacy of self-report instruments (e.g.,

Ashton & Goldberg, 1973; Jackson, 1975). Perhaps we feel justified in substituting self-reports for descriptions by others because we have found that, when the same items are used in these two methods, the same factorial structure tends to be found (Fiske, 1949; Norman, 1969).

There is still another rationale for having recourse to self-reports. We do not usually ask people to rate themselves on our more technical concepts, such as perceived external locus of reinforcement; we realize that people do not naturally think about themselves in such terms. Instead, we ask people to report on behaviors that we consider pertinent to those concepts, arguing that they can make adequate reports at that low level of abstraction. We then combine these item responses into scores according to our beliefs about which responses are indications of the traits we wish to estimate. In writing such items, we do try to use language that subjects seem likely to interpret the same way that we do. In so doing, we assume that each subject has in some degree the trait we want to measure. However, the adequacy or appropriateness of applying the same nomothetic variables to everyone is dubious, as Bem and Allen (1974), Kenrick and Stringfield (1980), and others have shown.

Do Personality Questionnaires Provide Operational Definitions?

In spite of the problems mentioned above, one could argue that we can develop a sound strategy for basic research in personality simply by using our self-report personality scales as operational definitions for the traits we want to study. Unfortunately, there is little reason to believe that this strategy will be successful. Insofar as it has been implicitly used in research during the last several decades, progress has been limited. In fact, it seems likely that we have achieved as much as we can hope to achieve by that approach.

There are several reasons why that strategy cannot achieve much success. First, it builds on a weak foundation: as we all know, the typical average intercorrelation among items in questionnaires is below .10 (e.g., Fiske, 1966); reports about the several behaviors subsumed under any of our standard trait labels covary only at a very low level. Second, very slight changes in wording can generate differences in responses. The best empirical evidence for that assertion comes from investigations of wording in opinion surveys (e.g., Turner & Krauss, 1978). Third, words have different meanings for different subjects. A clear case is the meaning of frequency terms, such as "often" or "occasionally" (Pepper, 1981; see also other papers in that sourcebook). Finally, as often occurs with operational definitions, each operation is somewhat distinctive: Different questionnaires aimed at the same trait yield scores that are clearly not interchangeable. When test constructors set out to measure the same general trait, their instruments show agreement ranging from good to only fair (e.g., Butt & Fiske, 1968), and even when their target concepts have been explicitly defined, as with needs in Murray's sense of the word, the resulting instruments may not agree on the levels of correlation between pairs of concepts (Fiske, 1973).

As instruments for basic research, we know that self-reports have critical and perhaps fatal weaknesses. By definition, self-reports use only one observer and so no estimate of interobserver agreement can be obtained. This obvious fact means that we face the difficult problem of distinguishing between effects arising from the subject as an observer and from the subject as the person being described. In addition, scores from self-report instruments do not have the stability over time that we need in such research: Do people's traits fluctuate over time as much as their test scores? It seems unlikely, but perhaps they do.

Still another influence is the interaction between the subject and the task of answering the questionnaire. Exactly what does the subject interpret the task to be? For example, does the subject's interpretation arouse self-defensiveness or a disposition to present himself or herself in a favorable light? Jackson (this volume) has developed a theory about how people decide on their responses to items. From this and other work (e.g., Kuncel, 1973), it is clear that our subjects do not always go about responding to our questions in just the way that we would like them to. Note that these are not systematic factors, constant over all subjects, that merely introduce a fixed bias into our data. Most regrettably, as in most other behavior, there are individual differences here that confound our efforts to create standardized measuring instruments.

The strategy of taking questionnaires as operational definitions of the traits they are designed to measure does have one important advantage: By simply asserting that those obtaining high scores on a set of questionnaires are high on the designated trait, it completely avoids the problem of the accuracy of the self-report responses. In contrast, the rationale for using self-reports about behaviors and attitudes as a basis for estimating trait strength has several weak points, some of which have been mentioned above. That rationale says that a person who is high on a trait will be likely to do certain things and have certain attitudes, and that we can ascertain these tendencies by asking the subject about them.

To find out whether a subject engages in certain behaviors, we ask rather general questions, such as "Do you often do ...?" Insofar as these can be taken as matters of fact, the accuracy of the response undoubtedly decreases with the time since the relevant events occurred, as various studies of accuracy of memories have shown. In addition, we must note that questionnaires rarely ask about a single specific event but rather ask about a set of events, and it is unlikely that the respondent recalls all of the relevant instances when deciding upon an answer. Perhaps we should change the wordings of our questions. The promising results obtained by Buss and Craik (1981) may have come from their asking whether the subject had ever performed each specific act. Survey researchers have found it helps to set a specific time period: "During the last month, have you ...?" [People constructing personality questionnaires will profit from *Asking Questions,* prepared by two people in the survey field (Sudman & Bradburn, 1982).]

The accuracy of answers to questions about attitudes and feelings is even more doubtful. Such accuracy is difficult or impossible to determine, because we obviously have no dependable alternative methods of assessment against which to compare the subjective responses. The provocative paper by Nisbett and Wilson (1977) provides grounds for doubting the accuracy of peoples' reports about their cognitive activity; subsequent rejoinders (e.g., Ericsson & Simon, 1980; Smith & Miller, 1978) do not disprove the assertion that the longer the interval between the inner experience and the report the less likely it is that the report will be accurate. [For a further discussion of this problem, see Fiske (1980).]

New Directions

Given these critical difficulties with personality questionnaires, what should we do? How should we direct or redirect our efforts to make more scientific progress? One possibility is to patch up our present approach and do the best we can with it. For example, we could develop a short standard list of important personality traits and define them carefully and explicitly. In particular, for each trait we could identify a set of situations where the trait is often manifested to some degree, situations that almost everyone encounters in daily living. We would then develop ways of assessing the strength of the trait shown by each person in each situation, using self-report questionnaires but supplementing them with reports of others where possible. Then we could calculate each person's mean and standard deviation over the values for the several situations. The mean would correspond to the traditional composite score. The standard deviation would tell us how consistent the person was with respect to that particular trait, that is to say, how well the mean score described the person.

Other measures could be derived from these data. In the two situations where the person shows the trait most strongly, how much does he or she show? Or we could determine the level the person generally reaches – say in 70% of the situations. Thus, the proposal is that other indices of a person's distribution of trait manifestations should be considered, and not just the central tendency.

Such scores might permit more adequate testing of some substantive personality theory. But, given the tendency of most psychologists to choose convenient and simple measurement strategies, I do not anticipate that the plan will actually be tried out, unless perhaps for some trait where consistency across situations has considerable theoretical or applied significance. Unfortunately, the execution of this plan requires some acceptable solution to the problem of developing a nomothetic classification of situations. Can we identify a set of situations that have the same psychological meaning for almost every person? Can we find even a small set of such situations for each trait? It seems unlikely that we can solve this problem. When a situation has the same meaning for all subjects, it is likely to be one that makes strong demands for conforming behavior and hence one that greatly reduces the extent of individual differences within it.

Another possibility is an intense re-examination of our present rationale for self-report instruments. Because the idea of just asking a question and getting a response seems to simple and so similar to what goes on in interviews (a source from which personality questionnaires were originally developed) and in everyday interactions, we have taken it too much for granted. But what do we really want our subjects to do, in answering our questions? Ideally, what would be the cognitive and decision processes involved? We have little systematic analysis of that matter. We do have some information about response sets and styles, gained from analyzing the responses themselves. We know a little about the processes, as reported by subjects who introspect immediately after giving a response (Kuncel, 1973), but we need much more research on the topic (Jackson & Paunonen, 1980). We do know that some of these processes, such as altering the question to make it easier to answer, occur in responding to opinion surveys (Belson, 1968). To investigate this area, we can adapt the methods of cognitive psychologists whose research is directed toward learning what goes on in people's heads.

Our problem comes from the fact that we want our respondents to aggregate, to summarize over instances. We are not asking them to retrieve from memory bits of factual information that have been stored as discrete entities. Instead, we ask them to consider a vaguely specified series of pertinent events and come up with a summarizing judgment. The task is much more difficult than that of an observer making a similar kind of judgment on the basis of a restricted period of observation.

The matter of aggregation also enters in as we go from item response to scores. For convenience, we arbitrarily give each keyed response a unit weight. The resulting score can be taken as indicating the range of situations and the variety of ways that the person manifests the trait. It ignores degrees of intensity or of relative frequency that are concealed within each positive response. It is not the way a person goes about arriving at a self-rating on a given trait, such processes probably being similar to those used in answering the items in questionnaires. All these considerations are in addition to questions about the availability of pertinent memories and the distortions in recollections of one's own behaviors.

Thus, the root of our difficulties in trying to measure traits from self-reports lies in the fact that traits are natural categories (as discussed earlier). A trait attribution is some kind of summarizing of a lot of discrete behaviors, behaviors taking different forms in different people. In practice, we leave this summarizing task to our subjects, permitting them to do it as they wish. I believe we take this easy way because we have never developed any satisfactory rationale for aggregating many behaviors into a single score. We could work out a theoretical notion of a trait score as derived in some way from distributions of an individual's pertinent behaviors over situations, each such behavior being assessed for rate of occurrence, for intensity, and perhaps also for duration. But we lack the consensual theory to guide us in determining the calculations to use in reducing these distributions to one score.

In re-examining and making explicit our current rationale for measuring traits by questionnaires, we must of course take into account the fact that our subjects are responding to our instructions and to the task we set for them, all within the context provided by the testing room. We know that their responses are influenced by the reason for their being there to be tested: Are they volunteers? Are they being tested for purposes from which they may benefit? We all realize that a major handicap in psychological research and measurement is the reactivity of subjects, the objects being studied.

Natural Descriptions

Another approach is based on a distinction between personality traits as properties of the outside, real world and traits as categories that people use to describe others. Many investigators in the personality domain seem to blur that distinction. They treat the natural categories that people use in everyday attributions to others as though they were based on real properties of people, which can be refined into scientific concepts. They have experienced great frustration, for reasons that have been brought out in the earlier pages of this paper.

The alternative approach is to treat traits as attributions that people make about themselves and others and to study the properties of these attributions. How do people make personality descriptions in everyday living? Goldberg (1981) and others have analyzed the descriptive terms that have become part of the language. But what terms do people use? Fiske and Cox (1979) have shown that people use different kinds of terms for different purposes. In the area of free self-description, recent work has been reviewed by Turner (1981). Free self-descriptions give us a considerable amount of information. In addition to providing us with protocols that can, if we wish, be coded into standard nomothetic variables, they tell us which variables are salient in the pictures that people have of themselves. And such self-portrayals have the advantage that the respondents can use their own language and do not have to force their self-impressions into the fixed molds of test constructors.

Relevance for the Individual

All of us already knew that any given trait described some people better than others and that the trait-relevant behavior of some people was more consistent over situations than that of others, but we needed the empirical demonstration of Bem and Allen (1974) to make us face up to that crucial fact and consider its implications. A major unresolved question is raised by that study: How are we to cope, in theory and in measurement, with the fact that each of our nomothetic variables describes some people well and others only poorly? Earlier, I suggested one initial pragmatic step that we can take: Describe people on a standard variable not only in terms of their average tendency but also by other indices of their distribution of manifestations over situations. But we still must be careful about the loose use of averages.

This fundamental issue stems of course from our wish to describe people in simple ways. It is easier to think about people as having a single value on each trait dimension than as having a distribution of tendencies. Once again, we see ourselves aggregating over diverse behaviors to obtain trait scores, and then averaging these scores to try to discover differences between groups of persons.

Note also that this crucial problem pervades all our work on personality measurement. Years ago, Campbell and I (Campbell & Fiske, 1959) introduced the notion of the trait method unit, and later (Fiske, 1973, 1976), I argued that such units had to be the focus of work on construct validity. But for any trait, each of our methods involves aggregating over a specified subset of trait manifestations. If the trait scores obtained by each method apply well to some people and poorly to others, how far can we hope to go in validating such a trait method unit?

Applications of Questionnaires

The preceding discussion has been concerned with the basic study of personality. Because of the many basic obstacles, we have made little scientific progress toward substantive knowledge in that area, and I see little reason to believe that appreciably more progress will be made if we continue our present methods and strategies (cf. Fiske, 1978). But my pessimistic view does not include a negative evaluation of our applied work. I think it is noteworthy that research on personnel selection is one of seven examples used by officials of the American Psychological Association in a 1981 letter protesting against the proposed cuts in the federal budget that would affect support for the behavioral sciences.

Especially when compared with other psychological tests, personality questionnaires do have limited utility in selecting people for jobs. Nevertheless, they are of value in vocational guidance and in counseling. They have some utility in clinical diagnosis. Self-report instruments can be of value in our efforts to understand maladjustment and perhaps can help in setting goals for psychotherapy. In all these applications the use of a standardized instrument has clear advantages over the use of human judgment, even that of experts. The more that is learned about human decision making, the more the evidence favors actuarial methods. Even when our instruments and other methods are developed from a rational or theoretical starting point, we have shown that we can identify self-report procedures that can be of value in practical situations. But, given the limitations of all self-report methods, there is a ceiling to what we can do.

We must accept the fact that no one standard instrument should be expected to be the best procedure for every kind of purpose. Accepting that proposition, we often develop an instrument solely for the particular goals of a given study. Insofar as we can specify a set of purposes or goals for which measurements of individuals are needed, we should compare procedures and identify the one or two best instruments. Although the differences in the usefulness of several instruments for any one purpose may not be large, we do need to use the most effective procedure in each particular application, accepting the obvious generalization that no self-report procedure will be ideal.

This recommendation does mean a lot of work for a relatively small gain in effectiveness of our measuring procedures. A major advantage, however, is that with repeated application of the standard instrument for each identified purpose, a body of information will be accumulated about the particular strengths and weaknesses of the instrument. Measurement must be approached pragmatically. Axiomatic formulations and logical analyses do help us to gain some perspective on what measurement is all about, but the final judgment on the adequacy of our measuring procedure must be based on empirical evidence.

Writing in 1921 about the rules that must hold for a property to be measurable, Campbell (1952) says, "The fact that the rules are true can be, and must be, determined by experiment in the same way as the fact that any other laws are true" (p. 119). If one thinks that it is inconceivable that such rules might not be true, one should note that each rule is "actually true only in certain conditions" (p. 119). Campbell was writing about measurement in physics, seemingly an easier task than measurement in psychology. The importance of his point becomes especially clear when we recall that in psychology, and particularly in personality, we have no ultimate criterion measurement, no ideal standard, against which to check the adequacy of our instruments. We can evaluate our procedures only in terms of relationships between independent measuring operations, examining not only the congruence between measurements intended to assess the same variable but also the patterns of relationship with measurements of variables that are theoretically related to our target construct, as in construct validation work.

Method Theory and Substantive Theory

Earlier, I argued that we needed to achieve a better understanding of the way people go about making their decisions in responding to self-report items. More generally, we need to develop a sound theory for our personality measurement. Some of the analyses and recommendations in my book, *Measuring the Concepts of Personality* (Fiske, 1971), were steps in that direction, although at that time I did not see them in this perspective. In a paper that has important implications for this area, "Verbal Reports as Data," Ericsson and Simon (1980) make a statement pertinent to our concerns: "... we must extend our analyses of the tasks that our subjects are performing to incorporate the processes they are using to produce their verbal responses. The expansion of theories to include a theory of the measuring instruments is commonplace in physics ... In the same way, experiments that record verbal responses of any kind need at least a rudimentary theory of how subjects produce such responses – in what memories the response information has been stored ..." (p. 216).

We sometimes forget that the natural sciences have to deal with problems of method variance, just as we do. The place to see this most clearly is not in the simple examples of measuring length that are found in discussions of the general theory of measurement, but in the more difficult measurement areas – for example, where the act of measuring affects the actual attribute in the object being measured. It is interesting that temperature can be measured in a wide variety of ways: In addition to the familiar use of expansion of liquids and the differential expansion of metals, there are the thermocouple, the resistance thermometer, and others. The important point is that each is based upon a different part of the established theory in physics. In making physical measurements, physicists have some theory pertinent to that measurement. As Kuhn (1961, p. 47) says, "... a quite highly developed body of theory is ordinarily prerequisite to fruitful measurement in the physical sciences ..."

The argument seems quite pertinent to measurement in behavioral science, including measurement by self-report. To measure well, we need a theory for our measuring procedures that is based on or derived from the substantive theory relevant to behavior, or more specifically, to the production of verbal responses and to decision making. Jackson's model (Jackson, this volume) is a step in the right direction.

In this connection, personality research can follow the lead of research on mental abilities, just as it did years ago with respect to psychometric theory. New theories of mental abilities are currently being developed. An example of one with an information-processing approach is that of Sternberg (1979). His analysis is based on the tasks involved in mental performance and draws heavily upon tests of specific kinds. In a subsequent paper (Sternberg, 1981), he urges the study of the specific mental processes that generate a subject's test performances. So the substantive theory is building upon conceptualizations of measurement tasks but eventually that theory will provide a guide to refinements in the theory and practice of measuring mental abilities.

We have always known that good measurement is necessary to carry out empirical tests of theory and to provide leads to new conceptualizations. But now we can see that good theory is needed to have good measurement. We must have an adequate theory of our measuring operations and, if current substantive theory does not provide it, we must develop the relevant theory ourselves. Psychological measurement involves psychological processes that we must understand (Fiske, in press). Self-report measurements have their own kinds of processes. Exactly what goes on in obtaining self-reports?

References

Ashton, S.G., & Goldberg, L.R. (1973). In response to Jackson's challenge: The comparative validity of personality scales constructed by the external (empirical) strategy and scales developed intuitively by experts, novices, and laymen. *Journal of Research in Personality, 7*, 1–20.

Belson, W.A. (1968). Respondent understanding of survey questions. *Polls, 3*, 1–13.

Bem, D.J., & Allen, A. (1974). On predicting some of the people some of the time: The search for cross-situational consistencies in behavior. *Psychological Review, 81*, 506–520.

Buss, D.M., & Craik, K.H. (1980). The frequency concept of disposition: Dominance and prototypically dominant acts. *Journal of Personality, 48*, 379–392.

Buss, D.M., & Craik, K.H. (1981). The act frequency analysis of interpersonal dispositions: Aloofness, gregariousness, dominance, and submission. *Journal of Personality, 49*, 175–192.

Butt, D.S., & Fiske, D.W. (1968). Comparison of strategies in developing scales for dominance. *Psychological Bulletin, 70*, 505–519.

Campbell, D.T., & Fiske, D.W. (1959). Convergent and discriminant validation by the multitrait-multimethod matrix. *Psychological Bulletin, 56*, 81–105.

Campbell, N.R. (1952). *What is science?* New York: Dover. (Originally published 1921).

Coleman, J.S. (1969). The methods of sociology. In Bierstadt, R. (Ed.), *A design for sociology: Scope, objectives, and methods* (Monograph 9). Philadelphia: American Academy of Political and Social Science.

Ericsson, K.A., & Simon, H.A. (1980). Verbal reports as data. *Psychological Review, 87*, 215–251.

Fiske, D.W. (1949). Consistency of the factorial structures of personality ratings from difference sources. *Journal of Abnormal and Social Psychology, 44*, 329–344.

Fiske, D.W. (1966). Some hypotheses concerning test adequacy. *Educational and Psychological Measurement, 26*, 69–88.

Fiske, D.W. (1971). *Measuring the concepts of personality*. Chicago: Aldine.

Fiske, D.W. (1973). Can a personality construct be validated empirically? *Psychological Bulletin, 80*, 89–92.

Fiske, D.W. (1976). Can a personality construct have a singular validational pattern? Rejoinder to Huba and Hamilton. *Psychological Bulletin, 83*, 877–879.

Fiske, D.W. (1978). *Strategies for personality research: The observation versus interpretation of behavior*. San Francisco: Jossey-Bass.

Fiske, D.W. (1980). When are verbal reports veridical? In Shweder, R. (Ed.), *New directions for methodology of social and behavioral science: Fallible judgments in behavioral research* (No. 4). San Francisco: Jossey-Bass.

Fiske, D.W. (in press). Measuring to understand and understanding measuring.

Fiske, S.T., & Cox, M.G. (1979). Describing others: There's more to person perception than trait lists. *Journal of Personality, 47*, 136–161.

Goldberg, L.R. (1981). Language and personality: Developing a taxonomy of trait-descriptive terms. In Fiske, D. (Ed.), *New directions for methodology of social and behavioral science. Problems with language imprecision*. (No. 9). San Francisco: Jossey-Bass.

Jackson, D.N. (1975). The relative validity of scales prepared by naive item writers and those based on empirical methods of personality scale construction. *Educational and Psychological Measurement, 35*, 361–370.

Jackson, D.N., & Paunonen, S.V. (1980). Personality structure and assessment. *Annual Review of Psychology, 31*, 503–551.

Kenrick, D.T., & Stringfield, D.O. (1980). Personality traits and the eye of the beholder: Crossing some traditional philosophical boundaries in the search for consistency in all of the people. *Psychological Review, 87*, 88–104.

Kuhn, T.S. (1961). The function of measurement in modern physical science. In Woolf, H. (Ed.), *Quantification: A history of the meaning of measurement in the natural and social sciences* (pp. 31–63). New York: Bobbs-Merrill.

Kuncel, R.B. (1973). Response processes and relative location of subject and item. *Educational and Psychological Measurement, 33*, 545–563.

Mervis, C.B., & Rosch, E. (1981). Categorization of natural objects. *Annual Review of Psychology, 32*, 89–115.

Nisbett, R.E. (1980). The trait construct in lay and professional psychology. In Festinger, L. (Ed.), *Retrospections on social psychology*. New York: Oxford University Press.

Nisbett, R.E., & Wilson, T.D. (1977). Telling more than we can know: Verbal reports on mental processes. *Psychological Review, 84*, 231–259.

Norman, W. (1969). "To see ourselves as others see us!": Relations among-self-perceptions, peer-perceptions, and expected peer-perceptions of personality attributes. *Multivariate Behavioral Research, 4*, 417–443.

Pepper, S. (1981). Problems in the quantification of frequency expressions. In Fiske, D.W. (Ed.), *New directions for methodology of social and behavioral science: Problems with language imprecision* (No. 9). San Francisco: Jossey-Bass.

Smith, E.R., & Miller, F.D. (1978). Limits on perceptions of cognitive processes: A reply to Nisbett and Wilson. *Psychological Review, 85*, 355–362.

Sternberg, R.J. (1979). The nature of mental abilities. *American Psychologist, 34*, 214–230.

Sternberg, R.J. (1981). Testing and cognitive psychology. *American Psychologist, 36*, 1181–1189.

Sudman, S., & Bradburn, N.M. (1982). *Asking questions: A practical guide to questionnaire design*. San Francisco: Jossey-Bass.

Turner, C., & Krauss, E. (1978). Fallible indicators of the subjective state of the nation. *American Psychologist, 33*, 456–470.

Turner, R.G. (1981). Using subject generated descriptors. In Fiske, D. (Ed.), *New directions for methodology of social and behavioral science. Problems with language imprecision* (No. 9). San Francisco: Jossey-Bass.

Wiggins, J.S. (1980). Circumplex models of interpersonal behavior. In Wheeler, L. (Ed.), *Review of personality and social psychology* (Vol. 1). Beverly Hills: Sage.

II. Item Generation and Scale Construction

Pragmatic Validity to Be Considered for the Construction and Application of Psychological Questionnaires

MICHAEL KASTNER

When introspective data are gathered by means of questionnaires, there are many ways in which results can become invalid. Every diagnostician is familiar with the feeling that the construct presented in a questionnaire is not clearly defined or that the test persons might interpret the items in varying ways. Existing test theories deal with "only" the syntactic aspects of questionnaire data. Too little attention is generally paid to semantic questions dealing with the way in which questionnaire scores are arrived at. Response set research also uses already existing data.

This contribution will investigate the processes involved in determining the meaning and understanding of a questionnaire, the manner in which these processes lead to final evaluations of questionnaire results, and the interpretation of these results. The testing of questionnaires is a diagnostic communication process in which various persons take part. A questionnaire also contains objects of meaning which can have different connotations for various persons

Table 1. Process most frequently used in determining meaning and understanding of questionnaires

Diagnostic communication process	Objects of meaning arranged in a sequence of decreasing invalidation
The designer of the test formulates	Construct
• The construct	
• The items indicating the construct	
• The response categories	Instruction
• The instructions	
• Interpretation aids	Item
The test person receives	
• Instructions	
• Items	Response category
and perceives and evaluates	
• The response category	
The diagnostician makes use of	
• The construct	
• The interpretation aids	Interpretation aids
• The items (sometimes)	
The contractor makes use of	
• The construct and/or interpretation aids	

taking part in the test. The process most frequently used for questionnaire testing is outlined in Table 1.

This chapter is an attempt to examine all possible "misunderstandings" which arise among persons participating in a test situation, with respect to the various objects of meaning contained in the questionnaire. This will be done in four steps:

1. It will be demonstrated with the help of empirical proof that misunderstanding occurs in the diagnostic communication process during questionnaire testing, thus potentially leading to invalidation of results.
2. Concrete examples of misunderstandings which lead to invalidations will be given.
3. A concept referred to as pragmatic language validation will then be introduced.
4. Pragmatic validation will be demonstrated and its effectivity will be proved.

Existence of Misunderstanding in the Diagnostic Process

In the first step it is necessary to ask whether empirical proof exists which shows that questionnaire results become invalid because of "misunderstandings" within the diagnostic communication process. If all participating persons and all the objects of meaning in the questionnaire (see Table 1) are systematically listed it becomes clear that it is meaningful to establish points of correspondence between them. Various persons have different interpretations of the meanings of various objects contained in a questionnaire.

Comparisons between such persons that are meaningful for questionnaire testing are presented in Table 2. If all the respective comparisons involved pro-

Table 2. Meaningful comparisons between persons and diagnostic processes

ns	Construct		Instruction		Item		Item response		Inter-pretation aids	
	T_1	T_2	T_1	T_2	T_1	T_2	T_1	T_2	T_1	T_2
st designer – test person			x		x		x	x		
st designer – psychologist	x	x	x	x					x	x
ychologist – test person			x							
ychologist – contractor	x	x							x	
veral psychologists	x	x							x	x
veral test persons			x	x	x		x			
veral contractors	x								x	

T_1, transformation of the symbol into the subjective meaning, on the part of the receiver;
T_2, transformation of the subjective meaning into the symbol, on the part of the sender

cesses of meaning and understanding which were in agreement with each other, then pragmatic language validation would not be necessary.

The first line in Table 2 deals with the question of whether the designer of the questionnaire and the test person have the same understanding of the instructions. If the test person does not behave in the intended fashion the whole test can become invalid. Or if various psychologists (see line 5 in Table 2) understand the interpretation aids on their evaluation sheets differently, then divergent interpretations can result from numerically identical questionnaire results. Table 2 would be of little informational value to a strict behaviorist or to a designer of empirical questionnaires, who are interested only in correlations with external criteria. According to Janke (1973), the best coefficients for criterion validity are lower than .40, so that there is an unexplained remaining variance of 84%. Even if regarded from the point of view of technical measurements, which would mean that semantic aspects were not taken into account, this error variance is surprising. The comparison of reactions to items which are kept constant will be included in the questionnaire testing. (Interaction questionnaires will not be used.)

The questionnaire aims at revealing differences between the persons. Interactions between persons and items are not desired and are seen as contributing to error variance.

Whenever several persons show different reactions to the same item, the following factors should be considered: (a) The desired adequate interpretation of and reaction to items, which depends on how pronounced a postulated latent trait is; (b) divergent interpretations of the items, an effect which is not desired; (c) divergent interpretations of response categories (not desired); (d) and finally, the possible combinations of adequate interpretations of items with inadequate reception of the response categories and vice versa.

If it can be proved that the data (reaction scores) are not generated in comparable ways, then methods which will make it possible to standardize these data must be developed. The potential invalidations mentioned above apply to the item responses, i.e., to the immediate development of test scores. Even if these are arrived at in the desired manner, the results of questionnaire testing can become totally invalid if the interpretation of the numerically determined score is not verbally communicated in accordance with the intended meaning. Thus, a method aimed at minimizing the invalidations which can potentially arise due to misunderstandings between participants in the diagnosis must take all objects of meaning into consideration. From the multitude of possible comparisons (Table 2), two specific examples will be explained to demonstrate that misunderstandings do arise in the process of diagnosis. The first is concerned with the interpretation of items.

1. Items from the FPI (Freiburg Personality Inventory by Fahrenberg, Selg, & Hampel, 1973) and
2. Specifications (interpretation aids) of the construct *'Gelassenheit'* (i.e., calmness, composure, tranquility, imperturbability) were each paired with the ideal item or the ideal specification "the person X is *gelassen* (calm,

composed, ...)". Persons belonging to different diagnostic groups were asked to judge on a scale from 1 to 9 to what extent the two items or specifications expressed the same human trait.

Ideal item and ideal specification	The person X is *gelassen*
Specimen item	The person X is generally very optimistic with regard to the future. How similar 1.....9?
Specimen specification	The person X is enterprising

Two-dimensional ALSCAL solutions show that test persons differ greatly in the extent to which they reduce or expand their semantic scope, their ability to differentiate between nuances of meaning. The most substantial differences (in relationship) were found between members of the contractor group and representative psychology students who had just recently begun their studies.

The most nearly similar results were found among psychology students shortly before graduation and psychologists. The substance of these results can be interpreted as follows:

Even items which, in the opinion of the respective test designer, fulfill statistical criteria for homogeneity can differ substantially with regard to the subjective interpretation of their similarity by the test persons.

The same applies to different interpretation aids for the same construct.

The differences in similarity patterns cannot be attributed to the differences between the various groups tested (psychologists, students, lay persons). With the help of both multidimensional scaling and cluster analysis it was possible to show that there were significant differences in the structures of the decision-making processes, which correspondend to group membership.

The similarity of the construct *Gelassenheit* to the items which are supposedly indications thereof and their interpretation aids is dependent on the manner in which it is semantically perceived by various persons and groups. The degree of semantic correspondence had a tendency to increase with the amount of psychological training the persons had been exposed to. This can be explained if it is assumed that the semantic scope of individuals converges in accordance with the degree to which a common cognitive structure exists among these for the use of words to describe persons.

The second example is concerned with the verbal evaluations of questionnaire results. Fifteen candidates for examinations in psychology wrote reports on one and the same case. Contractors and practicing psychologists evaluated these reports by means of a content analysis of categories such as "Based on the information in this report, how important is 'intellectual ability'?"

Of 31 initial categories, 12 remained in which the degree of correspondence between the evaluations was adequate. The data constituted the basis for a variance analysis with the following three factors: A = contractors, psychologists (did not prove significant); variant B = reports; and C = categories. The interaction between the reports and the categories led to the best explanation of variance.

This means that classifications of given categories vary from one report to the next. The factor reports also showed significant main effects, which will here be interpreted as demonstrating a lack of pragmatic language validity in the reports. Furthermore, the significant triple interaction seems to indicate that, depending on group membership (psychologists or contractors) and on the report, the importance of intellectual ability for a given case was sometimes judged as more and sometimes less pronounced.

Together with other studies, the studies described above have led to the assumption that relevant misunderstandings in the diagnostic process have an empirical basis. The question of the nature of this dissimilarity of results then arises.

The Nature of the Misunderstandings that Invalidate Questionnaire Testing

A further example study concerning item response follows. In this case the test persons were asked to respond to 10 FPI items. The study material included 23 qualitative questions, which had been selected by means of content analysis and were asked for every item. One item is discussed here as an example. In item 18, "To be honest, I sometimes enjoy tormenting others", the concept "to torment" is understood in various ways. Half the test persons associate "tormenting" with physical abuse in the sence of "beating"; about 20% think of "psychological terror" or "mental/emotional torture." Other test person regard "mental/emotional neglect" or "failure to fulfill needs" as "torture," etc. In other words, for half the test persons the response "does not apply" (which is available to all test persons) may mean:

"No, I do not enjoy tormenting others in the sense of physically beating them" (whereby failure to fulfill needs, for example, is not taken into consideration). For 50% of the test persons the response "does not apply" refers to the statement as a whole; for the other half it simply refers to "I enjoy." The statement "It is not true that I enjoy tormenting others" does not exclude the possibility that this might be considered necessary at times. Apart from this, the concept "sometimes" may lead a test person to respond "does not apply" because he feels that "always" or "most of the time" would be more appropriate. The various ways in which the response categories can be applied to either the statement as a whole or only to the first part ("I enjoy") are reflected in the fact that 65% of the test persons felt incapable of using the response categories in a way which would represent the items meaningfully. Those cases in which the responses limit themselves to physical torture, to situations which are not extreme, and to persons one does not hate are especially interesting. Restriction to situations which are not extreme excludes the sphere of action known as "war," whereas "mental/emotional tormenting" refers to the spheres of personal and professional relationships. Associations which lead away from the actual statement, e.g., with the film *Holocaust,* are also interesting: Viewers alter their understanding of the concepts of brutality and cruelty. Apparently the topicality of certain issues is also a relevant factor in the interpretation of the items.

This example for various types of misunderstandings is now followed by a description of approaches by means of which potential invalidations can be avoided.

Ways of Avoiding Questionnaire Invalidations: Pragmatic Language Validity

The very numerous studies on response sets in which the reactions of test persons were influenced by trick questions, SD (social desirability) control questions, item balancing, partializing of acquiescence, etc. are quite well known and will therefore not be discussed here. According to the tenets of the concept of pragmatic language validity, these methods cannot produce substantial results because they work with already existing data.

In my opinion, invalidation generally occurs at earlier stages. Research on the invalidation hypothesis (Janssen, 1978), which shows that questionnaires become most clearly invalidated when the transparency and the wisdom of the tests are most pronounced, especially under the influence of SD motivation, in no way contradicts the concept of pragmatic language validation, which attempts to assimilate contexts of meaning, including those of SD, for example.

Concepts for the evaluation of questionnaire contents have been incorporated into the concept of pragmatic language validation (cf. example in the previous section). This has been accomplished in part with the help of process questionnaires (cf. Cliff, 1968; Rogers, 1974; Turner & Fiske, 1968), which direct attention to variance at the expense of individual processes of evaluation.

Studies by Schneider-Düker and Schneider (1977) and the last study referred to above demonstrate the relevance of individual contexts of meaning to responses to the items. They emphasize that improvements to questionnaires are most likely to be possible in this area. Pragmatic language validation, in contrast to most other approaches, takes all objects of meaning in the diagnostic process and all participating persons into account. In my opinion, most studies on invalidation effects limit themselves to inquiring into item response. Pragmatic language validation deals with the question of the extent to which it can be guaranteed that concepts, sentences, and texts in a questionnaire are used in a sufficiently consistent way throughout the process of diagnostic communication, beginning with the theory of the test designer and ending with the understanding of the report by the contractor.

Pragmatic language validation is defined as follows:

1. A measurement made with the help of a questionnaire is valid if it corresponds to the intentions of the designer of the test. This intention is expressed verbally.
2. Pragmatic language validation of a measurement is achieved if the intended meaning of an item has, without the (or, if so agreed upon, with a minimum of) influence of external factors, generated the intended numerically represented reaction.
3. Provided that the second criterion above has been fulfilled, pragmatic language validation of the verbal interpretation of a numerical test value is achieved if its meaning is identical with that of the intended measurement.

All the essential components of the concept of pragmatic language validation are included in the simple definition: "Validity exists if one measures that which one has intended to measure." One measures (in fact) with the aid of something (a test), something one is supposedly familiar with, and nothing else. Thus validity means that empirical data must be brought into relation with a theory. In my opinion this can best be made clear by means of a discussion of facet theory.

Guttman (cited in Borg, 1981, p. 137) says: "A theory is a hypothesis which deals with the correspondence between a system of definitions for a universe of observations and one aspect of the empirical structure of these observations, together with a rationale for such a hypothesis." Figure 1 shows a breakdown of the universe of observation.

Validation is the attempt to confirm these hypotheses. Validity thus refers to *two* aspects of the universe of observations, the elements of empirical studies (stimuli, persons, reactions) *and* the theory postulating the structure of these observations.

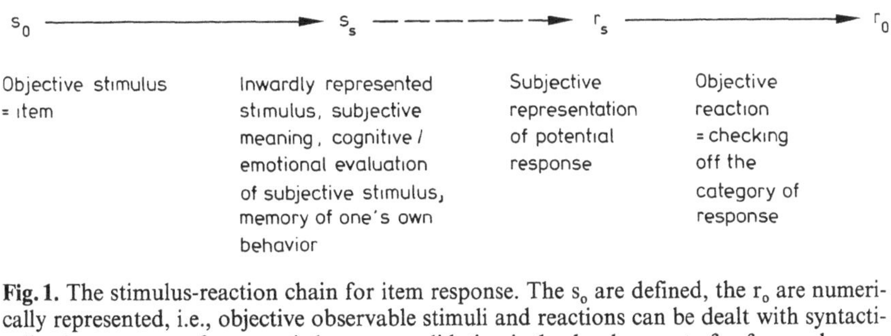

Fig. 1. The stimulus-reaction chain for item response. The s_0 are defined, the r_0 are numerically represented, i.e., objective observable stimuli and reactions can be dealt with syntactically. One concern of pragmatic language validation is the development of r_0 from s_0 by way of s_s and r_s. The degree to which this process is comparable when applied to various persons can be tested by applying highly standardized processes of evaluation to the field s_s, which encompasses cognitive/emotional evaluation, memory, test motivation, etc.

1. When the objective stimuli are not comparable, i.e., have not been derived from the same universe, the objective reactions are not comparable either. The stimuli do not represent the same facets.
2. When the s_s (subjective stimuli) are not comparable the above also applies for the r_0 (objective responses). They are not derived from the implicitly assumed universe of subjective stimuli.
3. When the r_s (subjective responses) are not comparable the above also applies for the r_0. What one person means in saying "yes" can be the same as what another person means by "no." The less comparable the cognitive/emotional evaluations, the situational and procedural contests of the remembered events and their relation to time, frequency, etc. are, the more readily does this also apply to r_s and r_0.

According to facet theory, validation is concerned with stimuli, persons, and reactions. Proof that stimuli (items) are representative of a universe of stimuli is a step toward sample selection, but is not a validation. Stimuli are defined in terms of the construct; they cannot be empirically tested for "truth."

With respect to stimuli, pragmatic language validation would require the definition of a universe of meanings for given contents or uses before appropriate sample items could be selected.

For this purpose, facets of meaning or usage would have to be defined. In my opinion, these can be derived from the field of psycholinguistics in the form of variables such as "conceptual ability", "adequacy with respect to one's own experience and behavior", and "clarity of meaning". The quantity S (stimuli) would then be a quantity of ordered structuples (with three facets of meaning, triplets). The quantity P (persons) could be defined in terms of facets such as age, sex, etc.

The contact between a person P and a stimulus S results in the reaction r_{ps}. The r's are fixed responses (yes/no), so that various ps combinations can result in the same R. Next, the stimuli are used as the common factor in correlating persons and reactions, and the persons are used to correlate stimuli and reactions. It must therefore be guaranteed that the stimulus for every SR combination will remain constant. If this is not the case the stimulus cannot consistently assume the function of correlating other factors. The same applies to the R's. The meanings of "yes" and "no" must always remain consistent if these correlations are to be comparable. It is interesting that facet theory defines "item" as a "structuple in S *together* with its structuple image in R." The primary concern of pragmatic language validation is the proof of this statement.

In principle, Fig. 1 also applies to other significant aspects of the diagnostic process, e.g., construct, instructions, and interpretation aid.

The concept of pragmatic language validation consists of two qualitatively different subconcepts:

1. First the construct which is to be comprehended must be defined as precisely as possible and facets must be deduced. Items are then formulated for all conceivable combinations of facets, whereby the latter also represent contexts of meaning.

2. Within the framework of the second subconcept the semantic qualities of these items are evaluated by a number of sample judges who should be as representative as possible and who should all stem from a defined linguistic population. Variables which seem appropriate for the evaluation of the objects of meaning described above have been derived from psycholinguistic findings, especially from those in the field of generative semantics (cf. Kastner, 1982). These variables are 'clarity of meaning,' 'conceivability,' and 'adequacy with respect to one's own experience and behavior.'

Selection of items takes place in the following manner: these are reformulated or eliminated until those items remain which have attained a minimum level of correspondence. The minimum value for the coefficient of correspondence (e.g., Krippendorff, 1970) must be decided on a priori. Pragmatic language validation is followed by a statistical analysis of items.

An Example of Pragmatic Language Validation

Within the context of several studies on mental stress a trans-situational, relatively persistent trait, i.e., 'stress tolerance,' was to be investigated by means of a questionnaire. For theoretical reasons and to limit the contexts of meaning, the questionnaire was developed to measure stress in one area of behavior, the area of car driving. The following facets of stress were deduced theoretically: 'intensity,' 'duration,' and 'control possibilities' for each situation. If the facets are only defined in terms of high/low there are eight possible combinations (Fig. 2).

Items were formulated for every eighth of the cube. These were then judged for the variables 'clarity of meaning,' 'conceivability,' and 'adequacy' on scales with values ranging from 1 to 9 by ten judges stemming from a defined linguistic population. After five revisions barely 60% of the original item pool re-

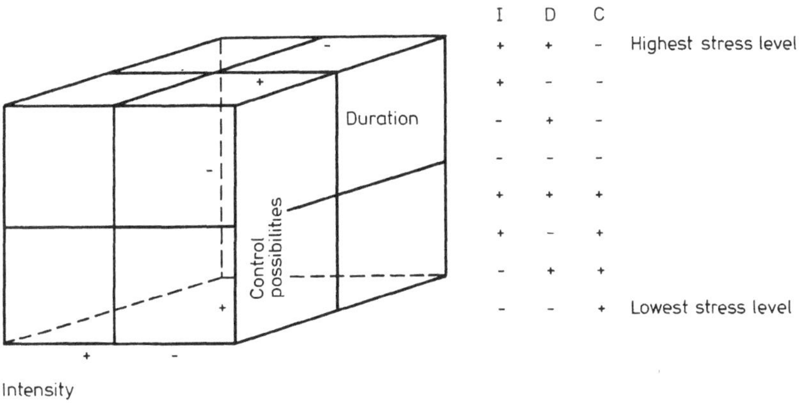

Fig. 2. Facet combinations for stress

mained, i.e., those which had reached a sufficiently high coefficient of correspondence (.80 according to Krippendorff, 1970).

In parallel with this procedure a second questionnaire was developed, with the same content as that described above. This questionnaire, however, was developed in the traditional manner, i.e., without pragmatic language validation. Both types of questionnaires (A = language-pragmatically validated, B = constructed in the traditional manner, using only statistical item analysis) were then administered to persons for whom physiological parameters derived from a test on stress and driving were available as exterior criteria. Two-factorial analysis of variance revealed significant differences between the two types of questionnaires with respect to the variables clarity of meaning and conceivability: these differences were in accordance with expectations. Significant interactions also showed that depending on the type of test, the evaluation of the items with respect to the variables clarity of meaning, etc. differed.

Next the test scores resulting from both types of questionnaire were correlated with pulse frequency (the most useful physiological parameter).

Type A scores (language pragmatically validated) had a higher correlation ($r = .53$) with the transformed baseline values of the pulse frequency than type B scores ($r = .28$).

The validated questionnaire thus shows a significantly stronger relation to the external criterion. The final step in the pragmatic language validation consisted in examination of the facet structure.

For the sake of clarity, 18 items were chosen at random from the type A questionnaire, and in accordance with their categorizations with regard to intensity, duration, and control possibilities and also to their codification, these were assigned to the appropriate fields of similarity (see Table 3).

The facets, along with the trait being measured, determine which items belong to which field. For this reason, stress tolerance scores were eliminated by means of partial coefficients. Partial correlations between the items were calculated. These constituted the basis for nonmetrical multidimensional scaling (Lingoes & Roskam, 1973).

A two-dimensional representation of the similarity structures showed that the items within any one field correlated very closely with each other.

This was demonstrated more successfully for the variables intensity and control possibilities than for the variable duration. An examination of the structure of the facets thus shows that the data can be fitted to the theory, supplying us with further proof of its validity.

Table 3. Assignment of items to the individual facets

Intensity	Duration	Control possibilities
11, 15, 27	55, 57, 60	22, 43, 65
5, 45, 74	31, 40, 52	20, 28, 56

In conclusion, the essential steps to the construction of a questionnaire according to the principles of pragmatic language validation are summarized again:

1. Unambigous definition of the construct in the context of a psychological theory and the derivation of facets
2. Examination of the use of language within the population to be tested, if possible in relation to the subject matter to be examined
3. Systematic combination of facets in accordance with the extent to which they are more or less pronounced, followed by formulation of the items in accordance with the resulting contexts of meaning
4. Determination of the desired measurements of correspondence
5. Evaluation of the items with regard to the variables clarity of meaning, conceivability, and adequacy by a sample of judges chosen from a defined language population
6. Reformulation and possible elimination of items showing inadequate levels of correspondence
7. Examination of facet structure

The other objects of meaning used in the diagnostic process (construct, instruction, interpretation aids) should also be examined with regard to the three above-mentioned variables and, if necessary, be reformulated. Another variable, 'replaceability of the item content by the response,' has proved useful for testing the response categories.

The attempt to establish the highest possible levels of correspondence when applying objects of meaning to the diagnostic communication process seems worthwhile, especially in view of the fact that a "syntactically" perfect method becomes useless when the theoretically presupposed relationship between the empirical and the numerical relationship is invalidated owing to varying interpretation processes or when the relationship between the given empirical factors themselves is questionable. The procedure involved in pragmatic language validation appears to be capable of minimizing the misunderstandings mentioned at the beginning of this chapter. It most definitely does not solve the old problem which arises in the philosophy of language, the problem of the meaning of the meaning. In my opinion this infinite regress in which language is explained by means of language can hardly be solved, especially for psychological terms.

The construction of a facet theory leads to the development of contexts of meaning which are very precisely defined: these would hardly have been conceivable with traditional methods of construction. The feedback between the empirical data and the theoretical statement, which is produced by examining the structure of the facets, usually indicates where the weak spots in the theory are to be found.

The evaluation of the objects of meaning by independent codifiers selected from a defined linguistic population leads to a strong correspondence of meaning processes, which benefits questionnaire testing as a whole. This can, however, lead to the conclusion that various questionnaire procedures will have to be developed for different linguistic subpopulations.

References

Borg, I. (1981). *Anwendungsorientierte multidimensionale Skalierung*. Berlin Heidelberg New York: Springer.

Cliff, N. (1968). Adjective check list and individual differences in perceived meaning. *Educational and Psychological Measurement, 28*, 1063–1077.

Fahrenberg, J., Selg, H., & Hampel, R. (1973). *Das Freiburger Persönlichkeitsinventar (FPI)*. Göttingen: Hogrefe.

Janke, W. (1973). Über die Konstruktion von Fragebögen. Bericht über ein Symposium: Das Dilemma von Persönlichkeitsfragebögen. In Reinert, G. (Ed.), *Bericht über den 27. Kongreß der Deutschen Gesellschaft für Psychologie in Kiel 1970* (pp. 41–48). Göttingen: Hogrefe.

Janssen, J.P. (1978). *Zur Validität von SD-verfälschten Persönlichkeitsfragebogen in Extremsituationen und beim Rollenspiel*. Köln: TÜV-Rheinland.

Kastner, M. (1982). *Ein Konzept zur internen Validierung psychologischer Fragebogenverfahren*. Wuppertal: Habilitationsschrift. Bergische Universität Wuppertal.

Krippendorff, K. (1970). Estimating the reliability, systematic error, and random error of interval data. *Educational and Psychological Measurement, 30*, 61–70.

Lingoes, J.C., & Roskam, E. (1973). Mathematical and empirical analysis of two multidimensional scaling algorithms. *Psychometrica Monograph, 38*, (4, Pt. 2).

Rogers, T.B. (1974). An analysis of two central stages underlying responding to personality items: The self-referent decision and response selection. *Journal of Research in Personality, 8*, 128–138.

Schneider-Düker, M., & Schneider, J.F. (1977). Untersuchungen zum Beantwortungsprozeß bei psychodiagnostischen Fragebögen. *Zeitschrift für experimentelle und angewandte Psychologie, 24*, 282–302.

Turner, C., & Fiske, D.W. (1968). Item quality and appropriateness of response process. *Educational and Psychological Measurement, 28*, 297–315.

It's *What* You Ask and *How* You Ask It: An Itemmetric Analysis of Personality Questionnaires[1]

ALOIS ANGLEITNER, OLIVER P. JOHN, and FRANZ-JOSEF LÖHR

Introduction

> "The sight of blood no longer excites me."
> "When I was a child, I was an imaginary playmate."
> "I become homicidal when people try to reason with me."
> "It's hard to concentrate in a room full of mice."[2]

Items from personality questionnaires have long been the butt of humorists and jaded graduate students. What makes these satirical items so funny is that they are instantaneously recognizable as having the correct form and yet their content is patently absurd. The fact that these items succeed as jokes suggests that at least for those familiar with personality scales there are some standard forms for items. This chapter describes three sets of formal item characteristics and demonstrates that the psychometric quality of personality items depends not only on content but also on form.

Historically, research on personality questionnaire construction has focused on the principles of scale construction and neglected the properties of the stimuli from which the scales are constructed. Yet, even the most sophisticated techniques for item grouping may never be able to remedy the flaws introduced by the initial item sample. The need for knowledge about the most basic units of questionnaire scales – the individual items – will be our major concern in this chapter; thus, we will primarily address questions related to the initial stages of test construction: How should the initial item pool be constructed? How should the items be written? How do the stimulus characteristics of the text influence the way in which subjects process the item?

For each of these questions, we try to identify sets of item characteristics that might facilitate adequate interpretation of and response to the individual items. We will describe a series of empirical studies in which we provide operational definitions of these item characteristics and evaluate and compare some widely used questionnaires in terms of the characteristics of their items. Finally, we will provide some initial evidence that these item characteristics are important for obtaining reliable and valid responses from subjects.

The empirical findings summarized here were obtained in a research project on the evaluation of personality questionnaires, which was conducted at the universities of Bonn and Bielefeld in West Germany.[3] To sample the domain of personality questionnaires as comprehensively as possible, we included in our studies a wide variety of frequently used instruments of Anglo-

American origin. In particular, we studied those questionnaires of Eysenck for which German editions were available by 1976, namely the MMQ (Eysenck, 1964), MPI (Eysenck, 1959a, 1959b, 1962), and EPI Forms A and B (Eysenck & Eysenck, 1964; Eggert, 1974); the translated parallel Forms A and B of Cattell's 16PF (Cattell & Eber, 1962, 1964); and the MMPI (Hathaway & McKinley, 1943, adapted by Spreen, 1963).[4] In addition, we included some German-developed questionnaires [i.e., Giessen Test (GT) by Beckmann & Richter, 1972; Persönlichkeits-Interessen-Test (PIT) by Mittenecker & Toman, 1951; Freiburger Persönlichkeits-Inventar (FPI) by Fahrenberg & Selg, 1970, and several questionnaires for children]. In this chapter we will summarize the most important findings from this project, focusing primarily on the former questionnaires, since they are of the most general interest. Their scale labels and the abbreviations used here are given in *Appendix A*.

Overview

This chapter consists of four sections, as outlined in Table 1. We will discuss the tasks of the researcher in constructing an item pool (the construction process) and those of the subjects who later respond to the resulting items (the response process). The lower part of Table 1 lists four sets of item characteristics associated with each stage, viz. (a) the logical relation between the trait construct and its indicator (the item); (b) surface elements of the item text; (c) semantic item properties which are assumed to affect the response process; and (d) item statistics which represent the aggregated response patterns of a sample of subjects. Each section of the chapter will focus on one of these four sets of item characteristics.

In the first section, we discuss some of the central issues that arise during the initial stages of the construction of personality questionnaires. In the construct-oriented approach, the test author first makes decisions about which trait constructs are to be measured and then devises new (or uses existing) construct definitions, which specify an appropriate item universe.[5] One aspect of such item universes is the relation between the items and the construct. We will define several types of potential verbal manifestations of traits and present an empirical study that compares the frequencies of these item types across various questionnaires and scales.

In the second section of the chapter, we discuss the next stage of the questionnaire construction process. As Table 1 shows, the researcher should write or select a set of items guided by the previously established construct definitions while keeping in mind certain rules of thumb about item writing. After a short literature review and a theoretical linguistic analysis, we will present some findings from an empirical study of the surface structures of current questionnaire items, including variables such as item length, syntactic characteristics, and response format. As Table 1 shows, the output of this stage of the researcher's activities, namely the string of words that make up the item,

Table 1. Item characteristics associated with different stages of item pool construction and item response processes, and the sections of this chapter where each is discussed

Stages	*Researcher* Constructs item pool			*Subjects* Respond to each item					Aggregated output
	Item generation		Output	Input	Processing stages			Output	
Specific tasks	Decisions about trait and its relation to observable events	Definition of relevant types of trait manifestations in *verbal* form	Writing or seclecting the items	Reading	Encoding	Comparing to stored information about oneself	Utility control during response selection	Response	Item response parameters
Item characteristics	Semantic trait-item relation (prototypicality)	Logical item-trait relations	Surface elements of item text: length, syntax, and response format		Comprehensibility Ambiguity	Abstractness Self-reference	Social norms and values	Endorsement	Item mean, variance, stability, item-test correlation
Section entitled	"Personality Traits and Personality Questionnaire Items"		"Surface Elements of Questionnaire Items: A Linguistic Analysis"		"Item Characteristics and Item Response Processes"			"The Prediction of Psychometric Characteristics"	

serves as the input to the subjects' item response processes. Consequently, before moving on to item selection based on statistical analyses of item responses, the researcher should check whether the response processes taking place are appropriate, that is, whether subjects process (understand and respond to) the item in the way intended by the researcher.

Thus, in the third section of the chapter, we discuss some frequently postulated item response processes and their associated item characteristics. The model of the item response process outlined in Table 1 suggests that items characterized by a high degree of ambiguity and low comprehensibility will be difficult to encode; abstractness and lack of self-reference of the item text can result in errors during the comparison stage; and references to social norms and values might bias response selection during the stage of utility control. All these item characteristics can affect the subject's decision to endorse the item. Thus, inasmuch as they lead to inappropriate processing of the item (i.e., distort the response process), a subject's response cannot be taken as an indication of his or her standing on the trait that the item was designed to assess.

Whereas the item characteristics discussed in the first three parts of the chapter were all derived directly from the texts of the items, the final section relates these logical, surface, and process characteristics to a variety of item parameters that are based on subjects' response patterns (i.e., item statistics). Using a multiple regression design, we investigate the extent to which the reliability and validity of item responses can be predicted from these item characteristics.

Whereas the present classification of item characteristics has been derived from the theoretical model outlined in Table 1, other authors have preferred to group item characteristics according to the methodology used to obtain measures of these variables. For example, Jones (1965) employed a two-fold classification: (a) sample specific (i.e., derived from subjects' ratings or responses) vs (b) intrinsic (i.e., denoting structural aspects of the item). Thus, using Jones' (1965) scheme and focusing on how we assessed these item characteristics, those discussed in the first and third sections would be grouped together as sample specific and intrinsic (based on judges' ratings of aspects of the item text); those discussed in the second section would also be intrinsic but would not be sample specific (scored directly and objectively from the item text); and those discussed in the last section would be sample specific but not intrinsic (derived from subjects' item responses). This classification corresponds directly to the three categories proposed by Goldberg (1968), viz. item ratings, lexicographic indices, and test-retest statistics, and to those used by Payne (1970), who labeled them judgmental, structural, and metric.

Personality Traits and Personality Questionnaire Items

Traits can be understood in Allport's (1937) sense transformational principles specifying those sets of equivalent stimulus conditions that consistently elicit similar responses from the individual. Alternatively, traits have been conceptualized as summarizing statements about stable trends in the behaviors and experiences of individuals (Hampshire, 1953). These conceptualizations imply two essential tasks for personality assessment. After deciding which behavioral domain is to be assessed, the researchers must first specify the set of stimulus conditions under which the behaviors of interest are likely to occur. Secondly, a set of rules must be identified which specify how various sets of behaviors can be aggregated. Similarly, the personality researcher who chooses to develop a questionnaire for personality assessment has to define the trait construct to be measured and to develop a set of items that inquire about trait-relevant behaviors and situations, the responses to which thus serve as indicators of the construct. Other important issues arising at later stages of the test construction process, for example, how items should be combined into scales, are discussed elsewhere (Burisch, this volume).

The Origin of Personality Questionnaire Items

In an exemplary program of test development that resulted in the publication of the Personality Research Form, Jackson (1967) started with the development of mutually exclusive, specific definitions of each construct, on the basis of reviews of the relevant research literature; then he and his coworkers generated an initial item pool for each construct with the help of a "grid of situations and behavioral sequences" (Jackson, 1970, p. 67). Moreover, for a subset of items, judges were given theoretically derived descriptions of target persons who exemplified the trait; then the judges were asked to rate the probability that the persons would endorse the items, to establish the degree to which the items could be considered relevant to the construct in question.

A more recent proposal for the task of item pool generation has been advanced by Buss and Craik (1983). In their act frequency approach to personality measurement, Buss and Craik (1983) began with a set of traits selected systematically from a structural model of interpersonal behavior (Wiggins, 1979). The task of identifying the corresponding observable behavior referents was delegated to a large sample of subjects who were asked to generate behavioral acts that could be viewed as manifestations of the traits. Another sample of subjects then rated the prototypicality of these acts vis-à-vis the traits. Thus, the assignment of behavioral acts to traits is based on explicit rules (i.e., prototypicality judgments) and on the consensus of a large number of speakers of a given language. These procedures capitalize on people's semantic knowledge about which behaviors are typical or indicative instances of a trait. The contention that the folk knowledge about personality that has been encoded into language may, in some respects, be as relevant to item generation as that of many personality researchers is supported by Buss and Craik's (1980, p. 389) finding that act prototypicality judgments showed considerable agreement between panels of personological "experts" and nonexperts.

The act-frequency approach is of limited usefulness if the object is to generate items for traits for which no names exist in the natural language and in cases where people cannot be expected to have well-elaborated semantic intuitions. These conditions may apply to many of the traits that are of interest to psychologists studying abnormal behavior and psychopathology. How should an item pool be constructed, if procedures similar to those suggested by Buss and Craik (1983) cannot be followed?

More than 25 years ago, Loevinger (1957, p. 659) postulated that "at the very least, the items in the pool should be drawn from an area of content defined more broadly than the trait expected to be measured"; that is, some of the items should assess other related traits against which the trait of interest can be discriminated. Within an item pool for a particular trait, the items should be "chosen so as to sample all possible contents which might comprise the putative trait according to all known alternative theories of the trait." Moreover, the various content domains "should be represented in proportion to their life-importance." These postulates were designed to ensure that evidence for the validity of a test or scale could also be interpreted as evidence for the validity of the underlying construct. Thus, Loevinger's recommendations are based on the assumption that researchers constructing questionnaire scales have already elaborated a nomological network in which the construct they wish to assess is embedded. However, many questionnaires were (and still are) constructed atheoretically, often for applied purposes (Goldberg, 1971). Consequently, Loevinger's (1957) recommendations have had little impact on the general practice of personality questionnaire construction.

In marked contrast to the ideals set out by Buss and Craik (1983), Jackson (1970), and Loevinger (1957), most authors of personality questionnaires have used combinations of the following three strategies to generate their items: (a) Constructing new items but leaving the rationale for item generation unexplicated (e.g., the items in Cattell's 16PF, whose origin is largely unknown); (b) using experts to supply what they regard as typical trait manifestations (e.g., some MMPI items); and/or (c) copying items from other questionnaires (e.g., many of Guilford's GZTS items).

The pervasiveness of "borrowing" as a strategy for generating item pools has been illustrated by Goldberg (1971, p. 335), who surveyed the history of American personality scales and concluded that "items devised around the turn of the century may have worked their way via Woodworth's Personal Data Sheet, to Thurstone and Thurstone's Personality Schedule, hence to Bernreuter's Personality Inventory, and later to the Minnesota Multiphasic Personality Inventory, where they were borrowed for the California Personality Inventory and then injected into the Omnibus Personality Inventory – only to serve as a source of items for the new Academic Behavior Inventory" (and, we may add, only to be translated and included in some new German personality inventories). Angleitner and Löhr (1980) attempted to assess the amount of item overlap among German personality scales by item wording comparisons.

Quite appropriately, then, Loevinger (1957, p. 658) characterized "the process by which the given investigator or group of investigators constructs or selects items to represent the content" as *idiosyncratic* and therefore *nonreproducible*. A major stumbling block to improved personality scales may arise from these defects in the initial item pools, since the use of highly objective, empirical-statistical methods such as item factor analysis or item discriminance analysis to select items from such pools will not correct for the initial subjectivity; what was left out in the first step cannot be reinserted and then selected to become part of the resulting trait scales. As a consequence, the decision as to which of many possible trait labels will eventually be used as the name for the resulting scale will largely reflect the test author's idiosyncratic preconceptions of the nature of the trait he or she has tried to assess.

What Kind of Items Do We Find in Questionnaires?

A comparison of Buss and Craik's (1983) act frequency items with those of traditional personality questionnaires shows that many act items refer to single instances of fairly specific behaviors, whereas questionnaire items often include intensity and frequency adverbs, thus assessing more generalized aspects of the ways in which individuals experience, and respond to, their environments. Apparently, at least some questionnaire items assess individual differences at the level of behavioral trends or habits. In our sample of questionnaires, the most common frequency adverbs were sometimes *(manchmal)*, often *(oft)*, always *(immer)*, and never *(nie)*. The most frequently used intensity adverbs were very *(sehr)* and much *(viel)* (see Löhr, 1983 a).

Most act-frequency items fall at roughly the same level of abstraction (i.e., specific behavioral acts), *because* Buss and Craik (e.g., 1983) made an explicit effort to eliminate "non-act" statements (e.g., trait attributions), general tendency and habit statements (e.g., "She tends to avoid parties"), and statements they considered too vague to constitute observable acts. The fact that only a subset of questionnaire items inquires about the respondents' acts suggests that personality questionnaire authors have not screened their items as carefully as Buss and Craik (1983) have done. In particular, critics suggest that the unsystematic construction of item pools has led to extremely heterogeneous mixtures of item types in contemporary personality questionnaires:

> The item sets of our questionnaires contain an odd mixture of questions of totally divergent logical and empirical status. Questions about concrete biographical data or about behaviors and experiences in specific situations appear next to items that ask the respondents to integrate behaviors and experiences that have arisen in specific or in completely vague situations across time and intensity, or to decide whether they behave in a particular way more frequently, or with higher intensity, than does some other, unspecified person. Besides that, the respondents are asked about their interests, preferences, and attitudes and requested to give evaluations of their own behaviors or those of others. Moreover, they are used as "trait construct-constructors" or "construct-validators" in such questions as "I am a timid, neurotic person." Items referring to "habits," "traits," and "types" stand side by side in one and the same questionnaire; particular behaviors and subaspects of just these behaviors are summed to one total score without hesitation. Some items ask for the frequency of behaviors;

others – listed in the same questionnaire – ask for the intensity of reactions. Yet other items represent weird mixtures of frequency and intensity aspects (e.g., I *sometimes* react *strongly* in certain situations). Furthermore, it is questionable whether responses to such items should be described by a cumulative or an increasing-probability item response model (Janke, 1973, p. 47, translated by the authors).

An Empirical Investigation of Item-Trait Relations

To assess whether Janke's characterization of the item pools of contemporary personality questionnaires is justified, a large set of items taken from various German-language personality questionnaires was classified. A second goal of this study was to find out whether differences in theoretical viewpoint and item selection strategies among test authors are related to differences in the kinds of items chosen as indicators of the trait. Finally, we wanted to investigate whether some types of items have better psychometric characteristics than others. This question is of great importance for the development of new questionnaires and will be addressed in the final section of this chapter.

The Category System. Guided by Janke's (1973 b) examples, Lennertz's (1973, pp. 59–60) description of consistent classes of logical item-trait relations, and our content analyses of some selected item sets, we developed a category system that would permit a systematic description of item-trait relations. An overview of this schema and some examples are given in Table 2. The central categories were: (a) Descriptions of *reactions,* which were further subdivided into *overt, covert,* and *bodily* reactions *(symptoms);* and (b) *trait attributions* which could be either *unmodified* or *modified* by, for example, situational context specifications or frequency qualifiers.

In addition, there were other categories representing (c) *wishes and interests;* (d) *biographical facts;* (e) *attitudes and beliefs;* (f) *reactions of other persons;* and (g) *bizarre item content.* These categories refer predominantly to items whose content is rather indirectly related to personality traits; that is, the evidential link between the item and the trait is more tenuous for these "indirect" item categories than for the first two categories. This distinction might be related to inter-item differences in response stability; as Goldberg (1963, p. 482) has pointed out, "the more an item reflects some aspect of behavior that is directly observable and easily identifiable the more stable the item; on the other hand, the more an item reflects some attitude, value, or other 'internal' state of mind the more unstable is the item."

Theory. The frequencies of these item types in questionnaires may vary with the theoretical orientation of the test author, the scale construction strategy applied, and the trait being assessed. Cattell (1957), for example, interprets his personality factors as *source* traits, which are thought to have a pervasive influence on every aspect of a person's way of experiencing and responding to the environment. Given this theoretical perspective, one might expect to find

Table 2. Item-trait relations: A category system

1. Descriptions of reactions
   This category contains items that are intended to assess
   a) *Overt* reactions of the test person that are – in principle – publicly observable (e.g., "I often go to parties");
   b) *Covert* or internal reactions that are private and generally not observable by others, such as internal sensations, feelings, and cognitions (e.g., "I think a lot about myself") and
   c) *Symptoms,* that is, physical reactions (e.g., "I sweat a lot")
2. Trait attributions
   Items classified in this category refer to dispositions of the test person. The traits attributed to the test person are usually expressed by adjectives and nouns (e.g., "I have good acting abilities"). These items are further subclassified in regard to whether they are unmodified or modified. Frequent modifications are specifications of frequency, duration, and situational contexts
3. Wishes and interests
   These items refer to the intention to engage in particular behaviors or the desire for something (e.g., "Sometimes I would really like to curse"). *Not* included here are those items that mention wishes and desires but specify that they are realized in actual behavior (e.g., "I like to spend my free time by myself")
4. Biographical facts
   This category contains items that focus on aspects of the past (e.g., "I had some trouble with the law when I was younger")
5. Attitudes and beliefs
   The items of this category refer to strongly held beliefs, opinions and attitudes about various kinds of general, social, and personal issues (e.g., "I think the law should be strictly enforced")
6. Others' reactions to the person
   This category subsumes items that describe behaviors and attitudes of other people toward the person (e.g., "At parties, I am seldom the center of attention")
7. Bizarre items
   Most of these items describe clearly unusual, strange, or even abnormal behaviors and experiences (e.g., "Somebody is trying to poison me")

a large number of different types of item-trait relations in Cattell's questionnaires. In contrast, Eysenck (e.g., 1947) had been influenced by Hull's behavioristic learning theory and developed a hierarchical model of personality. *Specific responses* to situational cues, which form the lowest level in his hierarchy, can be mapped into broader categories called *habitual response patterns,* which in turn combine into concepts at the *trait* level, such as sociability, impulsiveness, or activity. Finally, at the *type* level one finds "supraordinate" concepts such as extraversion, which are based on the observed intercorrelations among traits. Thus, since Eysenck's (1947) model was built up entirely from behavioral responses, there was no room for indirect trait indicators; item categories such as wishes and interests or attitudes and beliefs should therefore not be represented in item sets developed by Eysenck and his coworkers. Moreover, since Eysenck viewed specific responses as too unstable and unreliable to be useful for the assessment of personality characteristics, we expect his item sets to be drawn primarily from the second and third levels of his hierarchy (i.e., habitual responses and trait attributions) and therefore form fairly homogeneous sets of item types.

The test authors' preferences for different strategies of scale construction (see Burisch, this volume) by themselves provide only indirect clues as to the criteria they use in the construction of their initial item pools. For example, externally constructed questionnaires such as the MMPI may show highly heterogeneous mixtures of different types of item-trait relations. Finally, one can speculate that the intuitions of different test authors may converge on the kinds of items that are best suited for the assessment of a particular trait. For example, interpersonal traits such as sociability or dominance, which are often conceptualized in terms of observable social acts (e.g., Wiggins, 1979; Buss & Craik, 1983), might be assessed predominantly via items describing overt reactions.

Item Classification. The items of the German-language personality inventories used for adults were assembled in lists, each of which contained approximately 250 items. Each of 85 advanced psychology students, who were paid for their participation, was randomly assigned to one of the lists, and classified that item set according to the category system described above. Each item was categorized by at least nine judges.

To assess interjudge agreement, the frequencies of the seven main categories were computed for each item, and the category with the highest frequency was used as the key. The mean proportion of items that each judge had classified in agreement with the plurality of judges, averaged across the items of all ten adult questionnaires, was .79, whereas Kappa, a measure corrected for possible inflation by chance, was .61. For further analyses, each item was assigned to the category that had been selected by the majority of the judges. If none of the seven categories was chosen by more than 50% of the judges, the item apparently did not belong to just one category and was therefore left unclassified for the present purposes. Overall, only 8.7% of the items were not assigned to one of the seven main categories. The same set of procedures was used to assign items initially classified as trait attributions or reaction descriptions to the appropriate subcategories.

Results. In Table 3, the relative frequencies of the items in each category are reported for the item pools of the seven Anglo-American questionnaires included in this study; Table 4 presents the results separately for each scale. As Table 3 shows, the indirect item types were relatively infrequent (20%). The vast majority of items (63%) described various kinds of reactions, whereas less than 10% were trait attributions. The most frequent indirect reference categories were *wishes and interests* and *attitudes and beliefs*. The percentage of items referring to reactions of others and bizarre content was small.

Table 3. Relative frequencies of items in each category from the personality scales in seven questionnaires and the total set of 964 items

Questionnaire (no. of items)	Description of reactions				Trait attributions			Indirect references						Left unclassified	Number of main categories used
	1a Overt	1b Covert	1c Symptoms	Not subclassified	2a Unmod.	2b Mod.	Not Subclassified	3 Wishes	4 Biog.	5 Attds.	6 Others	7 Bizarre	Sum 3–7		
MPI (48)	18.8	41.7	2.1	8.2	18.8	4.2	2.0	0	0	0	0	0	0	4.2	2
MMQ (56)	19.6	23.2	17.9	8.9	10.7	7.1	7.2	0	1.8	0	0	0	1.8	3.6	3
EPI-A (57)	42.1	36.8	7.0	3.6	7.0	3.5	0	0	0	0	0	0	0	0	2
EPI-B (57)	24.6	22.8	14.0	12.3	7.0	5.3	1.7	0	1.8	0	0	0	1.8	10.5	3
16PF-A (171)	18.1	21.1	1.8	14.6	4.7	0	1.7	11.1	3.5	11.1	1.8	0	27.5	10.5	6
16PF-B (171)	17.5	24.0	3.5	10.6	1.2	.6	3.5	14.0	2.9	13.5	1.2	0	31.6	7.6	6
MMPI (404)	10.4	27.0	13.1	11.1	3.2	1.0	2.0	4.7	5.7	5.9	2.2	3.0	21.5	10.6	7
All items (964)	16.7	26.3	8.8	11.0	4.8	1.7	2.4	6.4	3.7	6.8	1.5	1.3	19.7	8.7	4.1

Unmod., unmodified; Mod., modified; Biog., biographical facts; Attds., attitudes and beliefs; Others, other's reactions to the subject.

Table 4. Relative frequencies of items in each category for the personality scales in seven Anglo-American questionnaires

Scales (no. of items)			Description of reactions				Trait attributions			Indirect references					Left completely unclassified	Number of main categories used
			1a Overt	1b Covert	1c Symptoms	Not subclassified	2a Unmod.	2b Mod.	Not subclassified	3 Wishes	4 Biog.	5 Attds.	6 Others	7 Bizarre		
MPI	E	24	37.5	12.5	0	8.3	29.2	4.2	0	0	0	0	0	0	8.3	2
	N	24	0	70.8	4.2	8.3	8.3	4.2	4.2	0	0	0	0	0	0	2
MMQ	N	38	5.3	23.7	26.3	5.2	15.9	7.9	10.5	0	2.6	0	0	0	2.6	3
	L	18	50.0	22.2	0	16.7	0	5.6	0	0	0	0	0	0	5.6	2
EPI-A	N	24	8.3	62.5	16.7	0	12.5	0	0	0	0	0	0	0	0	2
	E	24	62.5	16.7	0	8.3	4.2	8.3	0	0	0	0	0	0	0	2
	L	9	77.8	22.2	0	0	0	0	0	0	0	0	0	0	0	1
EPI-B	N	24	8.3	41.7	33.3	4.2	4.2	8.3	0	0	0	0	0	0	0	2
	E	24	37.5	12.5	0	20.8	8.3	4.2	4.2	0	0	0	0	0	12.5	2
	L	9	33.3	0	0	11.1	11.1	0	0	0	11.1	0	0	0	33.3	3
16PF-A	A	10	30.0	0	0	0	0	0	0	60.0	0	10.0	0	0	0	3
	C	13	15.4	30.8	7.7	15.3	0	0	0	7.7	0	0	15.4	0	7.7	3
	E	13	30.8	15.4	0	23.0	15.4	0	7.7	0	0	0	0	0	7.7	2
	F	13	30.8	0	0	0	7.7	0	7.7	7.7	0	7.7	0	0	39.5	4
	G	10	10.0	10.0	0	10.0	10.0	0	0	0	0	30.0	0	0	30.0	3
	H	13	30.8	23.1	0	23.0	15.4	0	0	7.7	0	0	0	0	0	3
	I	10	20.0	0	0	10.0	0	0	0	40.0	20.0	0	0	0	10.0	3
	L	10	20.0	30.0	0	20.0	0	0	0	0	0	20.0	10.0	0	0	3
	M	13	7.7	15.4	0	30.7	0	0	0	15.4	0	15.4	0	0	15.4	3
	N	10	20.0	10.0	0	10.0	0	0	0	0	0	30.0	0	0	30.0	2
	O	13	0	46.2	7.7	0	15.4	0	0	0	7.7	7.7	0	0	15.4	4
	Q1	10	0	36.0	0	10.0	0	0	10.0	10.0	10.0	30.0	0	0	0	5
	Q2	10	10.0	10.0	0	20.0	0	0	0	20.0	20.0	10.0	0	0	0	4
	Q3	10	30.0	10.0	0	40.0	0	0	0	0	0	20.0	0	0	0	2
	Q4	13	15.4	69.2	7.7	7.7	0	0	0	0	0	0	0	0	0	1

16PF-B	A 10	10.0	10.0	0	0	0	0	0	80.0	0	0	0	0	0	2
	C 13	15.4	38.5	0	15.3	0	0	0	15.4	7.7	7.7	0	0	0	4
	E 13	15.4	15.4	0	7.7	7.7	7.7	0	0	15.4	15.4	0	0	15.4	4
	F 13	23.1	15.4	0	7.7	7.7	0	15.4	15.4	0	7.7	0	0	7.7	4
	G 10	40.0	20.0	0	0	0	0	0	0	0	40.0	0	0	0	2
	H 13	30.8	30.8	0	23.0	0	0	7.7	0	0	0	0	0	7.7	2
	I 10	0	40.0	0	10.0	0	0	10.0	40.0	0	0	0	0	0	3
	L 10	10.0	30.0	0	0	0	0	0	0	10.0	30.0	10.0	0	10.0	4
	M 13	15.4	7.7	7.7	0	0	0	7.7	15.4	7.7	30.8	0	0	7.0	5
	N 10	20.0	30.0	0	10.0	0	0	0	20.0	0	20.0	0	0	0	3
	Q 13	7.0	61.5	7.7	7.7	0	0	0	0	0	7.7	0	0	7.7	2
	Q1 10	30.0	0	0	10.0	0	0	0	10.0	0	20.0	0	0	30.0	3
	Q2 10	10.0	10.0	10.0	10.0	0	0	1.0	0	0	20.0	10.0	0	20.0	4
	Q3 10	20.0	10.0	0	30.0	0	0	0	20.0	0	10.0	0	0	10.0	3
	Q4 13	15.4	30.0	23.0	23.0	0	0	0	7.7	0	0	0	0	0	2
MMPI	L 15	46.7	20.0	0	13.3	0	0	6.7	13.3	0	0	0	0	0	3
	F 64	7.8	12.5	9.4	4.7	3.1	1.6	0	1.6	9.4	12.5	3.1	17.2	17.2	7
	K 30	6.7	43.3	0	16.7	0	0	0	6.7	0	16.7	0	0	10.0	3
	Hs 33	0	0	87.9	3.0	3.0	3.0	3.1	0	0	0	0	0	0	2
	D 60	16.7	28.3	20.0	5.0	6.7	5.0	6.6	5.0	0	3.3	0	0	3.3	4
	Hy 60	8.3	23.3	35.0	13.4	1.7	3.3	1.7	3.3	0	8.3	0	0	1.7	4
	Pd 50	8.0	38.0	2.0	8.0	0	2.0	0	4.0	12.0	2.0	8.0	0	16.0	6
	Mf 60	13.3	23.3	1.7	3.4	5.0	0	0	21.7	8.3	6.7	0	0	16.7	5
	Pa 40	2.5	22.5	5.0	12.5	5.0	2.5	0	0	5.0	15.0	5.0	15.0	10.0	6
	Pt 48	4.2	52.1	6.3	14.5	4.2	2.1	8.3	2.1	2.1	0	0	0	4.2	4
	Sc 78	6.4	30.8	12.8	12.8	0	0	2.6	1.3	7.7	0	5.1	3.8	16.7	6
	Ma46	13.0	39.1	4.3	21.9	2.2	0	0	0	6.5	6.5	2.2	0	4.3	5
	Si 70	17.1	25.7	5.7	17.2	4.3	0	2.8	5.7	5.7	5.7	0	0	10.0	5
	Sd 39	5.1	38.5	17.9	7.7	5.1	5.1	2.6	2.6	2.6	2.6	5.1	0	5.1	6

Abbreviations as for Table 3

The four questionnaires published by Eysenck (i.e., MPI, MMQ, and EPI Forms A and B) were found to consist almost exclusively of items that require the respondent to provide reaction descriptions and trait attributions. Thus, the item types identified in Eysenck's questionnaires formed a homogeneous set consistent with his hierarchical model of personality. The scale-by-scale analyses (see Table 4) showed that Eysenck's Extraversion and Lie items were categorized primarily as *overt* reactions, whereas *covert* reactions and *physical symptoms* were the most frequent item categories found in his Neuroticism scales. A comparison of the distributions of category frequencies in EPI Forms A and B reveals that supposedly parallel scales were not entirely parallel with regard to the types of items used to assess the same construct. This is particularly true of the two Lie scales, which also have very low parallel test reliabilities (see Table 9).

Whereas only two or three categories were found in Eysenck's questionnaires, Cattell used a rather heterogeneous mixture of different types of item-trait relations in both forms of his 16PF; of the seven main categories, six were represented in Cattell's item sets. Overall, about 60% of these items involved self-descriptions of reactions (trait attributions being almost completely absent), whereas indirect references were much more frequent in Cattell's than in Eysenck's questionnaires. Specifically, the 16PF factors *A* and *I* (which supposedly assess warmth and tendermindedness) contained high percentages of items expressing wishes and interests. Since the parallel scales in Forms A and B of the 16PF different considerably in their category frequency distributions, the scale-by-scale analysis presented in Table 4 showed only a few trends for scales with the same label. In both forms, factor scales *C, O,* and *Q4,* which often load a second-order factor labeled Anxiety (Amelang, Sommer, & Bartussek, 1971; Gorsuch & Cattell, 1967; Timm, 1968), were characterized mostly by items that describe covert reactions. Similar to Eysenck's extraversion scales, factors *F* and *H* which form the second-order factor Exvia-Invia had many items referring to overt reactions (approximately 30%), but also contained items from several other categories. Finally, factor *G* (superego strength) was assessed predominantly by attitudes and beliefs (as well as some other item types), whereas the items of factor *N* (sophistication) represented a mixture of attitudes and beliefs, overt reactions, and covert reactions.

The MMPI clearly showed the most heterogeneous mixture of item types of all seven questionnaires analyzed. Apparently, Janke's (1973) description of "item hodge-podges" characterizes the MMPI item pool quite appropriately, even if the scales are considered individually. As the last column of Table 4 shows, the typical MMPI scale contained items from *five* different categories, whereas on average only two main item categories were found in the various Eysenck scales. In comparison with Cattell's and Eysenck's questionnaires, the MMPI had more items referring to physical symptoms. Given that the MMPI is primarily a clinical assessment instrument, this is not really surprising; however, although all clinical scales including Social Introversion (Si) had at least a few physical symptom items, most of these items were concentrated in the

Hypochondriasis (Hs) and, to a lesser extent, the Hysteria (Hy) scales. The modal category for all other clinical scales was that called *covert reactions*.

The MMPI was the only questionnaire that had bizarre items; they appeared in those scales where we would expect them – Paranoia (Pa) and Schizophrenia (Sc). And, again as might be expected, it was the validity scale *F* that contained the highest percentage of bizarre items. Finally, the MMPI Lie scale (*L*) was found to be similar to those developed by Eysenck in that the respondent's tendency to lie was assessed predominantly with items describing overt reactions, whereas the items of the correction scale *K* referred primarily to covert reactions.

Discussion. The finding that the items of most MMPI scales form much more heterogeneous sets of item-trait relations than Eysenck's scales might in part be attributed to the fact that the MMPI scales are generally longer. However, since the effect is still observed when the total item pools are compared (see Table 3), it seems possible that differences between scale construction strategies influence the heterogeneity of the item pools found in different questionnaires. In particular, the fact that the empirical external strategy, which was used to construct the MMPI scales, neglects both item content and scale homogeneity may result in a rather diverse set of different item types within the same scale. In contrast, the heavy reliance on item analysis typical of internal scale construction strategies may constrain the number of different item types.

The finding that the rather homogeneous item sets of Eysenck's questionnaires were consistent with his theory demonstrates how helpful the mere existence of a theoretical model can be for the generation of relevant types of trait indicators. Nevertheless, equal weighting of responses to different item types, such as habitual reactions and direct trait attributions, in the calculation of scale scores seems inconsistent with Eysenck's hierarchical model, which implies that habitual responses belong to a lower level of abstraction and are therefore more specific.

Heterogeneity of item types within a questionnaire scale is not necessarily undesirable in itself – as long as the nature of this heterogeneity is theoretically explicated and justified. For example, one may have a theory of assertiveness suggesting that highly assertive people report (a) engaging in observable assertive acts; (b) thinking a lot about acting assertively; and (c) having particular physical symptoms when deprived of the opportunity to act assertively. If, in addition, the theory states that such people (d) describe themselves as assertive, bold, and not timid; (e) express wishes and interest related to assertiveness; (f) report that they stood up for themselves at nursery school; (g) state that they admire assertive people and endorse the belief that assertiveness is necessary to make it in this world; and finally, (i) indicate that others have reacted to their self-assertion in various ways, then (and only then) could the use of eight different item types to assess assertiveness be justified. Using sets of items selected to cover each of these types (or facets – see Kastner, this volume), the researcher has to show that the theory is correct, that is, that the responses to all these different types of items are manifestations of the same underlying trait.

In all, the distributions of the item categories *within* trait scales are quite informative. The results suggest that scales that assess similar constructs tend to be measured by somewhat similar types of items, regardless of the many other differences among the questionnaires considered. All else being equal, Neuroticism (or Anxiety) scales were found to contain more items describing covert and physical reactions, whereas Extraversion and Lie scales were characterized by higher percentages of items referring to overt reactions. One wonders why these shared intuitions about what types of items are particularly suitable to measure certain kinds of traits have not yet been systematized and incorporated into a priori construct definitions.

One possibility for changing this unsatisfactory state of affairs can be derived from Buss and Craik's (1983) research on act frequencies and from other approaches that similarly view traits as categorical, prototype-based concepts (e.g., Hampson, 1982). Although Buss and Craik (1983) have concentrated their initial efforts on *interpersonal* traits (which, as the present results for the Extraversion scales suggest, tend to be conceptualized in terms of overt behavioral reactions), it is possible to generate prototypical instances of other classes of behavior as well. For example, Ashton and Goldberg (1973) and Jackson (1975) had fairly naive item writers generate items for traits that involve task-performance (achievement), values (tolerance), and self-related cognitions (self-esteem); the resulting scales had criterion validities superior to those of like-named scales from the empirically derived CPI (Gough, 1957).

The trait indicators obtained in such item generation studies could then be classified into different types, using a category system like the one proposed here. Thus, this approach would not only provide preliminary item pools, but also survey the item types relevant to the traits under investigation. In turn, this information can be used to elaborate and refine the construct definition (e.g., in terms of facets) and thereby help define central aspects of the item universe, from which further indicators of the trait construct could then be drawn.

These procedures, although far from perfect, would at least introduce some objectivity into the process of item pool generation. Compared with previous practices, which have often led to idiosyncratic, nonreproducible, and heterogeneous item pools, these procedures have the advantage of being explicit, quantifiable, reproducible, and open to evaluation in terms of intersubjective agreement. Even more important, they point to a way of satisfying the often-repeated postulate that these aspects of substantive validity (Loevinger, 1957) or content validity (Cronbach, 1970, p. 143) must be incorporated as an explicit part of the definition of the trait construct.

Situational Context in Questionnaire Items

We have already noted that many questionnaire items are modified by intensity and frequency qualifiers (Payne, 1970; Pepper, 1981); items requiring trait attributions sometimes specify at least some minimal situational context. Similarly, items such as "I feel anxious *when I speak in front of a group*" and "It takes me time to overcome my shyness *in new situations*" demonstrate that authors of personality inventories apparently felt that some situational context should be mentioned in the item. However, with the exception of a few S-R (stimulus-response) self-report inventories (see Knudson & Golding, 1974), authors of personality questionnaires have ignored the much-debated issue of situational specificity in human behavior (e.g., Mischel & Peake, 1982) when writing items for their scales. Test authors act as if they believe that the psychological meaning of situational characteristics can be captured by a conditional, temporal, or adverbial clause. Can it be taken for granted that a situational context presented in such a verbal form is adequate, representative, or sufficiently typical to permit a behavior-in-context rating? Also, is it sensible to attempt this within questionnaire items that typically consist of only one sentence? How indicative of the postulated trait is a behavioral act within a situation conceptualized in such a contrived way? These questions need to be investigated systematically before we can adequately construct a trait scale.

In recent years, psychologists have paid increasing attention to the characteristics of situations, and some taxonomies of situations (Magnusson, 1981, 1984; Van Heck, 1984) and of types of persons *within* situations (Cantor, 1981; Cantor, Mischel, & Schwartz, 1982 a, 1982 b) have been constructed. Thus, we believe that theory and methodology have advanced to a point where we can find empirical answers to the questions posed above. Before we develop new questionnaires, then, we should investigate the psychological characteristics of the settings in which the behaviors of interest typically occur. Only after that step can we construct items that assess the postulated trait across a representative sample of relevant situations. And, finally, we may need to find ways of describing these situations in a verbal form that will enable respondents to understand the kinds of situations to which the item refers.

Traits in Ordinary and Scientific Language

Whereas the concept of "life-importance" has not been applied to the construction of item pools, it has been considered in decisions about which of the extremely large number of *traits* should be selected for assessment (Goldberg, 1972). In general, sheer historical accident and societal pressures on psychologists to forecast significant personal outcomes have been more important than theoretical models of personality in determining the selection of traits measured by questionnaires (Goldberg, 1971). However, a few attempts have been made to base the decision about which traits to assess on empirical criteria, rather than on purely applied considerations or on subjective "armchair" theories. For example, life importance has been operationalized in terms of the frequency of a trait descriptor in spoken or written discourse about people (Goldberg, 1982; Gough, 1965), the number of synonymous expressions a language contains for the same trait (Cattell, 1943, 1946), or the universality of equivalent descriptive terms for the same trait across languages and cultures (Goldberg, 1981 a; John, Goldberg, & Angleitner, 1984). This kind of reasoning led Cattell (1943, 1946) to search Allport and Odbert's (1936) compilation of English person-descriptive terms (as well as relevant publications of personologists) for trait terms to be included in his "trait sphere," from which he derived some of the dimensions later measured by the 16PF. Similarly, Gough's (1957) construction of the CPI started with an informal analysis of "folk concepts" of personality, which he defined as "variables used for the description and analysis of personality in everyday life and in social interaction" (p. 295). Gough (1965) viewed such folk concepts as emerging directly from interpersonal behavior, and assumed that they have a "kind of immediate meaningfulness" and "universal relevance."

One implication of the view that the trait terms found in many natural languages provide convenient summary labels for individual differences in behavior is that we need a theory about how trait terms are used in everyday life. Moreover, some items in personality questionnaires require subjects to make trait attributions to themselves; responses to such items are taken as evidence for the presence or absence of a trait in a person without much theoretical reflection about the processes by which people arrive at such attributions. Finally, we seem to use trait concepts in both ordinary and scientific language contexts without making a clear distinction between the two.

When we ask our subjects in questionnaire items whether they see themselves as lively, outgoing, impulsive, or sociable, they will unquestionably answer according to their intuitive, everyday-language understanding of these terms. However, when we refer to Extraversion in a talk delivered at a conference, we assume that the audience has a fairly uniform understanding of this term. Its meaning is supposedly embedded in theoretical and empirical relations so that the hearer can distinguish between, for example, Eysenck's and Guilford's concepts of Extraversion when these names are mentioned. But, where is the transition between these two levels of language? Does the very labeling of a factor according to its marker items produce a scientific term? Or is the mere listing of short paraphrases of the high-loading items still part of everyday language, whereas a more abstract factor label, which is related to a relevant theoretical network, implies the existence of a scientific terminology? What status should then be assigned to those trait terms that are administered as rating scales to subjects and their peers to validate questionnaire factors?

Indeed, Cattell (1973) made an explicit effort "to avoid the pollution of meaning in scientific discussion" (p. 54) by inventing a "host of neologic gobbledegook" (Goldberg, 1980) for his structural dimensions. The problem with his approach is that it has not worked. Personality psychologists, like everybody else, communicate via the natural language. Moreover, personality assessment via questionnaires involves verbal communication among the assessor, the respondents, and the user, who may be a counselor or personnel manager with little knowledge of scientific terminology. Thus, to *really* understand what Cattell means by *Premsia, Harria,* and *Zeppia,* we must somehow manage to translate those terms back into their natural equivalents. Indeed, if those new terms turned out to be particularly useful in communicating about individual differences, they would soon become encoded in the natural language, just like Extraversion-Introversion (Goldberg, 1980).

It appears, then, that dealing with the natural languages is inevitable when personality is being assessed with a method so language-bound as a questionnaire. As a consequence, our scientific terms should be translatable into the everyday language of personality. If we want to use ordinary-language utterances as a source of psychological data (Fiske, 1981), we need an in-depth understanding of everyday-language *usage,* including an appreciation of the lack of precision and the context dependency of natural languages, as well as their power in human communication.

Thus, an important topic for further research is the usage of trait terms in self and peer descriptions. Some initial steps toward the development of semantic taxonomies for various types of personality-descriptive terms have been made in some West European languages (for a recent review, see John et al., 1984). When such taxonomies are mapped into recently developed situation taxonomies (e.g., Van Heck, 1984) and complemented with research on episode cognition (Forgas, 1982) and trait attribution (e.g., Kelley & Michela, 1980), our understanding of the differences and similarities between scientific and lay conceptions of traits will be much advanced.

Conclusions

There seems to be growing agreement among personality researchers of varying persuasions that the writing and selection of items should be preceded by an initial construction stage that involves some reflection about the trait construct and about the characteristics of relevant items (Fiske, 1971; Goldberg & Slovic, 1967; Jackson, 1971; Meehl, 1972; Mischel, 1972; Wiggins, 1973). Four issues that arise during this initial phase have direct implications for the practice of test development. First, rather than constructing measures for any odd trait and thereby contributing to the seemingly infinite proliferation of personality scales, the test developer should have a strong rationale for measuring a particular trait. Optimally, this rationale would be based on a structural theory of personality that reflects the "life-importance" of individual differences among people. Second, rather than "borrowing" items from other questionnaires or making up items on the spur of a creative moment, the test developer should begin the item-generation process by developing an explicit definition of the trait construct. This definition should include a description of the convergent and discriminant relations with other constructs and specify relevant types of trait manifestations, such as observable behavioral acts, trait attributions to oneself, or wishes and interests. Third, to avoid idiosyncratic and nonreproducible item pools (and consequently trait scales), exemplars for each of the theoretically derived item types (or facets) should, whenever possible, be generated by a sizable sample of people; the selection of items from these initial sets should be based on interjudge agreement on the relevance of the item content for the trait (e.g., estimates of endorsement probabilities, prototypicality), and discriminant item validity should already be taken into account at this stage. Finally, since the meaning of social behavior depends to a large extent on the context in which it is performed, the test developer should, when screening the initially generated item material, make a special effort to ensure that the relevant aspects of the situational context are included in the item text and that they are described as explicitly as possible.

Surface Elements of Questionnaire Items: A Linguistic Analysis

Following these decisions about the trait construct and about relevant item types, the next task of the test developer is to "translate" the theoretically elaborated trait manifestations into an appropriate verbal form. But, what is the most appropriate form to make an item a good indicator of the trait construct? How *should* items be written? At this stage of test construction, detailed knowledge about language would be of great help to questionnaire developers.

Responses to personality questionnaires are highly standardized verbal behaviors elicited by verbal stimuli and should, therefore, be of interest to psycholinguists and linguists. However, linguistic analyses of questionnaires and their items have been rare. Despite recent progress in research on text and discourse processing (Givon, 1979), these approaches are not yet sufficiently developed to provide sophisticated theories that could be applied to questionnaires. Indeed, little research by either linguists or personality psychologists has been directed at the investigation of syntactic and semantic characteristics of the sentences that are used in personality questionnaires.

A small number of studies have investigated the effects of syntactic characteristics of the item formulation on item response consistency. For example, Micklin and Durbin (1969) reported that larger differences between the structural properties of the sentences in otherwise parallel attitude scales were associated with less response consistency to such scales. Other studies have compared various response formats differing in the number of possible response alternatives (Jones, 1968), or analyzed how "?" or "middle" responses are used by subjects (Dubois & Burnes, 1975). Goldberg (1978, 1981 b) recently investigated the meaning of "middle" responses in a trait attribution paradigm. He argued that subjects could interpret the middle response option in four rather different ways. In particular, a middle response to an item can stand for (a) a situational attribution (e.g., "my behavior depends on the situation"); (b) an expression of uncertainty (e.g., "I do not know that aspect of myself well enough to make a decision"); (c) ambiguity of the item (e.g., "I am not sure what this item means"); and (d) neutrality (e.g., "I am average on this characteristic"). However, in the few questionnaires that offer the respondent a third response option (e.g., Cattell's 16PF and Eysenck's MPI), the middle responses are always counted as at least somewhat indicative of the trait and therefore increase the subject's total score.

Subjects frequently experience the dichotomous (sometimes trichotomous) response format as logically inconsistent with the item content. In our studies, subjects complained particularly about items that consisted of several separate clauses conjoined by *and* or *or* [e.g., MMPI item (131): "I like collecting flowers or growing indoor plants"] or contained unusual contextual specifications [e.g., MMPI item (171): "It makes me uncomfortable to put on a stunt at a party even when others are doing the same sort of things"]. Negations can also create considerable confusion, especially when a negated item does not apply, and thus the respondent should answer "false" or "no" (Peterson & Peterson, 1976).

Thus, it seems plausible that the wording of an item, as captured by surface characteristics such as response format, item length, and syntactic complexity of the sentence, should be related to the way the item is processed by the subjects who are trying to respond to it. Yet correlations between syntactic item characteristics and item response parameters are rarely substantial (Goldberg, 1968; Wiggins & Goldberg, 1965). One reason for the lack of more impressive empirical effects may lie in the fact that only a small number of relevant variables (often selected on an ad hoc basis) have been investigated in any one study. To overcome this deficiency, Löhr and Angleitner (1980) studied a more comprehensive set of precisely defined variables across a large sample of questionnaire items. A theoretical framework for the description of the surface structure of items will be introduced here and used to discuss their findings. The relations between item surface characteristics and item response reliability and validity will be presented in the fourth section of this chapter.

Linguistic Description of Item Surface Characteristics

According to psycholinguistic models of reading (see Foss & Hakes, 1978), the ease with which subjects read a sentence depends on the extent to which short-term memory is overloaded, and also on the structure of the sentence. Thus, errors during the initial stages of the item response process (i.e., reading and subsequent encoding) should increase with the length and complexity of the item and lead to low response stability. Findings by Wiggins and Goldberg (1965) support this reasoning; the correlation between item length and response consistency from first to second administration was $-.30$. To replicate and further explore this finding, Löhr and Angleitner (1980) devised three objective measures of item length, specifically, the numbers of words, of letters, and of clauses.

Although Chomsky (e.g., 1965) has stated that his theory of language cannot be directly interpreted as a theory of language *performance*, many models of comprehension incorporate some aspects of transformational grammar (Foss & Hakes, 1978). According to such models, each transformation in the grammar has an associated "reverse" transformation, that is, a set of operations which "detransform" the surface structure of a sentence into a semantic representation at the deep-structure level. In particular, these reverse transformations apply to the surface structure, which corresponds to the input string of words that make up the sentence. One implication of this type of model is that the comprehension of sentences that undergo more transformations should take longer and result in more errors than those that undergo fewer transformations. For example, a passive sentence should be more difficult to comprehend than the corresponding active one, since the inverse of the passive transformation has to be applied to it. Helferich (this volume) discusses some of the problems inherent in these models.

In addition to the three measures of item length, Löhr and Angleitner (1980) scored the number of passive verbs and syntactic negations as well as the tense (i.e., past, present, future) and the mood (i.e., indicative vs subjunctive) of the verb of the main clause. These measures seem to reflect the transformational complexity of the item's surface structure. The presence of personal pronouns such as *you* or *I* in the item's surface structure is another variable that could be viewed as an aspect of transformational complexity. That is, personality questionnaire items inquire about self-perceptions and retrospective accounts of self-related events, which seem to be represented within a part of semantic memory that is centered around the respondent's self (Hull & Levy, 1979; Rogers, 1977). Items whose surface structures already contain direct references to the respondent's self may require fewer transformations, and may therefore be more easily compared with self-relevant information already stored, than are items that do not contain any personal references.

Two other surface characteristics of questionnaire items that are beyond the reach of psycholinguistic theorizing are of a pragmatic nature, that is, they are specific to the particular format and communicative purpose of personality questionnaires: The respondents are expected to provide the researcher with information about themselves, but in order to do so they have to use the highly restricted and standardized response alternatives specified by the researcher. To elicit the desired information from the respondent, questionnaire authors have used a variety of response formats. Specifically, they have used as sentence types either direct questions or assertions, followed by response formats that differ in the number of response alternatives they permit. Several kinds of response formats can be distinguished; some require the same general response types to all questions (e.g., yes vs no or true vs false) whereas others consist of specifications of the item content (e.g., often–sometimes–never).

Surface Characteristics of Items in Contemporary Questionnaires

In Löhr and Angleitner's (1980) study, two judges scored 1624 items assembled from ten personality inventories on eleven variables, which can be grouped according to three aspects of the item's surface structure: Item *length* as indicated by number of words, letters, and clauses; item *complexity* assessed in terms of negations, passive voice, tense, mood, and personal reference; and finally, the item *format*, including the sentence type as well as number and kind of response options. As one should expect of such objectively defined measures, interjudge agreement was very high; overall, the two judges agreed on 98% of their ratings.

The results of this study show that many questionnaire authors do not even follow those guidelines that the relevant textbooks list as rules of thumb for item writing. Lienert (1969, pp. 63–64), for example, recommends keeping items short, and avoiding multiple clauses and negations. Yet, the average item in the set of 964 items compiled from seven Anglo-American questionnaires (see *Appendix A* for a list of the scales analyzed) was more than 12 words long (SD = 6.2) and consisted of two clauses (SD = 1.1). Moreover, almost a quarter of these items contained at least one negation. Double negations and passive verbs, however, were relatively infrequent (2% and 5%, respectively). Use of the past tense and subjunctive were found in 10.5% of the items; 4.5% contained *no* personal reference to the respondent. To evaluate these findings within a broader context of language use, comparison data for sentences found in other sources could be helpful. Thus, it might be interesting to investigate whether the text form "personality questionnaire" differs in some important ways from other text forms such as newspaper articles, autobiographies, and diaries, and whether such differences in surface structure reflect the particular communicative purposes of questionnaires.

There were some systematic differences in the items' surface characteristics among the seven questionnaires of Anglo-American origin included in this project. Cattell's 16PF items consistently had the highest scores on all three measures of item length. Whereas the items of the four Eysenck questionnaires (i.e., MPI, MMQ, EPI-A and -B) and the MMPI items averaged ten words and consisted of less than two clauses, the 16PF items had a mean length of 16 words and 2.5 clauses.

Comparisons of these questionnaires on the syntactic characteristics suggest that there is some correspondence between the logical relation of the item to the trait and the way it is phrased. That is, the surface structure of the item seems to reflect shared conventions about the phrasing of particular types of trait indicators. The most obvious example is the MMPI, which of all seven questionnaires contained the highest percentage of biographical items, and correspondingly had the highest percentage of items with the main verb in the past tense. More importantly, Löhr and Angleitner (1980) found that, compared with the other questionnaires, both forms of the 16PF had the highest percentages of items with subjunctive verb constructions and no direct references to the respondent. This finding reflects the much higher frequencies of inquiries about wishes and interests and about attitudes and beliefs in Cattell's item sets. Apparently, wishes and interests are often expressed as actions whose *hypothetical* nature is indicated by subjunctive verb forms, whereas attitudes and beliefs seem to be assessed predominantly in terms of categorical statements of a *general* nature, and therefore they may lack personal references in their surface structures.

Although we need to follow up these suggestive findings more systematically, it is evident that syntactic aspects of questionnaire items cannot be conveniently separated from semantic considerations (Fillmore, 1977). Indeed, our findings illustrate the complex interaction between the characteristics of trait constructs and the syntactic aspects of the items that psychologists construct to measure them. We hope that more rigorous theorizing and research in psycholinguistics will eventually increase our limited understanding of these intricate relations.

Item Characteristics and Item Response Processes

As Table 1 shows, the output of the researcher's item-writing efforts serves as the raw verbal input to the subjects who read the item and try to respond to it. Thus, whereas we took a linguistic perspective in the previous section and described and evaluated the syntactic surface characteristics of the item text with reference to the researcher's task of item *writing,* we will now discuss item characteristics that are relevant to the subject's task in *responding* to the item. Our perspective is that of cognitive psychology, and we will describe the cognitive stages and operations that need to be performed to arrive at a response. For each stage of this response process, we will identify the item characteristics that can be expected to facilitate or complicate the processing of the item, define, and measure them in a rating study, and finally, in the last section, use these measures to predict item response parameters such as item stability and validity.

Stages of the Response Process and Item Characteristics

Several different models have been proposed to describe the processes involved in responding to personality questionnaire items (e.g., Cliff, Bradley, & Girard, 1973; Kuncel, 1973; Nowakowska, 1970; Rogers, 1971, 1974a, 1974b; Schneider-Dueker & Schneider, 1977). Although these authors differ considerably in their methodological approaches (e.g., content analyses of thinking-aloud protocols, reaction time studies, pairwise ratings of the similarity between items), their models show a modest degree of convergence. Most of these models can be classified as three-stage, sequential processing models. When responding to a questionnaire item, the subjects first read the item and form an internal representation of its meaning (encoding stage). Second, they compare that meaning with internally stored information about themselves, and decide whether they agree with the item or not (item-self comparison stage). Before the response is marked on the answer sheet, the latent decision may also be checked for its utility, especially with regard to its congruence with social norms and values (utility-control stage).

Although Table 1 shows these hypothetical stages of the response process as if they were distinct and strictly sequential (see Rogers, 1974a), we do not claim that the operations implied by these processing stages are completely independent of each other or that they could not be executed in an interactive or parallel fashion. Rather, we view this model as an heuristic one that can help identify, for each stage of the response process, those item characteristics that might elicit processing difficulties at that stage. In particular, we will consider the following five questions: (a) Is the item difficult or easy to understand? (b) Is it possible to assign more than one meaning to the item, or is it unambiguous? (c) Does the item involve abstract information that may require additional complex processing or does it require only concrete information that is

Table 5. The rating scales used to assess the five response characteristics

Comprehensibility

1. You understand the item immediately upon first reading
2. After the first reading, you have to read at least parts of the item again
3. After the first reading, you find that at least one "aspect" is still completely unclear
4. You have to consciously apply grammatical rules to understand the item or read it at least three times

Ambiguity

1. The item is completely unambiguous
2. Only if you try to be very nitpicky can you discover a slight ambiguity, which is, however, of no practical consequence
3. If one reads the item carefullly and thinks about the possible answers, it is clear that the item cannot be answered unambiguously
4. The item is obviously ambiguous

Abstractness

1. The item is concrete in every respect
2. The important aspects of the item are worded in a concrete way; the overall impression is concrete
3. The important aspects of the item are worded in an abstract way, the overall impression is abstract
4. The item has almost no concrete reference

Self-Reference

1. The item refers strongly to personal experiences
2. The item refers predominantly to personal experiences. The respondent is the focal point of the statement
3. The respondent is mentioned in the item but is not the focal point of the statement
4. The respondent is either not mentioned at all in the item or "stands completely at the sidelines"

Evaluation

1. This item is as neutral when it is endorsed as when it is not endorsed
2. The item implies social norms; however, the individual's self-concept weighs more heavily in deciding how to respond
3. When responding to the item, one is likely to follow general value standards
4. The item expresses a clear positively or negatively valued standard

readily available and can be easily retrieved from memory? (d) Does the item refer to personally relevant information? (e) Is the item evaluatively neutral or is it socially desirable or undesirable to endorse the item? Corresponding to these five questions, five item characteristics were defined, and verbally anchored four-step rating scales were constructed to measure each of them. These rating scales are presented in Table 5.

Comprehensibility. Item comprehensibility is of obvious importance for the response process. The more difficult it is for subjects to comprehend the meaning of the item, the more likely it is that the item will be misunderstood, with the result that the response will not bear on the subject's real position. The importance of this item characteristic is reflected in various models of the response process, such as in Rogers' (1974a) stimulus encoding and Kuncel's (1973) meaning assignment stages. Causes of insufficient comprehensibility are uncommon words, complex sentence structures, unclear and confusing relations among clauses within sentences, and grammatical errors. In an attempt to construct a rating scale anchored in subjects' subjective reactions to items, each of the four steps of the scale were clearly labeled (see Table 5). Subjects were warned that comprehensibility and ambiguity are distinct concepts; an item that is difficult to comprehend may nevertheless have one perfectly clear and unambiguous meaning if enough time is spent trying to work out its meaning. Thus, a high degree of comprehensibility is particularly important to make sure that subjects with little verbal sophistication answer correctly, whereas subjects with high verbal sophistication are more likely to notice and to be bothered by ambiguity.

Ambiguity. Ambiguity has been traditionally defined as doubtfulness or uncertainty about the meaning of a stimulus; more specifically, an item is called ambiguous if its surface structure can be interpreted in more than one way, all of which are linguistically correct. The concept of ambiguity implies intraindividual uncertainty about the meaning of a stimulus, whereas interindividual differences in stimulus interpretation have been referred to as *equivocality* (Goldberg, 1963).

Since ambiguity is generally assumed to influence the interpretation of items, this item characteristic should be relevant at the encoding stage, the stage called stimulus comprehension by Rogers (1974a), intellectual evaluation of question and answer by Nowakowska (1970), and meaning assignment by Kuncel (1973). Item ambiguity can be due to the presence of words or phrases that have several meanings (Pepper, 1981), to relations among sentence clauses that are not unequivocal, or to incompatibilities between item and response format. The latter may stem from negations, or from conjunctions (e.g., *and, or*) in items that contain more than one main clause.

Item ambiguity can have two undesirable effects on response processing. First, the subject may not recognize the ambiguous nature of the item and may "misunderstand" it (i.e., interpret it in a way not intended by the author). A second possibility is that the subject does recognize the ambiguity but is not sure which of the two (or more) meanings is the intended one, thereby allowing some other variable unrelated to the item content, such as interpretive acquiescence (Messick, 1967), to influence the response.

Abstractness. We expect this item characteristic to influence the processing of items during the item-self comparison stage. Abstractness is related to Nowakowska's (1970) memory variable called "specific past experience," and refers to the extent to which an item inquires about abstract information. In particular, the more abstract the information required, the more likely it is that specific information stored in memory has to be further analyzed (e.g., integrated, supplemented by inferences) during the item-self comparison stage.

Concrete items refer to specific behaviors, and explicitly name relevant conditions, situations, people, or groups; they may even involve facts whose veridicality can be ascertained. In contrast, items that attribute to the respondent a general disposition, attitude, or wish are more abstract; these items require the interpretation of various past events (e.g., behaviors and experiences), their integration across different situations, comparisons with some unspecified standards, and other inferences. In other words, abstract items give the respondent considerable leeway in selecting information pertinent to the item and in integrating it into a response. Thus, the more abstract the item, the less likely it is that different subjects will arrive at a uniform understanding of its meaning.

Nisbett and Ross (1980, pp. 47–51) have reviewed evidence showing that concrete and vivid information is more easily recalled than is abstract information. Bellezza (1984) demonstrated that over a 1-week interval information about concrete nouns was more reliably retrieved from memory than was information about abstract nouns, and Payne (1970) showed that items rated as referring to explicit and clearly observable behaviors elicited more response stability than did items rated low on behavioral specificity. Thus, in addition to interindividual differences in understanding, the abstractness of the item content may lead to intraindividual response inconsistency.

Self-Reference. Self-reference is another item characteristic that is relevant to the item-self comparison stage, because it may influence the ease with which subjects can relate the item content to their own personal experiences or self-concepts. Self-reference is here defined as the degree to which the structure and content of the item taps the respondents' self-concept. An item with a high degree of self-reference permits the subjects to respond on the basis of their own perceptions and experiences. Self-reference is present in an item to the extent that the respondent is directly mentioned in the item, experiences or does something, is the object of an action, and/or is emotionally involved.

Evaluation. Items differ in the extent to which they invoke socioculturally determined values, norms, and standards. The more evaluatively extreme (i.e., either desirable or undesirable) the item content, the more likely it is that subjects will select the more socially desirable response. This item characteristic is particularly relevant to the final stage of the response process, namely utility control during response selection (Nowakowska, 1970; Rogers, 1971). Paulhus (this volume) differentiates among various mechanisms that might be involved in this process.

The Rating Study

In all, 1624 personality questionnaire items were rated by 230 paid judges who were advanced students of psychology or German literature. The instructions to the judges contained carefully written definitions of the five characteristics to be rated, several examples intended to anchor the steps of the rating scales, and several practice trials using pretested items (see Langer & Schulz von Thun, 1974). Each judge rated approximately 380 items on only one of the five item characteristics, resulting in 11–12 judges for each dimension and item. The original data were obtained by Löhr (1977) and Keren (1979), who dichotomized the verbally labeled four-step rating scales. The Comprehensibility scale was partitioned into "immediately understandable" (1) vs "not immediately understandable" (2+3+4); on the other four scales, the two higher (1+2) and the two lower (3+4) values were combined (see Table 5). All analyses summarized here were performed on these dichotomous data.

Overall, the mean interjudge agreement was 76%, and the mean value for Kappa was .50. Agreement among judges was consistently lower for the Ambiguity ratings than for the other four dimensions, agreement being highest on the Comprehensibility judgments. On the other hand, intrajudge consistency (assessed across items presented twice) exceeded 80% for Ambiguity, which was at least as stable as the other judgments. Thus, despite Löhr's (1977) and Keren's (1979) efforts to devise clear instructions, the judges seemed to have internally consistent but somewhat idiosyncratic conceptions of ambiguity.

Results. Table 6 presents the percentages of items that were classified by the majority of judges as ambiguous, abstract, value laden, not immediately understandable, and not self-referent; these proportions are presented separately for each of these five dichotomous dimensions and for each of the seven Anglo-American personality questionnaires described in this chapter.

Overall, more than 50% of the items in these personality questionnaires were not immediately understandable upon first reading. Cattell's 16PF was found to contain about twice as many items that were not easy to understand as either the MMPI or the four questionnaires constructed by Eysenck. Considering all seven questionnaires together, more than 25% of their items were classified as ambiguous. The 16PF had the highest percentage of ambiguous items, whereas Eysenck's questionnaires ranged from 10% (MPI) to 35% (EPI-A) ambiguous items. More than 40% of the items in this set had an ab-

Table 6. Item characteristics related to the response process: Percentage of items classified in each category for seven questionnaires. (Compiled from Löhr, in preparation)

Questionnaire	No. of items	Not immediately under-standable	Ambigous	Abstract	Not self-referent	Evalu-ative
MPI	48	41.7	10.4	68.8	12.5	47.9
MMQ	56	35.7	19.6	32.1	12.5	58.9
EPI-A	57	40.4	35.1	45.6	12.3	71.9
EPI-B	57	29.8	17.5	42.1	45.6	50.9
16PF-A	171	72.5	39.2	42.7	31.0	37.4
16PF-B	171	83.0	33.3	37.4	46.8	48.5
MMPI	404	40.6	22.5	43.6	36.1	47.0
All personality	964	52.9	27.1	42.9	33.7	48.1
Interest[a]	168	82.1	15.5	6.0	96.4	2.4
Verbal IQ[b]	26	92.3	3.8	0.0	100.0	0.0

[a] These percentage are based on eight 21-item vocational interest scales included in Mittenecker and Toman's (1951) Persönlichkeits-Interessen-Test and are given here for comparison only.

[b] The items of the 16PF scale B were not included with the other personality scales because that scale was devised to assess intelligence.

stract rather than concrete reference. With the exception of Eysenck's MPI, which had more than 60% abstract items, the questionnaires did not differ much from each other on this dimension. One third of the items lacked reference to the respondent's perceptions and personal experiences; the items of EPI-B and 16PF-B were particularly impersonal, whereas most MPI, MMQ, and EPI-A items did contain direct references to the respondent. Finally, almost 50% of the items were judged as highly value laden; among the seven questionnaires, the percentages ranged from 37% (16PF-A) to 72% (EPI-A).

Table 7 presents the relative frequencies of these item characteristics separately for each scale of the seven questionnaires. Scales assessing the same or similar constructs appear next to each other. The first section of Table 7 permits a comparison among three Extraversion, four Neuroticism, and three Lie scales, all constructed by Eysenck and his coworkers. With regard to the frequencies of difficult and ambiguous items, the three kinds of scales did not differ much from each other. The other three characteristics, however, showed some interesting differences. First, the Neuroticism scales had the most abstract items on average, followed by the Extraversion scales, whereas the Lie scales had a relatively large number of concrete items. Second, all four Neuroticism scales contained more self-referent items than any of the three Lie scales constructed by Eysenck; if the scales within each questionnaire are compared for self-reference, Neuroticism was always highest and the Lie scales were al-

Table 7. Item characteristics related to the response process: Percentage of items classified in each category for all scales. (Based on Löhr, in preparation)

Questionnaire	Scale (no. of items)	Not immediately understandable	Ambiguous	Abstract	Not self-referent	Evaluative
MPI	E (24)	33.3	4.2	62.5	20.8	50.0
EPI-A	E (24)	41.7	33.3	29.2	16.7	58.3
EPI-B	E (24)	45.8	29.2	41.7	58.3	54.2
MPI	N (24)	50.0	16.7	75.0	4.2	45.8
MMQ	N (38)	34.2	13.2	39.5	2.6	47.4
EPI-A	N (24)	37.5	41.7	62.5	0.0	79.2
EPI-B	N (24)	25.0	8.3	45.8	20.8	37.5
MMQ	L (18)	38.9	33.3	16.7	33.3	83.3
EPI-A	L (9)	44.4	22.2	44.4	33.3	88.9
EPI-B	l (9)	0.0	11.1	33.3	77.8	77.8
16PF-A	F (13)	53.8	23.1	38.5	46.2	15.4
16PF-B	F (13)	76.9	15.4	46.2	23.1	46.2
16PF-A	H (13)	61.5	15.4	30.8	7.7	15.4
16PF-B	H (13)	61.5	53.8	38.5	15.4	69.2
16PF-A	E (13)	84.6	46.2	53.8	0.0	69.2
16PF-B	E (13)	84.6	30.8	30.8	69.2	76.9
16PF-A	Q2 (10)	90.0	40.0	50.0	40.0	20.0
16PF-B	Q2 (10)	90.0	30.0	40.0	70.0	30.0
16PF-A	A (10)	50.0	20.0	10.0	60.0	10.0
16PF-B	A (10)	80.0	20.0	0.0	70.0	0.0
16PF-A	I (10)	40.0	30.0	0.0	40.0	10.0
16PF-B	I (10)	60.0	20.0	30.0	50.0	40.0
16PF-A	L (10)	90.0	40.0	50.0	40.0	20.0
16PF-B	L (10)	100.0	30.0	90.0	60.0	70.0
16PF-A	C (13)	61.5	38.5	53.8	15.4	30.8
16PF-B	C (13)	100.0	38.5	53.8	30.8	30.8
16PF-A	O (13)	61.5	69.2	46.2	15.4	53.8
16PF-B	O (13)	92.3	46.2	46.2	15.4	61.5
16PF-A	Q4 (13)	76.9	53.8	53.8	0.0	46.2
16PF-B	Q4 (13)	61.5	7.7	15.4	15.4	38.5
16PF-A	G (10)	90.0	20.0	70.0	50.0	70.0
16PF-B	G (10)	100.0	30.0	30.0	70.0	70.0
16PF-A	Q3 (10)	70.0	30.0	30.0	30.0	70.0
16PF-B	Q3 (10)	90.0	30.0	40.0	40.0	70.0
16PF-A	Q1 (10)	100.0	40.0	50.0	60.0	40.0
16PF-B	Q1 (10)	80.0	50.0	30.0	80.0	30.0
16PF-A	M (13)	76.9	46.2	38.5	38.5	30.8
16PF-B	M (13)	92.3	61.5	53.8	76.9	46.2
16PF-A	N (10)	90.0	70.0	60.0	50.0	60.0
16PF-B	N (10)	80.0	30.0	10.0	40.0	40.0
MMPI	L (15)	33.3	13.3	40.0	46.7	66.7
MMPI	F (64)	39.1	18.8	46.9	39.1	67.2
MMPI	K (30)	43.3	36.7	46.7	33.3	50.0
MMPI	Hs (33)	15.2	18.2	6.1	78.8	0.0
MMPI	D (60)	30.0	23.3	41.7	26.7	43.3

Table 7 (continued)

Questionnaire	Scale (no. of items)	Not immediately understandable	Ambiguous	Abstract	Not self-referent	Evaluative
MMPI	Hy (60)	41.7	25.0	35.0	45.0	31.7
MMPI	Pd (50)	36.0	22.0	62.0	32.0	64.0
MMPI	Mf (60)	30.0	6.7	26.7	36.7	25.0
MMPI	Pa (40)	45.0	32.5	75.0	30.0	50.0
MMPI	Pt (48)	39.6	33.3	58.3	12.5	66.7
MMPI	Sc (78)	43.6	25.6	51.3	23.1	64.1
MMPI	Ma (46)	63.0	32.6	52.2	21.7	52.2
MMPI	Si (70)	51.4	20.0	44.3	38.6	44.3
MMPI	Sd (39)	35.9	17.9	41.0	30.8	61.5

ways lowest. Third, whereas both Neuroticism and Extraversion scales contained approximately equal numbers of evaluative and neutral items, about 80% of the Lie scale items were classified as value laden, a finding which is quite consistent with the intended purpose of such scales.

All but two of the 16PF scales contained more than 50% items classified as not immediately understandable; on several scales [e.g., L (trust vs suspicion)], the percentage of such difficult items reached 90–100. Equally disconcerting was the high number of ambiguous items on the 16PF; the highest percentage of ambiguous items was concentrated on scales M and N, which supposedly assess aspects of cultural sophistication. As with Eysenck's Neuroticism scales, the 16PF scales that measure aspects of anxiety (C, O, Q4) had somewhat more abstract items and many more self-referent items than the other sets of scales. The fewest self-referent items were found for the scales G and Q1 (conscientiousness and traditionalism) and the cultural sophistication scales M and N. Finally, most of Cattell's scales were as value laden as the scales of the other test authors, with the exception of the cluster formed by the A, I, and L scales (warmth and sensitivity).

The distribution of the MMPI items on these characteristics generally mirrored the patterns found for similarly named scales constructed by Eysenck and by Cattell. For example, the MMPI Lie (L) scale had more concrete than abstract items, only about 50% self-referent items (i.e., it was the secondlowest MMPI scale on this characteristic), and a large percentage of value laden items. The Social Introversion (Si) scale was also similar to the Extraversion scales in this sample; its items were relatively unambiguous and self-referent. The Psychasthenia (Pt) and Schizophrenia (Sc) scales resembled the pattern obtained for Eysenck's Neuroticism and Cattell's Anxiety-related scales, namely high percentages of abstract, self-referent, and value laden items. Finally, the Hypochondriasis (Hs) scale should be mentioned for its exceptionally high values on most of these characteristics: 85% of its items were classified as immediately understandable, 82% as unambiguous, 94% as referring to concrete and specific events, and all 100% of them were classified as evaluatively neutral.

Table 7 also shows that the presumably parallel scales of EPI-A and -B and of 16PF-A and -B did not necessarily include items with similar characteristics; for example, all items of the EPI-B Lie scale were classified as immediately understandable, whereas only 56% of the EPI-A version of the same scale received that classification. Moreover, the Neuroticism scale of EPI-B contained three times as many evaluatively neutral items as did that of EPI-A. Similar examples can be found for a variety of "parallel" 16PF scales. Given such disparities, any claim that these scales are psychometrically equivalent may be hard to justify.

Discussion. These differences even among presumably parallel scales also imply that caution is necessary in the interpretation of the associations between scale content and the processing characteristics of the corresponding items. Nevertheless, we believe that the scale-by-scale analyses show three discernable trends. Neuroticism and related constructs tended to be measured by abstract and overwhelmingly self-referent items; their comprehensibility and ambiguity varied with the test and the test author. Extraversion items tended to be somewhat less abstract and less self-referent. Finally, Lie scale items tended to be relatively unambiguous, more concrete, less highly self-referent, and more value laden than either Neuroticism or Extraversion items.

How should the overall distributions of these characteristics be evaluated? Fortunately, the total battery of questionnaires classified by Löhr (1977) and Keren (1979) included a few vocational interest scales from a German personality and interest test (Mittenecker & Toman, 1951), as well as Cattell's 16PF intelligence scales. For comparison purposes, the percentages of processing characteristics for these two types of items are given in the last two rows of Table 6.

In contrast to the personality trait scales, vocational interest scales and IQ tests do not require the respondent to report or provide information about their past behaviors or personal experiences; instead they ask for a preference for a job and for the solution to a problem, respectively. Thus, the self-reference criterion crucial to the assessment of traits is largely irrelevant for interest and intelligence items. Quite appropriately, then, these items were found to be *uniformly not* self-referent. Moreover, the interest and IQ items, in contrast to the personality items, had extremely homogeneous distributions on the other item characteristics as well. With few exceptions, they were unambiguous and concrete, and did not involve social norms and values (see also Fiske, 1971, p. 222). Given that the IQ items were designed to differentiate subjects with high verbal skills from those with low ones, the finding that almost all IQ items were not easy to understand may actually indicate some construct validity for these classifications. On IQ tests, subjects are expected to try hard to think about each item and figure out the correct meaning; that there generally is only one correct interpretation is shown by the small percentages of ambiguous IQ (and interest) items. In instructions for personality questionnaires, however, subjects are told *not* to think or deliberate very much. The instructions for Cattell's 16 PF, for example, emphasize that one should *"Give the first, natural answer as it comes to you* ... Give the best answer you can at a rate not slower than five or six a minute" (emphasis in original), and those for Eysenck's EPI state that one should "Respond quickly ... we would like to assess your first reaction and not the result of long deliberations." Given this kind of instructional set, the effects of insufficient comprehensibility and ambiguity may be even more pronounced. Thus, in our opinion, the results presented here show that too many items of personality and validity scales have poor information processing characteristics: More than 50% are difficult to understand; 25% are ambiguous; and almost 50% are abstract and value laden.

Conclusions. Over the past decade, there has been increasing consensus in the assessment literature that the content of an item should make theoretical sense (Fiske, 1971; Goldberg & Slovic, 1967; Jackson, 1971; Meehl, 1972; Mischel, 1972; Wiggins, 1973). Thus, if the the goal of test construction is to maximize the content variance in item responses, successful and efficient communication of this content is imperative. This is even more important because responding to the items of paper-and-pencil inventories constitutes a highly constrained communication situation. The respondents are expected to provide information about themselves in a reliable and valid way. To do so, however, they have to use a notoriously fuzzy mode of communication, language, in a highly standardized format, their only means of response being the selection of inflexible alternatives. They cannot ask the test constructor, "What do you mean by that?" Thus, in order to ensure that communication is successful under the impoverished conditions of the testing situation, authors of personality questionnaires must make every effort to limit the effects of factors that are likely to introduce errors into this verbal process.

To summarize, then, items should be easy to understand; otherwise, differences between subjects in verbal sophistication and conscientiousness will introduce errors. Items should be unambiguous; otherwise, it is unclear what the subject responded to and thus what the response means. Items should be concrete; otherwise, a uniform understanding of the item cannot be guaranteed. Perhaps items should be self-referent; otherwise, subjects may be unable to relate the question to their own frames of reference and to provide meaningful answers. Items should be as neutral as possible; otherwise, some subjects are likely to be influenced as much by the value implications of their responses as by the item content. The data presented so far suggests that none of the authors of the personality questionnaires studied here have constructed item pools with all of those characteristics.

The Prediction of Psychometric Characteristics

In the preceding sections of this chapter, we have described and evaluated items on the basis of logical-semantic categories, linguistic surface-structure variables, and cognitive-processing characteristics. In this final part, we turn to those item characteristics that have traditionally been of the most interest to the psychometrically inclined psychologist, item *response* parameters obtained from a group of subjects. We will briefly describe these item statistics and their distributions in a large sample of items taken from personality and validity scales. Whereas the ultimate goal of itemmetric research should be the discovery of the relationships between item properties and *scale* validity, we will restrict ourselves here to the prediction of *item* response parameters. Using multiple regression analyses, we will examine the extent to which item stability and internal validity are influenced by the three kinds of item characteristics that we have discussed in the preceding sections.

Item Response Parameters

Item statistics were obtained by Angleitner (1976, 1981a), who administered the whole set of questionnaires to a sample of 102 normal adult subjects twice, with a test–retest interval of 2–3 weeks. The actual sample sizes varied from 81 to 99 subjects, depending on the questionnaire. Subjects filled out the questionnaires at home at their own pace. Frequencies of endorsement, frequencies of stable responses, and item-test correlations were used for the analyses described below.

Endorsement frequencies were transformed into adjusted *item means* to obtain an equivalent measure of central tendency independent of differences in response formats and keying among the questionnaires. For Eysenck's MPI, Cattell's 16PF, and the Giessen test (all of which offer more than two response options), the weights of the response options were adjusted to a range from 0 (minimum weight) to 1 (maximum weight), with equidistant intermediate weights. Then, for all reverse-keyed items, the response weights were subtracted from 1. The weights of items with dichotomous response formats and affirmative keying direction remained unaltered. Finally, item means were computed from the new weights and the corresponding endorsement frequencies. *Item variances* were also computed from these adjusted data.

Both test and retest data were transformed in this way, thus permitting the computation of reliability estimates. For the item means, the retest correlation was .98, and for the item variances it was .95. Given these high correlations, only the sample statistics from the first administration will be reported here. Table 8 presents the means and standard deviations (or percentages) for all item properties based on a set of 1051 items. In this set, the items from the interest and intelligence scales were eliminated, as were a large number of MMPI items, because their multiple keying did not permit the calculation of a single estimate of internal validity for each item. Specifically, this item sample con-

Table 8. Means and standard deviations of all item characteristics across 1051 items from personality and validity scales (Löhr, in preparations)

	Mean	SD	Percentages
I. *Logical item-trait relations*			
Description of reactions: Overt			20.7
Covert			27.2
Physical symptom			9.0
Not subclassified			10.3
Trait attribution			11.7
Indirect modes of self-description			14.7
Unclassified			6.4
II. *Item surface structure*			
Number of letters	67.98	32.20	
Number of words	12.40	5.70	
Number of clauses	1.97	1.04	
Negation: Negative phrasing			26.1
Tense: Past			6.4
Voice: Passive			3.8
Mood: Subjunctive			10.1
Impersonal phrasing: No first person pronoun			4.3
Sentence type: Question			15.4
Number of response alternatives	2.54	.97	
Keying direction: 'Yes'			58.6
III. *Aspects of response process*			
Not immediately understandable			52.0
Ambiguous			29.2
Abstract			47.1
Not self-referent			27.9
Evaluative (not neutral)			54.0
IV. *Psychometric characteristics*			
Item mean[a]	.48	.23	
Item variance[a]	.18	.06	
Item stability	.82	.07	
Item-test correlation[a]	.28	.20	

[a] Data from the first administration.

sisted of the seven questionnaires of Anglo-American origin (MPI, MMQ, EPI-A, and -B, 16PF-A and -B, and the MMPI scales L, D, and Si), plus the personality and validity scales of the German PIT, Giessen Test, and FPI.

As an estimate of the *internal validity* or discriminating power of each item, the point-biserial item-test correlation (part-whole corrected) was used. For all statistical analyses, these correlation coefficients were transformed to Fisher's Z. The reliability of the item validities (first with second administration) was .84.

The proportion of subjects who did not change their response from the first to the second administration was used as an index of *item stability*. Again, the multiple response formats used by three of the questionnaires caused a problem because the probability of changing responses increases with the number of possible response alternatives. Therefore, the response continuum was divided into two halves at its midpoint, regardless of the actual response format, thus redefining item stability with reference to the upper and lower halves of the response continuum. Response options that fell exactly at the midpoint were assigned at random. The stability index for items with multiple response formats was recomputed from the raw data (Löhr, in preparation); for the other items, it was adopted from Angleitner's (1981 a) report. Unlike the other item statistics, a reliability estimate of item stability was not available.

Relations Among These Item Statistics. The frequency distributions of these item statistics were unimodal and reasonably symmetric, with the exception of the item variances, which were extremely skewed. Given the relationship between item mean and variance, and the inconvenient shape of this distribution, item variance did not appear to be a very useful variable for regression analyses. The item mean can influence item stability and validity in the following ways: (a) The more extreme the item mean (i.e., closer to either 0 or 1), the more likely is the item to elicit a high degree of response stability. (b) The more extreme the item mean, the more likely is the item to have low internal validity (i.e., discriminating power). It follows from (a) and (b) that (c) a negative relationship between item stability and validity is to be expected. This phenomenon has been called the psychometric paradox (Goldberg, 1963; Nowakowska, 1970).

In these data, the relationship between item mean and stability was, as expected, curvilinear (U-shaped) and rather strong, the multiple R (using both linear and quadratic terms) being .66. The relationship between item mean and validity, however, was essentially linear and unexpectedly weak ($r = -.12$, multiple $R = .16$), although both the linear and the quadratic components were significant in this large item sample ($n = 1051$). And finally, a weak (again significant) *positive* correlation between item validity and stability ($r = .12$) indicated that the psychometric paradox did not seem to characterize these data. Moreover, an inspection of the bivariate scatterplots suggested no other types of relationships among the item statistics. In summary, the empirical relations among the item statistics suggest that item stability and validity as assessed by the item-test correlation can be treated as practically independent criterion variables. This finding will be important when we interpret the regression analyses.

Item Response Statistics from the Questionnaires in this Sample

Psychometric theory asserts that the consistency of item responses should approach the hypothesized stability of the behaviors being measured. Stability of response is, therefore, essential at both the item and the scale level. However, as in most studies of item response characteristics, one cannot help but be impressed by the degree of response inconsistency elicited by most personality questionnaire items. As Table 6 shows, almost 20% of the subjects changed their response to the average item over the 2-week test-retest interval. This figure is quite similar to the stability percentages that Goldberg (1963, p. 468) compiled 20 years ago for "some typical early" and for "six more recently developed" personality inventories.

In general, the item validities were relatively low. As Table 8 shows, the average item validity was .28, compared to .36 which is typical for carefully constructed verbal aptitude tests (Green, 1978). Moreover, about 4.8% of the item validities were *negative* in sign, 6.6% were zero, and 13.7% were about 0.1; yet, only one-third of these zero validities can be explained by extremeness of the corresponding item means. In contrast, the verbal aptitude test described by Green (1978) included only two items that had validities lower than .20 (their validities were .16). Obviously, a considerable number of personality questionnaire items have been constructed and selected so poorly that they fall into a range of validity that is characterized by zero discriminating power.

Table 9 presents the mean item stability, mean item-test correlation, the coefficient Alpha, and (when possible) the correlations among parallel scales for each scale of the seven Anglo-American personality questionnaires. The first section of Table 9 permits a comparison among the scales constructed by Eysenck and his coworkers. Overall, the Neuroticism scales were most internally consistent and obtained the highest parallel scale correlations; the Extraversion scales were somewhat less satisfactory. The relatively short Lie scales of the EPI had very low internal consistency values (Alphas of .66 and .61, respectively) and a low parallel test correlation ($r = .51$). In this sample, five of the ten Eysenck scales did not reach his goal (Eysenck, 1953, p. 300) that questionnaire scales should have an Alpha coefficient of at least .80. However, to obtain such high degrees of internal consistency in Neuroticism and Extraversion scales, given the enormous breadth of these constructs, their length would have to be substantially increased. Similarly, the retest reliabilities of Eysenck's scales did not meet his own standard (Eysenck, 1953, p. 301) of .90 (Angleitner, 1976, p. 328). However, since scale stabilities not only reflect response consistency at the item level but also the particular item composition of the scale, we believe that item response stability (corrected for endorsement frequency) may be the more important index. Indeed, item stability should be used as an item selection criterion early in scale construction, and the item stabilities should be reported in the test manual. Despite the generally accepted importance of stability of measurement, in none of today's widely used personality questionnaires has item stability been applied as an item exclusion criterion during the construction stage, not even in Jackson's otherwise exemplary PRF (Jackson, 1970).

As Table 9 shows, the mean item stabilities of the Eysenck scales generally exceeded 80% response consistency over an interval of 2–3 weeks; the item sta-

Table 9. Mean item stability, item-test correlation, coefficient Alpha, and parallel form reliabilities of seven personality questionnaires ($n = 105$)

Questionnaire	Scale	No. of items	Mean item stability	Mean item-test correlation[a]	Alpha	Parallel form correlation[a]
MPI	E	24	.78	.36	.81	
EPI-A	E	24	.84	.31	.77	.73
EPI-B	E	24	.84	.28	.73	
MPI	N	24	.80	.46	.88	
MMQ	N	38	.89	.36	.86	
EPI-A	N	24	.84	.48	.89	.85
EPI-B	N	24	.84	.39	.84	
MMQ	L	18	.86	.36	.77	
EPI-A	L	9	.82	.35	.66	.51
EPI-B	L	9	.89	.32	.61	
16PF-A	F	13	.77	.32	.70	.61
16PF-B	F	13	.76	.27	.62	
16PF-A	H	13	.76	.33	.70	.71
16PF-B	H	13	.73	.42	.78	
16PF-A	E	13	.72	.14	.40	.52
16PF-B	E	13	.80	.14	.39	
16PF-A	Q2	10	.76	.09	.26	.42
16PF-B	Q2	10	.73	.15	.37	
16PF-A	A	10	.75	.08	.24	.38
16PF-B	A	10	.78	.14	.36	
16PF-A	I	10	.79	.07	.19	.36
16PF-B	I	10	.80	.11	.28	
16PF-A	L	10	.78	.13	.34	.33
16PF-B	L	10	.78	.18	.43	
16PF-A	C	13	.73	.10	.29	.53
16PF-B	C	13	.75	.29	.66	
16PF-A	O	13	.72	.22	.52	.57
16PF-B	O	13	.70	.33	.68	
16PF-A	Q4	13	.73	.35	.73	.64
16PF-B	Q4	13	.71	.30	.67	
16PF-A	G	10	.75	.25	.56	.39
16PF-B	G	10	.77	.12	.33	
16PF-A	Q3	10	.73	.15	.37	.20
16PF-B	Q3	10	.75	.10	.26	
16PF-A	Q1	10	.75	.04	.10	.20
16PF-B	Q1	10	.74	−.02 (!)	−.07 (!)	
16PF-A	M	13	.77	.09	.29	.32
16PF-B	M	13	.76	.14	.39	
16PF-A	N	10	.74	.10	.26	.03 (!)
16PF-B	N	10	.76	−.04 (!)	−.15 (!)	
MMPI	L	15	.88	.28	.67	
MMPI	F	64	.92	.18	.74	
MMPI	K	30	.82	.26	.74	
MMPI	Hs	33	.88	.33	.83	
MMPI	D	60	.85	.16	.66	
MMPI	Hy	60	.85	.11	.56	

Table 9 (continued)

Questionnaire	Scale	No. of items	Mean item stability	Mean item-test correlation[a]	Alpha	Parallel form correlation[a]
MMPI	Pd	50	.84	.20	.71	
MMPI	Mf	60	.86	.18	.72	
MMPI	Pa	40	.87	.11	.44	
MMPI	Pt	48	.87	.37	.89	
MMPI	Sc	78	.89	.25	.86	
MMPI	Ma	46	.83	.11	.51	
MMPI	Si	70	.84	.23	.83	
MMPI	Sd	39	.87	.26	.86	
Means across items and scales						
Eysenck		218	.84	.37	.78	.72
Cattell		342	.75	.18	.40	.43
MMPI		404	.86	.23	.72	–

The item stabilities computed for the 16PF were corrected as described in the text
[a] Data from the first administration

bilities did not differ systematically from scale to scale and were only slightly lower on average than those of the MMPI scales. Overall, the psychometric characteristics of Eysenck's scales were fairly respectable, in particular when they are evaluated with reference to the other questionnaires in this sample, rather than in terms of Eysenck's absolute standards.

In each section of this chapter, in which we have compared the item sets of the seven questionnaires, we had to conclude that the items of Cattell's 16PF were particularly poor. Of all the questionnaires studied here, the 16PF had the longest, most complex, most difficult to understand, and most ambiguous items, and had the highest frequency of indirect types of trait indicators. The psychometric properties of the resulting scales are shown in Table 9; these findings are quite representative of those reported by other researchers (e.g., Bartussek, Weise, & Heinze, 1972). Since Cattell (e.g., 1973) rejects scale homogeneity as a relevant psychometric characteristic, it might be argued that evaluations of the 16PF scales have to focus on stability and parallel form reliability. However, these are also low (for a review, see Angleitner, 1976); Table 9 shows that the correlations between "parallel" scales were particularly low for those scales with extremely low internal consistency, perhaps suggesting that Cattell's scales could use more scale homogeneity.

All MMPI scales had item response stabilities well above .80. The average item-test correlations of the MMPI scales were lower than those of the Eysenck questionnaires, and the Alpha coefficients were, in light of the long scales, not very impressive. However, these results are based on a sample of normal adults and do not provide a complete appraisal of the MMPI, since that inventory was constructed primarily for clinical populations.

The Predictor Variables and their Interrelations

In the first three sections of this chapter we discussed three sets of stimulus characteristics of personality questionnaire items that might influence psychometric item and scale properties. Table 8 presents an overview of these variables, along with their distribution in the sample of 1051 personality and validity scale items. The empirical relations among these item characteristics, and between them and the four item response parameters, will be described by Löhr (in preparation). A summary of these analyses will now be presented here.

The correlations among the five response process characteristics were generally weak and in all cases much smaller in size than the reliabilities of the judgments, although five of the ten Phi coefficients were statistically significant due to the large sample size. Ambiguity correlated −.22 with comprehensibility and .26 with abstractness; although both correlations are in the logical direction, their size indicates that the judges were able to differentiate these three constructs from each other. Thus, we can conclude that these five ratings reflect fairly independent item characteristics.

Also of interest were the relations between these judged item characteristics and the more objectively scored item-surface characteristics decribed in the second section of this chapter. Only a few substantial relationships were found; most of them conformed to our expectations and thus provide some degree of construct validity for the rating-based measures. Specifically, the measures of item length (i.e., the number of letters and of sentence clauses) correlated approximately −.60 with the comprehensibility ratings; similarly, the greater the number of response options, the more likely was the item to be judged as difficult to understand (Phi = .30). Moreover, items whose text did not contain any personal pronouns were more likely to be classified as low in self-reference (Phi = .34).

Finally, there were a few substantial relationships between these two sets of item characteristics and the logical categories of item-trait relations (defined in Table 2). In particular, items classified as *indirect* trait indicators (i.e., items bearing an indirect relation to the trait to be assessed, such as wishes or attitudes) were likely to contain subjunctive verb forms (Phi = .48) and no personal pronouns (Phi = .50); with regard to their processing characteristics, such items were likely to be classified as not self-referent (Phi = .37).

Predicting Response Parameters

In order to abstract the general trends from the data, rather than focusing on the results from single variables, Löhr (paper in preparation) computed multiple regressions using each of the psychometric indices as criteria and each of the three sets of item stimulus characteristics as predictors. The findings from these analyses are summarized in Table 10.

Table 10. Multiple correlations between item characteristics and two criteria: Item stability and validity (item-test correlation). (Löhr, in preparation)

Predictors	Item sets considered				
	Total ($n=1051$)	Odd half ($n=526$)	Even half ($n=525$)	1st half[a] ($n=530$)	2nd half[b] ($n=521$)
	Item stability				
Logical relation	.27	.29	.28	.30	.29
Surface text	.44	.43	.47	.48	.46
Response process	.37	.36	.40	.40	.38
All	.51	.51	.55	.56	.54
	Item validity				
Logical relation	.34	.33	.38	.45	.23
Surface text	.40	.42	.40	.46	.43
Response process	.37	.40	.34	.49	.26
All	.50	.53	.52	.58	.48

The item characteristics are listed in Table 8.
[a] Items from the Giessen-Test, MMQ, EPI-A, FPI, and 16PF-B
[b] Items from the MPI, EPI-B, PIT, 16PF-A, and from MMPI scales L, D, and Si

The multiple correlation between item stability and *all* stimulus characteristics was .51. The item internal validities, as assessed by the item-test correlations, were also highly predictable ($R=.50$). Considering the three sets of stimulus characteristics separately, the surface text characteristics that were objectively scored and thus most reliable were the most powerful predictors of response stability ($R=.44$) and item validity ($R=.40$). The five response process variables were also quite predictive of item stability and validity (both $R=.37$); the categorical variables specifying the logical relations between item and trait were found to be least predictive. These coefficients did not shrink when separate subsamples of approximately 525 items each were used. Thus, the multivariate relations presented in Table 10 seem to hold independently of the particular composition of the item sample.

Conclusions. These findings provide impressive empirical support for our general hypothesis: The influence of "formal" item characteristics on the psychometric quality of personality questionnaires is both systematic and substantial. More specifically, our findings suggest that the surface structure of the verbal stimulus, if measured comprehensively, is an essential determinant of the reliability and validity of subjects' item responses. It appears, then, that authors of personality questionnaires would be well advised to spend more time and care in item writing. Second, our findings show that undesirable information processing characteristics of items can be identified with the rating methodology described here. It appears, then, that personality questionnaire authors would be well advised to incorporate criteria such as item comprehensibility, nonambiguity, concreteness, self-reference, and nonevaluative content, into the standard canon of item selection strategies. Finally, we found that even the logical item-trait relations were related to the item-response parameters, with the more indirect modes of self-description yielding less satisfactory item-response statistics. It appears, then, that personality questionnaire authors would be well advised to think more deeply about the kinds of items that make useful trait indicators.

Although there is clearly plenty of room for improvement, a beginning has already been made. Jackson (1967, 1970) used social desirability and ambiguity as item exclusion criteria during the construction of the initial item pool from which the PRF was developed. Moreover, his construct-oriented approach fostered convergent and discriminant item validity at the very beginning of the questionnaire construction process. More recently, Buss and Craik (1980, 1983) have developed explicit procedures for the generation of trait-relevant items that belong to only one class of logical item types (i.e., overt behavioral acts) and are, in addition, relatively concrete and specific.

Further improvements will not come easily. Meehl (1972) spelled out what will be necessary:

> An empirical showing that an item does not have certain undesirable properties, namely, systematic loadings on nuisance variables, is just as important as an empirical showing that it possesses the desirable properties of criterion discrimination and internal consistency. We must begin routinely to design our test-construction and test-validation research with an eye to negative properties. What makes this such a methodological and logistical pain in the neck is, of course, that the list of undesirable properties is considerably longer than the list of desirable properties! That is to say, given the structure of the human mind (a fact of the world and not a mere weakness of psychometric method or theory), during the course of scale-construction we may have to spend more time, money, brains, and energy measuring things we do not want the item to reflect, than we do measuring things we do want it to reflect (pp. 161–162).

The challenge lies ahead.

Notes

1 Order of authorship is alphabetical; this chapter represents a fully collaborative effort by the three authors, based in part on a paper delivered at the Bielefeld Symposium on Personality Questionnaires, which was held at the Center for Interdisciplinary Research, University of Bielefeld, June 17–20, 1982. Some of the analyses presented in this chapter are based on Franz-Josef Löhr's PhD dissertation (in preparation), a complete report of which may appear elsewhere.
We are grateful to Peter Borkenau, David Buss, William F. Chaplin, Donald Fiske, Sarah Hampson, Willem Hofstee, and Wolf Nowack for their comments on earlier drafts, and especially to Lewis R. Goldberg, the master wordsmith, whose untiring efforts helped improve the readability of this chapter considerably. Our research was supported by the Deutsche Forschungsgemeinschaft (DFG) An 106/1–3. Funds for the support of the second author during the writing of this report were provided in part by Grant MH-39077 from the National Institute of Mental Health (U.S. Public Health Service).

2 With the exception of the fourth statement, these "items" were written by Art Buchwald, the noted American humorist (as cited in Goldberg, 1974).

3 Parts of this project have been described in German by Angleitner (1976, 1981 a, 1981 b), Angleitner and Löhr (1980), Löhr and Angleitner (1980), and Löhr (1983 a, 1983 b). These reports are available from A. Angleitner, Fakultät für Psychologie und Sport, Universität Bielefeld, D-4800 Bielefeld 1, West Germany.

4 The German edition of Jackson's (1967, 1970) Personality Research Form (Stumpf et al., 1985) was not available when this project was begun.
5 There seems to be an increasing agreement among test developers of varying persuasions that responses to single items are too fragile to carry the weight of external analyses. Cattell and Comrey, for example, have advocated the factoring of clusters of items; analogously, most proponents of the criterion-group strategy would now probably prefer using homogeneous clusters of items to differentiate between their pairs of criterion samples. Thus, whatever the test developer's particular approach, the need for homogeneous item sets requires an initial construction stage involving some reflection about the trait construct and relevant items.

References

Allport, F.H. (1937). Teleonomic description in the study of personality. *Character and Personality, 6*, 202–214.

Allport, G.W., & Odbert, H.S. (1936). Trait-names: A psycholexical study. *Psychological Monographs, 47* (1, Whole No. 211).

Amelang, M., Sommer, E., & Bartussek, D. (1971). Persönlichkeitsstruktur und Studienrichtung. *Psychologische Beiträge, 13*, 7–15.

Angleitner, A. (1976). *Methodische und theoretische Probleme bei Persönlichkeitsfragebogen unter besonderer Berücksichtigung neuerer deutsch-sprachiger Fragenbogen.* Bonn: Habilitationsschrift, Psychologisches Institut der Universität Bonn.

Angleitner, A. (1981 a). *Teststatistische Kennwerte der Items aus 10 deutschsprachigen Persönlichkeitsfragebogen.* Bielefeld: Arbeitsberichte aus dem Projekt Persönlichkeitsfragebogen (No. 2), Universität Bielefeld.

Angleitner, A. (1981 b). *Teststatistische Kennwerte der Items aus 8 deutschsprachigen Persönlichkeitsfragenbogen für Kinder und Jugendliche.* Bielefeld: Arbeitsberichte aus dem Projekt Persönlichkeitsfragebogen (No. 3), Universität Bielefeld.

Angleitner, A., & Löhr, F.J. (1980). Itemüberlappung zwischen Persönlichkeitsfragebogen als Problem für Validitätsschätzungen. *Zeitschrift für Differentielle und Diagnostische Psychologie, 1*, 127–136.

Ashton, S.G., & Goldberg, L.R. (1973). In response to Jackson's challenge: The comparative validity of personality scales constructed by the external (empirical) strategy and scales developed intuitively by experts, novices, and laymen. *Journal of Research in Personality, 7*, 1–20.

Bartussek, D., Weiss, G., & Heinze, B. (1972). Reliabilität und faktorielle Validität des deutschen 16 PF-Tests von Cattell. *Arbeiten aus dem psychologischen Institut der Universität Hamburg, 19.*

Beckmann, D., & Richter, H.E. (1972). *Giessen-Test (GT). Ein Test für Individual- und Gruppendiagnostik. Handbuch.* Bern: Huber.

Bellezza, F.S. (1984). Reliability of retrieval from semantic memory: Noun meanings. *Bulletin of the Psychonomic Society, 22*, 377–380.

Buss, D.M., & Craik, K.H. (1980). The frequency concept of disposition: Dominance and prototypically dominant acts. *Journal of Personality, 48*, 379–392.

Buss, D.M., & Craik, K.H. (1983). The act frequency approach to personality. *Psychological Review, 90*, 105–126.

Cantor, N. (1981). Perceptions of situations: Situations prototypes and person-situation prototypes. In Magnusson, D. (Ed.), *Toward a psychology of situations: An interactional perspective.* Hillsdale: Erlbaum.

Cantor, N., Mischel, W., & Schwartz, J.C. (1981). Social knowledge: Structure, content, use and abuse. In Hastorf, A., & Isen, A. (Eds.), *Cognitive social psychology.* New York: Elsevier/North Holland.

Cantor, N., Mischel, W., & Schwartz, J.C. (1982). A prototype analysis of psychological situations. *Cognitive Psychology, 14*, 45–77.

Cattell, R.B. (1943). The description of personality: 2. Basic traits resolved into clusters. *Journal of Abnormal and Social Psychology, 38*, 476–507.
Cattell, R.B. (1946). *Description and measurement of personality*. New York: World Book.
Cattell, R.B. (1957). *Personality and motivation structure and measurement*. New York: World Book.
Cattell, R.B. (1973). *Personality and mood by questionnaire*. San Francisco: Jossey-Bass.
Cattell, R.B., & Eber, H.W. (1962). *Specimen set for the Sixteen Personality Factor Questionnaire "16 PF", experimental edition der deutschen Form A und B*. Champaign: Institute for Personality and Ability Testing.
Cattell, R.B., & Eber, H.W. (1964). *The Sixteen Personality Factor Questionnaire*. Champaign: Institute for Personality and Ability Testing.
Chomsky, N. (1965). *Aspects of the theory of syntax*. Cambridge, Mass.: M.I.T. Press.
Cliff, N., Bradley, P., & Girard, R. (1973). The investigation of cognitive models for inventory response. *Multivariate Behavioral Research, 8*, 407–425.
Cronbach, L.J. (1970). *Essentials of psychological testing*. New York: Harper & Row.
Dubois, B., & Burnes, J.A. (1975). An analysis of the meaning of the question mark response-category in attitude scales. *Educational and Psychological Measurement, 35*, 869–884.
Edwards, A.L. (1957). *The social desirability variable in personality assessment and research*. New York: Dryden.
Eggert, D. (1974). *Eysenck-Persönlichkeits-Inventar (EPI). Handanweisung für die Durchführung und Auswertung*. Göttingen: Hogrefe.
Eysenck, H.J. (1947). *Dimensions of personality*. London: Routledge & Kegan Paul.
Eysenck, H.J. (1953). Fragebogen als Meßmittel der Persönlichkeit: Eine experimentelle Untersuchung. *Zeitschrift für experimentelle und angewandte Psychologie, 1*, 191–335.
Eysenck, H.J. (1959a). *Das "Maudsley Personality Inventory" (MPI)*. Göttingen: Hogrefe.
Eysenck, H.J. (1959b). Der Maudsley Personality Inventory als Bestimmer der neurotischen Tendenz und Extraversion. *Zeitschrift für experimentelle und angewandte Psychologie, 6*, 167–190.
Eysenck, H.J. (1962). *The Maudsley Personality Inventory*. (Manual prepared by R.R. Knapp). San Diego: Educational and Industrial Testing Service.
Eysenck, H.J. (1964). *MMQ*. Göttingen: Hogrefe.
Eysenck, H.J., & Eysenck, S. (1964). *Manual of the Eysenck Personality Inventory*. London: University of London Press.
Fahrenberg, J., & Selg, H. (1970). *Das Freiburger Persönlichkeitsinventar (FPI) – Handanweisung*. Göttingen: Hogrefe.
Fillmore, C.J. (1977). The case for case reopened. In Cole, P., & Sadock, J. (Eds.), *Grammatical relations* (pp. 59–81). New York: Academic.
Fiske, D.W. (1971). *Measuring the concepts of personality*. Chicago: Aldine.
Fiske, D.W. (1981). *New directions for methodology of social and behavioral science: Problems with language imprecision*. San Francisco: Jossey-Bass.
Forgas, J.P. (1982). Episode cognition: Internal representations of interaction routines. In Berkowitz, L. (Ed.), *Advances in experimental social psychology* (Vol. 15). New York: Academic.
Foss, D.J., Hakes, D.J., & Hakes, D.T. (1978). *Psycholinguistics*. Englewood Cliffs: Prentice Hall.
Givon, T. (1979). *Syntax and semantics 12: Discourse and syntax*. New York: Academic.
Goldberg, L.R. (1963). A model of item ambiguity in personality assessment. *Educational and Psychological Measurement, 23*, 467–492.
Goldberg, L.R. (1968). The interrelationships among item characteristics in an adjective checklist: The convergence of different indices of item ambiguity. *Educational and Psychological Measurement, 28*, 273–296.
Goldberg, L.R. (1971). A historical survey of personality scales and inventories. In McReynolds, P. (Ed.), *Advances in psychological assessment* (Vol. 2, pp. 293–336). Palo Alto: Science and Behavior.

Goldberg, L.R. (1972). Some recent trends in personality assessment. *Journal of Personality Assessment, 36*, 547–560.
Goldberg, L.R. (1974). Objective diagnostic tests and measures. *Annual Review of Psychology, 25*, 343–366.
Goldberg, L.R. (1978). Differential attribution of trait-descriptive terms to oneself as compared to well-liked, neutral, and disliked others: A psychometric analysis. *Journal of Personality and Social Psychology, 36*, 1012–1028.
Goldberg, L.R. (1980, May). Some ruminations about the structure of individual differences: Developing a common lexicon for the major characteristics of human personality. *Meetings of the Western Psychological Association*, Honolulu, Hawaii.
Goldberg, L.R. (1981 a). Language and individual differences: The search for universals in personality lexicons. *Review of Personality and Social Psychology, 41(2)*, 141–165.
Goldberg, L.R. (1981 b). Unconfounding situational attributions from uncertain, neutral, and ambiguous ones: A psychometric analysis of descriptions of oneself and various types of others. *Journal of Personality and Social Psychology, 41(3)*, 517–552.
Goldberg, L.R. (1982). *From Ace to Zombie:* Some explorations in the language of personality. In Spielberger, L.D., & Butcher, J.N. (Eds.), *Advances in personality assessment* (Vol. 1). Hillsdale: Erlbaum.
Goldberg, L.R., & Slovic, P. (1967). Importance of test item content: An analysis of a corollary of the deviation hypothesis. *Journal of Counseling Psychology, 14*, 462–472.
Gorsuch, R.G., & Cattell, R.B. (1967). Second stratum personality factors defined in the questionnaire realm by the 16PF. *Multivariate Behavioral Research, 2*, 211–224.
Gough, H.G. (1957). *Manual for the California Psychological Inventory.* Palo Alto: Consulting Psychologists.
Gough, H.G. (1965). Conceptual analysis of psychological test scores and other diagnostic variables. *Journal of Abnormal Psychology, 70*, 294–302.
Green, B.F., Jr. (1978). In defense of measurement. *American Psychologist, 33*, 664–670.
Hampshire, S. (1953). Dispositions. *Analysis, 14*, 5–11.
Hampson, S.E. (1982). Person memory: A semantic category model of personality traits. *British Journal of Psychology, 73*, 1–11.
Hathaway, S.R., & McKinley, J.C. (1943). *Manual for the Minnesota Multiphasic Personality Inventory.* New York: Psychological Corporation.
Hull, J.G., & Levy, A.S. (1979). The organizational functions of the self: An alternative to the Duval and Wicklund model of self-awareness. *Journal of Personality and Social Psychology, 37*, 756–768.
Jackson, D.N. (1967). *Personality research form. Manual.* Goshen: Research Psychologists.
Jackson, D.N. (1970). A sequential system for personality scale development. In Spielberger, C.D. (Ed.), *Current topis in clinical and community psychology* (Vol. 2, pp. 61–96). New York: Academic.
Jackson, D.N. (1971). The dynamics of structured personality tests: 1971. *Psychological Review, 78*, 229–248.
Jackson, D.N. (1975). The relative validity of scales prepared by naive item writers and those based on empirical methods of personality scale construction. *Educational and Psychological Measurement, 35*, 361–370.
Janke, W. (1973). Das Dilemma von Persönlichkeitsfragebogen. Einleitung des Symposiums über Konstruktion von Fragebogen. In Reinhart, G. (Ed.), *Bericht über den 27. Kongreß der Deutschen Gesellschaft für Psychologie in Kiel 1970.* Göttingen: Hogrefe.
John, O.P., Goldberg, L.R., & Angleitner, A. (1984). Better than the alphabet: Taxonomies of personality-descriptive terms in English, Dutch, and German. In Bonarius, H.M., Van Heck, G., & Smid, N. (Eds.), *Personality psychology in Europe: Theoretical and empirical developments.* Lisse: Swets & Zeitlinger.
Jones, R.R. (1965). The relationships between item properties and scale reliability. *Oregon Research Institute Research Monograph, 5* (No. 1).

Jones, R.R. (1968, August). Differences in response consistency and subjects' preferences for three personality inventory formats. *Proceedings of the 76th Annual Convention of the American Psychological Association,* San Francisco.

Kelley, H.H., & Michela, G.L. (1980). Attribution theory and research. *Annual Review of Psychology, 34,* 457–504.

Keren, A. (1979). *Inhaltlich-semantische Analyse der Items aus fünf deutschsprachigen Persönlichkeitsfragebogen.* Universität Bonn: Masters Thesis.

Knudson, R.M., & Golding, S.L. (1974). Comparative validity of traditional versus S-R format inventories of interpersonal behavior. *Journal of Research in Personality, 8,* 111–127.

Kuncel, R.B. (1973). Response processes and relative location of subject and item. *Educational and Psychological Measurement, 33,* 545–563.

Langer, I., & Schulz von Thun, F. (1974). Messung komplexer Merkmale in Psychologie und Pädagogik – Ratingverfahren. Munich: Reinhardt.

Lennertz, E. (1973). Thesen zur Itemsammlung bei Persönlichkeitsfragebogen. In Reinert, G. (Ed.), *Bericht über den 27. Kongreß der Deutschen Gesellschaft für Psychologie in Kiel 1973.* Göttingen: Hogrefe.

Lienert, G.A. (1969). *Testaufbau und Testanalyse (3rd ed.).* Weinheim: Beltz.

Löhr, F.J. (1977). *Formale und inhaltliche Merkmale von Fragebogenitems – Zum Einfluß von Itemeigenschaften auf den Beantwortungsprozeß bei deutschen Persönlichkeitsfragebögen.* Universität Bonn: Masters Thesis.

Löhr, F.J. (1983a). *Häufigkeits- und Intensitätsadverbien in den Items von Persönlichkeitsfragebogen.* Bielefeld: Arbeitsberichte aus dem Projekt Persönlichkeitsfragebogen (No. 5), Universität Bielefeld.

Löhr, F.J. (1983b). *Sprachlogische und empirische Beziehungen in Persönlichkeitsfragebogen für Kinder. Eine empirische Untersuchung zur Bezugsebene der Items.* Bielefeld: Arbeitsberichte aus dem Projekt Persönlichkeitsfragebogen (No. 6), Universität Bielefeld.

Löhr, F.J. (In preparation). *Die Bedeutung von Itemeigenschaften für den Prozeß und das Ergebnis der Beantwortung von Persönlichkeitsfragebogen.* Bielefeld: Dissertation, Fakultät für Psychologie und Sportwissenschaft der Universität Bielefeld.

Löhr, F.J., & Angleitner, A. (1980). Eine Untersuchung zu sprachlichen Formulierungen der Items in deutschen Persönlichkeitsfragebogen. *Zeitschrift für Differentielle und Diagnostische Psychologie, 1,* 217–235.

Loevinger, J. (1957). Objective tests as instruments of psychological theory. *Psychological Reports, 3,* 635–694.

Magnusson, D. (1981). *Toward a psychology of situations: An interactional perspective.* Hillsdale: Erlbaum.

Magnusson, D. (1984). Persons in situations: Some comments on a current issue. In Bonarius, H.M., Van Heck, G., & Smid, N. (Eds.), *Personality psychology in Europe: Theoretical and empirical developments.* Lisse: Swets & Zeitlinger.

Meehl, P.E. (1972). Reactions, reflections, projections. In Butcher, J.N. (Ed.), *Objective personality assessment: Changing perspectives* (pp. 131–189). New York: Academic.

Messick, S. (1967). The psychology of acquiescence. In Berg, I.A. (Ed.), *Response set in personality assessment.* Chicago: Aldine.

Micklin, M., & Durbin, M. (1969). Syntactic dimensions of attitude scaling techniques: Sources of variation and bias. *Sociometry, 32,* 194–206.

Mischel, W. (1972). Direct vs. indirect personality assessment: Evidence and implications. *Journal of Consulting and Clinical Psychology, 38,* 319–324.

Mischel, W., & Peake, P.K. (1982). Beyond déjà vu in the search for cross-situational consistency. *Psychological Review, 89,* 730–755.

Mittenecker, E., & Toman, W. (1951). Der P.I.-Test. *Beihefte zur Wiener Zeitschrift für Philosophie, Psychologie, Pädagogik, 1.*

Nisbett, R., & Ross, L. (1980). *Human inference: Strategies and shortcomings of social judgment.* Englewood Cliffs: Prentice-Hall.

Nowakowska, M. (1970). A model of answering to a questionnaire item. *Acta Psychologica, 34*, 420–439.
Payne, F.D. (1970). *Structured personality inventory items: Test-retest response consistency and item properties*. Urbana-Champaign: Ph.D. Thesis, University of Illinois.
Pepper, S. (1981). Problems in the quantification of frequency expressions. In Fiske, D. (Ed.), *New directions for methodology of social and behavioral science: Problems with language imprecision*. (No. 9). San Francisco: Jossey-Bass.
Peterson, C.C., & Peterson, J.L. (1976). Linguistic determinants of the difficulty of true-false test items. *Educational and Psychological Measurement, 36*, 161–169.
Rogers, T.B. (1971). The process of responding to personality items: Some issues, a theory and some research. *Multivariate Behavioral Research Monographs, 6(2)*.
Rogers, T.B. (1974a). An analysis of the stages underlying the process of responding to personality items. *Acta Psychologica, 38*, 205–213.
Rogers, T.B. (1974b). An analysis of two central stages underlying responding to personality items: The self-referent decision and response selections. *Journal of Research in Personality, 8*, 128–138.
Rogers, T.B. (1977). Self-reference in memory: Recognition of personality items. *Journal of Research in Personality, 11*, 295–305.
Schneider-Dueker, M., & Schneider, F. (1977). Untersuchungen zum Beantwortungsprozeß bei psychodiagnostischen Fragebogen. *Zeitschrift für experimentelle und angewandte Psychologie, 24*, 282–302.
Spreen, O. (1963). *MMPI: Saarbrücken. Handbuch zur deutschen Ausgabe des Minnesota Multiphasic Personality Inventory*. Bern: Huber.
Stumpf, H., Angleitner, A., Wieck, T., Jackson, D.N., & Beloch-Till, H. (1985). *Deutsche Personality Research Form (PRF)*. Göttingen: Hogrefe.
Timm, U. (1968). Reliabilität und Faktorenstruktur von Cattells 16PF-Test bei einer deutschen Stichprobe. *Zeitschrift für experimentelle und angewandte Psychologie, 15*, 354–373.
Van Heck, G.L. (1984). The construction of a general taxonomy of situations. In Bonarius, H.M., Van Heck, G., & Smid, N. (Eds.), *Personality psychology in Europe: Theoretical and empirical developments*. Lisse: Swets & Zeitlinger.
Wiggins, J.S. (1973). *Personality and prediction: Principles of personality assessment*. Reading: Addison-Wesley.
Wiggins, J.S. (1979). A psychological taxonomy of trait-descriptive terms: The interpersonal domain. *Journal of Personality and Social Psychology, 37*, 395–412.
Wiggins, J.S., & Goldberg, L.R. (1965). Interrelationship among MMPI item characteristics. *Educational and Psychological Measurement, 25*, 381–397.

Appendix A: Labels of the Questionnaire Scales

MPI: Maudsley Personality Inventory

E: Extraversion-Introversion
N: Neutroticism

MMQ: Maudsley Medical Questionnaire

N: Neuroticism
L: Lie

EPI: Eysenck Personality Inventory (Forms A and B)

N: Neuroticism
E: Extraversion
L: Lie

16PF: Sixteen Personality Factor questionnaire (Forms A and B)

A: Affectia (outgoing, warm-hearted)
B: Scholastic Mental Capacity (intelligent)
C: Ego-Strength (emotionally stable)
E: Dominance (assertive)
F: Surgency (happy-go-lucky)
G: Superego Strength (conscientious)
H: Parmia (venturesome, uninhibited)
I: Premsia (tenderminded)
L: Protension (suspicious)
M: Autia (imaginative, bohemian)
N: Shrewdness (astute, polished)
O: Guilt Proneness (insecure)
Q1: Radicalism (liberal)
Q2: Self-Sufficiency (resourceful)
Q3: Strength of Self-Sentiment (controlled)
Q4: Ergic Tension (frustrated)
(Adjectival descriptors according to Cattell, 1973)

MMPI: Minnesota Multiphasic Personality Inventory

L: Lie
F: Infrequency
K: Correction
Hs: Hypochondriasis
D: Depression
Hy: Hysteria
Pd: Psychopathic Deviate
Mf: Masculinity-Femininity
Pa: Paranoia
Pt: Psychasthenia
Sc: Schizophrenia
Ma: Hypomania
Si: Social Introversion
Sd: Social Desirability (Edwards, 1957)

Methods of Personality Inventory Development – A Comparative Analysis

MATTHIAS BURISCH

Although the heated debates about the "best" way of developing personality inventories have largely disappeared from the journals, the issue has continued to hold sufficient interest to be investigated empirically. During the past 2 decades more than a dozen comparative studies have been published. The present chapter attempts to summarize them in a concise manner.

Three Strategies for Developing Personality Inventories

Deductive Strategy

Historically the oldest, the deductive viewpoint saw a questionnaire item mainly as a cheaper surrogate for a question a clinician might ask in the course of an interview. Contemporary deductive test constructors may have gained a more sophisticated understanding of the subtleties of language and personality, and they are certainly interested in a much wider array of personality dimensions than were their earlier predecessors. What is common to all of them and what distinguishes this approach from others, however, is that the concepts to be measured are chosen first and items fitting an implicit or explicit definition of the concepts are written next, the item writer's intuition being the guiding element. Provisional scales may later be purified by item analysis, but whatever items survive this stage are guaranteed to possess some substantive validity (at least for their creator).

External Strategy

Disenchantment with the early deductive inventories began in the 1920s, increased during the 1930s, and culminated in 1945 with the publication of Meehl's now classic paper "The Dynamics of 'Structured' Personality Tests." No longer would intuition be accepted as a basis for judging the adequacy of a personality item. As before, concepts were selected beforehand, but the crucial step was to operationalize them by some indicator outside the questionnaire domain, usually membership in a clinical or occupational category. The assembly of a large item pool, though not always as much a matter of "dust-bowl empiricism" as folklore would have it (Hathaway & McKinley, 1940, p. 249), was considered of secondary importance. Finally, items correlating sufficiently well with the external indicator were grouped together in a scale with the appropriate label, content validity or not.

Inductive Strategy

Lastly, in an attempt to get rid of the inevitable arbitrariness of preconceived personality dimensions or types and with the help of emerging computer technology, the inductive strategy was born. Normally more inclined to lay bare "the" structure of human personality than to predict outside criteria, inductivists – like externalists – start with a large, heterogeneous item pool, usually borrowed from existing inventories, but ideally looking "representative." Subjects' responses to this preliminary collection are then subjected to some variety of multivariate analysis likely to turn out clusters of correlating items, at least some of which are sufficiently similar in content to justify a common label. Although there are much more elaborate variants (e.g., Cattell & Tsujioka, 1964), the standard procedure is to assign each item to the cluster it is closest to, name the cluster, and create a scale by unit-scoring all keyed items. Note that in what can be seen as a reversion of the deductive strategy, the more abstract (scale) level follows rather than precedes the more specific (item) level of measurement.

Standards for Personality Inventories

Any comparison of instruments originating from one of the strategies outlined above is meaningful only insofar as it proceeds along the lines of meaningful standards. I propose that validity in its many facets should be one such standard. Though definitely more pragmatic, economy should be another. Before using these terms for comparative purposes, let me briefly discuss them.

Validity

It is neither possible nor necessary here to do justice to the many excellent treatises on how validity should be assessed. Following Campbell and Fiske (1959), I will distinguish convergent and discriminant validity. As someone who has applied personality scales in clinical practice and research, I will stress the importance of content validity or communicability. Finally, I will separate what I call "effectiveness" from convergent validity, although this distinction will turn out to make little difference for the outcome of the strategy comparison.

Convergent Validity and Effectiveness. As the convergent validity of a test I define its zero-order correlation with a criterion variable. I will restrict the term "criterion" to cases where this variable (a) is an indicator of the same construct as the test, i.e., where both are theoretically or semantically fairly close, *and* (b) is of superior "status" or "trustworthiness" compared with the test. It has become common to speak of criteria even if condition (b) does not hold; for example, scores on another, related test or even simple self-ratings are sometimes called criterion information. I prefer to use the term "quasi-criterion" in such circumstances, to make it clear that these measures are as much in need of validation as the test itself. Consequently, correlations with these are much less decisive than are correlations with criteria.

There is also the situation where some external variable of practical importance, such as student GPA, suicide risk in mental patients, or job satisfaction in clerks, must be predicted with the aid of whatever information happens to be available, including a battery of tests most or all of which bear no theoretical relationship to the target variable. Where it is more than a single predictor, multiple correlations, discriminant analysis his rate, or some other index of multivariate predictability is often used. I propose to call what is being assessed by such indices "effectiveness" rather than validity, because it is a different quality. The relative ineffectiveness of a hammer when it comes to extracting screws or sawing wood does not in the least diminish its usefulness for the purpose it was made for, sinking nails. Likewise, when an aggression scale or an inventory aimed at various needs in Murray's sense fails to predict dating frequency in college girls, this should not be assumed to tell us much about the instrument's merits per se. In a purely pragmatic context, of course, effectiveness is all that counts.

Discriminant Validity. If high effectiveness (in the sense of a zero-order correlation) means that a scale correlates with a theoretically unrelated target, discriminant validity requires that it does not. This makes it clear at once that discriminant validity is relevant in research and clinical contexts only, and not in prognosis contexts.

Unfortunately, it is an elusive quality. Not only can it never be attested affirmatively – can the next study of my scale not find a high correlation with a "wrong" criterion? – there is also no standard method of quantifying it. Therefore, in the few papers that have reported pertinent figures at all, the proportion of "stray shots" has been used as an indicator. A stray shot was counted whenever a scale correlated as highly with an "alien" criterion as with the criterion it was matched with, or even higher. This index is rough, because it does not register instances where the validity coefficient exceeds the second highest "wrong" correlation only minimally. Moreover, the index fails to take into account the number and dissimilarity of criterion variables. Jackson (1969) puts it nicely when he says that "there are two important 'rules' for finding that tests possess discriminant validity: *(a)* Keep the multitrait-multimethod matrix small and *(b)* select traits which are maximally dissimilar and methods which are maximally similar" (p. 34). Nonetheless, the index is straightforward and easily interpreted.

Content Validity. The filling in of a personality inventory is a communication process between subject and assessor. Wherever an accurate reception of the message is crucial, as is the case in clinical assessment, communicability of scale content becomes of prime importance. This requires that the scale possess content validity (in the sense of Holden & Jackson, 1979) plus a somewhat narrow-band "universe of content." Ideally, it should also satisfy the cumulative homogeneity model (Fiske, 1971, chap. 8). Measures of dimensions as broad as "maladjustment" may have their advantages (Peterson, 1965), but they certainly do not help much to clarify a clinical case.

Since content validity is a matter of expert judgment (but who are the experts?), it is not usually appraised in quantitative terms. Let me therefore point out here that the deductive strategy is the only one that makes a conscious effort to maximize it. Inductive scales will almost always contain at least some items that make one wonder how they came there. ("They just loaded on that factor.") Hard-nosed externalists, of course, shrug at content validity.

Economy

Economy is a simple term, but it will be broken up into three facets here: construction economy, administration economy, and redundancy.

Construction Economy. The sample size necessary for a serious item analysis may be comparable to that needed for a factor analysis or a cross-validated criterion group contrast. There is reason to doubt, however, that an item analysis is indispensable for the development of valid deductive scales (Ashton & Goldberg, 1973; Burisch, 1978, p. 100; Hermans, 1969; Jackson, 1975). Insofar as the deductive approach is essentially an armchair affair, it is undeniably the most economical one. Both inductive and external construction require much higher investments in terms of time and money.

Administration Economy. There is no logical reason why deductive scales should be shorter than others. In practice, however, it becomes hard to write more than a dozen or so nonrepetitive items hitting the core of a defined personality trait, particularly if the trait is reasonably specific and the cumulative homogeneity model (Fiske, 1971, chap. 8) is to be approximated. Lengthening a test beyond some limit may not only be uneconomical, but also detrimental to convergent validity (Burisch, 1984b).

Be that as it may, most test users, confronted with the choice of two 100-item inventories one of which produces 10 independent scores while the other produces only 2, would probably opt for the multiscale inventory, other things being equal.

Redundancy. Some of the early inventories fell into disrepute mainly because of their scales' high intercorrelations (cf. Goldberg, 1971). Obviously enough, a scale should be added to an existing set only if it adds some unique variance. The mean absolute within-inventory correlation is a rough indicator of redundancy and will be used as such in the comparisons that follow. Like my index of discriminant validity, this indicator has its limitations, one of them being neglect of criterion intercorrelations.

Should we, on a priori grounds, expect any one of the construction strategies to be superior here? Given that the most common inductive technique for item grouping is some variant of factor or component analysis, followed by orthogonal rotation, this strategy should indeed have an edge over the other two approaches. Externalists, on the other hand, tend to be most tolerant of the idea of item overlap, which results in some built-in redundancy for their inventories. No particular bets are warranted for the deductive approach.

Empirical Evidence

Looking for confirmation or disconfirmation of my conceptual analyses, I found 16 studies comparing two, or all three, of the above construction strategies empirically. The study by Borgen (1972) is representative for several analogous comparisons of SVIB (Strong Vocational Interest Blank) occupational vs basic interest scales. Likewise, Hedlund, Cho, and Wood (1977) stand for a number of studies which compared MMPI-168 clinical vs factor scales and are omitted here to save space. Table 1 summarizes what I found in terms of convergent validity or/and effectiveness, and also in terms of administration economy (i.e., scale length).

Section A of Table 1 contains four studies comparing all three strategies. Sections B, C, and D contain pairwise comparisons. The second, third, and fourth columns give some information on whether or not the design controlled a couple of important factors. If the inventories to be compared do not aim at identical constructs – and some are "easier" to measure than others – then this effect is confounded with any effects due to construction strategy. Individual items also differ in their ability to elicit generalizable information from respondents. Therefore, if inventories are developed from identical item pools, their constructors have the same chance at least to spot "good" items. If not only the basic pool is identical but also the set of items actually keyed, then the various inventories differ only in their grouping of items. In that case, the item factor is fully controlled.

It is probably fair to say that few of the studies reviewed are entirely satisfactory on methodological grounds. As can be gleaned from the subcaptions in the *Results* column, a number of effectiveness figures were not cross-validated, and the *Remarks* column points out some additional criticisms. Nevertheless, taken together, the 16 papers present a fairly coherent picture: *There is very little, if any, systematic variation in validity or effectiveness attributable to construction strategies.* Whether it is criteria, quasi-criteria, or targets, zero-order or multiple correlations, cross-validated or derivation sample figures that differ – whatever slight difference there is in one study tends to be reversed in the next. An exception is the excellent study by Broughton (1984), the last entry in section A, which found two deductive inventories leading the field by an appreciable margin. This study should (and will) be replicated, preferably using conventional true-false "statement" format items rather than adjectival self-rating scales. Pending such a replication, superiority claims in terms of

Source	Identical constructs?	Identical item pool?	Identical items?	Subjects	Criteria/targets	Results			*M* scale length	Number of scales in inventory	Remarks
A: All three strategies											
Goldberg (1972) Hase and Goldberg (1967)	No	Yes, CPI	No	152 Female students	*Criteria:* peer ratings for 5 traits. *Targets:* 8 variables such as GPA or dating frequency	Mean double-cross-validated *R* for:	5 criteria and 8 targets	5 criteria only			Several uncontrolled factors. RAT inventory not very "rational." *R*s as validity coefficients. Only EXT and RAT contained scales directly related to some criteria; in these cases mean $r = 0.24$ (EXT), .33 (RAT); see Hase and Goldberg, Table 7
						EXT	.25	.31	39	11	
						IND { FAC	.26	.36	17	11	
						IND { MSA	.24	.28	5	11	
						DED { THE	.26	.40	14	11	
						DED { RAT	.28	.37	37	11	
Mezzich, Damarin, and Erickson (1974)	Yes	Yes, MMPI	No	118 Depressives, 105 non-depressives	*Criterion:* psychiatric differential diagnosis	Biserial correlation with psychiatric diagnosis					EXT = MMPI standard key D. DED/IND is Wiggins' (1966) scale D, derived from a factor analysis of several short, deductively compiled scales
						EXT		.36	60	1	
						DED/IND		.18	33	1	
						DED		.26	44	1	
Burisch (1978)	Yes, for some pairs of inventories	Yes, FPI	For only 1 pair of inventories	138 Students	*Criteria:* peer ratings on 2 rating scale formats and 2 occasions	Mean correlation with criteria					STD = Factor-analytically constructed standard keys. EXT-S and STD, and EXT-D and DED, measure the same constructs. FAC and DED built on identical item subpool. Several uncontrolled factors
						EXT { EXT-S		.43	25	8	
						EXT { EXT-D		.36	9	8	
						IND { STD		.39	25	8	
						IND { FAC		.41	15	5	
						DED		.39	9	8	
Broughton (1984)	Yes	Yes, ACL	No	234 Male students	*Criteria:* peer ratings by 3–5 peers for 8 traits		Mean correlation with criteria	Mean double-cross-validated *R* with criteria			RAT is a set of scales developed by Gough and Heilbrun (1965). The IC scales are subsets of the RAT scales comprising items high in internal consistency. The PROT inventory was compiled using the rated "prototypicality" of items
						EXT	.22	.25	42	8	
						IND FAC	.15	.24	42	8	
						IND/DED IC	.22	.23	25	8	
						DED { PROT	.32	.28	42	8	
						DED { RAT	.28	.23	42	8	
B: External versus inductive strategy											
Crewe (1967)	No	Yes, MCI	Yes	2000 grade 9–12 boys and girls	*Targets:* teacher nominations for 7 characteristics such as conformity	Mean *R* with extreme group membership					*R*s as validity coefficients. Data had been part of the sample used to construct EXT, but not IND, scales
						EXT		.47	49	7	
						IND		.44	49	7	

							16 Major groups	10 Career groups			
						EXT	23.6%	23.0%	66	22	
						IND	20.1%	24.5%	12	22	
Overall (1974)	No	Yes, PSI	Yes	126 Psychiatric patients, 800 normals	*Target:* category membership	Hit rate of discriminant analysis					
						EXT		82.5%	26	5	
						IND		78.5%	26	5	
Hedlund, Cho and Wood (1977)[b]	Yes, for 1 pair of inventories	Yes, MMPI	Yes, for 1 pair of inventories	1117 psychiatric inpatients	*Target:* psychiatric diagnosis (6 most frequent categories)	Cross-validated hit rate of discriminant analysis					STD = Standard MMPI keys, 168 = MMPI-168 clinical scales, IND = MMPI-168 factor scales. *Rs* with psychiatric ratings on 14 dimensions were equally low for both strategies (figures not reported)
						EXT {STD		37%	56	13	
						EXT {168		39%	?	13	
						IND		40%	24	7	
Hornick, James, and Jones (1977)	No	Yes, PCQ	No	398 Firefighters	*Targets:* supervisor ratings of performance	Mean double-cross-validated *R* with target					IND inventory based on a principal-components analysis of 35 short deductive scales. Six resulting components entered into stepwise multiple regression analysis
						EXT		.46	61	2	
						IND		.49	24	6	
Klingler, Johnson, Giannetti, and Williams (1977)	No	Yes, MMPI	No	508 Male psychiatric patients	*Target:* psychiatric diagnosis (13 most frequent categories)	Hit rate of discriminant analysis					EXT = MMPI standard keys. IND/EXT inventory consisted of 4 factor-analytically derived scales + 6 quasi-external scales + 3 MMPI standard validity keys
						EXT		32%	56	13	
						IND/EXT		30%	?	13	
C: External versus deductive stragy											
Heilbrun (1962)	Yes	Yes, ACL	No	165 Students	*Quasicriterion:* selfreported number of friends	Biseral correlation of median-split scales with quasi-criterion					Correlation of EXT with DED scale = .75; item overlap of both not reported
						EXT		.12	34	1	
						DED		.06	?	1	
Ashton and Goldberg (1973)	Yes	For 3 inventories; CPI; for rest, no	No	168 Female students	*Criteria:* peer ratings of sociability, achievement, and dominance	Mean correlation with criteria					EXT = 3 external CPI scales. PSY, NPSY = scales written intuitively by psychology students or nonpsychologists, respectively
						EXT		.27	40	3	
						DED {PSY		.29	20	3	
						DED {NPSY		.18	20	3	
						DED {THE		.29	15	3	
						DED {RAT		.26	44	3	
						DED {PRF		.35	20	3	

Source	Identical constructs?	Identical item pool?	Identical items?	Subjects	Criteria/ targets	Results			*M* scale length	Number of scales in inventory	Remarks
Jackson (1975)	Yes	No	No	116 Female students	*Criteria:* peer ratings of self-esteem, social participation, and tolerance	Mean correlation with criteria					EXT = 16 randomly chosen items from each of 3 CPI standard scales. PSY = scales written intuitively by undergraduate psychology students. JPI = 3 scales from Jackson Personality Inventory
						EXT		.09	16	3	
						DED	PSY	.25	16	3	
						DED	JPI	.29	20	3	
Reilly and Echternacht (1979)	No	Yes	No	3072 air force personnel, 312 "men in general"	*Target:* membership in 1 of 8 "satisfied" USAF career groups	Mean double-cross-validated hit rate of classification procedure					Only 1 EXT scale per career group was used for classification. Several uncontrolled factors. Satisfaction within each career group was predicted better by DED than by EXT scales
						EXT		76.1%	17–38	8	
						DED		72.1%	15	13	
D: Inductive versus deductive strategy											
Knudson and Golding (1974)	No	No	No	64 Students	*Criteria (for PRF):* 7 peer trait ratings, 7 targets (e.g., dating frequency)	Mean *R* for	7 criteria and 7 targets	7 criteria only			*R*s (corrected for shrinkage) as validity coefficients. Peer ratings matched with 7 PRF scales only
						IND	SIR .10	.09	32	5	
						DED	RSR .17	.16	18	15	
						DED	ICL .23	.26	16	8	
						DED	PRF .28	.37	20	10	
Burisch (1984a)	Closely related constructs	No	No	Mixed sample $n = 101$	*Criteria:* peer ratings	Mean correlation with criteria					STD = 8 standard scales of FPI
						IND	STD	.33	25	8	
						DED		.38	5	23	

Abbreviations: ACL, Adjective Check List; CPI, California Psychological Inventory; DED, deductive scales; EXT, external scales; FAC, scales derived from factor analysis; FPI, Freiburger Persönlichkeitsinventar; ICL, Interpersonal Check List; IND, inductive scales; MCI, Minnesota Counseling Inventory; MMPI, Minnesota Multiphasic Personality Inventory; MSA, scales derived from multiple scalogram analysis; PCQ, Psychological Climate Questionnaire; PRF, Personality Research Form; PSI, Psychological Screening Inventory; RAT, scales from Hase and Goldberg's (1967) Rational inventory; RSR, Rational S-R-Inventory (a deductive regrouping of SIRs plus 101 additional items); SIR, Schedule of Interpersonal Response; STD, Standard scales; SVIB, Strong Vocational Interest Blank; THE, scales from Hase and Goldberg's (1967) Theoretical inventory.

[a] Representative for several studies comparing SVIB occupational with basic interest scales.

[b] Representative for several studies comparing MMPI-168 clinical (EXT) and factor (IND) scales.

Table 2. Discriminant validity and redundancy of inventories in three studies

Source	Discriminant validity: Percentage of stray shots			Redundancy: Mean absolute within-inventory correlation		
	DED	EXT	IND	DED	EXT	IND
Hase and Goldberg (1967)	RAT 0%	EMP 10%		RAT .29 THE .19	EMP .33	FAC .24
Burisch (1978)	DED 11%	EXT-S 24% EXT-D 18%	STD 18% FAC 8%	DED .24	EXT-S .67 EXT-D .43	STD .36 FAC .26
Burisch (unpublished)	DED 3%		IND 21%	DED .20		IND .32

convergent validity or effectiveness for any of the strategies would be premature.

A somewhat clearer differentiation emerges in Table 2, where we look at discriminant validity in the 3 papers that reported pertinent figures. The percentage of stray shots (as defined above) is everywhere lowest for deductive inventories and highest for external ones. No meaningful count was possible for Hase and Goldberg's (1967) inductive FAC and deductive THE inventories (derived from factor analysis and theoretically based, respectively), because too few scales had logically matching criterion variables. The good showing of the DED (deductive) scales in my unpublished study (the last entry in Table 2) is all the more remarkable because some of their constructs were very closely related (for details, see Burisch, 1984a, 1984b).

How about economy? As Table 1 shows, deductive scales are typically shortest and external scales longest, sometimes by considerable ratios. The equivalent pattern is seen in the right-hand half of Table 2, where redundancy figures are exhibited. (Hase & Goldberg's RAT inventory is an exception to the rule, but there a mean overlap of 2.9 items per scale pair had been deemed acceptable.) It could be argued that the lower reliability of short scales serves to attenuate within-inventory correlations, but in the three studies of Table 2 mean retest reliabilities were highly comparable.

The relatively high degree of redundancy of Hase and Goldberg's inductive inventory FAC and of the various inductive inventories in my two studies may seem surprising at first, in view of the fact that all these inventories had resulted from orthogonal rotations. One likely explanation is that customarily an item is assigned to the factor, and consequently the scale, where it loads maximally, even though it has one or more substantial loadings on other factors. Another is that factor analyses at the item level rarely extract a high percentage of the total variance; for good reasons, of course. In the case of inventory STD, for example, it was 27%. At any rate, all inductive inventories in Table 2 had at least one within-inventory correlation in the .60–.70 range.

Conclusion

When convergent validity and effectiveness, the most widely accepted standards, fail to guide our choice of a construction strategy, we must turn to other standards. Fortunately, the picture is much clearer when we look at discriminant validity, and quite unambiguous when it comes to economy. Although just three studies may be too slim a basis for drawing final conclusions, the existing evidence favors deductive inventories most and external inventories least. The same applies to content validity, *on average,* but since this is a subjective standard, there is room for disagreement. Finally, there is no doubt that deductive inventories are the most economical to construct and to use. Probably their scales are also most independent, but this may need replication.

What, then, should keep test constructors from using the deductive approach? There may be the infrequent situation where a completely novel phenomenon forces investigators to start from scratch. Lacking even the most rudimentary hunches, they may opt for regressing to the old shotgun external methods. Even in that rare instance, I would recommend contrasting extreme groups in terms of scale scores, not individual items, bearing in mind the latters' unreliability.

Secondly, whoever believes that inventories should measure "basic dimensions" of personality and that these must be "discovered" in the structure of correlation matrices, has no choice other than the inductive strategy.

An issue not yet finally resolved is the amount of technical sophistication – at the level of data-based item analysis – necessary to turn out a good deductive instrument. Jackson (1970, 1971), one of the most successful deductive test builders, has stressed the importance of a careful step-by-step procedure in the preparation of the Personality Research Form. On the other hand, the fate of Hase and Goldberg's (1967) deductive inventory THE, Ashton and Goldberg's (1973) and Jackson's (1975) experiments with naive item writers and no item analysis at all, and some published (Burisch, 1978) and unpublished minimum-effort experiences of my own have convinced me that this is a field where "you just don't get what you pay for" (Burisch, 1984b). What would have resulted, had an independent construction team branched off early in the development of the PRF, determined to shrink the initial item lists down to 20 each, using nothing but their brains? Nobody knows, and since it is good practice to end a chapter with a hint to future directions, I leave this one to be explored.

Summary

More than a dozen empirical investigations comparing the three major construction strategies for personality inventory scales – the deductive, the external, and the inductive strategies – are reviewed. It is concluded that all strategies produce instruments that predict criteria and other variables of interest about equally well. There is some evidence, however, that deductive inventories are best, and external inventories worst, in terms of discriminant validity. Moreover, deductive scales tend to be easiest to construct, most economical to administer, and least redundant. It is also argued on a priori grounds that deductive scale scores can normally be interpreted in a more straightforward fashion than others. In summary, then, the deductive approach is recommended for offering the most advantages.

Acknowledgements. This chapter is based on an invited address delivered at the Bielefeld Symposion on Personality Questionnaires, June 17–20, 1982, and overlaps substantially with the paper by Burisch (1984a). In particular, Table 1 is an updated version of the paper's Table 1, which is reprinted by permission of the copyright holder, the American Psychological Association. Thanks are due to Lewis R. Goldberg for unearthing a supplementary table offered in Footnote 4 to Hase and Goldberg (1967), over 15 years after the original publication. For further acknowledgements, see Goldberg (1983). I am also indebted to Manfred Amelang and Ross Broughton, who provided important information.

References

Ashton, S.G., & Goldberg, L.R. (1973). In response to Jackson's challenge: The comparative validity of personality scales constructed by the external (empirical) strategy and scales developed intuitively by experts, novices, and laymen. *Journal of Research in Personality, 7*, 1–20.

Borgen, F.H. (1972). Predicting career choices of able college men from occupational and basic interest scales of the Strong Vocational Interest Blank. *Journal of Counseling Psychology, 19*, 202–211.

Broughton, R. (1984). A prototype strategy for construction of personality scales. *Journal of Personality and Social Psychology, 47*, 1334–1347.

Burisch, M. (1978). Construction strategies for multiscale personality inventories. *Applied Psychological Measurement, 2*, 97–111.

Burisch, M. (1984a). Approaches to personality inventory construction: A comparison of merits. *American Psychologist, 39*, 214–227.

Burisch, M. 1984b). You don't always get what you pay for: Measuring depression with short and simple versus long and sophisticated scales. *Journal of Research in Personality, 18*, 81–98.

Campbell, D.T., & Fiske, D.W. (1959). Convergent and discriminant validation by the multitrait-multimethod matrix. *Psychological Bulletin, 56*, 81–105.

Cattell, R.B., & Tsujioka, B. (1964). The importance of factor-trueness and validity, versus homogeneity and orthogonality, in test scales. *Educational and Psychological Measurement, 24*, 3–30.

Crewe, N.M. (1967). Comparison of factor analytic and empirical scales. *Proceedings of the 75th Annual Convention of the American Psychological Association* (pp. 367–368).

Fiske, D.W. (1971). *Measuring the concepts of personality*. Chicago: Aldine.

Goldberg, L.R. (1971). A historical survey of personality scales and inventories. In McReynolds, P. (Ed.), *Advances in psychological assessment* (Vol. 2, pp. 293–336). Palo Alto: Science and Behavior.

Goldberg, L.R. (1972). Parameters of personality inventory construction and utilization: A comparison of prediction strategies and tactics. *Multivariate Behavioral Research Monographs, 72*(2).

Goldberg, L.R. (1983). *Out of the closet: An admission.* Unpublished manuscript.

Gough, H.G., & Heilbrun, A.B. (1965). *The adjective check list manual.* Palo Alto: Consulting Psychologists.

Hase, H.D., & Goldberg, L.R. (1967). Comparative validity of different strategies of constructing personality inventory scales. *Psychological Bulletin, 67*, 231–248.

Hathaway, S.R., & McKinley, J.C. (1940). A multiphasic personality schedule (Minnesota). I. Construction of the schedule. *Journal of Psychology, 10*, 249–254.

Hedlund, J.L., Cho, D.W., & Wood, J.B. (1977). Comparative validity of MMPI-168 factor and clinical scales. *Journal of Multivariate Behavioral Research, 12*, 327–330.

Heilbrun, A.B. (1962). A comparison of empirical derivation and rational derivation of an affiliation scale. *Journal of Clinical Psychology, 18*, 101–102.

Hermans, H.J.M. (1969). The validity of different strategies of scale construction in predicting academic achievement. *Educational and Psychological Measurement, 29*, 877–883.

Holden, R.R., & Jackson, D.N. (1979). Item subtlety and face validity in personality assessment. *Journal of Consulting and Clinical Psychology, 47*, 459–468.

Hornick, C.W., James, L.R., & Jones, A.P. (1977). Empirical item keying versus a rational approach to analyzing a psychological climate questionnaire. *Applied Psychological Measurement, 1*, 489–500.

Jackson, D.N. (1969). Multimethod factor analysis in the evaluation of convergent and discriminant validity. *Psychological Bulletin, 72*, 30–49.

Jackson, D.N. (1970). A sequential system for personality scale development. In Spielberger, C.D. (Ed.), *Current topics in clinical and community psychology* (Vol. 2, pp 61–96). New York: Academic.

Jackson, D.N. (1971). The dynamics of structured personality tests: 1971. *Psychological Review, 78*, 229–248.

Jackson, D.N. (1975). The relative validity of scales prepared by naive item writers and those based on empirical methods of personality scale construction. *Educational and Psychological Measurement, 35*, 361–370.

Klingler, D.E., Johnson, J.H., Giannetti, R.A., & Williams, T.A. (1977). Comparison of the clinical utility of the MMPI basic scales and specific MMPI state-trait scales: A test of Dahlstrom's hypothesis. *Journal of Consulting and Clinical Psychology, 45*, 1086–1092.

Knudson, R.M., & Golding, S.L. (1974). Comparative validity of traditional versus S-R format inventories of interpersonal behavior. *Journal of Research in Personality, 8*, 111–127.

Meehl, P.E. (1945). The dynamics of "structured" personality tests. *Journal of Clinical Psychology, 1*, 296–303.

Mezzich, J.E., Damarin, F.L., & Erickson, J.R. (1974). Comparative validity of strategies and indices for differential diagnosis of depressive states from other psychiatric conditions using the MMPI. *Journal of Consulting and Clinical Psychology, 42*, 691–698.

Overall, J.E. (1974). Validity of the Psychological Screening Inventory for psychiatric screening. *Journal of Consulting and Clinical Psychology, 42*, 717–719.

Peterson, D.R. (1965). Scope and generality of verbally defined personality factors. *Psychological Review, 72*, 48–59.

Reilly, R.R., & Echternacht, G.J. (1979). Validation and comparison of homogeneous and occupational interest scales. *Applied Psychological Measurement, 3*, 177–185.

III. Models of Item Responding and Self-Presentation

The Process of Responding in Personality Assessment

DOUGLAS N. JACKSON

My general purpose in this paper is to provide a formulation of the process of responding to a personality questionnaire item. In this venture I have four specific aims: (a) To outline the possible benefits of a process-oriented response model for personality assessment and to relate such a model to previous work; (b) to provide the elements of a threshold conception for personality assessment and to show how it can account for factors previously identified as the largest factors on tests of psychopathology; (c) to present a method for scaling personality item content based on response methods; and (d) to demonstrate how such item scale values can be used to evaluate an extension of the threshold concept to responses to personality item content.

The personality item is perhaps the simplest stimulus condition that the personality psychologist is called upon to deal with. In fact, psychologists with no interest in psychometrics wonder sometimes about the relevance of responses to personality items to other forms of behavior. Many are not persuaded of their importance as vehicles for studying the person. But the very simplicity of the conditions surrounding a response to a personality item gives it a great power. In many social situations there is a very large number of choices that might be elicited. But when we constrain responses to "true" or "false" or to a limited number of response options, we have a means of studying the response process with great precision.

In addition to the model that I will be presenting, a number of other models have been proposed over the years. Of particular interest are the well known approaches to attitude item scaling of Thurstone (1928), Guttman (1941), and Lazarsfeld (1959). These models, like that of Lord (1952) for ability items, focus on the individual item and its properties, particularly as these relate to some underlying attribute. In contrast to item-centered models, one might consider the possibility that a person can be described by a small number of parameters based on responses to a large number of items. Helmstader (1957) and Lumsden (1977) have described person operating characteristic curves for attitude items and ability items, respectively, similar to that proposed here for personality items. In these formulations, the respondent operating curve is a function relating the probability of a keyed response to a continuum of items having different degrees of valence or intensity for the attribute in question. In this sense, the operating curve for a person is the complement of the operating characteristic curve for items in the Lord and other similar models. More specifically in the area of personality assessment have been formulations by Goldberg (1963), who suggested that there might be a range of uncertainty around the individual's location on an underlying content dimension, and the work of Fiske (1966) and a number of his collaborators (Tyler, 1973; Kuncel, 1973; Kuncel & Fiske, 1974).

One problem that has plagued early efforts at applying precise quantitative models to investigating the response process in personality assessment has been the rather indifferent psychometric quality of personality scales. Many of these lacked convergent and discriminant internal structure in the sense that items showed the highest correlations with their own keyed scales. Because of the inevitable multidimensionality of personality scale content, attempts to apply homogeneity scaling to personality item content have often failed. It is my hope that through more refined techniques of personality scale construction and the procedures for multidimensional evaluation of item and scale properties, one may obtain a stronger foundation for identifying underlying processes.

The threshold theory of responding holds that each individual's response patterns can be represented by a different curve relating underlying item attributes, such as judged item desirability scale values, and the individual's probabilities of endorsement of the items. It is well known that for groups of respondents the probability of endorsing a personality item is a function of the item's desirability. Figure 1 describes this functional relation. The functional relation described in Fig. 1 was generated by investigating responses to the 432 items in the Differential Personality Inventory (DPI; Jackson & Messick, 1976), a 28-scale structured questionnaire designed to span the domain of psychopathology. Rather than score the DPI in terms of its content scales, 24 arbitrary scales were generated which were heterogeneous as to content but each

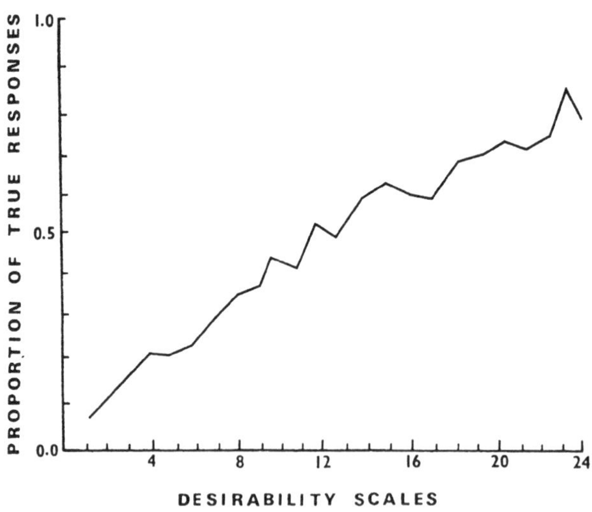

Fig. 1. Mean proportion of true responses as a function of desirability

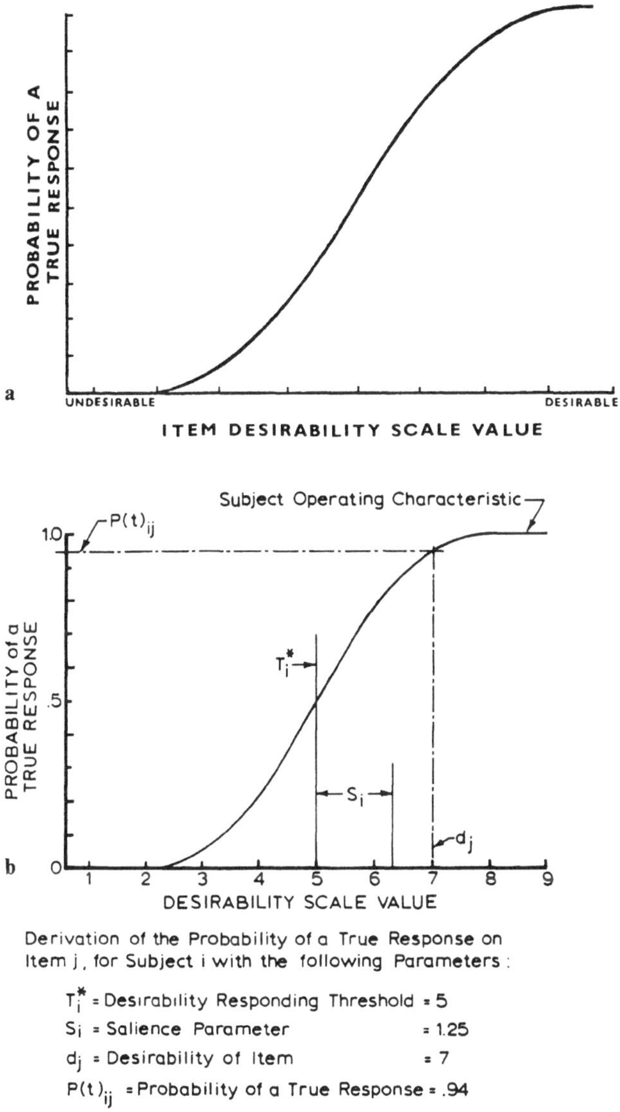

Fig. 2 a. Typical theoretical subject operating characteristic curve; **b** visual presentation of the method of deriving the probability of a „true" response to an item for a subject, given the operating characteristic curve

at a particular level of desirability. This was accomplished by first ranking the 432 items in terms of their judged desirability scale value (Messick & Jackson, 1961) and designating the 18 least desirable items as "Scale 1", the second 18 items as "Scale 2", etc. It will be observed from Fig. 1 that there is a lawful relation between desirability and probability of responding, confirming observations made in unpublished works by Wherry and Horst and later by Edwards (1957). But it should be recognized that this relationship describes groups of items and respondents; it provides an incomplete picture of individual response processes (Norman, 1967). But to the extent that a typical respondent is like the average depicted in Fig. 1, it is possible to draw a theoretical respondent operating characteristic curve as in Fig. 2. Figure 2 represents the probability of a true response for an individual respondent (rather than for a group of respondents) as a function of item desirability as a normal ogive. (This theoretical curve shows response probabilities asymptoting at 0.0 and 1.0 at the extremes, something which did not happen in the empirical data because items extreme in desirability had been removed and because there typically is a 1% or 2% rate of nonpurposeful responding.) This curve is described by two parameters, the desirability responding *threshold* and the *salience* of the desirability dimension in determining the individual's response. It is important to reemphasize that this *subject* operating characteristic must be differentiated from *item* operating characteristic curve of test theory (Lord, 1980). The latter is based on examining the responses of many persons to a single item, while the subject operating characteristic is based on a single subject's responses to many items. Thus, there are as many subject operating curves as there are subjects. Although, in general, the curve is a monotonically increasing function, individual variations permit the construction of a more-or-less unique curve for each individual.

The Response Threshold

The response threshold describes the point on the curve which marks the transition from a *false* to a *true* response in the case of dichotomous items, or, generally, the point at which the individual begins to endorse items along a quantitative dimension. For a particular individual, response probabilities below .5 are below threshold, and those at or above .5 are above threshold. Once the threshold is established it is possible to locate the point on the desirability dimension corresponding to the threshold, as illustrated in Fig. 3. Figure 3 illustrates two subjects showing markedly different thresholds. Subject A endorses items lower on the desirability scale than does subject B.

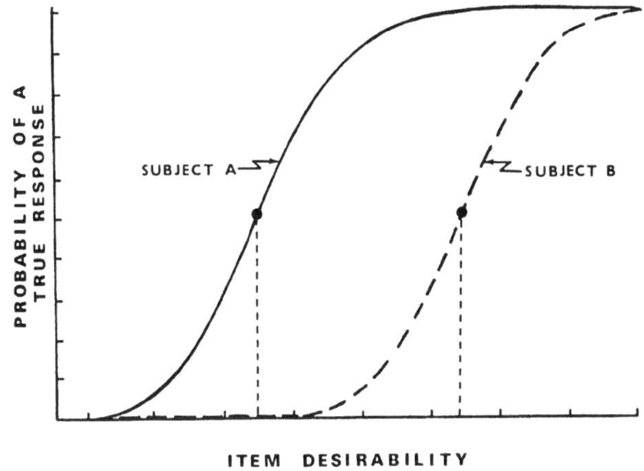

Fig. 3. Theoretical subject operating characteristic curves of two subjects showing extreme thresholds. Subject A has a low threshold, while Subject B has a high threshold

Salience

Salience psychologically is defined in terms of a subject's sensitivity to the desirability dimension as reflected in the patterning of responses. A subject with a higher salience or sensitivity parameter will show a steeper curve, as illustrated by subject C in Fig. 4. Subject D's curve shows a less steep slope and hence a lower salience. The limiting cases are: for high salience a step function with a probability of a true response of 0.0 below the threshold and 1.0 above

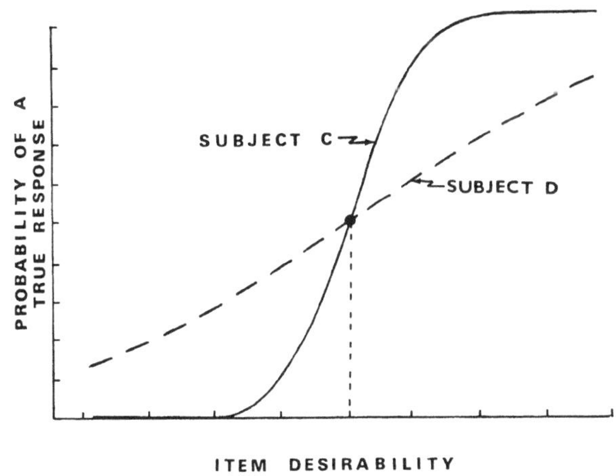

Fig. 4. Theoretical subject operating characteristic curves of two subjects showing extreme salience parameters. Subject C has a high salience value while Subject D has a low salience value

the threshold, and for low salience a horizontal line with zero slope, indicating an absence of an effect due to item desirability. (Negative slopes are possible, although very rare, usually indicating random, nonpurposeful responding.)

A Monte Carlo Study of Desirability Thresholds

In a series of studies conducted more than 2 decades ago Jackson and Messick (1961, 1962) reported a number of factor analyses of the MMPI in which two large dimensions accounted for major portions of the variance. Figure 5 illustrates the kind of results which typically emerged from these studies. True- and false-keyed subscales were separated on one factor, while the second factor showed consistently very high levels of association with the average judged item desirability of scales. The Jackson-Messick characterization of these two

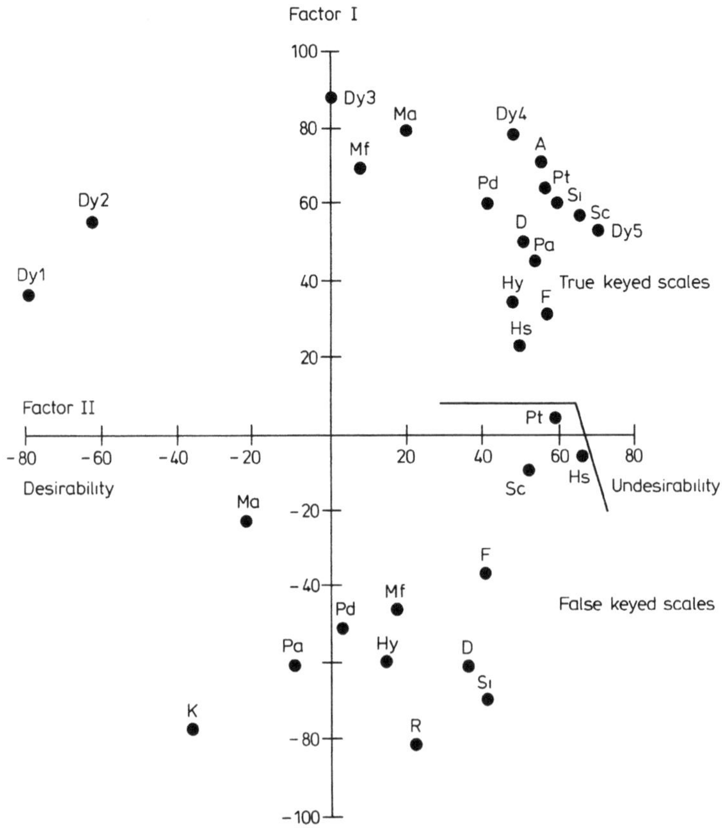

Fig. 5. Factor space defined by the first two factors of the Jackson and Messick (1961) factor analysis of MMPI scales

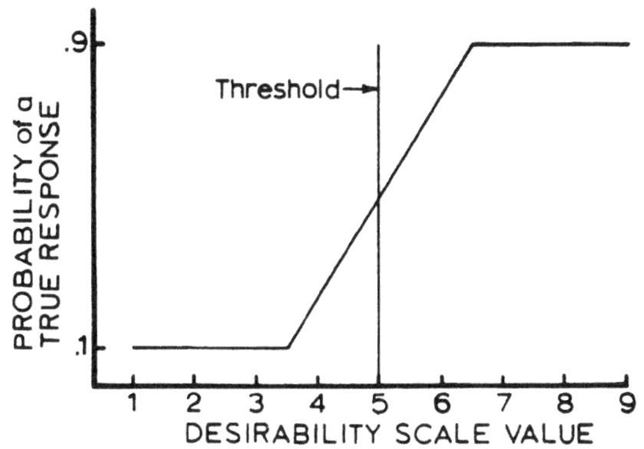

Fig. 6. Basic form of the subject operating characteristic curve used in simulation

dimensions as being respectively due to acquiescence and desirability was challenged by Block (1965) and by Rorer (1965). In considering the criticisms of these authors, two issues became clear to me: (a) the emergence of broad general dimensions probably could not be accounted for by specific item and scale content; and (b) an understanding of underlying processes would do much to resolve alternative interpretations of controversial findings.

The question arose as to whether or not the structure observed repeatedly on the MMPI might be attributable to the processes thought to underlie the threshold model. In a doctoral dissertation conducted under my supervision Rogers (1971) programmed a computer to simulate the responses of a large number of hypothetical subjects. Each "subject" was assigned an arbitrary threshold value based on a random algorithm. The program instructed each subject to respond "true" to items above their threshold and "false" to items below their threshold with a certain graded probability for the region of uncertainty around the threshold, as illustrated in Fig. 6. The only information available to the computer was the set of MMPI desirability scale values, a distribution of 100 subject thresholds, and the above instructions. The 100 subjects' responses were scored on the same MMPI scales as used by Jackson and Messick (1961), intercorrelated, and factored by principal axes. Two large eigenvalues emerged, accounting together for 82% of the variance (Fig. 7). The resulting rotated dimensions are presented in Fig. 8. Comparison with Fig. 2 indicates a marked similarity between simulated and real data. In both cases there is a complete separation of true- and false-keyed scales and an ordering from left to right of desirable and undesirable scales. Rank correlations between the pattern of factor loadings for the first two dimensions on real and simulated data sets were .93 and .83, respectively.

It should be recognized that Rogers (1971) used only one parameter in his simulation instead of the two proposed by Jackson. Even though other anal-

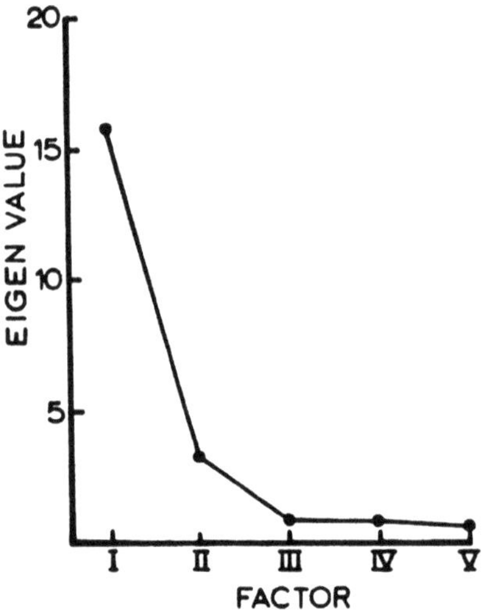

Fig. 7. Plot of eigenvalues of the first five factors of the simulated data

yses have pointed to the potency of the salience parameter in accounting for response variance, the results of the simulation study indicate that the threshold parameter alone can generate a structure very similar to that yielded by the MMPI. While the results from the simulation study do not *prove* that the hypothesized processes operate in MMPI responses, they do lend support to these hypotheses by suggesting that such processes could account for the observed regularities. Rogers also reported a second series of analyses showing that the consistency reported by Rorer and Goldberg (1965) between original and reversed MMPI items could be well accounted for by the threshold model. The crux of the argument is given in Fig. 8, which illustrates the basis for such consistencies. Given that a correlation of .87 exists between original and reversed MMPI desirability scale values (Edwards & Oakland, personal communication), the expectation is that a "true" response to an original item will generally imply a false response to a reversal and vice versa. The item "I am not easily angered" has a relatively high desirability scale value, while its logical reversal, "It is not true that I am easily angered," has a much lower scale value for a true response. Thus the desirability of a "true" response to the original is approximately equal to a "false" response for the reversal. The small inconsistencies between original and reversed items when scored in a "content" direction were consistently predicted by Rogers using derivations from the threshold model.

Thus, the evidence implies that subjects neither employed blind acquiescence tendencies to any substantial degree nor responded consistently to

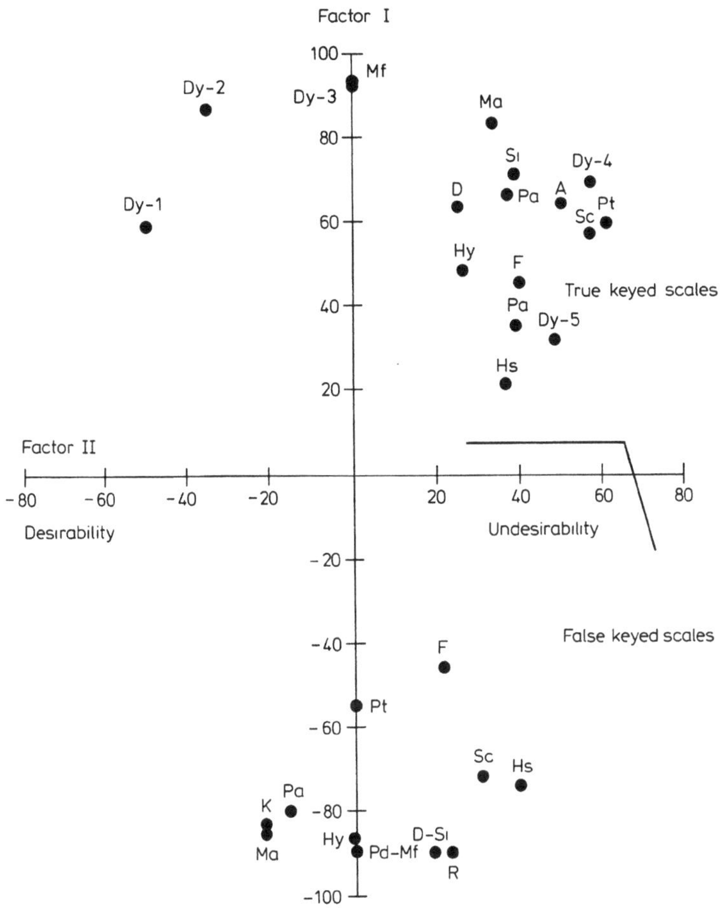

Fig. 8. Factor space defined by the first two factors of the simulated data

homogeneous content, but, rather, showed an almost psychophysical precision in locating a threshold and using it consistently over a wide range of content and of direction of wording and of keying.

Voyce and Jackson (1977) undertook an extensive series of studies on the Differential Personality Inventory. A number of estimates of the two subject parameters of the model were investigated, including those akin to psychophysical methods for estimating threshold. These are summarized in Table 1. The best methods were also the simplest; the intercept of the subject operating characteristic proved to be an excellent indicant of threshold, while the slope proved to be an excellent indicant of salience. Both judged desirability and judged frequency of endorsement were investigated. Of particular interest in Table 1 are the factor loadings on the first dimension of −.92 and −.95 (for

Table 1. Rotated factor loadings of parameter estimates

Parameter	Desirability		Frequency	
	I	II	I	II
Ascending estimate	.55	.65	.70	.44
Descending estimate	.83	−.25	.78	−.30
Threshold	.91	.23	.93	.07
Biserial	−.01	.99	.05	.99
Porportion of true responses	−.92	−.12	−.95	−.08
Intercept	.95	.04	.95	.12
Slope	−.01	.99	.05	.99

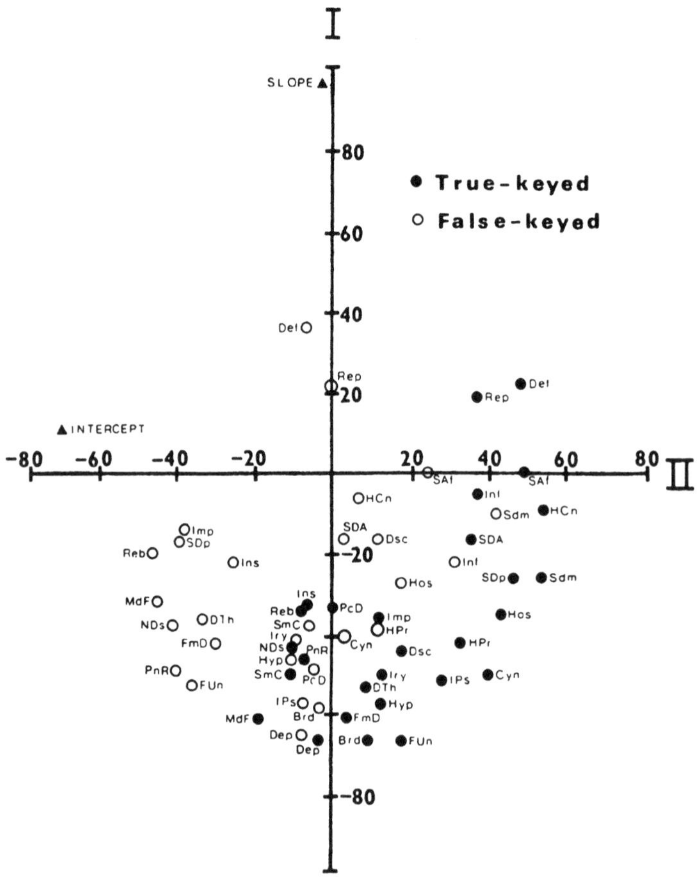

Fig. 9. Factor space defined by the first two factors of the DPI response data

frequency scale values) for the proportion of true responses by a subject. This implies that the lower a respondent's threshold for responding on the desirability dimension, the larger the proportion of true responses. This process quite probably underlies what Morf and Jackson (1972) labeled acceptance acquiescence. Another interesting observation is that the slope parameter measured by the biserial correlation between a subject's tendency to endorse items and their desirability scale values loaded .99 on the second dimension, adding to credibility to the interpretation of this factor as representing salience or sensitivity to the underlying item desirability.

Voyce and Jackson also factor analyzed responses to the separately scored true- and false-keyed subscales of the DPI in an analysis that also included the intercept and slope measures of threshold and sensitivity of threshold and salience. The results are summarized in Fig. 9, a plot of rotated factor loadings. Slope marked the largest factor, with a loading of .96, while intercept marked the second, with a loading of .71, the highest loading being on the second factor. There were statistically significant correlations between the patterning of loadings on Factor I and their desirability scale values. The separation of true- and false-keyed subscales, although significant, was not as clear as in the results with the MMPI, raising further questions as to whether or not "acquiescence" is a proper designation for the second factor. The possible basis for the separation of true- and false-keyed subscales can be discerned from Fig. 10, a frequency distribution of desirability scale values for true responses for 432 DPI items. It is noteworthy that when true- and false-keyed items are plotted separately, the distribution is distinctly bimodal. True-keyed items are less de-

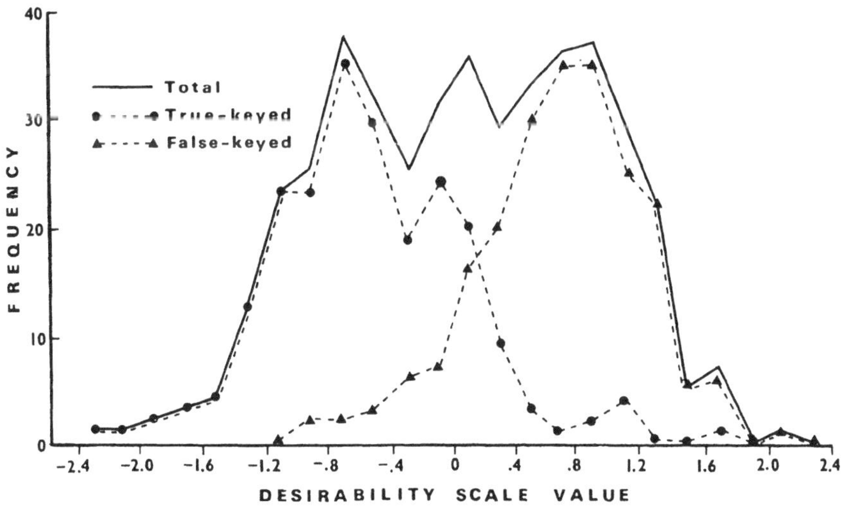

Fig. 10. Frequency distribution of desirability scale values of 432 DPI items. (The distributions of true- and false-keyed items are plotted separately)

sirable, something to be expected in measures of psychopathology. A person with a threshold near the middle of the desirability scale value distribution would endorse the false-keyed items and reject the true-keyed items. This would lead to a negative correlational component between true- and false-keyed scales, causing them to load on opposite sides of a factor. But this process is not inextricably linked to the direction of keying. If true-keyed scales contained more desirable items or if false-keyed scales contained less desirable items, there would not be a clear separation between them, as was the case with the DPI. Further, because of clearer content measurement on the DPI, the two largest factors account proportionally for only half the variance accounted for by the two largest factors of the MMPI.

In summary, the research results on applications of the threshold theory to measures of psychopathology suggest a number of conclusions: (a) response style dimensions previously identified as due to acquiescence and desirability can be reinterpreted as due to individual differences in threshold and salience or sensitivity for responding in terms of the desirability level of personality items; (b) these processes are readily measurable in tests of psychopathology by employing the intercept and slope of the best-fitting straight line of the subject operating characteristic; (c) these processes serve to define the two largest factors in the MMPI and the DPI; (d) these processes account for only half as much variance on the DPI as on the MMPI; (e) the threshold concept serves to clarify and subsume processes previously described as "acceptance acquiescence."

Extensions of the Threshold Model to Content Responding

Basic Structure Content Scaling

Since the threshold model requires scale values for personality items, a method of obtaining multidimensional scale values for each of the keyed scales or components in a personality questionnaire was required. Jackson and Helmes (1979) report such a method based on conventional component analysis suitable for large sets of items. The method analyzes response data in such a way as to provide scale values or estimates of the magnitude of items on content dimensions. Thus the method incorporates not only formal content characteristics as they might be observed by independent judges, but also the structure of responses to the items as these are elicited in the assessment situation.

A brief description of the Jackson-Helmes scaling method is in order. If a personality inventory is administered to a number of respondents and an item factor analysis is undertaken, items are likely to show loadings on a number of content factors, as well as loadings on stylistic factors, particularly those associated with desirability. Unidimensional judgment scaling techniques, such as scaling items in terms of a dominance dimension, are likely to fail to do justice to the multidimensionality of item content, as well as to the response determinants linked to desirability scale values. Multidimensional scaling techniques can be applied to personality items, but there are at least two important reasons why they are unequal to the task of scaling large numbers of personality items: (a) multidimensional scaling typically requires a large number of judgments, which increase geometrically as the number of items increases arithmetically, making it impractical to scale sets of personality items of any substantial size; (b) there is evidence from our laboratory that the structure derived from multidimensional scaling is different from that derived from response methods. The latter typically are confounded with stylistic variance, which do not appear in judgments.

The problem of identifying different response patterns among subjects was approached by Jackson and Helmes (1979) by assuming that each subject could be considered as a vector in a multidimensional space and responds to each item with respect to a one-dimensional attribute. Subjects might be represented by different vectors reflecting a different pattern or ordering of true and false responses, but it is assumed that there are usually fewer vectors than there are respondents. Rather than among items or tests, the similarities are identified among respondents. Thus, if a set of items, say from three different scales, such as achievement, aggression, and dominance, were represented in a multidimensional space, different respondents might show differing patterns of true and false responses, depending upon their location on each of these dimensions and upon their tendencies to respond desirably or undesirably. Assuming that these consistencies could be represented as vectors in the space, individual subjects might be grouped into types of clusters in such a way that item projections on the combined vectors which reflect subjects of a similar type could represent scale values for each identified type. There are at least three important advantages to such a procedure: (a) It can efficiently handle large numbers of items, much larger than either multidimensional scaling methods or unidimensional methods which require the scaling of the same stimuli on several separate dimensions; (b) it is not necessary in advance to specify the nature or number of dimensions under investigation; and (c) such a method incorporates the relevant influences which determine responses to personality items.

The appropriate derivations and computing formulas for the procedure are outlined in Jackson and Helmes (1979). In general, there is a close analogy between the calculation of item scale values in basic structure content scaling and the calculation of component scores in principal components factor analysis. Whereas in traditional components or factor analysis correlations are evaluated among tests and measures on underlying dimensions are obtainable for persons, basic structure content scaling reverses this procedure, seeking to analyze a correlational structure among persons and locating items in terms of their magnitudes as projections on these dimensions.

An illustration would be helpful. Jackson and Helmes scaled 352 items comprising the 22 scales of Form E of the Personality Research Form (PRF; Jackson, 1984). Table 2 provides a summary of the results for six items for the Dominance scale of the PRF. The first three of these were all true keyed and

Table 2. Scale values and items for the dominance scale

Item no.	Scale value	Item
317	4.73	I would like to be an executive with power over others
229	4.41	The ability to be a leader is very important to me
9	3.68	I feel confident when directing the activities of others
75	−4.23	I avoid positions of power over other people
207	−4.38	I feel uneasy when I have to tell people what to do
163	−4.89	I have little interest in leading people

had the most extreme positive scale values, while the last three were false keyed and had the most extreme negative scale values for the Dominance scale. A total of 22 dimensions were obtained, corresponding to the 22 scales on the PRF. In general the items keyed on a particular scale yielded the most extreme scale values for a particular scale, with the average of the keyed items several times larger than for the nonkeyed items. Although it was recognized that scale values derived in this way would not be identical with those derived from conventional unidimensional judgment methods, some degree of relationship would be expected. We therefore used content scale values in a study of their correlation with judged scale values as reported by Rogers (1973), who had scaled PRF items from the Autonomy and Impulsivity scales. The correlation between our content scale values when considering the set of autonomy items only was .96 for an orthogonal rotation and .98 for an oblique rotation, while the correlations for impulsivity items only were .94 and .95 for orthogonal and oblique rotations, respectively. These data together with the indications of a strong correspondence between extreme scale values and the PRF scoring key provided us with sufficient confidence to proceed in using these scale values for the evaluation of the threshold model for content responding.

A Two-Dimensional Cumulative Model for Responding to Personality Items

The elements of the model for content responding are summarized in Fig. 11. Whereas the probability of a true response in terms of desirability scale values could be represented in a two-dimensional figure, the addition of content scale values requires at least a three-dimensional geometric representation. In this instance, an individual is appraising at least two components when he responds to a personality item, namely, its location on the relevant content dimension and on the desirability dimension in relation to his or her own threshold and sensitivity to these two dimensions. Of course, such a model assumes that items are univocal in terms of content, in the sense that they measure one and only one content dimension well. A more complicated and less interesting model might be represented in the case of the PRF as a 22-dimensional model where every dimension enters into every response pattern. This in a sense might be more realistic but it is surely less parsimonious.

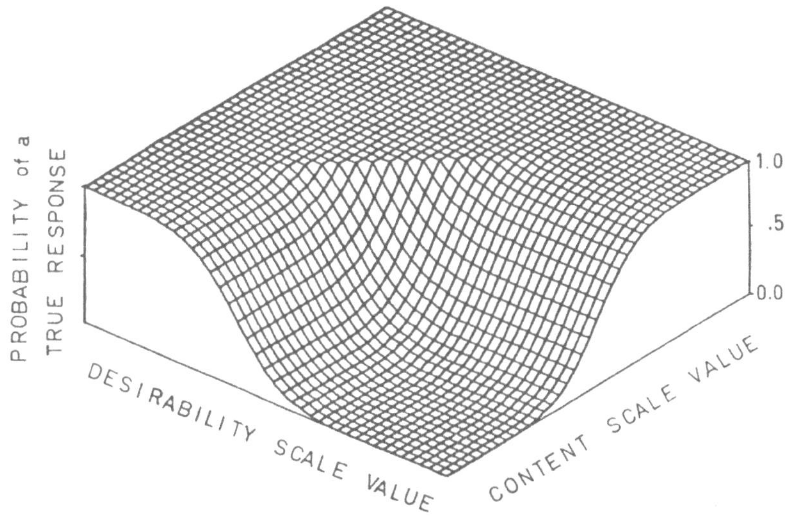

Fig. 11. A two-dimensional cumulative model

Helmes (1978), working at The University of Western Ontario, has conducted a series of studies to evaluate the threshold model as it applies to content responding. In implementing this investigation, Helmes used the content scaling technique previously described and undertook an analysis of the relationship between subjects' saliences for content responding and their PRF scale scores. When scales were considered individually, this correlation proved to be .97 (it was .82 when the entire set of PRF items was used). What Helmes sought to do was to use this connection between salience and scale score to test which particular items an individual would respond to on the PRF. Helmes utilized the connection between salience and scale score to use saliences indirectly in making predictions about item responses. Thus, for example, if one individual has a scale score of 8 and another has a scale score of 10, a scale score salience model would predict that the eight items to which the first individual responds in the keyed direction are those with the most extreme scale values. The second individual would respond to the same eight items in the keyed direction and also to the next two most extreme items. Note that this is a quite specific prediction. Helmes points out that it thereby avoids the simple tautology that an individual with a scale score of 10 would answer ten items in the keyed direction. The prediction specifies exactly which ten items would be answered in the keyed direction. Table 3 summarizes some of Helmes' results. It will be observed that the use of scale scores predicts response patterns quite well, and significantly better than invariant models based upon item p values or desirabilities. The addition of a second dimension to scale content, desirability, was not particularly potent for PRF items. While it resulted in a small but significant improvement for university students, it was

Table 3. Results for cumulative models based upon scale scores

Model	Sample								
	University			High school			Pooled		
	Correct predictions	Percent-age	Kappa[a]	Correct predictions	Percent-age	Kappa[a]	Correct predictions	Percent-age	Kappa[a]
Scale content	21090	65.12	.303	67448	63.66	.274	88538	64.00	.281
Scale content, desirability	21196	65.45	.310	67697	63.89	.278	88893	64.26	.286

[a] All values of kappa are significantly greater than zero at the .001 level.

not significant for high school students. This is not surprising, given the efforts to suppress desirability on the PRF. While Helmes also attempted to evaluate the second parameter, namely threshold, he did not combine the two in a single model for predicting responses. Presumably, the two combined would predict responses better than either one would separately. A question might be raised about the absolute magnitude of the percentages reported in Table 3. A rate of prediction that hovers in the vicinity of 64% might not be considered high enough. But it should be noted that we are dealing here with the characteristic problem of predicting a single response, namely, that these individual items, although substantially reliable when aggregated, are not highly reliable individually. A 16-item scale with a reliability of .85 will be comprised of items showing average reliabilities in the low .2 range. Under the circumstances, the accuracy of prediction should be taken as a comparative issue rather than as an absolute matter.

Some Experimental Results

A series of experimental studies has been undertaken by Fekken (1983), at The University of Western Ontario, on some implications of the threshold theory as it applies to the process underlying changes in responding to personality scale content.

Threshold theory suggests that an individual will find responding to items near his or her threshold more "difficult" than responding to items far from the threshold. This hypothesis was evaluated in two ways. First, the proportion of response changes to items falling in the threshold range (i.e., the 25% of items nearest an individual's threshold) was compared with the proportion of response changes to items falling outside the threshold range. Subjects completed 10 content scales (160 items) of the PRF on two occasions, 1 week apart. A response change was defined as a change from a "true" to a "false" response to an item on retest or vice versa. A significantly higher proportion of response changes occurred to items in the threshold range than to items outside the threshold range. Further, when subjects were divided into two groups based on a median split on salience of desirability responding to the set of PRF items, the difference in the proportion of items changed inside and outside the threshold range was more pronounced for the high- than for the low-salience group.

The second way in which the original hypothesis was evaluated was by requiring the threshold model to predict *which* item responses an individual would change. For example, if an individual changed 25 item responses on retest, the threshold model would predict these are more likely to be the 25 items nearest the threshold. This proved to be the case to a statistically significant degree. Other promising results have emerged with regard to response latencies. To be consistent with earlier results of Fiske (1966; Kuncel & Fiske, 1974) and his group with a different formulation, one would expect latencies to be highest nearer the individual threshold, on the assumption that these choices are more difficult. This was also borne out.

Implications for a Structural Theory of Motivation

Returning for a moment to Fig. 10, I would like to comment on the implications of the ideas presented here for understanding behavior outside the assessment situation in real life situations. But I should note first that I do not believe that the processes which account for responding to personality items stylistically or in terms of content are unique to the assessment situation, but rather, that these represent a microcosm of behavior in the real world. The question is how to represent what appears to be the often unpredictable and difficult to understand behavior of a person operating in a situation. My suggestion is that the threshold model outlined here may have some relevance. If we substitute for an item the concept of a situation, which, like an item, elicits a certain response, and also consider that a response relevant to a particular situation might be scaled both in terms of its desirability and in terms of its strength as reflecting a particular personality dimension, and if we further assume that individuals may vary in their sensitivity to the response-evoking potentials of different situations, then the relevance of the threshold concept to understanding motivation more generally immediately becomes clear.

Consider a particular situation. An individual is dining in a restaurant. A waiter spills soup on the individual under circumstances which lead the individual to believe that this might have been a deliberate act. Does the individual respond aggressively? The answer to this question can be conceptualized as being a function of the individual's threshold on and sensitivity to the aggression dimension as well as the appraisal of this response on the desirability dimension in terms of the individual's threshold and sensitivity to responding desirably. If we knew the scale values of alternative responses in terms of the desirability and aggression dimensions, a prediction of which response was elicited might be made. Of course, in the real world a prediction is more complicated, because people do not necessarily restrict their behavior to a binary choice – they can scale their response in terms of aggression and desirability. Two people might both reprimand the waiter, but one with much greater intensity than the other. The difficulties of experimenting with such a formulation should be recognized, but I believe that research directed at the threshold model's broader implications might bear fruit.

Overview

I have outlined a formulation to account for the major dimensions in responding to personality measures of psychopathology, provided evidence to illustrate how such a formulation might operate with simulated data, and shown how it operates empirically on measures of psychopathology. We have also seen how items might be scaled in terms of their response-evoking potential for reflecting personality dimensions, and illustrated the application of such scale values in accounting for individual responses and in predicting response change. Finally, I have sought to touch upon the broader implications for understanding the structuring of behavior in the real world. But much research needs to be done to evaluate the relevance of such a model.

References

Block, J. (1965). *The challenge of response sets.* New York: Appleton-Century-Crofts.
Edwards, A.L. (1957). *The social desirability variable in personality assessment and research.* New York: Dryden.
Fekken, C. (1983). *Comparison of 4 models for predicting person reliability.* London/Ontario: Doctoral dissertation, University of Western Ontario.
Fiske, D.W. (1966). Some hypotheses concerning test adequacy. *Educational and Psychological Measurement, 26*(1), 69–88.
Goldberg, L.R. (1963). A model of item ambiguity in personality assessment. *Educational and Psychological Measurement, 23*, 467–492.
Guttman, L. (1941). The quantification of a class of attributes: A theory and method of scale construction. In Horst, P. (Ed.), *The prediction of personal adjustment* (pp. 319–148). New York: Social Science Research Council.
Helmes, E. (1978). *A multidimensional approach to personality inventory responding.* London/Ontario: Doctoral dissertation, University of Western Ontario.
Helmstader, G.C. (1957). Procedure for obtaining separate set and content components of a test score. *Psychometrika, 22*, 381–393.
Jackson, D.N. (1984). *Personality research form* (3rd ed.). Port Huron: Research Psychologists Press.
Jackson, D.N., & Helmes, E. (1979). Basic structure content scaling. *Applied Psychological Measurement, 3*(3), 313–325.
Jackson, D.N., & Messick, S. (1961). Acquiescence and desirability as response determinants on the MMPI. *Educational and Psychological Measurement, 21*, 771–790.
Jackson, D.N., & Messick, S. (1962). Response styles on the MMPI: Comparison of clinical and normal samples. *Journal of Abnormal and Social Psychology, 65*, 285–299.
Jackson, D.N., & Messick, S. (1976). *Differential Personality Inventory.* Department of Psychology, The University of Western Ontario, London (Canada).
Kuncel, R.B. (1973). Response processes and relative location of subject and item. *Educational and Psychological Measurement, 33*, 545–563.
Kuncel, R.B., & Fiske, D.W. (1974). Stability of response process and response. *Educational and Psychological Measurement, 34*, 743–755.
Lazarsfeld, P.F. (1959). Latent structure analysis. In Koch, S. (Ed.), *Psychology: A study of a science* (Vol. 3, pp. 476–543). New York: McGraw-Hill.
Lord, F.M. (1952). The relation of the reliability of multiple-choice tests to the distribution of item difficulties. *Psychometrika, 17*, 181–194.
Lord, F.M. (1980). *Applications of item response theory to practical testing problems.* Hillsdale: Erlbaum.
Lumsden, J. (1977). Person reliability. *Applied Psychological Measurement, 1*, 477–482.
Messick, S., & Jackson, D.N. (1961). Desirability scale values and dispersions for MMPI items. *Psychological Reports, 8*, 409–414.
Morf, M.E., & Jackson, D.N. (1972). An analysis of two response styles: True responding and item endorsement. *Educational and Psychological Measurement, 32*, 329–353.
Norman, W.T. (1967). On estimating psychological relationships: Social desirability and self report. *Psychological Bulletin, 67*, 273–293.
Rogers, T.B. (1971). The process of responding to personality items: Some issues, a theory and some research. *Multivariate Behavioural Research Monographs, 6*(2).
Rogers, T.B. (1973). Ratings of content as a means of assessing personality items. *Educational and Psychological Measurement, 33*, 845–858.

Rorer, L.G. (1965). The great response-style myth. *Psychological Bulletin, 63*, 129–156.
Rorer, L.G., & Goldberg, L.R. (1965). Acquiescence in the MMPI? *Educational and Psychological Measurement, 25*, 801–817.
Thurstone, L.L. (1928). The measurement of opinion. *Journal of Abnormal and Social Psychology, 22*, 415–430.
Tyler, L.E. (1973). *Response stability, person-item distance and homogeneity*. Chicago: Doctoral dissertation, University of Chicago.
Voyce, C.D., & Jackson, D.N. (1977). An evaluation of a threshold theory for personality assessment. *Educational and Psychological Measurement, 37*, 383–408.

Self-Deception and Impression Management in Test Responses *

Delroy L. Paulhus

> Man is what he believes — *Chekhov*
>
> Convictions are more dangerous enemies of truth than are lies — *Nietzsche*

Introduction

In psychological assessment, we aim for the most accurate description of some cognitive or behavioral attribute. In assessment involving self-reports, this objective is invariably haunted by the possibility of misrepresentation. Certainly we would be sceptical of self-reports of intelligence, perhaps because of its universal desirability. Among the few qualities typically rated as even more desirable than intelligence is having a good personality. Thus it seems dangerous to ignore the possibility that at least some respondents systematically misrepresent their own personality.

The venerable literature on socially desirable responding (SDR), which peaked in the 1960s, attests to a fear on the part of many psychologists that SDR is a major threat to accurate assessment and should be controlled (e.g., Bernreuter, 1933; Edwards, 1957; Ellis, 1946; Jackson & Messick, 1962; Meehl & Hathaway, 1946). Such concerns have continued on into the 1980s (Kiecolt-Glaser & Murray, 1980; Linehan & Nielson, 1981; Rock, 1981; Sarason, Levine, Basham, & Sarason, 1983). Indeed, the 1974 revision of the *Standards for Educational and Psychological Tests* recommends attention to any "attempt to by the examinee to present a socially desirable conforming or false picture ..." An equally vocal school of assessment psychologists continues to deny that a correlation between social desirability and content scales indicates a need for control. These psychologists insist that such dimensions are much more substance than style (Block, 1965; Heilbrun, 1964; McCrae & Costa, 1983).

Without a clear reconciliation, the emphasis of personality assessors has shifted from the extremely polarized positions of the 1960s. The new look claims that respondents on self-reports are attempting to convey a certain self-concept or role to the assessor. For example, in Hogan's socioanalytic theory (Cheek & Hogan, 1984; Hogan, 1983; Mills & Hogan, 1978), responses to self-

* This work was supported by a research grant from the Social Science and Humanities Research Council of Canada.

report inventories are said to be guided by underlying self-images which are unconscious and not situationally consistent. Although organized for a positive self-presentation, these self-images do not involve conscious dissimulation. Similar but less elaborate theories have been proposed by Wiggins (1966), Rogers (1974), Baumeister (1982), and Taylor, Carithers and Coyne (1976).

While this new emphasis has blunted the sometimes harsh battles over the social desirability issue, at least two problems central to personality assessment have been left in limbo (Strosahl, Linehan, & Chiles, 1984). The first concerns the relationship between socially desirable responding and adjustment. The second is whether social desirability should be routinely controlled in developing and administering self-report instruments.

In this paper, I will try to show how this controversy, as well as a number of other unsolved problems, may be resolved by a new emphasis on an old distinction. I will use the term *impression management* to refer to conscious dissimulation of test responses designed to create a favorable impression in some audience. In contrast, the term *self-deception* will refer to any positively biased response that the respondent actually believes to be true (these purposely vague definitions will be clarified later). Although researchers have alluded to this distinction over the years, its conceptual potential has been underestimated. I will try to show how the distinction yields surprisingly straightforward solutions to the lingering questions about adjustment and control.

Some History

Varieties of Terminology

In the beginning there was Freud. By touting the unconscious as a central component in psychic behavior, he provided the requisite feature for lying to oneself – a bicameral mind. Even the well-adjusted, socialized individual was assumed to inhibit and disguise both from himself and from others the driving forces of sexual and aggressive motivation. Such defense mechanisms were held to be largely unconscious in operation. Although Freud did not use the term explicitly, subsequent commentators on his work have cited the concept of self-deception as being a central mechanism in psychoanalytic theory. For example, Sackeim and Gur (1978) argue that self-deception is a necessary condition for repression. Mischel (1974) holds that all neurotic behavior is self-deceptive. Hilgard (1949) goes even further, to say that self-deception is a feature of all defense mechanisms.

Several philosophers have proposed definitions. Sartre (1943/1966) discusses a theory of self-deception using the French term *«mauvaise foi»* (literal) meaning "bad faith," the term has been figuratively translated as "self-deception" (Kaufmann, 1956). Self-deception is said to be a free choice to persuade oneself that a conflict does not exist. Sartre's term, like his concept, has a moralistic tone. The self-deceiver's refusal to take responsibility for his actions is said to indicate an "inner disintegration at the heart of being" (p. 70). Kierkegaard's (1843/1959) concept is similarly moralistic: An individual may accept the responsibility of the self as an ethical agent of his behavior or deny the reality of responsibility as a self-deceiver. The fact that Sartre and Kierkegaard see self-deception as a moral issue places their theories beyond the scope of a purely psychological analysis.

More recently, Demos (1960) has defined self-deception in a straightforward way as simultaneously believing *p* and not-*p*. Individuals are said to be conscious of both but fail to notice that they have a conflict or be unable to notice it. Unfortunately, Demos is unclear about whether the not-noticing is motivated or not. Moreover his claim that both beliefs are conscious is problematic. Murphy (1975) has also argued for the importance of attention in self-deception.

Bach (1981) has provided the most psychological analysis in the philosophy literature. Rather than believing both *p* and not-*p*, the self-deceiver is said to believe only *p*. Since he desperately wants not-*p* to be true, he avoids thinking about *p* through processes of rationalization, jamming, and/or evasion. In a sense, not-*p* becomes true by default. Other, more restricted definitions are given by Fingarette (1969) and Sarbin (1981). For a detailed review see Lockard and Paulhus (in press).

The definition given by Sackeim and Gur (1978) is the most important for our purposes, because it is stated as a set of necessary and sufficient conditions for confirming that self-deception exists. The four criteria are (a) the individual holds two contradictory beliefs; (b) the two beliefs are held simultaneously; (c) the individual is not aware of holding one of the beliefs; and (d) the unawareness of one belief is motivated (p. 150).

This definition is clearly the most systematic and will be used as the working definition of self-deception in this chapter. To evaluate its utility in the context of test responses, we must review the empirical work.

Assessment of Self-Deception and Impression Management

A wide array of methods have been applied to the assessment of individual differences in SDR. For instance, several researchers developed instruments on a rational basis: they wrote questions that biased respondents should answer in a predictable way e.g., the Marlowe-Crowne scale (Crowne & Marlowe, 1964), the Self- and Other-Deception Questionnaires (Sackeim & Gur, 1978), and the MMPI Lie scale (Hathaway & McKinley, 1943). Other instruments were developed by comparing the responses under "look-good" instructions to responses under standard conditions. The best-differentiating items were included in the scale. Among such instruments are Wiggins' Sd scale (Wiggins, 1959) and Ruch's Honesty scale (Ruch, 1941). A third approach involves selecting statements which have extremely high (or extremely low) desirability values when rated by judges, e.g., Edwards' SD scale (Edwards, 1957). Finally, the most recent method involves comparing scores on a social desirability inventory under normal conditions with scores under bogus pipeline conditions (Millham & Kellogg, 1980).

Given the dramatically differing methodologies, it is not surprising that the resulting instruments often show minimal correlations with one another. We have known for some time that social desirability is multidimensional (Messick, 1960; Wiggins, 1966). It seems reasonable to suspect some systematic relation between the method of scale development and the nature of the resulting measure of desirable responding. For the most part, scale developers have not made a direct connection between their methodology and the construct they were attempting to measure. I will return to address this issue later. For the moment, I will try to partition the various SDR scales by the similarity of the concept to impression management or to self-deception.

Impression Management. The vast majority of instruments developed to assess individual differences in SDR seem to be aimed at impression management. The definitions typically included the term "lying," – the conscious, purposeful deception of others. Perhaps the first such instrument was Ruch's (1941) Honesty scale. Others include the MMPI Lie scale (Hathaway & McKinley, 1943), the Eysenck Personality Inventory Lie scale (Eysenck & Eysenck, 1964), the Faking scale for 16PF (Winder, O'Dell, & Karson, 1975), the Positive Malingering (Mp) scale (Cofer, Chance, & Judson, 1949), Cattell's (1965) Unwilling to Admit Frailties scale (MI 219), Sackeim and Gur's (1978) Other-Deception Questionnaire, Ling's Lie scale (Amelang & Bartussek, 1970) and the Jackson-Messick Defensiveness scale (Kusyszyn & Jackson, 1968).

Discussions of such constructs focused on the respondent's conscious objective of fooling the test administrator. The respondent's behavior was assumed to be instrumental, aimed at winning a new job, or impressing an experimenter or teacher whose good graces were worthy of wooing. A smaller number of these instruments have been developed to measure faking bad or malingering (Winder et al., 1975).

Other measures were aimed at impression management as a goal in itself. The high scorer's behavior is not instrumental to some other purpose but is directed at getting the target to like them as a nice, upright, healthy person. These include Crowne and Marlowe's (1964) Need for Approval measure and Snyder's (1974) Self-Monitoring scale.

Self-Deception. This set of measures have in common a different concept of SDR – a less conscious attempt to look good to oneself. The respondent's motivation for the positive bias is assumed to be the protection of self-beliefs, including maintenance of self-esteem.

The first known attempt to measure self-deception was described by Frenkel-Brunswik in 1939. She compared the self-reports of 40 students in a graduate class with the ratings of four judges who knew them well. The self-deceptive tendency of each student was indexed in a variety of ways, e.g., the number of contradictions between the subjects' and the judges' reports of everyday behavior. Evidence was reported for the following individual differences in self-deception: (a) Distortion of negative traits into positive ones; (b) omission of major traits in free descriptions; (c) justification of defects; and (d) minimizing the importance of defects. These tendencies were generally found to co-occur in the same individuals.

In her discussion, Frenkel-Brunswik makes a distinction between sincere and insincere self-reports. Unfortunately, her procedure of directly soliciting self-reports is likely to have encouraged some degree of impression management. Consequently, all the intriguing correlates of her self-deception measures are tainted by the confounding of self-deception with impression management.

About the same time, the developers of the MMPI were assembling the validity scales designed to pick up individuals with systematic tendencies to bias or contaminate responses. The authors felt that the Lie scale (Hathaway & McKinley, 1943) was effective in detecting extreme, conscious tendencies to fake good. This was later replaced by the K scale "to detect the more common and often unconscious varieties of defensiveness" (Meehl & Hathaway, 1946, p. 561). Interestingly, the authors warned that the instrument "was not assumed to be measuring anything which in itself is of psychiatric significance" (p. 544). The scale was developed empirically by selecting items which best distinguished between subjects diagnosed as abnormal but who had normal profiles and normal subjects. Subsequent studies of the K scale confirmed that it was distinct from the Lie scale but failed to clarify its conceptual meaning (e.g., Gynther & Brilliant, 1968; Heilbrun, 1964; Palmer, 1970).

Cattell and coworkers developed a series of motivation distortion scales (Cattell, 1965; Cattell, Horn, Sweney, & Radcliffe, 1964; Schanberger, 1967) to assess the biasing effects of motivation on self-reports. One scale is said to measure autism – the tendency to perceive reality as one wishes, in a way that makes one comfortable. The relation of this construct to self-deception becomes unclear in light of Cattell's (1965) comments that autism is a mostly conscious form of self-enhancement and that it is equivalent to an eccentric, nonpractical style of thinking (p. 367).

Jackson and Messick (e.g., Kusyszyn & Jackson, 1968) developed two measures of SDR: (a) The Defensiveness scale assessing deliberate dissimulation and (b) the Desirability scale assessing a bias in self-regard. Given their interest in these issues it is surprising that they have not reported any psychometric or validity studies on these scales.

The most explicit assault on measuring self-deception was directed by Sackeim and Gur (Gur & Sackeim, 1979; Sackeim, 1983; Sackeim & Gur, 1978, 1979). They developed the Self-Deception Questionnaire (SDQ) by writing 20 questions about threatening thoughts and feelings e.g., "Have you ever felt hatred toward any of your parents?" and "Have you ever wanted to rape or be raped by someone?." Most of the questions have a psychoanalytic flavor: The assumption is that everyone experiences such sexual and aggressive impulses, but some people deny to themselves that such feelings have occurred. A critical feature of these questions is that no one but the respondent could possibly confirm the truth or falsehood of the response. The events in question are entirely intrapsychic and unavailable to outside observers. Thus, any bias observed under fully anonymous conditions must be honestly held by the respondent. In contrast, Sackeim and Gur's Other-Deception Questionnaire contained questions about undesirable *overt* behaviors which an individual would find difficult to deny to himself.

Another feature of the SDQ is worth noting. The respondent answers by marking a seven-point Likert scale anchored by "Not at all" (=1) to "Very much so" (=7). The scoring, however, is dichotomous. A point is awarded for self-deception only for extreme denial of the threatening thought, that is, a response of "1" or "2." Thus the SDQ score indexes a systematic *exaggeration* in denying threatening thoughts and feelings.

Most of the research on the SDQ has used the original 20 items – rationally devised but not statistically refined. Moreover, the original keying was negative for all items, thus confusing self-deception scores with acquiescence. A recent revision has rectified these problems with the SDQ and ODQ in a new instrument called the Balanced Inventory of Desirable Responding (BIDR). Both scales now have a balanced key, and items with low part-whole correlations have been replaced (Paulhus, 1984a).

The construct validity of the SDQ has been supported in a series of experimental and correlational studies (Gur & Sackeim, 1979; Paulhus, 1982, 1984; Sackeim, 1983; Sackeim & Gur, 1978, 1979). For instance, Gur and Sackeim (1979) investigated subjects' ability to recognize their own voice on a tape recording containing several voices speaking the same phrase. On some trials subjects would deny hearing their voice although psychophysiological measures indicated that they were aware that the voice was theirs. These false denials were interpreted as instances of self-deception. The rate of false denials was positively related to scores on the SDQ. Thus experimentally induced instances of self-deception were predictable from scores on the self-report measure. In sum, the SDQ is clearly the most clearly conceptualized and well-validated measure of self-deception currently available.

The Empirical Relation of Self-Deception to Impression Management

The preceding partitioning of self-deception and impression management scales was based on the theoretical rationales provided by the various scale developers. That is, the scales discussed under the rubric "impression management" were conceived to measure similar constructs and likewise for those discussed under "self-deception." Factor analytic studies have supported this conceptual partitioning with some notable exceptions.

Only a handful of studies have explored the underlying structure of SDR measures (Edwards & Walsh, 1964; Liberty, Lunneborg, & Atkinson, 1964; Jackson & Messick, 1962; Wiggins, 1964). In one such study, Wiggins (1964) uncovered one SDR factor (alpha) which included the Edwards SD scale and the MMPI K scale; a second SDR factor (gamma) included the MMPI Lie scale and the positive malingering scale. These results have two major implications. First, social desirability scales do not converge on one underlying construct but diverge into two factors which are consistent with the conceptual partitioning into self-deception and impression management presented above. The second implication is that Edwards' SD scale is associated with the self-deception cluster. Several other studies have replicated these findings (e.g., Edwards & Walsh, 1964; Jackson & Messick, 1962; Liberty et al., 1964; Paulhus, 1984a).

In 1965, Damarin and Messick reviewed this literature and spelled out a two-factor theory of SDR. This paper contained the first clear-cut argument for distinguishing available measures on the basis of conscious and unconscious biases in self-regard. The former was labeled "propagandistic bias," that is, a purposive, systematic distortion aimed at a specific audience. The second was labeled "autistic bias," the tendency to distort responses to be consistent with self-attitudes.

I would argue that most compelling evidence for the validity of the two-factor model comes from the three studies I recently reported (Paulhus, 1984a). Study 1 was an exploratory factor analysis of the traditional social desirability scales along with Sackeim and Gur's (1978) Self-Deception Questionnaire (SDQ) and Other-Deception Questionnaire (ODQ). The result are displayed

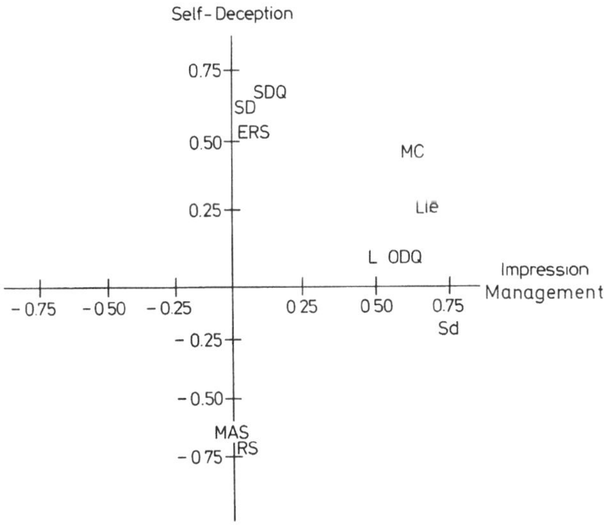

Fig. 1. Loadings of measures of desirable responding. *L* EPI Lie scale, *Lie* MMPI Lie scale, *SDQ* Self-Deception Questionnaire, *ODQ* Other-Deception Questionnaire, *MC* Marlowe-Crowne scale, *SD* Edwards social desirability scale, *Sd* Wiggins social desirability scale, *MAS* Taylor's Manifest Anxiety Scale, *RS* Byrne's Repression-Sensitization scale, *ERS* Block's Ego-Resiliency scale

in Fig. 1. Also included in Fig. 1 are several measures factor analyzed in a separate study (Paulhus, 1983).

As in previous studies, the Edwards SD scale, Block's ERS, and Byrne's R-S scale mark the alpha factor, and the Wiggins Sd scale marks the gamma factor. Moreover, the SDQ and ODQ loadings strongly support the two-factor model: The SDQ is the best marker of alpha, supporting its interpretation as self-deception. The ODQ is the best marker of gamma, supporting the interpretation as impression management. Note that the Marlowe-Crowne scale loads highly on both factors, indicating that its original designation as a lie scale was overly simplistic.

Study 2 in Paulhus (1984a) used confirmatory factor analyses to show the superiority of this two-factor model over a competing model proposed by Millham (1974). Study 3 provided experimental support for the interpretation of alpha and gamma as self-deception and impression management. Respondents completed the battery of desirability measures under one of two conditions, (a) *anonymous,* in a large group testing situation where no names were requested; or (b) *public,* in small groups where the experimenters requested names and indicated that they would check the answers. Results indicated that responses to measures loading high on the impression management factor were significantly more socially desirable in the public condition than in the anonymous condition. In comparison, the scales marking the self-deception factor did not change as much. Thus, impression management scales like ODQ and Sd are more responsive to situational changes in the demand for a positive self-presentation.

Some Resolutions

Self-Deception and Adjustment

We are now in a better position to address one of the questions lingering from the controversy about interpreting the major MMPI factors. MMPI researchers held that the first factor represented overall mental health or adjustment as evidenced by various external criteria of adjustment (Block, 1965; Heilbrun, 1964; Welsh, 1956). Critics emphasized the fact that the first factor was highly correlated with measures of SDR, especially the Edwards SD scale (Jackson & Messick, 1962; Edwards, 1957).

A rather simple postulate reconciles these positions: Well-adjusted individuals have a positively biased view of themselves. This bias will be manifested in tendencies to (a) ignore minor criticisms, (b) discount failures, (c) avoid negative thoughts, and (d) have a high expectancy of success in new endeavors. In contrast, the anxious or depressed individual accepts criticism and failures as being informative of his abilities and character. This comparison corresponds to Byrne's (1964) distinction between the repressor and the sensitizer. More recently, several writers have given arguments for the adaptive value of positive self-illusions (Lazarus, 1983; Sackeim, 1983; Taylor, 1983). This postulate is certainly disturbing, given the traditional view that insight into one's motivation and mistakes is the key to psychological health (e.g., Gough, 1965; Murphy, 1975; Rogers, 1959).

Nonetheless an array of empirical findings supports this postulate. A recent series of correlational studies certainly favors this view. The SDQ is highly negatively correlated with standard measures of psychopathology, including Beck's Depression Inventory (Roth & Ingram, 1985; Sackeim, 1983) and the Manifest Anxiety Scale (D. L. Paulhus, 1983, Correlates of self-deception, unpublished data). The SDQ is positively correlated with measures of adjustment including Rosenberg's Self-Esteem scale and Block's Ego-Resiliency Scale (D. L. Paulhus, 1983, Correlates of self-deception, unpublished data).

Further support derives from new findings in the clinical and social psychology literature. Consider first the provocative new work on "depressive realism": A growing body of research suggests that depressed individuals are *less* susceptible than nondepressed to a number of biases which distort reality in a self-serving fashion (e.g., Alloy & Abramson, 1979; Golin, Terrell, & Johnson, 1977; Nelson & Craighead, 1977). For example, Lewinsohn, Mischel, Chaplain, and Barton (1980) had subjects meet with a confederate who evaluated them. When asked to guess how well they had done, nondepressed subjects overestimated the interviewer's evaluation of them. Depressed subjects, however, were significantly more accurate in guessing the interviewers' ratings.

Other normal biases which are less evident in depressives include the false-consensus effect (Tabachnik, Crocker, & Alloy, 1983), the illusion of control (Alloy & Abramson, 1979; Golin et al., 1977), and defensive attributions (Feather, 1983; Kuiper, 1978). A wide range of other biases have been confirmed in normals, e.g., beneffectance, the hindsight bias, the optimism bias (Greenwald, 1980; Nisbett & Ross, 1980).

It is difficult to argue in light of all this evidence that insight is necessarily the sign of a healthy individual. On the contrary, a certain tendency toward self-deception may be a prerequisite to good adjustment. A resilient set of defenses would be of great advantage in surviving the slings and arrows of daily fortune. Clearly there are limits to the adaptive value of self-deception. If the self does not accommodate to major irrefutable threats, it risks a more serious psychological breakdown in the extreme. Moreover, there is evidence that individuals prone to self-deception also deny *physical* symptoms (Linden, Paulhus, & Dobson, in press). The ignoring of a temporary stomach ache may permit one to carry on with work or recreation. If, however, the stomach ache is the sign of a developing ulcer, ignoring it is dangerous because it precludes active coping behavior (Lazarus, 1983; Breznitz, 1983). When behavioral coping is fruitless, positive illusions can at least maintain the psychological health of the patient (Taylor, 1983).

If the reader is now convinced that self-deception is characteristic of the happy, well-adjusted person, the controversy over the MMPI alpha factor may be honorably settled. Self-deception contributes to ego-resiliency, self-esteem, and self-confidence, while warding off anxiety and depression. In addition, because of an optimistic, positivistic bias, the self-deceiver tends to say good things about himself (sometimes exaggeratedly so) on social desirability scales like the Edwards SD scale. In sum, then, the MMPI alpha factor is tapping a positive self-bias which facilitates self-confidence and well-being.

Control of Socially Desirable Responding

The considerations in the previous section raise serious questions about the traditional recommendations for controlling social desirability in self-reports (see APA Standards for Educational and Psychological Tests). When conceived as a nuisance variable, socially desirable responding was an appropriate target for purging. When content and stylistic variance are one and the same, the bathwater is jettisoned only at risk to the baby. Indeed, several studies have shown that, once SDR has been controlled with the Edwards or Marlowe-Crowne scales, measures related to the alpha factor (e.g., ego-resiliency, anxiety) lose predictive power (Borkenau & Amelang, 1985; Edwards, 1970; McCrae & Costa, 1983). Since adjustment is confounded with the self-deception component of SDR, the latter should never be controlled in assessments of adjustment e.g., self-esteem, ego-resiliency, anxiety, and depression.

The tendency toward an honestly held positive self-bias may underlie other personality constructs besides adjustment. For example, measures of perceived control (Paulhus, 1983; Rotter, 1966) concern the expectancy of control over one's reinforcements. Those scoring as Internals relative to Externals have an over-optimistic expectancy of success (e.g., Phares & Lamiell, 1974), show more dissonance reduction (McCann, Zanna, & Higgins, 1980), and forget negative information (Phares et al., 1968). Other constructs entailing a positive bias include social dominance (Wiggins, 1979), hopelessness (Beck et al., 1974), and achievement motivation (Weiner, 1978). The control of self-deception in measuring any of these constructs will be hazardous to predictive validity.

On the other hand, impression management remains a contaminant in interpreting self-reports. The problem does not arise so much in the anonymous group-test situations typical in scale development, but in typical applications in laboratory studies, clinical settings, and personnel selection, where anonymity is impossible (Zerbe & Paulhus, 1984): when self-report inventories are administered, an individual who consciously fakes good will score high on those content measures with clear-cut desirability implications. The same individual should also score high on an accompanying IM scale. One could simply disregard protocols where the IM score exceeded a certain level (Dahlstrom & Welsh, 1960). More sophisticated approaches will be discusses in the next section.

Specific Techniques. In an earlier paper I discussed three categories of techniques for controlling SDR (Paulhus, 1981). Rational techniques are features built into a self-report instrument to preclude desirable responding, e.g., forced choice between options balanced on desirability. Covariate techniques involve statistically correcting an observed relation by partialing out the variance due to SDR e.g., partial correlation, regression. Factor analytic controls involve the removal of SDR variance from an item correlation matrix before the construction of content scales, e.g., target rotation, factor deletion. All these techniques now require a second look, given the measurable separation of self-deception and impression management.

The covariate and factor techniques can be dealt with in straightforward fashion. If one wished to correct for both types of SDR, one would control the variance due to each variable. In general, this would require inclusion of both self-deception and impression management scales in the inventory.

The rational techniques raise more abstruse problems. Consider the technique of equating options for social desirability in a forced-choice format. This task should be difficult to the extent that the content dimension is intrinsically confounded with SDR. Attempting to equate options on an anxiety scale, for instance, would be difficult and ultimately fruitless. Indeed, one risks creating strange options which are unbalanced on a host of unknown variables (Meehl, 1970). In general, the forced-choice format is contraindicated for control of self-deception.

The technique is still useful for controlling impression management. Recall that items asking about overt behaviors were minimally subject to self-deception. Such behavioral reports would still be subject to impression management unless the options were equated for desirability.

Another rational technique involves the use of statements with neutral desirability. If neither response is more socially desirable than the other, it is assumed the respondent will focus on the item content. Again, it is difficult to write neutral items to tap adjustment, although Block (1965) had some success. Such neutral items would be useful in controlling self-deception, because the latter is said to be elicited only by extreme threats. In contrast, items with extremely high or low desirability would provoke such a threat. Impression management may also be usefully controlled by asking about behaviors with neutral desirability value.

Finally, it bears repeating that self-deception is controlled by asking only about overt behaviors. A corollary is that constructs entailing self-deception will be difficult to assess with items about overt behavior.

New Directions

A Closer Look at Self-Deception

The time has come to consider a number of questions surrounding the claim that self-deception is being tapped by such measures as the SDQ and SD scales. First, how do we know that the socially desirable reports of high scorers (alphas) are not in fact accurate accounts of their good character? After all, there is substantial evidence that they are popular, well-adjusted people (Block, 1965; Heilbrun, 1964).

I agree that alphas are likely to be accurate in reporting a lack of anxiety and unhappy thoughts as probed by many items on the SD and R-S (Repression-Sensitization) scales. Furthermore, it seems reasonable that the self-confidence and self-liking addressed by other items should follow from lack of anxiety. What is harder to accept is the type of claim alphas make on the SDQ. They deny ever having sexual fantasies or hateful thoughts about their parents, enjoying their bowel movements, or feeling angry or guilty. (Recall that responses are counted as self-deceptive only if the denial is extreme.) Behavioral measures also corroborate the unrealistic degree of their positive bias. High scorers on the SDQ have been shown to deny hearing their own voice when physiological measures indicate they have heard it (Gur & Sackeim, 1979). They also exhibit the hindsight bias more than low scorers (Paulhus, 1983: Correlates of self-deception, unpublished data). Finally, one notable group scoring very low on the SDQ is depressives (Roth & Ingram, 1985; Sackeim & Gur, 1979). As documented earlier, depressives fail to show a variety of biases evident in nondepressives. In sum, my reading of the literature is that alphas are positively biased to such a degree that they often distort reality.

Nonetheless, a demonstration that alphas are unrealistically biased is not equivalent to demonstrating that they are deceiving themselves. It is equivalent if we define self-deception in the most general sense as an honest belief in a false characterization of the self. Hence we can argue that alphas are in a self-deceived *state* while withholding judgment on its origin. However, it may be preferable to restrict the term self-deception to the motivated unawareness of one of two conflicting cognitions. This usage is compatible with that of most concerned writers (Demos, 1960; Fingarette, 1969; Sackeim & Gur, 1978). As a complement, I will use the term *auto-illusion* to represent self-biases which result from cognitive or informational biases. Nisbett and Ross (1980) have detailed a number of cognitive biases involving nonmotivational mechanisms of information processing. Although nonmotivational, these biases result in a favorable self-image. Informational biases derive from social restrictions on availability of information. For instance, people avoid bearing bad news, including criticism, to others (Tesser & Rosen, 1974). This social convention should induce a biased self-view in most people.

The critical question now becomes whether alphas are characterized by self-deception or auto-illusions (or both). Self-deception in the pure sense has only been demonstrated in two studies (Gur & Sackeim, 1979; Sackeim, 1983). As detailed earlier, Gur and Sackeim asked subjects to pick out their own voices from a tape of several students reciting the same phrase. Psychophysiological records showed a relatively reliable response whenever the subject's own voice came on. At an oral level, however, subjects often denied hearing their voice. The authors considered the GSR (galvanic skin response) and oral reports to be indicators of separate cognitions which were sometimes in disagreement. Evidence that this separation of cognitions was motivated followed from an additional manipulation. Subjects who had just undergone a failure experience showed a higher rate of discrepancies (e.g., false denials) than those experiencing success. A similar study is reported by Sackeim (1983). Perhaps most importantly, individuals scoring high on the SDQ exhibited a higher rate of false denials.

Few would deny that this study is a creative and sophisticated investigation of a well-defined phenomenon. Nonetheless, its value in demonstrating self-deception is restricted in at least one important sense – the time-frame is rather short. The contradictory cognitions were simultaneously held for only the briefest time. Only while the individual's voice was being played (a 5-s duration) could the two conficting cognitions be simultaneously registered. There is no suggestion of any long-term storage of conflicting cognitions. This short duration is not consistent with the anecdotal examples of self-deception typically cited, e.g., a child with a love/hate attitude toward a parent. Admittedly, the study of such chronic cases would remove the research from the controlled conditions of the laboratory into the realm of case studies with questionable scientific and ethical status. I shall dub such cases *chronic* self-deception, in contrast to the *acute* instance demonstrated by Sackeim and Gur (cf. Paulhus, 1984b). Perhaps the SDQ taps a tendency toward acute rather than chronic self-deception, which may involve highly idiosyncratic concerns.

The notion of acute self-deception bears some resemblance to Byrne's (1964) construct of repressive style. The repressor is said to habitually avoid attending to negative thoughts and threatening information. The R-S scale (which correlates .50 with the SDQ) has an extensive research literature supporting its conception as a cognitive style. In contrast, the emphasis in self-deception is on its motivational basis. Virtually any behavior might be called upon to serve the needs of self-deception (Sackeim, 1983). Nonetheless, repressive style and acute self-deception are similar in providing mechanisms which respond to threat and induce a state of positive self-bias including freedom from anxiety. Such a bias would then be autonomous, being maintained by cognitive inertia until disconfirmed (McGuire, 1960; Ross, 1977; Tesser & Paulhus, 1976).

We can now return to the question of whether the alpha factor measures are tapping self-deception, auto-illusions, or simply the resulting sense of well-being. The last seems true of Edwards's SD, Byrne's R-S, and the anxiety scales. Their item content generally concerns the psychological comfort of being positively biased. There is no provocation of self-deception in responding to "I am happy most of the time" or "My hands and feet are usually warm enough." On the SDQ, however, the items are designed to elicit defensiveness. Consider the item, "Have you ever enjoyed your bowel movements?" The question is threatening even if the respondent had never given it much thought before (Butcher & Tellegen, 1966). Presumably few people could accurately deny they had ever enjoyed a bowel movement. Nonetheless, admitting it seems shameful, as if anything associated with feces could not honorably be considered pleasurable. Some respondents giving false denials may have considered the possibility before and now glibly report their previous negative conclusion as part of a chronic self-deception. Those who had not previously considered it would still find the idea offensive and deal with it using some self-defensive technique. Some form of self-deception is implicated, given that the truth is "yes" and the honest response is "no."

Given the high intercorrelations among the three types of measures, the alpha factor seems to simultaneously tap (a) adjustment, (b) auto-illusions, and (c) self-deception. We are left with an intriguing question that I will not try to answer here: Why should individuals with self-deceptive tendencies also tend to exhibit auto-illusions?

A Closer Look at Impression Management

Impression management is far from a unified concept. In this section I will describe three distinct usages of this appellation and consider the implications for assessment. Briefly the three usages are: (a) impression management as strategic simulation (e.g., Edwards, 1970; Jones & Pittman, 1982); (b) impression management as a motive (e.g., Crowne & Marlowe, 1964); and (c) impression management as a skill (e.g., Collins, Paulhus, & Graziano, 1983; Danheiser & Paulhus, 1981; Snyder, 1974).

Among the writers who see impression management as strategic, the most extreme group holds that each situation has a uniquely situated identity which is the culturally acknowledged best image to portray that situation (Alexander & Knight, 1971). Jones and Pittman (1982) have narrowed a taxonomy of those who use impression management by distinguishing five major types: (a) The ingratiator, who seeks to appear likable; (b) the intimidator, who seeks to appear threatening; (c) the self-promoter, who seeks to appear competent; (d) the supplicant, who seeks to appear helpless; and (e) the exemplifier, who seeks to appear virtuous. While these types may not be exhaustive, they do cover the four poles of the interpersonal circumplex which is said to circumscribe the domain of interpersonal behavior (Leary, 1957; Wiggins, 1979). The ingratiator and the intimidator are impression managing on the nurturance-hostility dimension; the self-promoter and the supplicant are impression managing on the dominance-submission dimension.

Jones and Pittman see all five types of impression management as *strategic*. The actor engages the role for its instrumental value in increasing his power over a particular target. Clearly impression management covers far more ground. To begin with, it is necessary to distinguish "acquisitive" self-presentation from "defensive" self-presentation (Arkin, 1981; Lennox & Wolfe, 1984). In fact, such impression management behaviors are often engaged in as ends in themselves, i.e., motives. The ingratiator sometimes wants nothing more than the affection of his target: such approval motivation has been described in considerable detail by Crowne and Marlowe (1964) and more recently by Millham and Jacobson (1978). The self-promoter is often motivated to achieve respect and status among his peers, not by the opportunities for instrumental gain. Similarly, intimidation, supplication, and exemplification have intrinsic motivational value in some of the people some of the time. For a detailed review of the range of motives represented in the circumplex see Wiggins and Broughton (in press).

The distinction between impression management as strategic or motivational has direct implications for assessment. The gamma factor of SDR involves measures which were developed in terms of strategic dissimulation. High scorers were considered to be purposely faking good to win a job, impress an experimenter, etc. By this view, the same respondents would presumably fake bad if the situation called for it (Meehl & Hathaway, 1946, p. 539; cf. Winder et al., 1975). In fact, gammas would presumably tend to fake any profile which they perceive to maximize their strategic outcomes in that specific context. This description is reminiscent of the Machiavellian personality (Christie & Geis, 1979), particularly the Tactics factor. There should be a high correlation between Mach Tactics and lie scales in situations where looking good is advantageous. As far as I know, these propositions remain untested.

Let us now consider the measurement of impression management as a motive. Although the gamma factor measures were typically developed as lie scales, there is some evidence that they are tapping a motivation to be liked. Indeed, the Marlowe-Crowne scale was originally conceived as a lie scale (Crowne & Marlowe, 1964). Detailed research on the behavior of high (as opposed to low) scorers indicated a consistent personality syndrome – a strong need for approval (Crowne & Marlowe, 1964). However, this syndrome may result from the unique conjoint nature of the Marlowe-Crowne scale: it combines impression management and self-deception (Paulhus, 1984a). Thus, need for approval may be an emergent personality *type* rather than a simple trait. That is, the unique character of this individual may emerge from a willingness to fool others combined with lack of self-insight.

Nonetheless, no known research has examined the personality of individuals scoring high on gamma factor scales. If these scales, like the Marlowe-Crowne scale, are tapping approval motivation rather than dissimulation, we should see patterns of conformity and approval-seeking even where there is no instrumental advantage to such behavior.

As noted earlier, several other common types of impression management might be enacted for their intrinsic benefits rather than instrumental to some external payoff. Thus, the self-promoter may gain self-esteem by selling himself to others. For instance, there is evidence that a positive self-presentation tends to become internalized if no contrary information is available (Gergen, 1965; Jones, Gergen, & Davis, 1962; Jones & Wortman, 1973). Similarly, the portrayal of hostility and submission may be intrinsically rewarding to some people some of the time.

Finally, let us consider impression management as a skill. Social skills as a whole cover a wide variety of abilities, styles, and temperament, along with moderating situations and attributes, e.g., sex, age, attractiveness (Hogan &

Briggs, 1983). Snyder (1974) has emphasized the importance of one trait which he calls self-monitoring. As originally defined, the high self-monitor is one "who out of a concern for social appropriateness, is particularly sensitive to the expression and self-presentation of others in social situations and uses these cues as guidelines for monitoring his own self-presentation" (p. 528). Although a motivation is implied in "concern for social appropriateness," Snyder's theoretical emphasis and research has been on the ability component. Factor analyses have confirmed that social skill is one component of the measure (Briggs, Cheek, & Buss, 1980). There is now evidence that self-monitors can communicate emotions accurately on command (Snyder, 1974), can control their behavior to impress others (Arkin, Gabrenya, Appelman, & Cochrane, 1979; Shaffer, Smith, & Tomarelli, 1983), can detect deception in others (Krauss, Geller, & Olson, 1976), detect ingratiation in others (Jones & Baumeister, 1976), and generally make accurate predictions about their social environment (Berscheid, Graziano, Monson, & Dermer, 1976).

It is important to note that the self-monitoring scale shows little correlation with the Marlowe-Crowne scale measuring need for approval (Danheiser & Paulhus, 1981; Snyder, 1974). Thus skill and motivation in impression management appear to be independent. This independence has provoked some recent research examining the behavior of the various combinations of high and low skill and motivation. For instance, Danheiser and Paulhus (1981) found that the most popular members of a continuing group were those high in skill and high in motivation. The least popular were those high in motivation but low in skill. Like the proverbial schlemiel, they wanted friends desperately but their inept overtures offended others. This "schlemiel effect" was replicated in a subsequent laboratory study (Collins, Paulhus, & Graziano, 1983).

This research illustrates the value of measuring different levels of impression management separately. By studying such combinations of skill, motivation and tactics, we will surely come closer to understanding the complexities of social interactions. Such understanding will receive a significant boost when the nature of the gamma factor is clarified.

Conclusions

The thrust of this chapter has been to highlight the distinction between self-deception and impression management. I began by tracing the distinction to a few seminal papers in the philosophical and psychological literature. The application of this distinction to the old social desirability controversy provided some rather elegant resolutions. I concluded that the major dimension of adjustment (the first factor of the MMPI) is intrinsically intertwined with a self-deceptive bias in self-regard. Several other central dimensions of personality also involve a component of self-deception. Consequently, any attempt to control self-deception in measuring these constructs will undermine predictive power. On the other hand, impression management is a contaminating factor and should generally be controlled during both the development and the administration of tests.

A detailed analysis of self-deception indicated a need to distinguish self-deception (the motivated unawareness of one of two conflicting cognitions) from auto-illusions (a self-bias resulting from cognitive or informational biases). In addition, I made a distinction between chronic self-deception (where the conflicting cognitions remain available in memory over an extended period) and acute self-deception, where the conflicting cognitions are simultaneously available only for a brief period.

Finally, an in-depth analysis indicated the potential for assessment of impression management as a tactic, as a motive, and as a skill. The joint characterization on more than one of these components has vast potential for improving prediction.

My hope is that this paper has answered some lingering questions and framed some new questions in a testable fashion. It is now clear that the distinction between self-deception and impression management offers theoretical and methodological benefits. Self-deception, in particular, appears to play a theoretical role in a number of personality constructs. The ability to measure self-deception and impression management separately also has important methodological benefits. These center on improved predictive power based on a clearer understanding of when and how to control socially desirable responding.

Acknowledgements. I would like to thank Bill Graziano, Abe Tesser, and Jerry Wiggins for comments on an earlier draft of this paper.

References

Alexander, C.N., & Knight, G.W. (1971). Situated identities and social psychological experimentation. *Sociometry, 34*, 65–82.

Alloy, L.B., & Abramson, L.Y. (1979). Judgment of contingency in depressed and nondepressed students: Sadder but wiser? *Journal of Experimental Psychology: General, 108, 4*, 441–485.

Amelang, M., & Bartussek, D. (1970). Untersuchungen zur Validität einer neuen Lügenskala (An investigation of the validity of a new lie-scale). *Diagnostica, 16*, 103–122.

Arkin, R.M. (1981). Self-presentation styles. In Tedeschi, J.T. (Ed.), *Impression management theory and social psychological research.* New York: Academic.

Arkin, R.M., Gabrenya, W.K., Appelman, A.S., & Cochrane, S.T. (1979). Self-presentation, self-monitoring, and the self-serving bias in causal attributions. *Personality and Social Psychology Bulletin, 5*, 73–76.

Bach, K. (1981). An analysis of self-deception. *Philosophy and Phenomenological Research, 41*, 351–370.

Baumeister, R.F. (1982). A self-presentational view of social phenomena. *Psychological Bulletin, 91*, 3–26.

Beck, A., Weissman, A., Lester, D., & Trexler, L. (1974). The measurement of pessimism: The Hopelessness scale. *Journal of Consulting and Clinical Psychology, 42*, 861–865.

Bernreuter, R.G. (1933). Validity of the personality inventory. *Personality Journal, 11*, 383–386.

Berscheid, E., Graziano, W.G., Monson, T., & Dermer, M. (1976). Outcome dependency: Attention, attribution and attraction. *Journal of Personality and Social Psychology, 34*, 978–989.

Block, J. (1965). *The challenge of response sets.* New York: Appleton-Century-Crofts.

Borkenau, P., & Amelang, M. (1985). The control of social desirability in personality inventories: A study using the principal-factor technique. *Journal of Research in Personality, 19*, 44–53.

Breznitz, S. (Ed.). (1983). *The denial of stress.* New York: International Universities Press.

Briggs, S.R., Cheek, J., & Buss, A.H. (1980). An analysis of the self-monitoring scale. *Journal of Personality and Social Psychology, 38*, 679–686.

Butcher, J.N., & Tellegen, A. (1966). Objections to MMPI items. *Journal of Consulting Psychology, 30*, 527–534.

Byrne, D. (1964). Repression-sensitization as a dimension of personality. In Maher, B. (Ed.), *Progress in experimental personality research* (Vol. 1). New York: Academic.

Cattell, R.B. (1965). *The scientific analysis of personality*. Harmondsworth: Penguin.

Cattell, R.B., Horn, J.L., Sweney, A.B., & Radcliffe, J.A. (1964). *The motivation analysis test, MAT.* Champaign: Institute of Personality and Ability Testing.

Cheek, J., & Hogan, R. (1984). Self-concepts, self-presentations and moral judgments. In Suls, J. & Greenwald, A. (Eds.), *Psychological perspectives on the self* (Vol. 2). Hillsdale: Erlbaum.

Christie, R., & Geis, F.L. (1970). *Studies in Machiavellianism.* New York: Academic.

Cofer, C.N., Chance, J., & Judson, A.J. (1949). A study of malingering on the MMPI. *Journal of Psychology, 27*, 491–499.

Collins, J.E., Paulhus, D.L., & Graziano, W.G. (1983, August). Is self-monitoring a skill or a motive? *Meeting of the American Psychological Association,* Anaheim.

Crowne, D.P., & Marlowe, D. (1964). *The approval motive: Studies in evaluative dependence.* New York: Wiley.

Dahlstrom, W.G., & Welsh, G.S. (1960). *An MMPI handbook.* Minneapolis: University of Minnesota Press.

Damarin, F., & Messick, S. (1965). *Response styles as personality variables: A theoretical integration of mutivariate research* (Research Bulletin 65-10). Princeton: Educational Testing Service.
Danheiser, P., & Paulhus, D.L. (1981, March). Self-monitoring and need for approval as impression management styles: Skill versus need. *Meeting of the Southeastern Psychological Association,* Atlanta.
Demos, R. (1960). Lying to oneself. *Journal of Philosophy, 57,* 588–595.
Edwards, A.L. (1957). *The social desirability variable in personality assessment and research.* New York: Dryden.
Edwards, A.L. (1970). *The measurement of personality traits by scales and inventories.* New York: Holt, Rinehart & Winston.
Edwards, A.L., & Walsh, J.A. (1964). Response sets in standard and experimental personality scales. *American Educational Research Journal, 1,* 52–61.
Ellis, A. (1946). The validity of personality questionnaires. *Psychological Bulletin, 43,* 385–440.
Eysenck, H.J., & Eysenck, S.B.G. (1964). *The manual of Eysenck Personality Inventory.* London: University of London Press.
Feather, N.T. (1983). Some correlates of attributional style: Depressive symptoms, self-esteem, and Protestant Ethic values. *Personality and Social Psychology Bulletin, 9,* 125–135.
Fingarette, H. (1969). *Self-deception.* New York: Humanities.
Frenkel-Brunswik, E. (1939). Mechanisms of self-deception. *Journal of Social Psychology, 10,* 409–420.
Gergen, K.J. (1965). Interaction goals and personalistic feedback as factors affecting the presentation of self. *Journal of Personality and Social Psychology, 1,* 413–424.
Golin, S., Terrell, F., & Johnson, B. (1977). Depression and the illusion of control. *Journal of Abnormal Psychology, 86,* 440–442.
Gough, H.G. (1965). A validational study of the Chapin Social Insight Test. *Psychological Reports, 17,* 355–368.
Greenwald, A.G. (1980). The totalitarian ego: Fabrication and revision of personal history. *American Psychologist, 35,* 603-618.
Greenwald, A.G. (1982). Is anyone in charge? Personalysis versus the principle of personal unity. In Suls, J. (Ed.), *Psychological perspectives on the self* (Vol. 1). Hillsdale: Erlbaum.
Gur, R.C., & Sackeim, H.A. (1979). Self-deception: A concept in search of a phenomenon. *Journal of Personality and Social Psychology, 37,* 147–169.
Gynther, M.D., & Brilliant, P.J. (1968). The MMPI K^+ profile: A reexamination. *Journal of Consulting and Clinical Psychology, 32,* 616–617.
Hathaway, S.R., & McKinley, J.C. (1943). *Manual for the Minnesota Multiphasic Personality Inventory.* New York: Psychological Corporation.
Heilbrun, A.B. (1964). Social learning theory, social desirability and the MMPI. *Psychological Bulletin, 61,* 377–387.
Hilgard, E.R. (1949). Human motives and the concepts of self. *American Psychologist, 4,* 374–382.
Hogan, R. (1983). A socioanalytic theory of personality: In Page, M.M. (Ed.), *Nebraska symposium on motivation, 1982.* Lincoln: University of Nebraska Press.
Hogan, R., & Briggs, S. (1983). Noncognitive measures of social intelligence. *Meeting of the American Psychological Association,* Anaheim.
Jackson, D.N., & Messick, S. (1962). Response styles and the assessment of psychopathology. In Messick, S., & Ross, J. (Eds.), *Measurement in personality and cognition.* New York: Wiley.

Jones, E.E., & Baumeister, R.F. (1976) The self-monitor looks at the ingratiator. *Journal of Personality, 44*, 541–559.

Jones, E.E., & Pittman, T.S. (1982). Toward a general theory of strategic self-presentation. In Suls, J. (Ed.), *Psychological perspectives on the self* (Vol. 1). Hillsdale: Erlbaum.

Jones, E.E., & Wortman, C. (1973). *Ingratiation: An attributional approach.* Morriston, N.J.: General Learning Press.

Jones, E.E., Gergen, K.J., & Davis, K.E. (1962). Some determinants of reactions to being approved or disapproved as a person. *Psychological Monographs, 76* (2, Whole No. 521).

Kaufmann, W. (1956). *Existentialism from Dostoevsky to Sartre.* Cleveland: World Publishing.

Kiecolt-Glaser, J., & Murray, J.A. (1980). Social desirability bias in self-monitoring data. *Journal of Behavioral Assessment, 2*, 239–247.

Kierkegaard, S. (1959). *Either/Or* (Vol. 2) (W. Lowrie, Trans.). New York: Anchor. (Original work published 1843).

Krauss, R., Geller, V., & Olson, C. (1976). Modalities and cues in the detection of deception. *Meeting of the American Psychological Association,* Washington.

Kuiper, N.A. (1978). Depression and causal attributions for success and failure. *Journal of Personality and Social Psychology, 36*, 236–246.

Kusyszyn, I., & Jackson, D.N. (1968). A multimethod factor analytic appraisal of endorsement and judgment methods in personality assessment. *Educational and Psychological Measurement, 28*, 1047–1061.

Lazarus, R.S. (1983). Costs and benefits of denial. In Breznitz, S. (Ed.), *The denial of stress.* New York: International Universities.

Leary, T. (1957). *Interpersonal diagnosis of personality.* New York: Ronald Press.

Lennox, R., & Wolfe, R. (1984). Revision of the Self-Monitoring Scale. *Journal of Personality and Social Psychology, 46*, 1349–1364.

Lewinsohn, P.M., Mischel, W., Chaplain, W., & Barton, R. (1980). Social competence and depression: The role of illusory self-perceptions? *Journal of Abnormal Psychology, 89*, 203–212.

Liberty, P.G., Lunneborg, C.E., & Atkinson, G.C. (1964). Perceptual defense, dissimulation, and response styles. *Journal of Consulting Psychology, 28*, 529–537.

Linden, W., Paulhus, D.L., & Dobson, K.E. (in press). The effect of response styles on the report of psychological and somatic distress. *Journal of Consulting and Clinical Psychology.*

Linehan, M.M., & Nielsen, S.L. (1981). Assessment of suicidal ideation and parasuicide: Hopelessness and social desirability. *Journal of Consulting and Clinical Psychology, 49*, 773–775.

Lockard, J.S., & Paulhus, D.L. (in press). *Self-deception: An adaptive mechanism?* New York: Prentice-Hall.

McCann, C.D., Zanna, M.P., & Higgins, E.T. (1980). Attitude change following induced compliance: An individual difference perspective. *Meeting of the Canadian Psychological Association,* Calgary, June 1980.

McCrae, R.R., & Costa, P.T. (1983). Social desirability scales: More substance than style. *Journal of Consulting and Clinical Psychology, 51*, 882–888.

McGuire, W.J. (1960). A syllogistic analysis of cognitive relationships. In Rosenberg, M.J., Hovland, E.I., McGuire, W.J., Abelson, R.P., & Brehm, J.W. (Eds.), *Attitude organization and change.* New Haven: Yale University Press.

Meehl, P. (1970). Nuisance variables and the ex post facto design. In Radner, M., & Winokur, S. (Eds.), *Minnesota studies in the philosophy of science* (Vol. 4). Minneapolis: University of Minnesota Press.

Meehl, P.E., & Hathaway, S.R. (1946). The K-factor as a suppressor variable in the MMPI. *Journal of Applied Psychology, 30*, 525–564.

Messick, S. (1960). Dimensions of social desirability. *Journal of Consulting Psychology, 24*, 279–287.

Millham, J. (1974). Two components of need for approval score and their relationship to cheating following success and failure. *Journal of Research in Personality, 8*, 378–392.

Millham, J., & Jacobson, L.I. (1978). The need for approval. In London, H., & Exner, J.E. (Eds.), *Dimensions of personality*. New York: Wiley.

Millham, J., & Kellogg, R.W. (1980). Need for social approval: Impression management or self-deception? *Journal of Research in Personality, 14*, 445–457.

Mills, C., & Hogan, R. (1978). A role theoretical interpretation of personality scale item responses. *Journal of Personality, 46*, 778–785.

Mischel, T. (1974). Understanding neurotic behavior: From "Mechanism" to "Intentionality". In Mischel, T. (Ed.), *Understanding other persons* (pp. 216–259). Oxford: Blackwell.

Murphy, G. (1975). *Outgrowing self-deception*. New York: Basic Books.

Nelson, R.E., & Craighead, W.E. (1977). Selective recall of positive and negative feedback, self-control behaviors and depression. *Journal of Abnormal Psychology, 86*, 397–388.

Nisbett, R., & Ross, L. (1980). *Human inference: Strategies and shortcomings*. Englewood Cliffs: Prentice-Hall.

Palmer, W.H. (1970). *Actuarial MMPI Interpretation: A replication and extension*. Doctoral dissertation, University of Alabama, Birmingham, AL.

Paulhus, D.L. (1981). Control of social desirability in personality inventories: Principal-factor deletion. *Journal of Research in Personality, 15*, 383–388.

Paulhus, D.L. (1982). Individual differences, self-presentation, and cognitive dissonance: Their concurrent operation in forced compliance. *Journal of Personality and Social Psychology, 43*, 838–852.

Paulhus, D.L. (1983). Sphere-specific measures of perceived control. *Journal of Personality and Social Psychology, 44*, 1253–1265.

Paulhus, D.L. (1984a). Two-component models of socially desirable responding. *Journal of Personality and Social Psychology, 46*, 598–609.

Paulhus, D.L. (1984b). Self-deception: An information-processing model. *Meeting of the American Psychological Association*, Toronto.

Phares, E.J., & Lamiell, J.T. (1974). Relationship of internal-external control to defensive preferences. *Journal of Consulting and Clinical Psychology, 42*, 872–878.

Phares, E.J., Ritchie, D.E., & Davis, W.L. (1968). Internal-external control and reaction to threat. *Journal of Personality and Social Psychology, 10*, 402–405.

Rock, D.L. (1981). The confounding of two self-report assertiveness measures with the tendency to give socially desirable responses in self-description. *Journal of Consulting and Clinical Psychology, 49*, 743–744.

Rogers, C.R. (1959). A theory of therapy, personality and interpersonal relationships as developed in the client-centered framework. In Koch, S. (Ed.), *Psychology: A study of a science* (Vol. 3). New York: McGraw-Hill.

Rogers, T.B. (1974). An analysis of two central stages underlying responding to personality items: The self-referant decision and response selection. *Journal of Research in Personality, 8*, 128–138.

Ross, L. (1977). The intuitive psychologist and his shortcomings: Distortions in the attribution process. In Berkowitz, L. (Ed.), *Advances in experimental social psychology* (Vol. 10). New York: Academic.

Roth, D.L., & Ingram, R.E. (1985). Factors in the Self-Deception Questionnaire: Associations with depression. *Journal of Personality and Social Psychology, 48*, 243–251.

Rotter, J.B. (1966). Generalized expectancies for internal vs external control of reinforcement. *Psychological Monographs, 80*, No. 1 (Whole No. 609).

Ruch, F.L. (1941). A technique for detecting attempts to fake performance on a self-inventory type of personality test. In McNemar, Q., & Merrill, M.A. (Eds.), *Studies in personality* (pp. 229–234). New York: McGraw-Hill.
Sackeim, H.A. (1983). Self-deception, self-esteem, and depression: The adaptive value lying to oneself. In Masling, J. (Ed.), *Empirical studies of psychoanalytic theories*. Hillsdale: Erlbaum.
Sackeim, H.A., & Gur, R.C. (1978). Self-deception, self-confrontation and consciousness. In Schwartz, G.E., & Shapiro, D. (Eds.), *Consciousness and self-regulation: Advances in research* (Vol. 2, pp. 139–197). New York: Plenum.
Sackeim, H.A., & Gur, R.C. (1979). Self-deception, other-deception, and self-reported psychopathology. *Journal of Consulting and Clinical Psychology, 47*, 213–215.
Sarason, I.G., Levine, H.M., Basham, R.B., & Sarason, B. (1983). Assessing social support: The social support questionnaire. *Journal of Personality and Social Psychology, 44*, 127–139.
Sarbin, T.R. (1981). On self-deception. *Annals of the New York Academy of Sciences, 364*, 206–235.
Sartre, J.P. (1966). *Being and nothingness* (H. Barnes, Trans.). New York: Washington Square. (Original work published 1943).
Schanberger, W.J. (1967). A motivational distortion scale for the Sixteen Personality Factor Questionnaire. *Meeting of the Western Psychological Association*, San Francisco.
Shaffer, D.R., Smith, J.E., & Tomarelli, M. (1982). Self-monitoring as a determinant of self-disclosure reciprocity during the acquaintance process. *Journal of Personality and Social Psychology, 43*, 163–175.
Snyder, M. (1974). Self-monitoring of expressive behavior. *Journal of Personality and Social Psychology, 30*, 526–537.
Strosahl, K.D., Linehan, M.M., & Chiles, J.A. (1984). Will the real social desirability scale please stand up? Hopelessness, depression, social desirability, and the prediction of suicidal behavior. *Journal of Consulting and Clinical Psychology, 52*, 449–457.
Tabachnik, N., Crocker, J., & Alloy, L.B. (1983). Depression, social comparison and the false consensus effect. *Journal of Personality and Social Psychology, 45*, 688–699.
Taylor, J.B., Carithers, M., & Coyne, L. (1976). MMPI performance, response set, and the "self-concept" hypothesis. *Journal of Consulting and Clinical Psychology, 44*, 351–362.
Taylor, S.E. (1983). Adjustment to threatening events: A theory of cognitive adaptation. *American Psychologist, 38*, 1161–1173.
Tesser, A., & Paulhus, D.L. (1976). Toward a causal model of love. *Journal of Personality and Social Psychology, 34*, 1095–1105.
Tesser, A., & Paulhus, D.L. (1983). The definition of self: Private and public self-evaluation maintenance strategies. *Journal of Personality and Social Psychology, 44*, 672–682.
Tesser, A., & Rosen, S. (1974). The reluctance to transmit bad news. In Berkowitz, L. (Ed.), *Advances in experimental social psychology* (Vol. 8). New York: Academic.
Weiner, B. (1978). Achievement strivings. In London, H., & Exner, J.E. (Eds.), *Dimensions of personality*. New York: Academic.
Welsh, G.S. (1956). Factor dimensions A and R. In Welsh, G.S., & Dahlstrom, W.G. (Eds.), *Basic readings on the MMPI in psychology and medicine*. Minneapolis: University of Minnesota Press.
Wiggins, J.S. (1959). Interrelationships among MMPI measures of dissimulation under standard and social desirability instructions. *Journal of Consulting Psychology, 23*, 419–427.
Wiggins, J.S. (1964). Convergences among stylistic measures from objective personality tests. *Educational and Psychological Measurement, 24*, 551–562.
Wiggins, J.S. (1966). Substantive dimensions of self-report in the MMPI item pool. *Psychological Monographs, 80* (22, Whole No. 630).

Wiggins, J.S. (1979). A psychological taxonomy of trait-descriptive terms: The interpersonal domain. *Journal of Personality and Social Psychology, 37*, 395–412.
Wiggins, J.S., & Broughton, R. (1985). The interpersonal circle: A structural model for the integration of personality research. In Hogan, R., & Jones, W.H. (Eds.), *Perspectives in personality: Theory, measurement and interpersonal dynamics* (Vol. 1). Greenwich: JAI.
Wiggins, N. (1966). Individual viewpoints of social desirability. *Psychological Bulletin, 66*, 68–77.
Winder, P., O'Dell, J., & Karson, S. (1975). New motivational distortion scales for the 16-PF. *Journal of Personality Assessment, 39*, 532–537.
Zerbe, W., & Paulhus, D.L. (1984). *Social desirability effects in organizational research: A review and extension.* (Manuscript under review).

Psychometric Models for Analysis of Data from Personality Questionnaires

Willem K. B. Hofstee and Nico G. Smid

This chapter attempts to deal with the problem: How should responses to existing personality questionnaires be analyzed so as to extract a maximum of valid information from these responses? After a brief overview of the alternatives to taking the unweighted sum of the item scores, we concentrate on one of these alternatives, namely methods of scoring that account for the relevance of a questionnaire scale for the individual (Fiske, this volume) or its salience (Jackson, this volume). Through secondary analysis of questionnaire data collected by Brokken (1978) and Luteijn (1974) we will test the incremental validity of a more sophisticated alternative scoring method of this kind. On the theoretical side, we pay special attention to the notion of moderator effects associated with these approaches. Both our empirical findings and our theoretical arguments lead us to the conclusion that the burden of proof in demonstrating the validity of a sophisticated approach is on its proponents.

Two preliminary remarks should be made on the limitations of our study. In the first place, we take incremental predictive validity as the criterion for improvements in the statistical analysis of responses to personality questionnaires. This predilection follows the spirit of Fiske's (this volume) emphasis on the applied rather than the theoretical value of personality assessment – an emphasis that was earlier incorporated into the title of Wiggins' *Personality and Prediction* (see Wiggins, 1973, p. iii) and is also prominent in Hofstee's (1984) psychometric conception of personality. We do not wish to preclude other, less pragmatic criteria for improvement in the analysis of questionnaire data. It seems to us, however, that better prediction is a minimal requirement.

The second, more arbitrary limitation is in the selection of existing personality questionnaires as a point of reference. We do not deal with questionnaire construction. In particular, we do not ask how personality questionnaires should be constructed to justify more sophisticated analyses. Instead, we take the point of view of the users of more or less standard instruments, who ask themselves whether they can extract more information from the responses than is given by the usual unweighted sum of the item scores.

Analyzing Questionnaire Data

Stating a general model for the analysis of responses to personality questionnaires is relatively simple. The data to be analyzed consist of the endorsements of particular response options to a number of questionnaire items. The aim of the analysis is to find a numerical function to be applied to these responses, so that a scale score X results for each individual, which should either be maximally valid in predicting an external criterion, or maximally reliable (internally consistent) in the case of internal analysis.

Mostly, numerical values are attached to the response options in an a priori manner, thus restricting the analysis to finding a rule for combining these values. The popular strategy of scale construction is therefore a mixed strategy combining a priori with external or internal approaches. In an early study, however, Wilde (1962) applied a purely internal strategy. In essence, his procedure consisted of treating each of the three response options (yes, ?, no) to his n items as a separate pseudovariable and factor analyzing the set of $3n$ pseudovariables (these data are of course redundant, but Wilde used an algorithm that does not require nonsingularity). Wilde's results were interesting: For example, the weight attached to the middle response in the lie scale items was systematically higher than the weights for the yes and no responses. Hofstee (1963) dichotomized Wilde's weights and found high correlations between the weighted and unweighted sum scores. For practical purposes, probably little or no gain should be expected from highly differentiated score weightings. Wilde's example does show, however, that the probabilities of endorsing the successive response options are not necessarily a monotonic function of the person's position on the underlying construct. The following procedures may therefore be recommended for questionnaires containing three or more response options per item: If an external strategy is followed, the criterion should be regressed on the response options, and the regression should be inspected or tested for monotonicity or linearity; in the case of internal analysis, the total score at a certain stage in an iterative procedure takes the place of the criterion in external analysis. The procedures can be brought under the general heading of "canonical scaling" (Gifi, 1984), i.e., a scaling procedure whereby the weights for response options are chosen so as to maximize a relationship with another variable.

The next step to be taken in the analysis of questionnaire data is the construction of a rule for combining the item scores into a scale score. Procedures for item selection may be considered a part of this analysis, since the elimination of an item is equivalent to deciding upon a zero weight for that item. In practice, items are usually given weights of 1, −1, or 0 on the basis of a priori, internal, or external considerations (see Burisch, this volume) and are then summed to a total score.

A first alternative to the "unweighted" (except for deletions and reversals) sum is the application of differential weightings to the items, for example according to their item-test correlations or loadings on their first factor. A minor comment on this procedure is that, logically, regression weights for predicting the total score from the item score, or factor weights, rather than correlations or factor loadings, should be taken. More important is the old psychometric truth (e.g., Gulliksen, 1950) that weighted and unweighted sums will be more highly correlated as the number of items is larger. Also in external analysis, little gain is to be expected from using differential multiple regression weights (Wainer, 1976). So, the usefulness of multivariate procedures at this stage is mainly restricted to item selection (zero versus nonzero weights) and checking the direction of scoring (positive versus negative weights).

Modern test theory (e.g., Fischer, 1974) has provided us with far more sophisticated models for the analysis of individual differences. Outside the area of intelligence and achievement testing, some application of these models have taken place in the area of attitude measurement (for an overview see Jansen, 1983). The field of personality assessment has been slow to comply with the stringent restrictions that these models impose. The pragmatic position that is taken here would require the demonstration of increased predictive validity as a justification for the use of modern test theory. While there is little doubt that purer scales would result, we have insufficient reason to predict that these scales would also be more valid.

Having arrived at the level of scale scores, the question is what models are to be applied to these scores to maximize predictive validity. Throughout the history of personality questionnaires a permanent criticism has been that a particular scale score may not mean the same thing with respect to different individuals, and that these individuals should therefore not automatically receive the same predicted criterion score. That criticism has mostly been translated into the application of suppressor and moderator models. A further distinction can be made between suppressor and moderator variables that are measured independently, and variables that are derived from the same responses upon which the scale score is based. We will focus upon the latter case, since we have restricted ourselves to analyzing responses on existing personality questionnaires.

A suppressor model was implied in attempts to partial out stylistic variance (i.e., variance associated with response styles such as acquiescence and response set or social desirability set) from the scale scores of personality questionnaires, to retain content-determined scores. Both this research paradigm and the subsequent attempts to exploit sets and styles as variables in their own right have been unsuccessful (see, e.g., Nunnally, 1978; Wiggins, 1973) and have virtually been abandoned since Rorer's (1965) frontal attack on the "great response style myth."

In the area of personality assessment, the moderator approach has received vigorous support from Bem and Allen's (1974) "On Predicting Some of the People Some of the Time" (see also Amelang & Borkenau, this volume). In this approach, the idea is not so much that scores are contaminated with artifactual variance that has to be partialled out, as in the suppressor model, but rather that a certain scale may be relatively irrelevant for predicting the behavior of a subset of individuals. Before we turn to an investigation which we carried out to test the incremental validity of a particular moderator model a number of general remarks have to be made, since the moderator approach is less transparent than is generally realized.

The Moderator Model

The moderator model (see, e.g., Roe, 1983; Wiggins, 1973) tends to give rise to misconceptions in everyday discussions and, to some extent, in the literature. Saunders' (1956) classic moderated regression equation offers the best possibilities of circumventing these misconceptions:

$$\hat{Y} = a + bX_1 + cX_2 + dX_1X_2 \tag{1}$$

where
$\hat{Y}$ is the predicted criterion variable,
X_1, X_2 are predictor variables, and
a, b, c, d are regression weights.

A first observation is that Eq. (1) carries no moderator *variable,* but only a moderator term, i.e., X_1X_2. The functioning of the two predictor variables is perfectly symmetrical. Note that in the Frederiksen and Melville (1954) study, in which compulsiveness was found to moderate the relationship between interest and GPA, it could have been equally well concluded that interest moderated the relationship between compulsiveness and GPA. A moderator effect is present if and only if the moderator term X_1X_2 has a nonzero weight in predicting the criterion Y.

In many applications one of the predictors, say X_2, is arbitrarily taken as the moderator variable; subjects are then divided into two groups according to their scores on X_2, which is treated as a dichotomy, i.e., X_2 is 1 or 0. This treatment may be represented as a special case of Eq. (1) by substituting 1 and 0, respectively, for X_2:

$$\begin{aligned} {}_1\hat{Y} &= (a + c) + (b + d)X_1 \\ {}_0\hat{Y} &= a + bX_1 \end{aligned} \tag{2}$$

where the prior subscripts refer to groups 1 and 0. The reversed operation is easily carried out: If, through separate linear regression analyses in the two groups, it has been found that

$$\begin{aligned} {}_1\hat{Y} &= v + wX_1 \\ {}_0\hat{Y} &= a + bX_1 \end{aligned} \tag{3}$$

then c in Eq. (1) can be solved as v − a, and d as w − b; consequently, the two formulas in Eq. (3) can be merged into one moderated regression equation:

$$\hat{Y} = a + bX_1 + (v - a)X_2 + (w - b)X_1X_2 \tag{4}$$

in which the symmetry between X_1 and X_2 has been restored.

One may of course enforce asymmetry by setting c = 0:

$$\hat{Y} = a + bX_1 + dX_1X_2 \tag{5}$$

That would constitute an inferior approach, however, since any independent contribution that X_2 could make to predicting Y is being disregarded; another way to state this is that the intercept of the regression function of Y on X_1 is no longer allowed to vary according to the value taken by X_2. When X_2 is dichotomous, Eq. (5) will resolve into:

$$\begin{aligned} {}_1\hat{Y} &= \mathrm{a} + \mathrm{w}X_1 \\ {}_0\hat{Y} &= \mathrm{a} + \mathrm{b}X_1 \end{aligned} \tag{6}$$

In general, the consequence would be that Y would be systematically underpredicted in one group and overpredicted in the other.

The counterpart to Eq. (6) is a model in which the intercepts, not the slopes, are allowed to vary according to X_2:

$$\begin{aligned} {}_1Y &= \mathrm{v} + \mathrm{b}X_1 \\ {}_0\hat{Y} &= \mathrm{a} + \mathrm{b}X_1 \end{aligned} \tag{7}$$

This model appears to be relevant in research on social discrimination (cf. Gael et al., 1975a, b). Again, the two equations can be merged into one:

$$\hat{Y} = \mathrm{a} + \mathrm{b}X_1 + (\mathrm{v} - \mathrm{a})X_2 \tag{8}$$

Contrary to the terminology of some authors (e.g., Roe, 1983), Eq. (8) is not a moderator model, since the moderator term carries no weight. Thus, the observation that the regression lines in two groups do not coincide is insufficient reason to speak of a moderator effect: A moderator effect is only present when the regression lines do not run parallel.

Differential validity, i.e., inequality of the correlations between X_1 and Y in the two groups, is also insufficient reason to conclude the presence of a moderator effect. The slope coefficients may be written as:

$$\begin{aligned} &\frac{{}_1\mathrm{s}(Y)}{{}_1\mathrm{s}(X_1)}\,{}_1\mathrm{r}(X_1, Y) \\ &\frac{{}_0\mathrm{s}(Y)}{{}_0\mathrm{s}(X_1)}\,{}_0\mathrm{r}(X_1, Y) \end{aligned} \tag{9}$$

If

$$\frac{{}_1\mathrm{r}(X_1, Y)}{{}_0\mathrm{r}(X_1, Y)} = \frac{{}_1\mathrm{s}(X_1)\,{}_0\mathrm{s}(Y)}{{}_1\mathrm{s}(Y)\,{}_0\mathrm{s}(X_1)} \tag{10}$$

then the two slopes are identical irrespective of the values of the correlations, and no moderator effect is present. This situation would occur, for example, when subjects whose scores on X_1 and Y form a bivariate normal distribution are divided into two groups of unequal size on the basis of their X_1 scores, say, the bottom 10% and the top 90%. Naturally, the regression of Y on X_1 in both groups would still be the same as before, but the validity in the bottom group would be much lower than in the top group, owing to greater restriction of range. The observation that differential validity does not logically imply a moderator effect is of utmost importance, since most of the alleged demonstrations of moderator effects in the literature have been presented in terms of differential validity (see also Bem & Allen, 1974).

Zedeck (1971) has proposed a search for variables that predict the algebraic difference $Z_y - Z_x$ between standardized criterion and predictor scores (rather than the absolute difference; see Ghiselli, 1956). This procedure, however, amounts to finding a linear combination of the original predictor and the "moderator", so the approach does not constitute a moderator model.

We conclude at this point that the moderated regression equation is a comprehensive and flexible model for studying moderator effects, and that other approaches may easily lead to confusion. Conclusions about the presence or absence of a moderator effect should be based upon finding a nonzero or zero weight for the moderator term in predicting a criterion. It has been objected that the statistical testing of a moderator effect involves a contradiction, since it is impossible for the linear and the product terms to simultaneously satisfy the conditions of linearity and homoscedasticity (Mellenbergh & Pannekoek, 1979; Sockloff, 1976). However, the test may be sufficiently robust to against the inevitable violation (Roe, 1983).

Several authors have noticed that a predictor can be used as its own moderator, namely, by substituting $X_2 = X_1$ into Eq. (1):

$$\hat{Y} = \mathrm{a} + (\mathrm{b} + \mathrm{c})X_1 + \mathrm{d}X_1^2 \tag{11}$$

which is simply a quadratic regression equation. The consequences of this substitution have not been fully discussed, however. Fiske (this volume), for example, proposes to calculate an intrapersonal standard deviation of the manifestations of a person's trait on different occasions (items) as a consistency measure to supplement the traditional total score. If the item scores were dichotomous, however, the person standard deviation (say, X_2) would be a transformation of the proportion of scale responses (say, X_1):

$$X_2 = (X_1 - X_1^2)^{1/2} \tag{12}$$

If the consistency measure X_2 were then used as a "moderator variable" in predicting a criterion Y, the result of substituting Eq. (12) into Eq. (1) would be:

$$\hat{Y} = \mathrm{a} + \mathrm{b}X_1 + \mathrm{c}(X_1 - X_1^2)^{1/2} + \mathrm{d}X_1(X_1 - X_1^2)^{1/2} \tag{13}$$

which would amount to a complicated nonlinear regression equation for predicting Y from the traditional total score.

Instead of the intraperson standard deviation we could use the variance, since Fiske's reasoning does not dictate a preference for one of these indices over the other. In the case of binary items,

$$X_2 = X_1 - X_1^2 \tag{14}$$

Substitution into Eq. (1) gives:

$$\hat{Y} = \mathrm{a} + (\mathrm{b}+\mathrm{c})X_1 + (\mathrm{d}-\mathrm{c})X_1^2 - \mathrm{d}X_1^3 \tag{15}$$

which is a cubic regression function. Thus Fiske's proposal can be translated into the proposition that a cubic function of the traditional total score should be taken when trying to predict a criterion Y. In our opinion, the prior probability of finding stable nonzero weights for quadratic and cubic terms in regression equations is low (see also Wiggins, 1973). Our analysis therefore seems to have implications for the credibility of the original proposal.

Incremental Validity of a Threshold Model

Jackson (this volume) has proposed a threshold model for personality assessment in which a salience parameter, reflecting a subject's sensitivity to the underlying dimension represented by the items, is added to a threshold parameter, reflecting that subject's standing on the dimension. The threshold and salience parameters are the intercept and the slope, respectively, of the "respondent operating characteristic curve," i.e., the regression of the subject's item responses on the value that the items have on the dimension.

Adopting these formal characteristics of the threshold model, we questioned whether the predictive validity of existing questionnaires could be enhanced by using Jackson's individual parameters, in particular his salience/slope parameter, in addition to the traditional total score. Since the salience parameter stands for the relevance of a questionnaire scale for the individual, a moderator model is appropriate in testing its incremental validity. Like Jackson, we used the linear regression of the subject's item scores on the dimension values of the items.

An analytical caveat should be put forward before we turn to the empirical study. The slope parameter of the linear intraperson regression function may be expressed as:

$$r_{pd}\frac{s_p}{s_d} \tag{16}$$

in which:

s_p is the within-person standard deviation of the item responses,

s_d is the standard deviation of the dimension values of the items, and

r_{pd} is the within-person correlation between the item responses and the dimension values.

In comparison of individuals, s_d is a constant. The slope parameter therefore consists of two variable components, r_{pd} and s_p. In the preceding section, we have expressed our doubts as to the predictive usefulness of s_p. In the case of r_{pd}, a warning flag should be raised with respect to its reliability in regular questionnaire scales. We estimate that the modal number of items in such scales is around 20, so that the standard error of r_{pd} is quite high. In addition, the individual item responses (not the dimension values) tend to be very unreliable. So one should not have high prior expectations about the effect of introducing a salience parameter in a predictive validity study. By way of compensation, however, we staged a good many opportunities for such an effect to show up.

Method

Two sets of data were made available by our colleagues Frank Brokken and Frans Luteijn, both at the University of Groningen, The Netherlands. The first set, to be referred to as SPEL data, consisted of the responses of 200 paid student subjects to the items of the seven scales of the Standard List of Personality-Descriptive Adjectives (SPEL; cf. Hofstee, Brokken, & Land, 1981), with peer ratings on the same seven scales by a close acquaintance of each subject as criteria. The SPEL is a very carefully constructed instrument, in which the scales were formed not only on the basis of the relationships between the items but also on the basis of their positions in an Osgood semantic space. The second set, to be referred to as NPV data, consisted of the responses of 464 persons who approached the local Institute of Multidisciplinary Psychotherapy (IMP), to the items of the seven scales of the Dutch Personality Inventory (NPV; Luteijn, 1974), with independent psychiatric ratings upon intake as criteria. The NPV is also a very carefully constructed inventory. Table 1 presents the scale labels and relevant statistics of SPEL and NPV.

For each subject, the following predictor scores were used:

x_j, the unweighted sum of the item scores for scale j ; $j=1,...7; 8,...14$;

a_j, the intercept parameter of the linear regression of the item scores of the subject on the dimension values of the items in scale j; and

b_j, the slope parameter.

The dimension associated with scale j was operationalized as the average (across individuals) response to the item. This operationalization may be seen as a substitute for the social desirabilities of the items used by Jackson (this volume), with which they presumably correlate highly. On the other hand, the average response may be interpreted independently: the intercept parameter records the position of the individual on the scale compared with the average individual, while the slope parameter records how well the individual profile of the item scores corresponds with the average profile.

To test the incremental validity of the a and b parameters, stepwise regressions of the criterion measures on the predictors were carried out for each

Table 1. Scale labels and relevant statistics of SPEL and NPV

SPEL scale	*n*	*m*	*s*	Alpha	*r*
Culture	24	12.13	8.24	0.79	0.17
Emotional stability	26	28.04	11.50	0.79	0.63
Agreeableness	22	41.82	8.76	0.75	0.18
Irritableness	21	19.56	9.61	0.77	0.23
Conscientiousness	19	36.08	7.94	0.77	0.60
Introversion	17	20.82	8.63	0.69	0.18
Conservatism	6	7.79	3.58	0.75	0.51

NPV scale	*n*	*m*	*s*	Alpha	r_1	r_2	r_3
Inadequacy	21	24.39	9.47	0.86	−0.12	0.10	0.16
Social inadequacy	15	15.29	7.06	0.83	−0.10	0.06	0.14
Rigidity	25	21.99	8.87	0.77	−0.16	0.16	0.14
Injustice	19	18.68	7.39	0.77	−0.16	0.24	0.08
Self-sufficiency	16	9.05	4.74	0.68	−0.11	0.11	0.03
Dominance	17	12.71	5.57	0.72	0.07	0.02	−0.12
Vigor	19	18.28	6.77	0.68	0.06	−0.04	−0.14

n, number of items; *m*, mean score; *s*, standard deviation; Alpha, coefficient alpha; *r*, zero-order validity against peer rating; r_1, r_2, r_3, zero-order validity against psychiatric rating on Stability, Neuroticism, and Anxiety

scale-criterion combination. In the first step, the validity of x was computed to serve as a baseline. In the second, a was added, which has essentially the same interpretation as x, with the expectation that it would make no contribution to the validity. In the third, a^2 was added, to check whether any moderator effects found in the last step could be explained in terms of a nonlinear relation between a and the criterion (see above). In the fourth step, the moderator term ab was introduced to complete the prediction model.

Seven analyses were performed on the SPEL data, each time with peer ratings on the same scale as a criterion, and 21 on the NPV data, since the three criteria that were available were not specific to one of the seven questionnaire scales.

Results and Discussion

The prime result can be stated briefly: In none of the 28 stepwise regression analyses did any of the added person parameters increase the correlation between the traditional total score x and the criterion to a significant ($p < .01$) extent. In five analyses, the difference between a multiple correlation and the zero-order validity of x was of borderline ($p < .05$) significance; in only one of these cases, however, was the moderator term responsible for the increase in predicted variance of the criterion.

Table 2. Median intercorrelations between total score (x), intraindividual intercept (a), slope (b), and correlation between items and dimension (r)

a	0.5		
b	0.0	−0.8	
r	0.0	−0.8	0.9
	x	a	b

In an attempt to discover any artifacts that might be responsible for these null results, we hit upon a high negative correlation between the intercept and slope parameters, ranging between −.59 and −.95 for the 14 scales. Table 2 gives the median intercorrelations between x, a, b, and the intraindividual correlation coefficient r between the item scores and the dimension values. While we had conceived of the intercept parameter a as an approximate replica of x, the correlation between the two is only in the order of .5. Table 2 further shows that the intraindividual r behaves in the same way as b.

The relation between x, a, and b can be clarified if the intraindividual regression equation is written as follows:

$$a_i + b_i D_g - \hat{x}_{ig} = 0 \tag{17}$$

where
a_i is the intercept parameter for individual i;
b_i is the slope parameter for i;
D_g is the dimension value of the item g (g = 1,...k) and
$\hat{x}_{ig}$ is the regression of the item score on the dimension

Summation of all items and division by the number of items gives:

$$a_i + b_i \bar{D} - k^{-1} x_i = 0 \tag{18}$$

where $\bar{D}$ is the average dimension value of the items, thus a constant, and x_i is the individual's total score on the scale in question, since the sum of the regressed scores equals the sum of the scores.

Equation (18) shows that each of the three variables is a linear function of the other two. If b shows little variation the correlation between a and x will be high, as it was in the Jackson study. The high negative correlation between a and b in our data points to relatively low variation in x. In all cases, however, one variable can be left out, since it is perfectly redundant given the other two.

In our analysis of the questionnaire data, we tested the incremental validity of the moderator term ab. In view of the high negative correlation between a and b, however, this moderator term adds little to the a^2 term, which had already been partialled out. It therefore appears that the moderator term bx would have been a more felicitous choice with the present data. Since $x_i = ka_i + k\bar{D}b_i$, the new moderator term bx is equal to $ka_ib_i + k\bar{D}b_i^2$. In other words, instead of changing the moderator term we might add b^2 to the original analysis.

Thus, a second analysis was performed, in which x, b, and bx were taken as predictors. Again in no case did the moderator term show significant ($p < .01$) incremental validity. In two of the 28 cases, the predictive gain was of borderline ($p < .05$) significance. Thus the null results of the first analysis were essentially repeated.

Conclusions

The question raised in this chapter was whether the users of personality questionnaires should consider other methods of scoring than the traditional total score per scale. In particular, we asked whether a moderator model is useful in which some other function of an individual's item scores (e.g., their standard deviation or the slope of their regression on an underlying dimension) representing the relevance of the questionnaire scale for the individual should be used as a "moderator variable." We attempted to deal with this question through psychometric reasoning and secondary analysis of empirical data.

The answer is negative: None of the recommendations for more sophisticated scoring models receive empirical support from our results, which lends support to Burisch's (this volume) plea for simplicity. Moreover, our psychometric analyses indicate that sophisticated scoring methods are subject to a logical minefield in which they may easily explode, the remains leading to the conclusion that nothing much was added in the first place. It was shown, for example, that the moderator "variable" is a poor concept to begin with; that a finding of differential validity is insufficient reason to infer moderator effects; that supposed moderator effects can be reduced in some cases to supposed nonlinearity of one variable; and that the addition of intraindividual intercept and slope parameters to the scale score suffers in part from redundancy. We recommend that any novel scoring procedure be given to a psychometrician to try and tear it apart, and that it not be put into practice until the psychometrician has given up. We also recommend that investigators realize how fallible their data are, and how tenuous therefore are any models except the most undemanding.

Our reasoning does not necessarily extend to studies in which questionnaire data are supplemented with other variables that are external to these data. We are inclined, however, to transfer a certain amount of generalized suspiciousness to such cases. It should be realized, for example, that Bem and Allen (1974) have demonstrated differential validity, not incremental validity of a moderator term. We predict that Wiggins' (1973) conclusions about the elusiveness of moderator effects would not be subject to drastic changes if the later developments were taken into account.

Acknowledgements. The authors are indebted to Frank Brokken and Frans Luteijn for providing the data on which the secondary analyses were performed; to Henk Camstra and Bert Lisser for their prompt and capable processing of the data; and to Jos ten Berge, Frits Zegers, and the present editors for reviewing the draft version of this chapter.

References

Bem, D.J., & Allen, A. (1974). On predicting some of the people some of the time: the search for cross-situational consistencies in behavior. *Psychological Review, 81*, 506–520.

Brokken, F.B. (1978). *The language of personality.* Groningen: Doctoral dissertation, University of Groningen.

Fischer, G. (1974). *Einführung in die Theorie psychologischer Tests.* Bern: Huber.

Frederiksen, N., & Melville, S.D. (1954). Differential predictability in the use of test scores. *Educational and Psychological Measurement, 14*, 647–656.

Gael, S., Grant, D.L., & Ritchie, R.J. (1975a). Employment test validation for minority and nonminority telephone operators. *Journal of Applied Psychology, 60*, 411–419.

Gael, S., Grant, D.L., & Ritchie, R.J. (1975b). Employment test validation for minority and nonminority clerks with work sample criteria. *Journal of Applied Psychology, 60*, 420–426.

Ghiselli, E.E. (1956). Differentiation of individuals in terms of their predictability. *Journal of Applied Psychology, 40*, 374–377.

Gifi, A. (1984). *Nonlinear multivariate analysis.* Leiden: DSWO.

Gulliksen, H. (1950). *Theory of mental tests.* New York: Wiley.

Hofstee, W.K.B. (1963). Enkele notities over G. J. S. Wilde's „Neurotische labiliteit, gemeten volgens de vragenlijstmethode". *Nederlands Tijdschrift voor de Psychologie, 18*, 481–499.

Hofstee, W.K.B. (1984). What's in a trait: reflections about the inevitability of traits, their measurement, and taxonomy. In Bonarius, H., van Heck, G., & Smid, N. (Eds.), *Personality psychology in Europe: theoretical and empirical developments* (pp. 75–81). Lisse: Swets & Zeitlinger.

Hofstee, W.K.B., Brokken, F.B., & Land, H. (1981). Constructie van een standaard-persoonlijkheids-eigenschappen-lijst (SPEL). *Nederlands Tijdschrift voor de Psychologie, 36*, 443–452.

Jansen, P.G.W. (1983). *Rasch analysis of attitudinal data.* Nijmegen: Doctoral dissertation, University of Nijmegen.

Luteijn, F. (1974). *De konstruktie van een persoonlijkheidsvragenlijst (de N.P.V.).* Groningen: Doctoral dissertation, University of Groningen.

Mellenbergh, G.J., & Pannekoek, J. (1979). *The moderator effect reconsidered.* Amsterdam: Report of the Psychological Laboratory, University of Amsterdam.

Nunnally, J.C. (1978). *Psychometric theory* (2nd ed.). New York: McGraw-Hill.

Roe, R.A. (1983). *Grondslagen der personeelsselektie.* Assen: Van Gorcum.

Rorer, L.G. (1965). The great response style myth. *Psychological Bulletin, 63*, 129–156.

Saunders, D.R. (1956). Moderator variables in prediction. *Educational and Psychological Measurement, 16*, 209–222.

Sockloff, A.L. (1976). The analysis of non-linearity via linear regression with polynomial and product variables: An examination. *Review of Educational Research, 46*, 267–291.

Wainer, H. (1976). Estimating coefficients in linear models: it don't make no nevermind. *Psychological Bulletin, 83*, 213–217.

Wiggins, J.S. (1973). *Personality and prediction: Principles of personality assessment.* Reading: Addison-Wesley.

Wilde, G.J.S. (1962). *Neurotische labiliteit gemeten volgens de vragenlijstmethode.* Amsterdam: Doctoral dissertation, University of Amsterdam.

Zedeck, S. (1971). Problems with the use of "moderator"-variables. *Psychological Bulletin, 76*, 295–310.

On Linguistic Variables Influencing the Understanding of Questionnaire Items

HEDE HELFRICH

Understanding of Questionnaire Items as a Source of Response Variance and Bias

During the phase of empirically oriented personality research, methodological problems concerning questionnaires have mainly been discussed with respect to test statistical properties (cf. Löhr & Angleitner, 1980, p. 218). Unfortunately, validity coefficients, expressed as correlations between test scores and an external criterion, generally remained relatively low [according to Janke (1973) between .20 and .30]. One reason for this might be that research focused on responses to items, but rarely on the conditions leading to responses. What seems necessary is the reconstruction of the entire process of responding to an item, and the specification of relations between the components which constitute this process (cf. Fiske, 1982; Schwarzer, 1982). The aim of such an approach is the elimination of methodological artifacts in a more direct way.

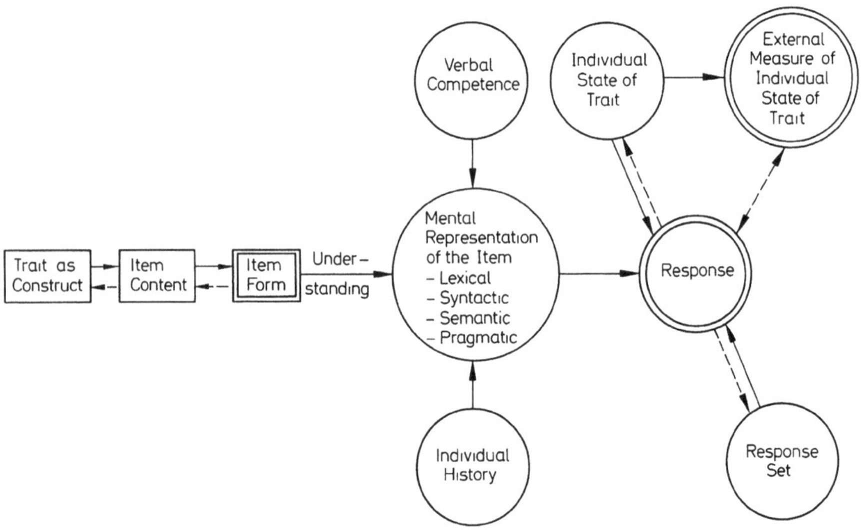

Fig. 1. Response to an item as a process. ═ observable components, —— constructs, → direction of processes influencing the response, - - →direction of inferences made by the researcher

Figure 1 is a schematic showing the process of response to an item. The components of this process may be observable elements, such as the item response and the item form, or mere constructs, such as the underlying trait and the item content. Full arrows indicate the direction of processes influencing the response of an individual. Broken arrows refer to the inferences that have to be made to relate the responses to an underlying trait.

Empirically oriented personality research has concentrated almost exclusively on the relation between response and individual state of trait, and on the interaction with response sets. Implicitly, it has been assumed that the understanding and the mental representation of items is similar for all individuals. However, understanding itself may be a source of response variance and bias. There are two components of understanding which may contribute to deviations from the representation intended by the researcher: direction and degree of understanding.

Direction of Understanding

Understanding may be influenced either by ambiguously formulated items or by the individual history of the respondent. Item ambiguity has been discussed by Löhr & Schütte (1982). For example, an item may be ambiguous because it is not clear whether a negation includes the whole sentence or merely part of the sentence.

However, even linguistically unambiguous items may cause differing mental representations. Especially words that have a strong evaluative character may have different connotations for different respondents, depending on their individual histories. An example is given in a study by Hörmann, Pieper, and Engelkamp (1976), who have found that sentences referring to the state of loneliness are evaluated by younger persons in a completely different way than by older persons.

Degree of Understanding

Although items may be formulated unambiguously and without evaluative terms, the degree of understanding might remain inadequate. Possible reasons are a complicated syntactic structure of items, differential verbal competence of respondents, or too short a response time.

Where the problem of item structure has received attention, suggestions for maximum simplicity have often been given. For example, Edwards (1957) cautions against "compound and complex sentences" and "the use of double negatives" (cf. Micklin & Durbin, 1969, p. 195). According to Lienert (1969, p. 64) "telegraphic shortness" should be avoided as well as "fussy length."

Systematic attempts to treat formulations of items as a source of response variance and bias have been made by Micklin and Durbin (1969) and by Löhr and Angleitner (1980). Two problems arise in the context of these studies, which have investigated syntactic variables such as negations, use of the passive voice, and sentence complexity:

1. Given the relatively moderate correlation ($r = -.39$) between differences in sentence structure of parallel test forms and parallel test reliability in the Micklin & Durbin study, it seems questionable whether the formulation of items has a substantial influence on the responses.
2. Certain syntactic features may be intrinsically related to the trait to be measured. Thus, the use of passive voice is highly correlated with items indicating neuroticism (Löhr & Angleitner, 1980, p. 232).

Reconstruction of Understanding as a Time-Dependent Process

Apparently, an isolated investigation of formal syntactic properties of items is not sufficient. We may ask whether modes of linguistic description and issues of psycholinguistic research would yield an appropriate framework for the analysis of understanding an item. Central importance in contemporary linguistic theory attaches to the distinction between surface and deep structure (cf. Hörmann, 1981). This distinction has been introduced to account for

1. The logical similarity of such sentences as
   "The boy hit the ball."
   "The ball is hit by the boy."
2. The logical difference between such sentences as
   "John is eager to please."
   "John is easy to please."

In a very crude simplification, surface structure can be equated with item form, and deep structure with item content. The distance between the two may vary as a function of item formulation.

Psycholinguistic experiments on the understanding of sentences indicate that the process of understanding may be described as a progression from surface to deep structure representation. This progress has been demonstrated for memory as well as for comprehension. An example is a study conducted by Sachs (1967). In this experiment, subjects had to listen to passages of connected discourse consisting of sentences that had to be recognized at various time intervals. Four types of sentence were used as test materials. Examples are the following:

Base sentence: He sent a letter about it to Galileo, the great Italian scientist.
Semantically changed: Galileo, the great Italian scientist, sent him a letter about it.
Passive: A letter about it was sent to Galileo, the great Italian scientist.
Form changed, without changing the meaning: He sent Galileo, the great Italian scientist, a letter about it.

The subjects' task was to decide whether or not a test sentence was identical with the original they had heard in the preceding passage. Any one of the four types of sentences could appear as the original and/or as a test sentence.

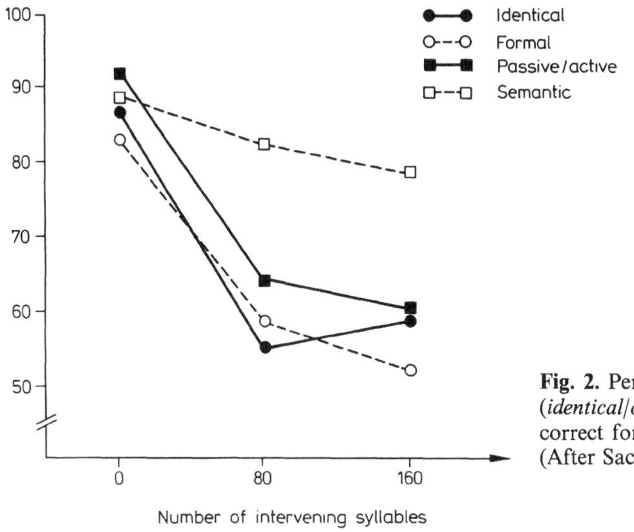

Fig. 2. Percentages of judgements (*identical/changed*) that were correct for each test type. (After Sachs, 1967)

Figure 2 shows the results as a function of number of syllables intervening between sentence and recognition test. The recognition memory declined much more rapidly for the form of a sentence than for the meaning. When the test sentence immediately followed the original sentence, all changes could be recognized. When 80 syllables (roughly 27 s) were interpolated, syntactic changes remained unnoticed, while semantic changes were recognized even after 160 syllables (roughly 46 s). Immediately after presentation, the surface form of a sentence not only is still present in memory, but predominates the content of the sentence. Questions concerning the content of the sentences at that time are responded to faster when they have the same syntactic surface form as the original sentence. However, after a few seconds, this difference completely disappears (Layton & Simpson, 1975).

Given that the process of understanding has not been completed immediately after presentation of an item, and given that response times to questionnaire items vary between individuals, a source of response bias may emerge. At the time when they give their responses, some individuals may have come to a deep structure representation of the item, while others have not. One might conclude that items should be constructed in such a way that the distance from the deep structure, or its mental representation, is minimal. But what are the characteristics of such a deep structure?

Mental Representation of Linguistic Structures

Based on the lingustic distinction between deep and surface structure (Chomsky, 1957, 1965), early psycholinguistic studies tried to make evident the psy-

Table 1. Example of a kernel sentence and transformational operations in early transformational grammar

Sentence form		Example
SAAD:	Simple-active-affirmative-declarative (=kernel sentence)	The boy has hit the ball.
Q:	Question	Has the boy hit the ball?
P:	Passive	The ball has been hit by the boy.
N:	Negation	The boy has not hit the ball.
PQ:	Passive-question	Has the ball been hit by the boy?
PN:	Passive-negation	The ball has not been hit by the boy.
NQ:	Negation-question	Has not the boy hit the ball?
PNQ:	Passive-negation-question	Has not the ball been hit by the boy?

chological simplicity of the so-called SAAD or kernel sentences (Mehler, 1963; Miller, 1962). Transformations from kernel sentences to various surface forms (see Table 1) have been interpreted as time-consuming operations.

It has been hypothesized that the more transformations, e.g., negation and passivation, a sentence contains, the more difficult it will be to perceive or memorize (Mehler, 1963; Miller, 1962). Although the hypotheses have often been confirmed, the results did not exclude more parsimonious explanations, such as differential sentence length, frequency of usage, or amount of information (cf. Engelkamp, 1974). However, the most critical objections to these experiments have been of a theoretical nature:

1. Some of the so-called syntactic operations have semantic implications. Negation of a sentence, in particular, changes the content. Consequently, this aspect has been revised in the more recent version of Chomsky's transformational grammar, where negation, like passive voice, is incorporated into deep structure (Chomsky, 1965).
2. It may be generally doubted that modes of linguistic description can be applied to psychological operations without modifications.

In the next two sections, these two aspects – semantic implications of syntactic factors and noncorrespondence between linguistic and psychological operations – will be exemplified with negation and passive voice.

Reconsideration of Syntactic Factors Determining Understanding: Negation

Not all negations are more difficult to process than their affirmative counterparts. Processing difficulty depends on the scope of negation and the semantic implications associated with negation. Moreover, even sentences that are affirmative in form may contain "psychological" negatives.

1. *Scope of Negation.* Negations vary with respect to extension or "scope" (Jackendoff, 1969). Negations with unspecific scope, i.e., negations which extend over the entire sentence, are not more difficult to process than their affirmative counterparts. Processing difficulty increases, however, when negation only refers to a word group or a single word (Hörmann, 1971; Wason & Johnson-Laird, 1972).
2. *Degree of Semantic Implication.* Lexical meanings of negated elements of a sentence may be different with respect to their specificity or their degree of "semantic implication" (Hörmann, 1971). Examples for low and high degrees of semantic implication are given in Table 2. The difficulty of processing a negation increases with the degree of semantic implication of the negated elements. The higher the degree of semantic implication, the stronger the positive assertion of the state of affairs is implied. Processing of negation will, therefore, entail an extra expense of effort (Hörmann, 1971).

Table 2. Example of a difference in degree of semantic implication. (After Hörmann, 1971)

Low:	The pupil has not found the book
High:	The river has not washed away the bank

3. *Psychological Negations.* Certain lexical units (verbs, adjectives) are negatively evaluated and are therefore psychologically equivalent to negatives.

Table 3. Examples of psychological (____) and syntactic (- - - -) negations from personality questionnaires

I have no enemies who really wish to harm me. (MMPI)

Bad words, often terrible words, come into my mind and I cannot get rid of them. (MMPI)

It wouldn't make me nervous if any members of my family got into trouble with the law. (MMPI)

It is all right to get around the law if you don't actually break it. (CPI)

I do not have a great fear of snakes. (CPI, MMPI)

I have never had any breaking out on my skin that has worried me. (MMPI)

There is something wrong with a person who can't take orders without getting angry or resentful. (CPI)

I do not dread seeing a doctor about sickness or injury. (CPI)

It's no use worrying my head about public affairs; I can't do anything about them anyhow. (CPI)

I would be ashamed not to use my privilege of voting. (CPI)

I have never deliberately told a lie. (CPI)

It makes me angry when I hear of someone who has been wrongly prevented from voting. (CPI)

When added to a syntactic negation they have an effect comparable to a double negative sentence (Boysson-Bardies, 1970; Sherman, 1976). Personality questionnaires often contain such hidden double negatives. Examples drawn from various questionnaires are given in Table 3.

Reconsideration of Syntactic Factors Determining Understanding: Passive Voice

The use of passive constructions has been found to occur with particular frequency in scales measuring neuroticism (Löhr & Angleitner, 1980). While, according to early psycholinguistic research, passive constructions should be more difficult to comprehend than active sentences (e.g. Gough, 1965), later research has shown that it is not the passive voice per se which affects difficulty of processing. The modifying influence derives from semantic or pragmatic constraints built up by the words of a sentence. Slobin (1966) and Herriot (1969) found that passives were more difficult to process than actives only if they were semantically or pragmatically reversible, i.e., if the relations expressed by the nouns can be interchanged without leading to an implausible sentence (see Table 4).

Table 4. Examples of reversible and nonreversible sentences

Type	Example
Reversible	The dog is chasing the cat
Semantically nonreversible	The girl is watering the flowers
Pragmatically nonreversible	The doctor treated the patient

A special kind of semantic constraint is provided by so-called truncated passives such as "English is spoken here." Such passives are much more common in our speech than full passives. Slobin (1968) showed that a truncated passive, i.e., a passive without an explicit agent, is processed somewhat differently from a full passive. While full passives are likely to be changed to active forms, truncated passives tend to be recalled verbatim, and not as full passives or as actives.

However, Franks and Bransford (1974) pointed out that context can influence the way in which truncated passives are processed. If the context supplied information about the deleted actor verbatim memory for the truncated passives decreased, and subjects tended to recognize alternative sentence forms (actives and full passives) expressing the meaning of the truncated passives plus the contextually given actor. An example of the stimulus material is:

Truncated sentence: After the harvest a huge feast was served.
Context sentence: Mrs. Brown who did it was a very good cook.

Based on those results one might question whether a purely syntactic model is appropriate for the description of the mental representation of verbally mediated events. An attempt to reconstruct the mental representation of sentences as elementary action schemes is provided by a model initiated by Fillmore (1968, 1977) and developed by natural language scientists (e.g. Schank, 1975). According to this model the relations existing between different concepts, as expressed in a sentence, are specified as case relations. These cases are not identical with the cases of school grammar but rather describe functional relationships which are at the same time semantic and syntactic. Such functional relations are identified as "agent," "patient," "recipient," "instrument," or "location."

The verb is of central importance within this framework. It constitutes the predicate of which the case relations are the arguments. The semantic complexity of the verb determines the number and kind of possible arguments. The psychological significance of the verb in speech perception has been demonstrated by Hörmann, Lazarus, and Lazarus (1975, cited according to Hörmann, 1978). They presented subjects with sentences degraded by white noise. If the verb had been correctly perceived the probability of correct recall of the whole sentence was significantly higher than if either the subject or the object had been correctly perceived and not the verb.

Starting from the framework of case grammar, predictions concerning the comprehensibility of questionnaire items can be derived which are partially contrary to the predictions based on purely formal syntactic properties. Comprehensibility of an item should be related to the salience of the intended predicate-argument structure in the surface form. Given the centrality of the verb, an item should be easier to comprehend if the verb contains the intended relations as possible arguments. Therefore, item 243 of the CPI should be easier to comprehend than item 306, although, unlike item 306, it is formulated in a passive voice.

Item 243 (CPI): I am often bothered by useless thoughts [which keep running through my mind].
Item 307 (CPI): I have nightmares [every few nights].

The verb "to bother" contains the intended case relations – patient and agent – as possible arguments, while the modal verb "to have" refers to the more unspecific arguments of an owner and an owned object.

Reconsideration of Syntactic Factors Determining Understanding: Focus

Since the functional case relations have been defined without reference to either a "logical" or a "grammatical" subject, reason might suggest that the traditional subject of a sentence is of minor psychological significance. The use of active and passive voice would then be psychologically equivalent.

However, Ertel (1974, 1977) has shown that the psychological significance of the grammatical subject lies in its property to focus one of the nominal units in a sentence. The subject is the grammatical category in which a speaker or hearer anchors his cognitive construction. Thus, place relations such as "in front of" and "behind" – normally interpreted from the speaker's or hearer's own perspective – experience a shift of perspective toward the person who is being referred to as the subject of a sentence (Ertel, 1977). Moreover, indefinite number terms like "some" or "all" may change their meanings according to their function as sentence subject or object. When used in subject position, these lexical indefinite terms tend to be perceived as referring to definite elements of a set (Hörmann, 1982).

Returning to the psychological distinction between active and passive voice, we may draw the following conclusion. Whether the active or passive voice should be preferred in item construction depends on the intended perspective. In neuroticism scales, where the role of the respondent is primarily that of a "patient," the passive voice should be easier to comprehend than the active voice.

Summary

Apart from response sets, understanding of questionnaire items itself may constitute a source of response bias. The understanding of an item may be conceived as a time-dependent process leading from the surface form to the content of the item. To minimize psychological complexity, items should be formulated in such a way that the distance between "surface structure" and "deep structure" is minimal. It is argued that syntactic properties of items, such as passive voice or negation, do not per se sufficiently account for psychological complexity. Using the theoretical framework of case grammar as well as empirical evidence from psycholinguistic research, predictions concerning processing difficulty have been derived, which are partially in contrast to predictions derived from a purely syntactic model.

References

Boysson-Bardies, B. de (1970). Syntax and semantics in memorization of negation. In Flores d'Arcais, G.B.J., & Levelt, W.J.M. (Eds.), *Advances in psycholinguistics* (pp. 237–245). Amsterdam: North-Holland.

Chomsky, N. (1957). *Syntactic structures*. The Hague: Mouton.

Chomsky, N. (1965). *Aspects of the theory of syntax*. Cambridge/Mass.: M.I.T. Press.

Edwards, A.L. (1957). *Techniques of attitude scale construction*. New York: Appleton-Century-Crofts.

Engelkamp, J. (1974). *Psycholinguistik*. Munich: Fink.

Ertel, S. (1974). Satzsubjekt und Ich-Perspektive. In Eckensberger, L.H., & Eckensberger, U.S. (Eds.), *Bericht über den 28. Kongreß der Deutschen Gesellschaft für Psychologie in Saarbrücken 1972* (Vol. 1, pp. 129–139). Göttingen: Hogrefe.

Ertel, S. (1977). Where do the subjects of sentences come from? In Rosenberg, S. (Ed.), *Sentence production. Developments in research and theory* (pp. 141–167). Hillsdale: Erlbaum.
Fillmore, C.J. (1968). The case for case. In Bach, E., & Harms, R. (Eds.), *Universals in linguistic theory* (pp. 1–88). New York: Holt, Rinehart, & Winston.
Fillmore, C.J. (1977). The case for case reopened. In Cole, P., & Sadock, J. (Eds.), *Grammatical relations* (pp. 59–81). New York: Academic.
Fiske, D.W. (1982, June). What can we do with personality questionnaires? *Bielefeld Symposium on Personality Questionnaires*, Bielefeld.
Franks, J.J., & Bransford, J.D. (1974). Memory for syntactic form as a function of semantic context. *Journal of Experimental Psychology, 103*, 1037–1039.
Gough, H.G. (1956). *California Psychological Inventory (CPI)*. Palo Alto: Consulting Psychologists.
Gough, P.B. (1965). Grammatical transformation and speed of understanding. *Journal of Verbal Learning and Verbal Behavior, 4*, 107–111.
Herriot, P. (1969). The comprehension of active and passive sentences as a function of pragmatic expectations. *Journal of Verbal Learning and Verbal Behavior, 8*, 166–169.
Hörmann, H. (1971). Semantic factors in negation. *Psychologische Forschung, 35*, 1–16.
Hörmann, H. (1978). *Meinen und Verstehen*. Frankfurt/M.: Suhrkamp.
Hörmann, H. (1981). *Einführung in die Psycholinguistik*. Darmstadt: Wissenschaftliche Buchgesellschaft.
Hörmann, H. (1982). Hidden determinants of understanding. In LeNy, J.-F., & Kintsch, W. (Eds.), *Language and comprehension* (pp. 251–260). Amsterdam: North-Holland.
Hörmann, H., Pieper, U., & Engelkamp, J. (1976). Zur psychologischen Problematik sog. Altersdialekte. *Psychologische Rundschau, 27*, 12–27.
Jackendoff, R.S. (1969). An interpretive theory of negation. *Foundations of Language, 5*, 218–241.
Janke, W. (1973). Über die Konstruktion von Fragebögen. In Reinert, G. (Ed.), *Bericht über den 27. Kongreß der Deutschen Gesellschaft für Psychologie in Kiel 1970* (pp. 41–48). Göttingen: Hogrefe.
Layton, P., & Simpson, A.J. (1975). Surface and deep structure in sentence comprehension. *Journal of Verbal Learning and Verbal Behavior, 14*, 658–664.
Lienert, G.A. (1969). *Testaufbau und Testanalyse* (3rd ed.). Weinheim: Beltz.
Löhr, F.-J., & Angleitner, A. (1980). Eine Untersuchung zu sprachlichen Formulierungen der Items in deutschen Persönlichkeitsfragebogen. *Zeitschrift für Differentielle und Diagnostische Psychologie, 1*, 217–235.
Löhr, F.-J., & Schütte, W. (1982). *Zur linguistischen Analyse von Fragebogenitems – eine Pilot-Studie*. Bielefeld: Arbeitsbericht aus dem Projekt Persönlichkeitsfragebogen (No. 1), Universität Bielefeld.
Mehler, J. (1963). Some effects of grammatical transformations on the recall of English sentences. *Journal of Verbal Learning and Verbal Behavior, 2*, 346, 351.
Micklin, M., & Durbin, M. (1969). Syntactic dimensions of attitude scaling techniques: Sources of variation and bias. *Sociometry, 32*, 194–206.
Miller, G.A. (1962). Some psychological studies of grammar. *American Psychologist, 17*, 748–762.
Sachs, J.S. (1967). Recognition memory for syntactic and semantic aspects of connected discourse. *Perception and Psychophysics, 2*, 437–442.
Schank, R.C. (1975). *Conceptual information processing*. Amsterdam: North-Holland.
Schwarzer, R. (1982, June). Convergent and discriminant validity in personality assessment: Techniques for distinguishing trait and method variance. *Bielefeld Symposium on Personality Questionnaires*, Bielefeld.
Sherman, M.A. (1976). Adjectival negation and the comprehension of multiply negated sentences. *Journal of Verbal Learning and Verbal Behavior, 15*, 143–157.
Slobin, D.J. (1966). Grammatical transformations and sentence comprehension in childhood and adulthood. *Journal of Verbal Learning and Verbal Behavior, 5*, 219–227.

Slobin, D.J. (1968). Recall of full and truncated passive sentences in connected discourse. *Journal of Verbal Learning and Verbal Behavior, 7*, 876–881.
Wason, P.C., & Johnson-Laird, P.N. (1972). *Psychology of reasoning. Structure and content.* London: Batsford.
Weinert, A.B. (1982). *Deutscher CPI: Testanweisung und Test.* Bern: Huber

IV. Problems of Convergent and Discriminant Validation

Evaluation of Convergent and Discriminant Validity by Use of Structural Equations

RALF SCHWARZER

Introduction

The multitrait-multimethod (MTMM) matrix is a correlation matrix of a set of traits, each of which is measured by the same set of methods. Such a matrix can be generated when there are at least two traits being measured by at least two different methods. Two measures of the same trait should intercorrelate highly in order to indicate "convergent" validity. In addition, the correlation between two methods designed to measure the same trait should be substantially higher than the correlation between two traits when they are measured by the same method. This would be called "discriminant" validity. The idea of analyzing a multitrait-multimethod matrix to determine convergent and discriminant validity was introduced by Campbell and Fiske in 1959. Several generalizations have so far been proposed (Fiske, 1982).

The correlations among variables, all of which are measured by the same method, are included in the monomethod triangles. All other parts of the matrix are heterotrait-heteromethod blocks. There are two types of correlations in each of them: the monotrait values and the heterotrait values. The first are located on the diagonals of each block representing the convergent validities (validity diagonals). The second are the heterotrait-heteromethod correlations.

Campbell and Fiske (1959, pp. 82–83) specify four criteria for the consideration of validity. First, to demonstrate convergent validity, the entries in the validity diagonals should be significant and sufficiently large. The other three criteria focus on discriminant validity. The validity diagonal values should be higher than the values lying in its column and row in the heterotrait-heteromethod blocks. That is, a validity coefficient for a variable should be higher than the coefficients obtained between that variable and any other variable which is designed to assess another construct and which is measured by different methods. Third, a validity diagonal value should be higher than its corresponding value in the monomethod triangle. That is, a variable should correlate more highly with itself when measured by a different method than with measures designed to assess different traits but employing the same method. Finally, the same pattern of trait interrelationship should be shown in all of the heterotrait triangles.

These rather informal rules and heuristic strategies have been revised by several authors. Jackson, for example (1975), suggested that a more profound technique would be one which provides (a) a means of separating trait and method variance components, (b) the capability of identifying as many dimensions as there are traits to be evaluated, (c) a basis for evaluation of evidence of success, and (d) the location of an individual on a dimension which is not biased by method variance. These requirements are met by the structural equation approach, also known as path analysis or the confirmatory factor analysis approach. This paper will deal with that perspective exclusively (Bentler, 1980; Bentler & Weeks, 1980; Blalock, 1982; Duncan, 1975; Heise, 1975; Jöreskog & Sörbom, 1978, 1979, 1981; Rezmovic & Rezmovic, 1981; Schmitt, 1978; Schmitt, Coyle & Saari, 1977).

Basic Ideas of the Structural Equation Approach

The basic ideas of the structural equations approach are the path analytic decomposition of variances and the specification of more or less complex or restricted models to be tested by linear regression methods. One assumption of the approach lies in the existence of latent variables which are seen as responsible for the variation and covariation of the observed variables. Each observed variable is composed of a trait influence and a method influence and, in addition, by a uniqueness or a disturbance. This simple situation can be written as a structural equation: $x = \lambda_1 T + \lambda_2 M + u$. The equation can be illustrated by a path diagram. Latent variables usually are circled, while observed variables are depicted in a rectangle (see Fig. 1).

If there are three traits and three methods, for example, there will be nine observed variables associated with nine disturbances. The variation and covariation are to be seen as caused by six latent variables, three exerting method influence and three exerting content influence. A measurement model is dinstinguished from a structural model. The equations for the measurement model are the following:

$$
\begin{aligned}
x_1 &= \lambda_1 T_1 + \lambda_{10} M_1 + u_1 \\
x_2 &= \lambda_4 T_2 + \lambda_{11} M_1 + u_2 \\
x_3 &= \lambda_7 T_3 + \lambda_{12} M_1 + u_3 \\
x_4 &= \lambda_2 T_1 + \lambda_{13} M_2 + u_4 \\
x_5 &= \lambda_5 T_2 + \lambda_{14} M_2 + u_5 \\
x_6 &= \lambda_8 T_3 + \lambda_{15} M_2 + u_6 \\
x_7 &= \lambda_3 T_1 + \lambda_{16} M_3 + u_7 \\
x_8 &= \lambda_6 T_2 + \lambda_{17} M_3 + u_8 \\
x_9 &= \lambda_9 T_3 + \lambda_{18} M_3 + u_9
\end{aligned}
$$

Each of the x-variables here is composed of a trait factor T_1–T_3, a method factor M_1–M_3, and a uniqueness u_1–u_9.

The structural model (Fig. 2) is subject to theory-derived specifications by the investigator. In Fig. 2 all six latent variables are allowed to be correlated.

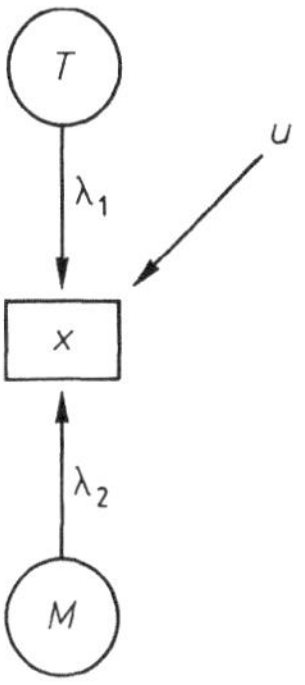

Fig. 1. An observed variable, x, composed of trait variance (T), method variance (M), and uniqueness (u)

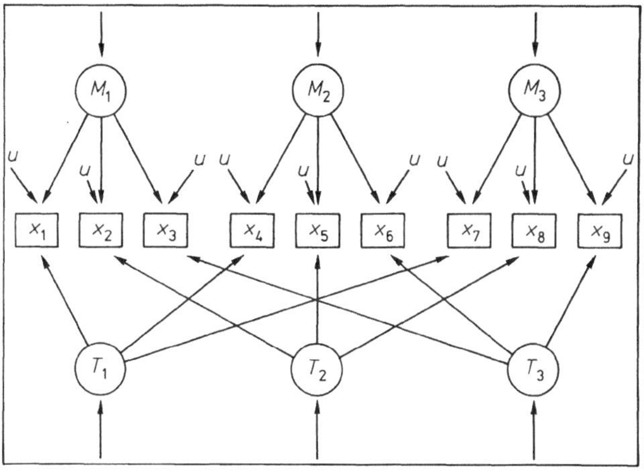

Fig. 2. Model with three traits and three methods

Therefore, this is a six-factor oblique design: 15 factor intercorrelations therefore have to be estimated. The uniqueness terms (u) are usually specified as uncorrelated with all latent variables and with each other. Nine parameters have to be estimated here. In addition, 18 factor loadings are specified as free, all others are fixed at zero. This can be seen in the matrix notation below (Table 1).

In all, $15+9+18=42$ parameters have to be estimated, based on a matrix of 45 observed variances and covariances. So there are three degrees of freedom left, or three overidentifying restrictions. By the way, three traits and three methods are the minimal situation if one wants to specify an overidentified full model. A smaller number of factors requires constraint of parameters and a restricted model.

Table 1. Specification of the factor loadings; 18 parameters are free, all others are fixed at zero

	Trait 1	Trait 2	Trait 3	Method 1	Method 2	Method 3
X_1	1	0	0	2	0	0
X_2	0	3	0	4	0	0
X_3	0	0	5	6	0	0
X_4	7	0	0	0	8	0
X_5	0	9	0	0	10	0
X_6	0	0	11	0	12	0
X_7	13	0	0	0	0	14
X_8	0	15	0	0	0	16
X_9	0	0	17	0	0	18

Table 2. Specification of the covariance matrix of latent variables in the orthogonal model where trait factors and method factors are not correlated with each other

	Trait 1	Trait 2	Trait 3	Method 1	Method 2	Method 3
Trait 1	0					
Trait 2	19	0				
Trait 3	20	21	0			
Method 1	0	0	0	0		
Method 2	0	0	0	22	0	
Method 3	0	0	0	23	24	0

(Nos. 1–18 are identical with Table 1).

Now we turn to three suggested standard models for analyzing a MTMM matrix. First, the full model is the most general design and allows for correlations between all latent variables. Second the orthogonal model, which was proposed by Jöreskog (1971 b), is consistent with the previous ideas of Campbell and Fiske (1959). In this case it is assumed that trait factors and method factors are not correlated with each other. For our specimen model with three traits and three methods this restriction can be shown by the covariance matrix of the latent variables (Table 2). The nine parameters, indicating correlations between trait factors and method factors, are fixed at zero. Therefore only 6, instead of 15, factor correlations have to be estimated. This seems to be the most useful model in MTMM situations. "This is our way of defining each method factor to be independent of the particular traits that the method is used to measure. In other words, method factors are sources of variation and covariation in the data that remain after all trait factors have been eliminated" (Jöreskog, 1971 b, p. 128).

The "equal method effects" model would be even more restricted. In addition to the orthogonal model, the effects of the latent method variables on the

Table 3. Specification of the equal methods effects model

	Trait 1	Trait 2	Trait 3	Method 1	Method 2	Method 3
X_1	1	0	0	2	0	0
X_2	0	3	0	2	0	0
X_3	0	0	4	2	0	0
X_4	5	0	0	0	6	0
X_5	0	7	0	0	6	0
X_6	0	0	8	0	6	0
X_7	9	0	0	0	0	10
X_8	0	11	0	0	0	10
X_0	0	0	12	0	0	10
Trait 1	0					
Trait 2	13	0				
Trait 3	14	15	0			
Method 1	0	0	0	0		
Method 2	0	0	0	16	0	
Method 3	0	0	0	17	18	0

observed variables are assumed to be constant across all such effects of a given method. All paths leading from one latent method variable to the manifest variables are constrained to be equal. On these assumptions, the Campbell-Fiske criteria for discriminant validity are generally valid. As Alwin (1974, p. 96) states, "Since this set of assumptions does allow valid inferences from the use of their criteria for discriminant validity, I shall refer to the model involving these assumptions as the 'implicit' Campbell-Fiske model." In the 3 trait and 3 method case, by this, 6 additional degrees of freedom are gained, yielding 18 overidentifying restrictions. Table 3 provides the corresponding specifications for the measurement model and for the covariance matrix of the latent variables.

An Example with Three Traits and Three Methods

To illustrate the basic ideas discussed so far, a specimen matrix is now presented. Winne and Marx (1981) presented a paper on convergent and discriminant validity in self-concept measurement. They discussed the theoretical facets of academic, physical and social self-concept. Up to now, most attempts to demonstrate discriminant validity among these facets of self-concept have failed. The three traits of self-concept were measured by three different methods. The first is the Sears Self-Concept Inventory. The second is a new instrument by the authors themselves asking the students to compare themselves with their peers. The subjects had to respond to 18 items like, "How many other students are smarter than you?" on a five-point scale anchored by "almost everyone" to "almost no one." The responses were summed to produce scores for academic, physical, and social comparison, each based on six items. The third instrument instructed students to "tell how you feel about how you rank," by responding on a five-point scale to nine items like, "I feel (great, badly) about how popular I am." The responses were summed to produce scores for academic, physical, and social satisfaction, each based on three items. So there are three traits (academic, physical, and social self concept) measured by three methods (Sears, comparison, satisfaction). The MTMM matrix is presented in Table 4. All three standard models discussed earlier were tried out. The full model and the equal method effects model yielded unfavorable results, i.e., their goodness of fit was poor, the numbers of iterations exceeded 250, or their results were anomalous (e.g., negative disturbances and factor loadings above unity). The orthogonal model, however, turned out to be adequate. Table 5 shows the results. There are several goodness of fit indices which prove that this orthogonal model fits our matrix of observed covariances nearly perfectly (Table 6).

The average of the residual is only .02, that is, the original correlation matrix is reproduced very well. The nine observed variables are clearly determined by three construct dimensions. Especially the academic and physical dimensions produce high loadings. Also, there are three clear method factors contributing differently to the variation of the observed variables. They are correlated with each other (.577, .697, .572). The self-concept dimensions are also correlated with each other. Physical and social self-concepts are correlated ($r=.298$), which is a familiar degree of relationship in this context. The other two correlations are negative. This is in line with the suggestions of the authors. They claim a compensatory self-concept model, that is, low academic self-concept may be compensated by a high social self-concept. This cannot be detected at the level of observed variables. Recall that all significant values in the MTMM matrix had been positive. Only the structural equations approach reveals that true interrelationships between underlying sources of covariation.

Table 4. Multitrait-multimethod matrix consisting of Academic (1), Physical (2), and Social (3) self-concept measured by Sears Inventory (A) and comparison (B), and satisfaction (C) rating scales. (Winne & Marx, 1981)

	A1	A2	A3	B1	B2	B3	C1	C2	C3
A1	1.000								
A2	.370	1.000							
A3	.480	.540	1.000						
B1	.490	−.030	−.030	1.000					
B2	.220	.770	.330	.140	1.000				
B3	.110	.350	.370	.060	.540	1.000			
C1	.610	−.010	.100	.600	−.020	−.050	1.000		
C2	.230	.730	.420	−.020	.700	.390	.140	1.000	
C3	.220	.440	.550	−.070	.400	.480	.080	.560	1.000

Table 5. Results for the orthogonal model

LISREL estimates (maximum likelihood)

λ

	ξ_1	ξ_2	ξ_3	ξ_4	ξ_5	ξ_6
A1	0.396	0.0	0.0	0.821	0.0	0.0
A2	0.0	0.737	0.0	0.610	0.0	0.0
A3	0.0	0.0	0.383	0.722	0.0	0.0
B1	0.625	0.0	0.0	0.0	0.484	0.0
B2	0.0	0.700	0.0	0.0	0.682	0.0
B3	0.0	0.0	0.479	0.0	0.577	0.0
C1	0.718	0.0	0.0	0.0	0.0	0.580
C2	0.0	0.631	0.0	0.0	0.0	0.642
C3	0.0	0.0	0.530	0.0	0.0	0.642

ϕ

	ξ_1	ξ_2	ξ_3	ξ_4	ξ_5	ξ_6
KSI 1	1.000					
KSI 2	−0.473	1.000				
KSI 3	−0.752	0.398	1.000			
KSI 4	0.0	0.0	0.0	1.000		
KSI 5	0.0	0.0	0.0	0.577	1.000	
KSI 6	0.0	0.0	0.0	0.697	0.572	1.000

δ

A1	A2	A3	B1	B2	B3	C1	C2	C3
0.170	0.083	0.331	0.368	0.026	0.450	0.162	0.192	0.291

Squared multiple correlations for x variables

A1	A2	A3	B1	B2	B3	C1	C2	C3
0.830	0.917	0.669	0.632	0.974	0.550	0.838	0.808	0.709

Table 6. Measures of goodness of fit for the whole model employing the LISREL V program ($n = 181$)

1. Chi-square with 12 degrees of freedom	10.74	(probability level = 0.551)
2. Jöreskog goodness of fit index	0.978	
3. Jöreskog adjusted goodness of fit index	0.918	
4. Tucker-Lewis coefficient	1.00	
5. Bentler's Delta	0.988	
6. Root mean square residual	0.021	

Table 7. Decomposition of variances

Variable	Trait	Method	Uniqueness
Sears Academic	.157	.674	.170
Sears Physical	.543	.372	.083
Sears Social	.147	.521	.331
Academic comparison	.391	.234	.368
Physical comparison	.490	.465	.026
Social comparison	.229	.333	.450
Academic satisfaction	.516	.336	.162
Physical satisfaction	.398	.412	.192
Social satisfaction	.281	.412	.291

To learn more about the coefficients, a decomposition of variances can be performed (Table 7). The values can be decomposed by dividing them into trait and method variance, each equal to the corresponding squared factor loading. As can be seen, the physical facet of self-concept is assessed in the most reliable way, whereas the opposite is true for the social facet. Especially the social comparison measure is strained by 45% of uniqueness. On the whole, there are equal amounts of trait variance and method variance in the observed variables.

Decomposition of Reproduced Correlations

The last section demonstrated by use of an example what can be done in an elegant way to obtain information about convergent and discriminant validity. An additional way of gaining even more information about the data is to decompose the reproduced correlations, which is less elegant and very time consuming, but is illustrative and useful. First, a theoretical description is given. Afterwards the idea will be applied to our example.

The correlation between observed variables can be decomposed with respect to the interrelationship of latent traits and methods. Let us take two correlated observed variables x and y. The question is, by which sources the intercorrelation is caused. Figure 3 a illustrates the assumption that the total correlation of x and y is due to two different traits T_1 and T_2 ($r_{xy}=atb$). (t, m, p, and q are factor intercorrelations; a, b, c, and d are path coefficients.) In the special case of trait orthogonality $t=0$ and, therefore, $r_{xy}=0$. In the special case of trait unity, $t=1$ and the correlation $r_{xy}=ab$, which is identical to a "one trait-two indicator situation" (two congeneric tests). Figure 3 b illustrates the assumption that the total correlation of x and y is due to two different methods, M_1 and M_2 ($r_{xy}=cmd$). If there is no correlation between the methods, the covariance between x and y also vanishes. If the two methods become similar we will obtain a monomethod situation ($r_{xy}=cd$). Figures 3 c and

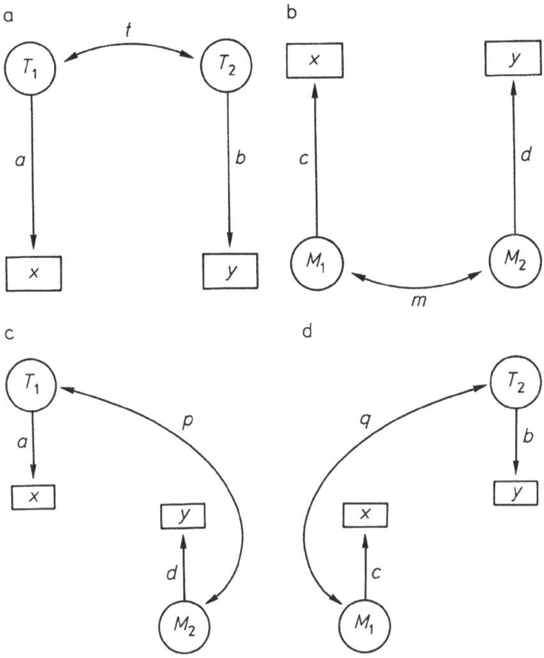

Fig. 3 a–d. Decomposition of a correlation r_{xy}. **a** By two traits; **b** by two methods; **c** by one trait and one method; **d** by one trait and one method

d illustrate the assumption that the total correlation of x and y is due to a correlation between trait T_1 and method M_2 ($r_{xy}=apd$) or between T_2 and M_1 ($r_{xy}=cqb$). From a theoretical point of view such correlations should be zero in order to obtain discriminant validity, but in practice these trait-method interrelationships occur. Two strategies are possible: one is to explore such correlations in order to learn about the data, and the other is to specify only orthogonal models, which exclude unwanted effects because they are not hypothesized. The first yields more information, while the second is more parsimonious and confirmatory.

Following this second strategy we now transfer the decomposition rules to the three kinds of correlations within a MTMM matrix. Figure 4a illustrates the monotrait-heteromethod case (MTHM). As an example, one value r_{xy} is selected from a validity diagonal to be decomposed with respect to trait and method influences. The correlation $r_{xy}=ab+cmd$ consists of two parts, one due to a common trait and the other due to separate methods. Minimal convergent validity is demonstrated by $ab>cmd$. In the case of two orthogonal methods ($m=0$) the term "cmd" becomes zero; then they can be treated as uniqueness. In any case the term "ab" has to be as high as possible.

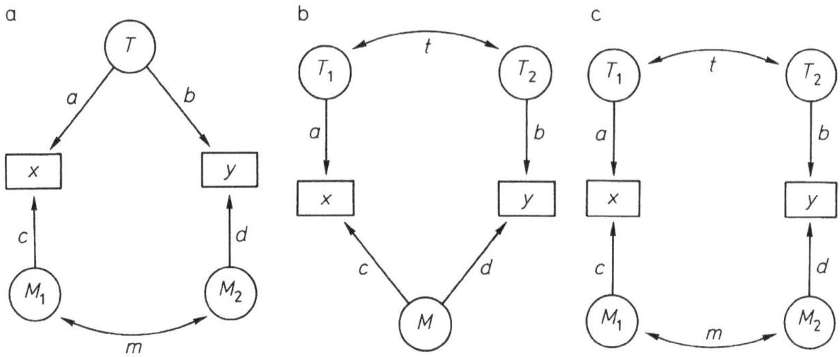

Fig. 4 a–c. Decomposition of a correlation r_{xy}. **a** By one trait and two methods; **b** by two traits and one method; **c** by two traits and two methods

Figure 4b illustrates the heterotrait-monomethod (HTMM) case, that is, a coefficient in the monomethod triangles is to be decomposed. The coefficient $r_{xy} = atb + cd$, the first part being due to the separate traits and the second due to the common method. A dominant method effect is given by $cd > atb$. In the case of trait orthogonality ($t = 0$) the total intercorrelation of the two observed variables is caused by the fact that they share the same method. At least, low trait intercorrelations are needed for discriminant validity to be obtained.

Figure 4c illustrates the heterotrait-heteromethod (HTHM) case, that is, coefficients located below and above the validity diagonals. The coefficient $r_{xy} = atb + cmd$ is influenced by traits and methods. It is expected that $atb \approx cdm$. If intermethod correlations are too high they will be too influential. If intertrait relationships are too high they will predominate. A balance is desirable to obtain discriminant validity. Both the traits and the methods should be very dissimilar from each other, and the correlation should be as low as possible.

It should be recalled that in none of three cases is there any trait-method intercorrelation, because we have specified an orthogonal model in advance, based on the assumption that such intercorrelations should be zero as they otherwise represent a threat to construct validity. Note that the decomposition of reproduced correlations is only a supplement to the analysis by the structural equation approach. Lisrel does not contain any procedures like these. Therefore such decomposition lacks parsimony because each correlation coefficient has to be decomposed (or at least a selection of correlation coefficients).

Let me now return to our example and decompose 3 of the 36 reproduced correlations. First, one coefficient is selected from the validity diagonal (MTHM case). The physical self-concept (2) measured by the Sears Inventory (A) is associated with itself, measured by the comparison method (B); $r = .756$.

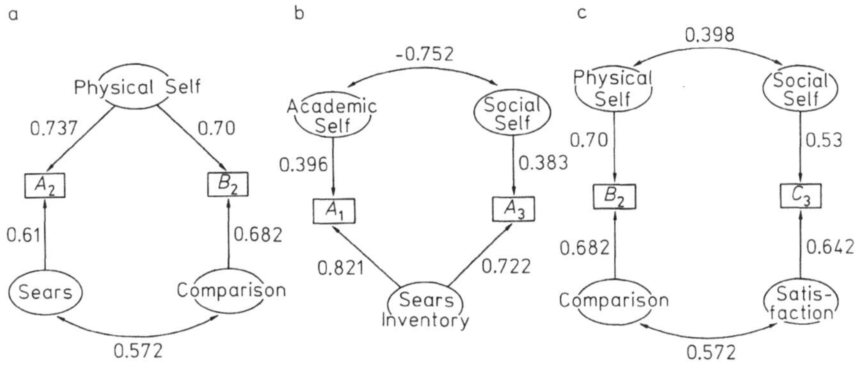

Fig. 5 a. Decomposition of a monotrait-heteromethod correlation coefficient of .756, proving convergent validity; **b** decomposition of a heterotrait-monomethod correlation coefficient of .479, proving a strong method effect; **c** breakdown of a heterotrait-heteromethod correlation coefficient of .398

Figure 5a shows the decomposition. The trait influence is $.737 \times .70 = .516$, and the method influence is $.61 \times .572 \times .682 = .238$, which leads us to the conclusion that the correlation is mostly due to the same underlying trait, therefore demonstrating convergent validity.

In Fig. 5b one value is selected from a heterotrait-monomethod (HTMM) triangle. The correlation between academic (1) and social (3) self-concept is $r = .479$, both measured by the Sears Inventory (A). This is a very interesting case, because the correlation is positive even though the two underlying traits are correlated negatively ($r = -.752$). Here we have a strong positive method effect of $.821 \times .722 = .593$, in contrast to a weak negative trait effect of $.396 \times .383 \times -.752 = -.114$, producing a positive correlation of $r = .479$. Sharing of the same method appears to be the reason why observed measures of academic and social self-concept are positively correlated in contrast to their underlying traits. As can be seen, our decomposition strategy has proven a strong method effect.

Finally, a heterotrait-heteromethod (HTHM) value will be decomposed (Fig. 5c). Physical self-concept (2) measured by the comparison method (B) and social self-concept (3) measured by the satisfaction method (C) are correlated with a coefficient of .398. This is exactly the same correlation as is estimated between the two underlying traits ($r = .398$). But the trait effect is only $.70 \times .398 \times .53 = .148$, whereas the method effect is $.682 \times .572 \times .642 = .25$. Therefore, this correlation seems to be predominantly influenced by method variance.

In sum, these selected findings are in line with the assumptions of convergent and discriminant validity of the variables at hand.

Three Traits and Two Situations: The State-Trait Personality Inventory

As noted earlier, three traits and three methods are the minimum situation if one wants to specify an overidentified full model. A smaller number of factors requires constrained parameters and a restricted model. What kind of restriction is chosen to be adequate will depend on the theory. A standard procedure could be to apply the equal method effects model that is characterized by equal loadings within each of the two method factors. Then, the three trait factors are allowed to be correlated among each other as well as the two method factors are. But method factors are not allowed to correlate with trait factors.

This strategy was applied to data which we obtained in one of our educational research projects using the State-Trait Personality Inventory (STPI). The STPI is an instrument designed to assess three constructs at a state level and at a trait level. It was developed by Spielberger (1979) and his coworkers. The German version is still in the developmental stage. The three traits are anxiety, curiosity, and anger. The state (S) condition is evoked by asking the subjects to describe their present feelings. The trait (T) condition is evoked by asking them how they generally feel. Each subscale consists of ten items. So there are six subscales referred to as State-Anxiety, State-Curiosity, State-Anger, Trait-Anxiety, Trait-Curiosity, and Trait-Anger. Subjects respond to the STPI by rating themselves on a four-point scale (Schwarzer, 1984; Schwarzer & Schwarzer, 1982; Schwarzer, Jerusalem & Lange, 1982).

Table 8. Correlation matrix of the STPI ($n = 1739$)

	SANXIET	SCURIOS	SANGER	TANXIET	TCURIOS	TANGER
SANXIET	1.000					
SCURIOS	−0.006	1.000				
SANGER	0.576	−0.011	1.000			
TANXIET	0.598	−0.096	0.385	1.000		
TCURIOS	−0.008	0.724	0.010	−0.134	1.000	
TANGER	0.439	0.167	0.456	0.505	0.220	1.000

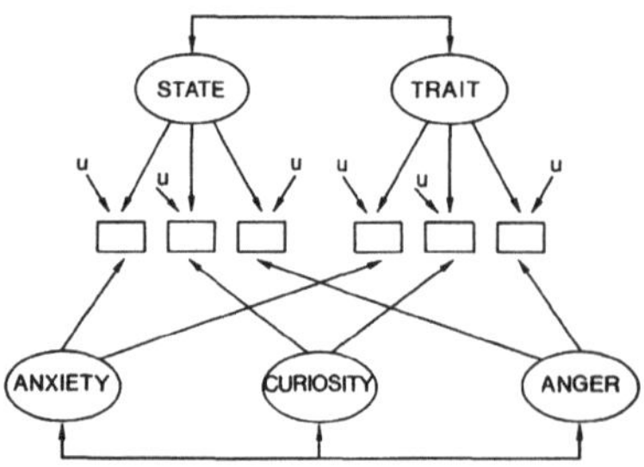

Fig. 6. Model for the STPI without correlations among the traits and the situations

In 1980, these scales were given to 1531 students who attended grades 6 or 9. The sample was divided into four groups according to sex and grade level. For these four subsamples many LISREL runs were performed without finding a satisfactory solution.

In 1981, the same sample of students, who now were attending grades 7 or 10, was retested ($n = 1739$). The correlation matrix is depicted in Table 8, and the orthogonal model, in Fig. 6.

The equal methods effects model turned out to be inadequate. The two situations – state and trait – were too similar to each other and did not account for distinctive variance. Therefore, it was necessary to fix their intercorrelation at 1, which means a loss of the original diagnostic concept. This time the estimates were not bad. Again, they could be improved by allowing the distur-

Table 9. Parameter estimates

LISREL estimates (maximum likelihood)

λ

	ξ_1	ξ_2	ξ_3	ξ_4	ξ_5
SANXIET	0.644	0.0	0.0	0.141	0.0
SCURIOS	0.0	0.716	0.0	0.141	0.0
SANGER	0.0	0.0	0.499	0.141	0.0
TANXIET	0.864	0.0	0.0	0.0	0.106
TCURIOS	0.0	0.993	0.0	0.0	0.106
TANGER	0.0	0.0	0.842	0.0	0.106

ϕ

	ξ_1	ξ_2	ξ_3	ξ_4	ξ_5
ξ_1	1.000				
ξ_2	−0.124	1.000			
ξ_3	0.718	0.204	1.000		
ξ_4	0.0	0.0	0.0	1.000	
ξ_5	0.0	0.0	0.0	1.000	1.000

δ

	SANXIET	SCURIOS	SANGER	TANXIET	TCURIOS	TANGER
SANXIET	0.531					
SCURIOS	0.0	0.470				
SANGER	0.263	0.0	0.712			
TANXIET	0.0	0.0	0.0	0.241		
TCURIOS	0.0	0.0	0.0	0.0	0.004	
TANGER	0.0	0.0	0.0	0.0	0.0	0.278

Squared multiple correlations for x variables

SANXIET	SCURIOS	SANGER	TANXIET	TCURIOS	TANGER
0.469	0.530	0.288	0.759	0.996	0.722

bances of S-Anxiety and S-Anger to be correlated. This final solution will be discussed in the following section.

Table 9 presents the estimates. The first three factors are content dimensions for anxiety, curiosity, and anger. The weightings are meaningful and consistent with previous research. The fourth and fifth factors have to be interpreted as a single method or situation factor, because their intercorrelation was fixed at 1 in advance. The other correlations are meaningful. Anxiety and

Table 10. Measures of goodness of fit for the whole model

Chi-square with	3 degrees of freedom	99.79	(probability level = 0.000)
	Goodness of fit index	0.954	
	Adjusted goodness of fit index	0.677	
	Root mean square residual	0.046	
	Tucker – Lewis coefficient	.825	
	Bentler's Delta	.973	

Table 11. Standard errors

	λ				
	ξ_1	ξ_2	ξ_3	ξ_4	ξ_5
SANXIET	0.040	0.0	0.0	0.125	0.0
SCURIOS	0.0	0.042	0.0	0.125	0.0
SANGER	0.0	0.0	0.049	0.125	0.0
TANXIET	0.039	0.0	0.0	0.0	0.236
TCURIOS	0.0	0.047	0.0	0.0	0.236
TANGER	0.0	0.0	0.036	0.0	0.236

	ϕ				
	ξ_1	ξ_2	ξ_3	ξ_4	ξ_5
KSI 1	0.0				
KSI 2	0.073	0.0			
KSI 3	0.036	0.058	0.0		
KSI 4	0.0	0.0	0.0	0.0	
KSI 5	0.0	0.0	0.0	0.0	0.0

	δ					
	SANXIET	SCURIOS	SANGER	TANXIET	TCURIOS	TANGER
SANXIET	0.027					
SCURIOS	0.0	0.041				
SANGER	0.022	0.0	0.031			
TANXIET	0.0	0.0	0.0	0.030		
TCURIOS	0.0	0.0	0.0	0.0	0.070	
TANGER	0.0	0.0	0.0	0.0	0.0	0.043

anger are highly associated with each other. The Theta Delta matrix shows the uniquenesses as specified. S-Curiosity is strained by a disturbance of .712. The squared multiple correlations also make it clear that the three state measures are not well represented in this solution, in contrast to the three trait measures.

Table 10 shows the goodness of fit indices. The χ^2 is significant owing to the large sample size ($n = 1739$). The other indices are satisfactory. Especially Bentler's Delta (.97) indicates a good fit. Also, the standard errors (Table 11) are tolerable. However, the t values (Table 12) show that the six loadings on the method factor are not significant and would therefore be better omitted, leaving three trait factors only. This is also true for the correlation between anxiety and curiosity and for the disturbance of T-Curiosity.

Table 13 shows the residuals and the normalized residuals. Two of the residuals exceed the 0.10 limit, and five of the normalized residuals exceed the 2.0 limit. Due to these indices it must be concluded that the search for method or situation effects in this MTMM matrix was not successful, although there

Table 12. *t* Values

	λ				
	ξ_1	ξ_2	ξ_3	ξ_4	ξ_5
SANXIET	16.244	0.0	0.0	1.128	0.0
SCURIOS	0.0	17.160	0.0	1.128	0.0
SANGER	0.0	0.0	10.266	1.128	0.0
TANXIET	22.228	0.0	0.0	0.0	0.448
TCURIOS	0.0	21.068	0.0	0.0	0.448
TANGER	0.0	0.0	23.567	0.0	0.448

	ϕ				
	ξ_1	ξ_2	ξ_3	ξ_4	ξ_5
KSI 1	0.0				
KSI 2	− 1.696	0.0			
KSI 3	19.829	3.500	0.0		
KSI 4	0.0	0.0	0.0	0.0	
KSI 5	0.0	0.0	0.0	0.0	0.0

	δ					
	SANXIET	SCURIOS	SANGER	TANXIET	TCURIOS	TANGER
SANXIET	19.777					
SCURIOS	0.0	11.338				
SANGER	11.898	0.0	23.283			
TANXIET	0.0	0.0	0.0	8.010		
TCURIOS	0.0	0.0	0.0	0.0	0.052	
TANGER	0.0	0.0	0.0	0.0	0.0	6.451

Table 13. Residuals

	σ					
	SANXIET	SCURIOS	SANGER	TANXIET	TCURIOS	TANGER
SANXIET	0.966					
SCURIOS	−0.037	1.002				
SANGER	0.513	0.093	0.981			
TANXIET	0.571	−0.061	0.324	1.000		
TCURIOS	−0.064	0.726	0.116	−0.095	1.001	
TANGER	0.404	0.138	0.435	0.533	0.182	0.998
	Residual variances and covariances					
	SANXIET	SCURIOS	SANGER	TANXIET	TCURIOS	TANGER
SANXIET	0.034					
SCURIOS	0.031	−0.002				
SANGER	0.063	−0.104	0.019			
TANXIET	0.027	−0.034	0.060	0.000		
TCURIOS	0.056	−0.001	−0.106	−0.039	−0.001	
TANGER	0.035	0.029	0.021	−0.029	0.038	0.002
	Normalized residuals					
	SANXIET	SCURIOS	SANGER	TANXIET	TCURIOS	TANGER
SANXIET	1.044					
SCURIOS	1.325	−0.051				
SANGER	2.400	−4.357	0.577			
TANXIET	0.979	−1.418	2.417	0.011		
TCURIOS	2.389	−0.042	−4.433	−1.629	−0.026	
TANGER	1.364	1.218	0.816	−1.062	1.555	0.049

is evidence of a good fit by the indices. A respecification should exclude the two method factors. But this is beyond the scope of the present paper.

Two Traits and Four Methods

The Problem

If there are fewer than three traits or methods the full model will not be identified, which means that no unique solution exists. Therefore, a restricted model has to be specified. To illustrate this case, an example is chosen which has already been reanalyzed by Kenny (1976).

Jaccard, Weber, and Lundmark (1975) studied the attitudes towards cigarette smoking and capital punishment by means of four methods: semantic differential, Likert, Thurstone and Guilford scaling procedures. The correlations

Table 14. Correlation matrix to be analyzed

	C1	P1	C2	P2	C3	P3	C4	P4
C1	1.000							
P1	0.290	1.000						
C2	0.780	0.230	1.000					
P2	0.280	0.840	0.290	1.000				
C3	0.810	0.190	0.770	0.180	1.000			
P3	0.260	0.810	0.310	0.890	0.240	1.000		
C4	0.760	0.100	0.710	0.090	0.810	0.080	1.000	
P4	0.270	0.840	0.240	0.910	0.230	0.850	0.150	1.00

of the eight measures are presented in Table 14. The correlations between the four methods measuring only one of the two attitudes are very high, indicating convergent validity. The values in the validity diagonals are much higher than any other value in the matrix, indicating discriminant validity.

Due to the small sample size ($n=35$) the analysis has to be considered as illustrative only.

Kenny (1976) applied confirmatory factor analysis to these data. He overcame the identification problem by specifying two factors only, namely cigarette smoking factor and capital punishment factor. Each attitude was equipped with four indicators representing the four methods. To check for method effects he allowed each method to be correlated; for example, cigarette smoking measured by the Likert method was allowed to correlate with capital punishment measured by the same method. So his design contained the following three parameters: eight factor loadings (four at each factor), eight disturbances, four intercorrelated disturbances (method effects) and one interfactor correlation. This adds up to 21 free parameters facing 36 correlations, which means that there are 15 overidentifying restrictions (degrees of freedom). Kenny obtained a χ^2 of 10.35, indicating a satisfactory goodness of fit.

The following reanalysis is performed to illustrate an alternative model to cope with the identification problem based on the same number of overidentifying restrictions.

The Model Specification and the Parameter Estimates

The structural equation model was specified as an equal method effects model, that is, the two observed variables affected by each of the four methods should have equal loadings and also trait and method factors should be uncorrelated. In addition, all four indicators of each factor were constrained to be equal. This is a very restricted model (Table 15), which demands estimation of only 21 parameters, leaving 15 degrees of freedom.

The model turned out to fit the data in a satisfactory manner (Table 16). The coefficients of Tucker-Lewis and Bentler indicate a perfect solution, whereas the indices provided by Jöreskog are less positive. It has to be taken into account that $n=35$. The correlations are therefore unstable.

Table 15. Analysis of parameter specifications in Kenny's data (Kenny, 1976, p. 152) with two traits and four methods

Parameter specifications

	λ					
	ξ_1	ξ_2	ξ_3	ξ_4	ξ_5	ξ_6
C1	1	0	2	0	0	0
P1	0	3	2	0	0	0
C2	1	0	0	4	0	0
P2	0	3	0	4	0	0
C3	1	0	0	0	5	0
P3	0	3	0	0	5	0
C4	1	0	0	0	0	6
P4	0	3	0	0	0	6

	ϕ					
	ξ_1	ξ_2	ξ_3	ξ_4	ξ_5	ξ_6
KSI 1	0					
KSI 2	7	0				
KSI 3	0	0	0			
KSI 4	0	0	8	0		
KSI 5	0	0	9	10	0	
KSI 6	0	0	11	12	13	0

δ								
	C1	P1	C2	P2	C3	P3	C4	P4
1	14	15	16	17	18	19	20	21

Table 16. Measures of goodness of fit for the whole model (LISREL V)

Chi-square with 15 degrees of freedomes	11.63	(probability level = 0.0707)
Jöreskog goodness of fit index	0.723	
Jöreskog adjusted goodness of fit index	0.336	
Tucker-Lewis coefficient	1.03	
Bentler's Delta	0.96	
Root mean square residual	0.057	

The parameter estimates (Table 17) show very high loadings for the two trait factors and rather low loadings for the four method factors, all constrained to be equal within one dimension. This means convergent validity. The trait factor intercorrelation turned out to be .20, which is not too far from Kenny's solution ($r = .25$), indicating discriminant validity (see Fig. 7). The methods factor intercorrelations are rather high, demonstrating that these methods are not as dissimilar as is desirable for validation purposes.

Table 17. LISREL estimates (maximum likelihood)

	λ					
	ξ_1	ξ_2	ξ_3	ξ_4	ξ_5	ξ_6
C1	0.856	0.0	0.310	0.0	0.0	0.0
P1	0.0	0.906	0.310	0.0	0.0	0.0
C2	0.856	0.0	0.0	0.334	0.0	0.0
P2	0.0	0.906	0.0	0.334	0.0	0.0
C3	0.856	0.0	0.0	0.0	0.302	0.0
P3	0.0	0.906	0.0	0.0	0.302	0.0
C4	0.856	0.0	0.0	0.0	0.0	0.278
P4	0.0	0.906	0.0	0.0	0.0	0.278

	φ					
	ξ_1	ξ_2	ξ_3	ξ_4	ξ_5	ξ_6
ξ_1	1.000					
ξ_2	0.196	1.000				
ξ_3	0.0	0.0	1.000			
ξ_4	0.0	0.0	0.699	1.000		
ξ_5	0.0	0.0	0.603	0.635	1.000	
ξ_6	0.0	0.0	0.579	0.537	0.597	1.000

δ

C1	P1	C2	P2	C3	P3	C4	P4
0.837	0.200	0.236	0.030	0.132	0.134	0.214	0.069

Squared multiple correlations for x variables

C1	P1	C2	P2	C3	P3	C4	P4
0.837	0.800	0.764	0.970	0.868	0.866	0.786	0.931

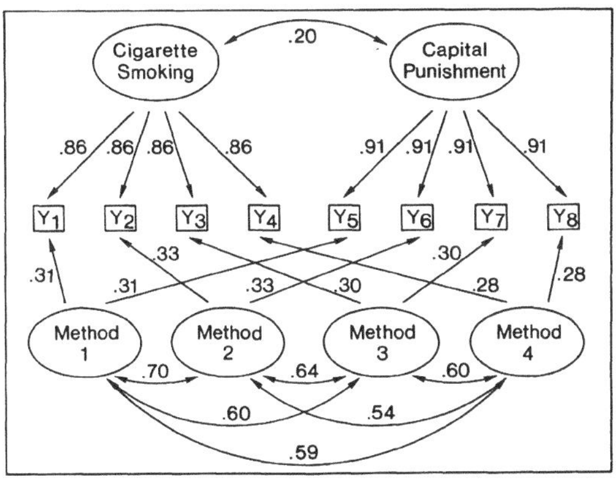

Fig. 7. A model with two traits and four methods

Table 18. Analysis of residuals in Kenny's data (Kenny, 1976, p. 152) with two traits and four methods

Residuals

Sigma

	C1	P1	C2	P2	C3	P3	C4	P4
C1	0.992							
P1	0.248	1.116						
C2	0.805	0.224	1.080					
P2	0.224	0.892	0.263	0.961				
C3	0.789	0.208	0.797	0.216	0.956			
P3	0.208	0.877	0.216	0.884	0.243	1.045		
C4	0.783	0.202	0.783	0.202	0.783	0.202	1.024	
P4	0.202	0.870	0.202	0.870	0.202	0.870	0.229	0.966

Residual variances and covariances

	C1	P1	C2	P2	C3	P3	C4	P4
C1	0.008							
P1	0.042	−0.116						
C2	−0.025	0.006	−0.080					
P2	0.056	−0.052	0.027	−0.0039				
C3	0.021	−0.018	−0.027	−0.036	0.044			
P3	0.052	−0.067	0.094	0.060	−0.003	−0.045		
C4	−0.023	−0.102	−0.073	−0.112	0.027	−0.122	−0.024	
P4	0.068	−0.030	0.038	0.040	0.028	−0.020	−0.079	0.034

Normalized residuals

	C1	P1	C2	P2	C3	P3	C4	P4
C1	0.032							
P1	0.226	−0.430						
C2	−0.112	0.030	−0.306					
P2	0.325	−0.224	0.148	0.165				
C3	0.096	−0.101	−0.122	−0.213	0.189			
P3	0.290	−0.279	0.506	0.026	−0.018	−0.179		
C4	−0.104	−0.545	−0.323	−0.642	0.125	−0.674	−0.096	
P4	0.399	−0.129	0.215	0.181	0.167	−0.088	−0.450	0.147

Table 18 shows the reproduced correlations and the residuals. This table can be the starting point for a decomposition of correlations, which would underline the very impressive convergent validities and the mere absence of method effects for the example at hand.

Conclusions

The superior method of analyzing an MTMM is now the structural equation approach, which usually is realized by running the LISREL program. Until now this procedure has not been widely used because of its difficulty and because of lack of availability. In some years, when researchers have become more familiar with it, increased use of it can be predicted.

Problems arise with small samples, nonlinear relationships, and nonnormally distributed variables. But this is common to most multivariate procedures and therefore cannot be seen as a specific shortcoming of the structural equation approach.

Another problem may be that a full model is not always testable. If all correlations among latent variables and all uniquenesses are to be estimated at least three traits and three methods are necessary for identification of the model. Even if these preconditions are fulfilled the model still may be empirically underidentified (Kenny, 1979). On the other hand, a full model is not necessarily always the best one. LISREL provides several means of constraining parameters to test a restricted model with theoretical assumptions in mind. As Alwin (1974) has suggested, an orthogonal model and an equal method effects model are in line with the original philosophy of Campbell and Fiske (1959).

To sum up, I would like to list the advantages of the structural equation approach to a MTMM matrix:

1. It allows testing of explicit hypotheses referring to underlying latent variables rather than to relationships among manifest variables. Specific statements of the nature of assumptions that disclose the researcher's intentions are necessary.
2. It allows the estimation of trait and method impact on each measure as well as the estimation of the uniqueness associated with each measure. This allows decomposition of effects, providing variance components that may be attributed to different sources of variance according to the previously established specification. Also, an estimate of reliability can be obtained by subtracting the uniqueness from unity.
3. It is possible to determine the location of individuals on an underlying latent trait continuum.
4. It allows the estimation of correlations between methods, between traits, and between traits and methods if the model is identified. It provides an empirical test of the number of factors that yield the best fit to the data.
5. The fit of the model to the data can be tested empirically. Several indices could be used for this purpose: a chi-square value for overall goodness of fit, a matrix of residuals, the Tucker-Lewis coefficient, and Bentler's Delta. The difference of goodness of fit of competitive models can be tested.
6. It allows specification of alternate models with different kinds and degrees of restriction, but replications of the final solution are necessary. An elegant way to do this is to analyze one model for several groups simultaneously.
7. It is the most general procedure. The design need not be factorial. If, for example, one trait in one of the methods is missing, the analysis can still be done.

8. A decomposition of selected reproduced correlations reveals convergent validities and method effects in detail.
9. Finally, the method is illustrative and therefore the results are easily understandable for the reader.

Summary

The traditional procedure in analyzing a multitrait-multimethod matrix is intuitive and informal. One modern strategy for obtaining precise information on convergent and discriminant validity is an approach in which all traits and methods are specified as latent variables. This can be seen as a special case of confirmatory factor analysis or path analysis. This strategy is applied here (a) to the distinction between three facets of self-concept, (b) to the validation of anxiety, curiosity, and anger measured both as a trait and as a state, and (c) to the validation of two attitudes concerning cigarette smoking and capital punishment. The parameters were estimated by the LISREL V program. The results encourage further applications in educational research.

References

Alwin, D.F. (1974). Approaches to the interpretation of relationships in the multitrait-multimethod matrix. In Costner, H.L. (Ed.), *Sociological methodology 1973–1974* (pp. 79–105). San Francisco: Jossey-Bass.

Bentler, P.M. (1980). Multivariate analysis with latent variables: Causal modeling. *Annual Review of Psychology, 31*, 419–456.

Bentler, P.M., & Bonett, D.G. (1980). Significance tests and goodness of fit in the analysis of covariance structures. *Psychological Bulletin, 88*, 588–606.

Bentler, P.M., & Weeks, D.G. (1980). Linear structural equations with latent variables. *Psychometrika 45*, 289–308.

Blalock, H.M. (1982). *Conceptualization and measurement in the social sciences.* Beverly Hills: Sage.

Campbell, D.T., & Fiske, D.W. (1959). Convergent and discriminant validation by the multitrait-multimethod matrix. *Psychological Bulletin, 56*, 81–105.

Duncan, O.D. (1975). *Introduction to structural equation methods.* New York: Academic.

Fiske, D.W. (1982). Convergent-discriminant validation in measurements and research strategies. In Brinberg, D., & Kidder, L. (Eds.), *New directions for methodology of social and behavioral science: Forms of validity in research* (No. 12, 77–92). San Francisco: Jossey-Bass.

Heise, D.R. (1975). *Causal analysis.* New York: Wiley.

Jaccard, J., Weber, J., & Lundmark, J. (1975). A multitrait-multimethod analysis of four attitude assessment procedures. *Journal of Experimental Social Psychology, 11*, 149–154.

Jackson, D.N. (1975). Multimethod factor analysis: A reformulation. *Multivariate Behavioral Research, 10*, 259–276.

Jöreskog, K.G. (1971 a). Simultaneous factor analysis in several populations. *Psychometrika, 36*, 409–426.

Jöreskog, K.G. (1971 b). Statistical analysis of sets of congeneric tests. *Psychometrika, 36*, 109–133.

Jöreskog, K.G., & Sörbom, D. (1978). *Lisrel: Analysis of linear structural relationships by the method of maximum likelihood (Version IV).* Chicago: NER.

Jöreskog, K.G., & Sörbom, D. (1979). Advances in factor analysis and structural equation models. Cambridge, Mass.: Abt. Books.

Jöreskog, K.G., & Sörbom, D. (1981). LISREL V. *Analysis of linear structural relationship by maximum likelihood and least squares methods* (Research report 81–8). Uppsala: University of Uppsala.

Kenny, D. (1976). An empirical application of confirmatory factor analysis to the multitrait-multimethod matrix. *Journal of Experimental Social Psychology, 12*, 247–252.

Kenny, D.A. (1979). *Correlation and causality*. New York: Wiley.

Rezmovic, E.L., & Rezmovic, V. (1981). A confirmatory factor analysis approach to construct validation. *Educational and Psychological Measurement, 41*, 61–72.

Schmitt, N. (1978). Path analysis of multitrait-multimethod matrices. *Applied Psychological Measurement, 2*, 157–173.

Schmitt, N., Coyle, B.W., & Saari, B.B. (1977). A review and critique of analysis of multitrait-multimethod matrices. *Multivariate Behavioral Research, 12*, 447–478.

Schwarzer, R. (1984). Worry and emotionality as separate components in test anxiety. *International Review of Applied Psychology, 33*, 205–220.

Schwarzer, R., & Schwarzer, C. (1982). Achievement anxiety with respect to reference groups in school. *Journal of Educational Research, 75*, 305–308.

Schwarzer, R., Jerusalem, M., & Lange, B. (1982). A longitudinal study of worry and emotionality. In Schwarzer, R., van der Ploeg, H., & Spielberger, C.D. (Eds.), *Advances in test anxiety research* (Vol. 1). Lisse: Swets & Zeitlinger.

Spielberger, C.D. (1979). *State-trait personality inventory*. Preliminary professional manual. University of South Florida, Tampa, Fla.

Tucker, L.R., & Lewis, C. (1973). A reliability coefficient for maximum likelihood factor analysis. *Psychometrika, 38*, 1–10.

Winne, P.H., & Marx, R.W. (1981). Convergent and discriminant validity in self-concept measurement. *Annual Meeting of the AERA*, Los Angeles.

An Example of Convergent and Discriminant Validation of Personality Questionnaires

GEORG RUDINGER and NORBERT DOMMEL

Introduction

Within the last 5 years efforts at validating personality questionnaires via the multitrait-multimethod strategy (MTMM) originally proposed by Campbell and Fiske (1959; Jackson & Paunonon, 1980) have been redoubled. This interest is of course spurred on by the realization that what is actually being measured in any personality instrument is not solely the trait itself but rather the trait confounded with the method used. Rezmovic and Rezmovic (1981) succinctly summarize this state of affairs by saying that "each measure is a trait-method unit in which observed variance is a combined function of variance due to the construct being measured and the method used to measure that construct" (Rezmovic & Rezmovic, 1981, p. 61). In any attempt to introduce new personality questionnaires it has become standard practice to include some form of multitrait-multimethod analysis. While this practice is straightforward in itself, many different statistical approaches have been suggested for this purpose (Jackson, 1975; Hubert & Baker, 1978). In fact, the variety of different analyses has justified a general review and critique of approaches (Schmitt, Coyle, & Saari, 1977). Of the many proposals suggested for MTMM, the approach via confirmatory factor analysis seems to be the most straightforward and promising in this context (Schmitt, 1978; Rezmovic & Rezmovic, 1980, 1981).

Subsequent sections contain a discussion of this type of convergent and discriminant validation, using Jackson's Personality Research Form (PRF) in the German version as an example. For our present purpose three methods are considered (questionnaire, peer-ratings, self-ratings), each of which is presumed to measure 14 common traits. This represents a classic case of the multitrait-multimethod matrix layout proposed by Campbell and Fiske (1959). Our present work is similar to a secondary analysis carried out by Rezmovic and Rezmovic (1980), except that they used only two methods in an MTMM paradigm, viz. the PRF questionnaire in the original version and peer-ratings, analyzed by exploratory factor analysis.

In this paradigm several traits are measured by various methods. In all, the number of variables observed is equal to the number of traits times the number of methods. All variables are then correlated to form an MTMM matrix. This basic approach proposed by Campbell and Fiske was rather straightforward, in that discriminant validation pertains to low correlations among variables in the matrix, which are theoretically independent regardless of the method involved. Convergent validity, on the other hand, pertains to high correlations among variables, which measure the same trait or are theoretically related regardless of the method involved. Many papers discuss the decomposition of this matrix, and there is no need to discuss these points here. The reader is referred to the contribution by Schwarzer (this volume) and to the original paper by Campbell and Fiske (1959).

The main purpose of this paper is to give a practical demonstration of path analysis strategy in analyzing a large MTMM matrix. Schmitt (1978) gave four reasons for adopting this strategy. First, Campbell and Fiske originally proposed that the researcher, after constructing an MTMM matrix, inspect different diagonals in the matrix (heterotrait-monomethod, heterotrait-heteromethod, monotrait-heteromethod). This merely visual inspection necessarily leads to a subjective comparison of the correlations. Second, this strategy may seem adequate for rather small research projects (three traits and three methods), but is quite inadequate with large matrices. Third, the reliability of methods may be confounded with discriminant and convergent validity. Finally, and this is related to the point above, the ideal state of affairs, in which the methods used and the traits measured do not correlate seems highly unlikely at the empirical level. These reasons make a merely visual inspection of an MTMM matrix seem quite inappropriate. This fault is also inherent in Fiske's system (1973, 1976), albeit understandable in light of the methods then available. What is needed is an overall test for the many different assumptions inherent in this analysis.

This type of overall analysis has already been performed by different approaches, e.g., a main component factor analysis with the correlation matrix (Tucker, 1958; Jackson, 1975). In this approach the variance is decomposed statistically and not theoretically. In other words, this strategy ignores the fact that the researcher definitely does have some very fundamental assumptions about his data. Schmitt (1978) therefore argues in favor of an overall model test of an MTMM matrix via the analysis of linear structural relationships by maximum likelihood (ML). Here different model alternatives are suggested for discovering sources of variance in the observed data, i.e., not only the basic model with the full number of trait factors and method factors are tested, but also different model alternatives, as only trait factors or only method factors. This point will be made more evident in the subsequent sections. However, an important point here is that each of the models does specify a distinct hypothesis which after formulation is subsequently tested.

The strategy proposed involves testing these models by means of the computer program LISREL V (Jöreskog & Sörbom, 1981). Since a detailed discussion of this general model is way beyond the scope of this paper, the reader is referred to the paper cited above for more information.

Methods

Data Used in the Analysis

As stated above, there are three methods in our analysis, the PRF questionnaire by Jackson in the German version (Stumpf, Angleitner et al., 1985), peer-ratings, and self-ratings.

The PRF contains 254 items and forms 14 traits, which are of interest in the present analysis. Each trait was measured on a scale of 1 through 14. They contained the following constructs:

Achievement (AC)	Impulsivity (IM)
Affiliation (AF)	Nurturance (NU)
Aggression (AG)	Order (OR)
Dominance (DO)	Play (PL)
Endurance (EN)	Social recognition (SR)
Exhibition (EX)	Succorance (SU)
Harm avoidance (HA)	Understanding (UN)

In the subsequent discussion and figures these variables will be denoted by x_1 through x_{14} (AC 1 through UN 1).

The second method was the use of peer-ratings. Each subject (S) was rated by seven peers on 14 traits separately on a scale of 1 through 9. Since the variables involved in the present analysis were standardized, the mean of the seven peer-ratings on each trait was used. (Had the analysis involved a covariance matrix instead of a correlation matrix, a true score estimate could have been obtained from the seven peer-ratings by the use of generalizability theory. In the case of standardization of the variables the true score estimate is identical to the mean.) The peer variables will be denoted by x_{15} through x_{28} (AC 2 through UN 2).

The final method used was self-rating. Each subject was asked to rate himself on each of the 14 traits on a scale of 1 through 9. This rating was very similar to the peer-ratings above. These scores will be denoted by x_{29}–x_{42} (AC 3 trhough UN 3). In all, there were 107 Ss in the sample.

Method of Analysis

For those readers familiar with LISREL V (Jöreskog & Sörbom, 1981) the following presentation will contain this terminology. For an explanation of this form of analysis the reader is referred to Fig. 1. The variables x_1 through x_{42} (in accordance with the conventions stated above) are enclosed in rectangles and represent the observed variables. The theory implies that the observed variables are influenced by the 14 traits, which cannot be directly observed and must be construed. These are termed latent variables ξ_1 through ξ_{14}. In addition to the 14 traits we also assume that each x-variable is also influenced by its specific method factor (latent variables, ξ_{15} through ξ_{17} in the bottom half

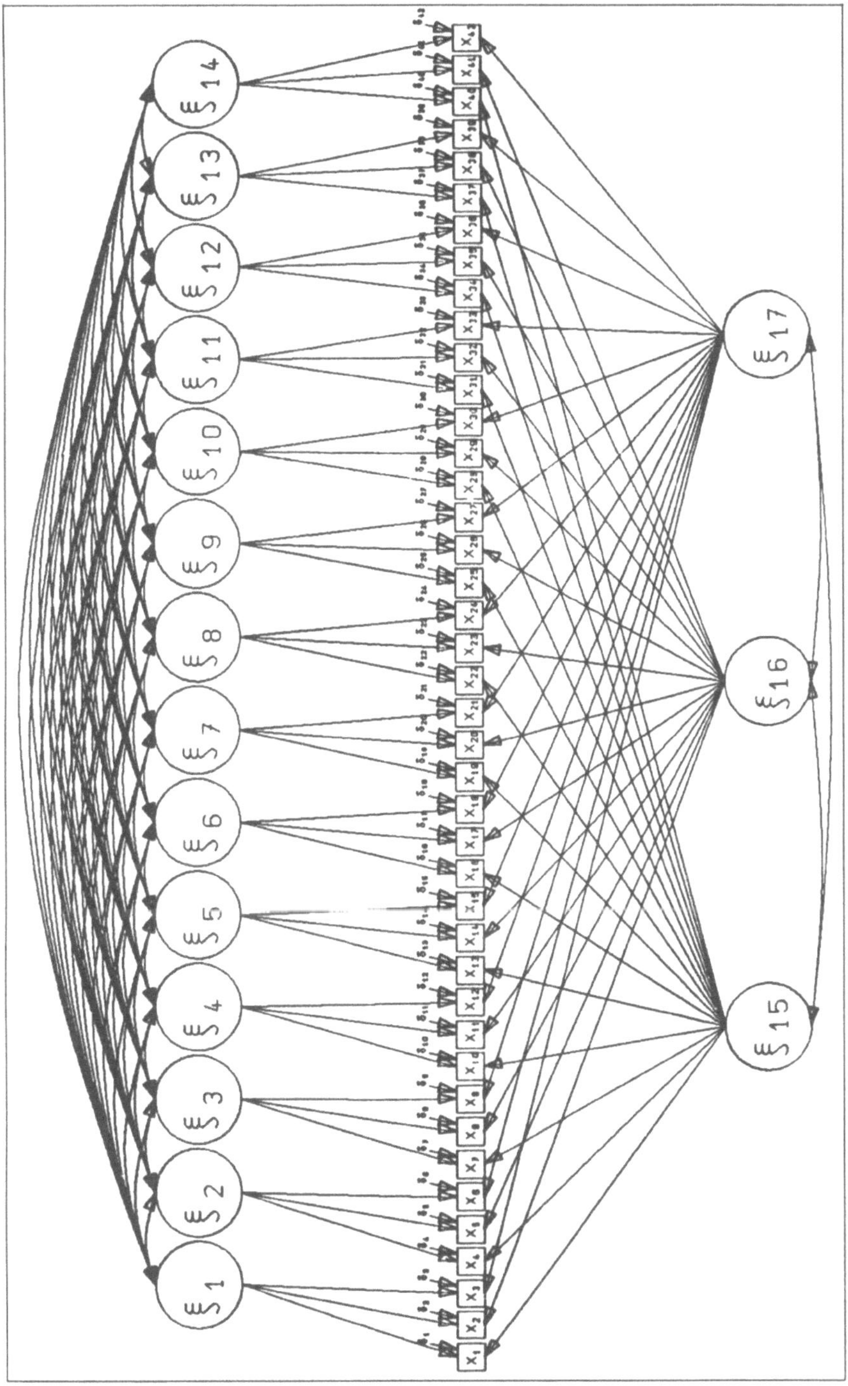

Fig. 1. Full MTMM-PRF model (model 1); the frame indicates correlations between the set ξ_1–ξ_{14} with the set ξ_{15}–ξ_{17}.

of the figure). The path coefficients between the latent level and the observed level are denoted by Λ. Thus the latent variables translate into

ξ_1 – AC	ξ_{10} – OR
ξ_2 – AF	ξ_{11} – PL
ξ_3 – AG	ξ_{12} – SR
ξ_4 – DO	ξ_{13} – SU
ξ_5 – EN	ξ_{14} – UN
ξ_6 – EX	ξ_{15} – method factor: questionnaire
ξ_7 – HA	ξ_{16} – method factor: peer-rating
ξ_8 – IM	ξ_{17} – method factor: self-rating
ξ_9 – NU	

Finally, each x-variable is also influenced by an error term (measurement error) denoted by δ_1 through δ_{42}. These effects are also symbolized by paths between variables. The paths or influences may be translated into a series of equations. Thus variable x_1 is influenced by ξ_1 and ξ_{15} plus the measurement error:

$$x_1 = \lambda_{1,1}\xi_1 + \lambda_{1,15}\xi_{15} + \delta_1$$

This leads to 42 equations for the 42 observed variables x, which can be summarized in matrix algebra as:

$$X = \Lambda_x\xi + \Theta_\delta$$

where X denotes a vector of 42 elements.

Λ_x denotes a 42,17 matrix (x-variables times 17 ξ_{17} variables, the matrix of path coefficients),

and finally,

Θ_δ denotes a diagonal matrix containing uncorrelated measurement error.

The model depicted in Fig. 1 also contains assumptions about influences between the latent variables ξ. This model is a full model, in that there are influences between each and every ξ variable. This implies a path between the members of each possible combination of two ξ variables analogous to the paths between the method factors below. In the full model there are also paths between the members of every possible pair of ξ variables (trait factor) above and the members of every possible combination of two factors (ξ_{15} through ξ_{17}) below. This signifies that all ξ variables are correlated. The paths between the latent variables go in both directions (contrary to the Λ paths above, from latent variable to observed variable) and are denoted by φ coefficients. Thus, in this model $\varphi_{15,16}$ and $\varphi_{16,15}$ are equal.

Another way to describe the absence or presence of paths between selected ξ variables is the pattern matrix φ. This matrix represents a correlation matrix, of symmetrical and diagonal elements. The pattern matrix for the model of

	1	2	3	4	5	6	7	8	9	10	11	12	13	14	15	16	17
1	0																
2	1	0															
3	1	1	0														
4	1	1	1	0													
5	1	1	1	1	0												
6	1	1	1	1	1	0											
7	1	1	1	1	1	1	0										
8	1	1	1	1	1	1	1	0									
9	1	1	1	1	1	1	1	1	0								
10	1	1	1	1	1	1	1	1	1	0							
11	1	1	1	1	1	1	1	1	1	1	0						
12	1	1	1	1	1	1	1	1	1	1	1	0					
13	1	1	1	1	1	1	1	1	1	1	1	1	0				
14	1	1	1	1	1	1	1	1	1	1	1	1	1	0			
15	1	1	1	1	1	1	1	1	1	1	1	1	1	1	0		
16	1	1	1	1	1	1	1	1	1	1	1	1	1	1	1	0	
17	1	1	1	1	1	1	1	1	1	1	1	1	1	1	1	1	0

Fig. 2. φ Matrix for the full model 1

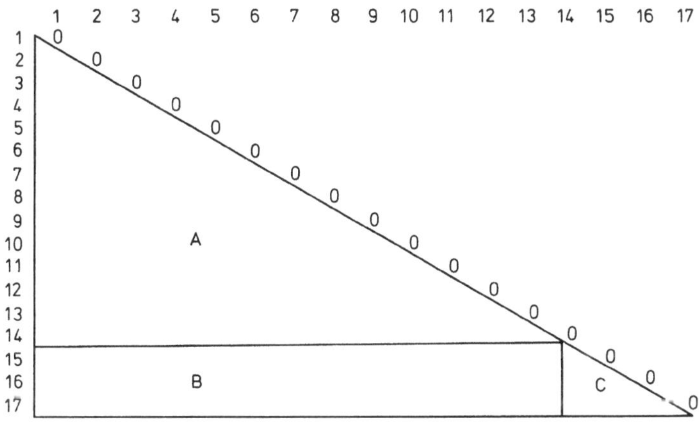

Fig. 3. φ Matrix for different alternatives of model 1

Fig. 1 is represented in Fig. 2. Since the diagonal elements are equal to 1.0 and need not be estimated, they are represented by 0 in the matrix. Each path that will be estimated is represented using a 1. In the present case there is a correlation between each ξ variable and each of the others, so that below the diagonal each entry is '1'. This pattern matrix will become quite useful in specifying submodels of this full model.

As mentioned above, the LISREL V computer program will estimate all the specified path coefficients simultaneously by minimizing the maximum likelihood function (ML). In addition to these estimates the program output provides a chi-square test statistic for the overall fit of the specified model to the observed data. The program computes an ML estimate from the observed data with the model specifications and reproduces this correlation matrix. The chi-square test statistic is based on the hypothesis that this reproduced matrix is arrived at by the model specifications against no model specifications (unconstrained Σ-matrix). The degrees of freedom (*df*) associated with a particular chi-square value are:

$$0.5\,k(k+1)-t$$

where k is the number of observed variables (in our case $k=42$), and t is the number of path coefficients to be estimated. The probability level of chi-square is the probability of obtaining a chi-square value larger than the value actually observed given that the model is correct (Jöreskog & Sörbom, 1981). Thus a large chi-square value and small probabilities relative to degrees of freedom indicate a bad fit for the specified model. Small chi-square values and relatively large probabilities indicate a good fit of the model to the observed data.

Model Specification and Hypotheses

Following Schmitt's suggestions, in analyzing an MTMM matrix different alternative models can be specified and tested against each other. Two models can be compared if both contain the same number of observed and latent variables, by subtraction of the chi-square values and subtraction of the degrees of freedom for each model. This will again yield a chi-square value with degrees of freedom. This chi-square test statistic can show whether there is a significant improvement of one model over the other. For models which do not have the same number of variables a rough measure of improvement in one model over the other can be gained by mere inspection of the differences in chi-square and the gain or loss of degrees of freedom. A rule of thumb indicated by Jöreskog for this procedure is that a significant drop in chi-square compared with a small loss in degrees of freedom indicates an improvement of one model over the other (Jöreskog, personal communication).

For the present analysis the specifications from Schmitt (1978) were followed. In all, 16 models were tested. The models are summarized in Table 1 which includes a model specification, the number of parameters (path coefficients) to be estimated in each model, the number of ξ variables postulated, the chi-square test statistic, and the associated degrees of freedom. As already mentioned, each of these models concerns some hypothesis about what our variables measure and their source of variance.

The models can be divided into four groups at a conceptual level. The first group includes model 1, and models 7 through 12. (Model 1 has already been outlined in the method of analysis section.) Models 7 through 12 are each submodels of model 1. This can easily be demonstrated in a comparison of Figs. 2 and 3 (each denotes a φ pattern matrix). The subdiagonal of the matrix in Fig. 2 can be divided into two triangles, A and C, and a rectangle, B. Each '1' triangle A denotes a correlation between traits, each '1' rectangle B denotes a

Table 1. Summary of models 1–16[a]

Model	Specification	PAR	ξ	χ-square	*df*
1	14 Correlated traits, 3 correlated methods with trait-method interrelationship	262	17	913.33	641
2	14 Correlated traits, 1 method	231	15	1058.09	672
3	1 Trait, 3 Correlated methods	132	4	2075.03	771
4	14 Correlated traits	175	14	1217.58	728
4′	14 Uncorrelated traits	84	14	1889.65	819
5	3 Correlated methods	87	3	2573.84	816
6	'Single factor'	84	1	2916.40	819
7	No trait-method interrelationship	220	17	980.21	683
8	No trait interrelationship	171	17	1384.92	732
9	No method interrelationship	259	17	948.11	644
10	No trait-method, no trait interrelationship	129	17	1540.19	774
11	No trait-method, no method interrelationship	217	17	1024.35	686
12	No trait, no method, no trait-method interrelationship	126	17	1591.95	777
13	'No factor model'	0	42	3216.81	903
14	'Hypothesized model'	136	17	1385.62	767
15	'Mokken scale model'	159	17	1336.41	744
16	Combined 'hypothesized Mokken scale model'	162	17	1207.70	741

PAR, number of free parameters to be estimated in the model
[a] Models 1–13 are in line with the suggestions of Schmitt (1978); models 14–16 are guided by theoretical content-oriented thoughts.

correlation between a trait and a method; each '1' in triangle C denotes a correlation between two methods. Thus, model 7, for example (no trait-method interrelationships), takes the form of the φ pattern matrix of model 1, except that there are zeroes in rectangle B. In this way each of the models in this group can be specified.

The second group of models contains models 2, 3, and 6. Model 6 assumes a single factor as the source of variance in the observed data. This could be the case, for example, when there is an overwhelming experimental effect in the design. Model 2 assumes a single method factor and the 14 traits, while model 3 reverses the situation, with 3 method factors and a single trait. Again, the model specifications indicate a certain hypothesis about the data. Model 3, for example, only measures 1 latent trait with 3 methods.

The third group contains models 4, 4′, and 5. Here the source of variance is attributed to one side, i.e., only 14 traits or 3 methods are accountable.

Model 4′ is a more stringent submodel of model 4 (correlated vs uncorrelated traits).

The fourth group specifies models 14, 15, and 16. These models were derived by specification against a theoretical or empirical background. The relationships in model 14 among the ξ variables were inferred from theory. Model 15 was the hypothesized relationship among the ξ variables in keeping with the results obtained from a Mokken scale analysis at the item level of the PRF carried out at the University of Bonn (Chaselon, Noack, Voss, & Zimmermann), while model 16 represents a combination of the two approaches. These models were included for demonstration purposes and will be taken up again in the discussion.

The reader will note that model 13 was not included in the above-mentioned groups. This becomes somewhat more reasonable in the conceptual translation of the model specifications. Model 13 assumes 42 ξ variables, so that the number of ξ variables equals the number of x-variables. Furthermore, there is no relationship among the latent variables. Each variable measures something unique. It actually represents a test of the observed correlation matrix. The results for each of the analyses carried out are summarized in the chi-square values and the associated degrees of freedom in Table 1. None of the models in the analysis fit the data (high chi-square values and low probabilities).

Discussion

Discussion of the results should begin with model 13. Had this model fitted the data, then no further analysis would have been necessary, since the observed variance is unique to each x-variable. This model also represents one end of a continuum of the tested models. The chi-square value for all other models should be below this value (3216.81). Still within the limits of the measurement model with invariant structural zeroes, at the other end of the continuum we find model 1 (Fig. 1). This postulates the full number of ξ variables (17) and relationships among all of them. Thus, all other chi-square values should be above this value (913.33). Still the model did not fit the data, and consequently no further analysis would ordinarily be required. However, to identify possible sources of variance in the data all other specified analyses were carried out nonetheless.

A detailed discussion, including a comparison of all the proposed models (hypotheses), is far beyond the scope of this paper. Thus, this report will concentrate on some of the more striking relationships. First models within groups and then members of different groups will be compared.

In group 1 all models were compared with model 1. Although there is always a statistically significant drop in the chi-square statistic in relationship to the degrees of freedom, some members, viz. model 7 and model 11, do not have such a striking improvement in the goodness of fit. This leads to a first tentative conclusion that the associated method factors do not have a major effect on the variance.

In group 2 this first tentative evidence receives further support. Model 6 represents the hypothesis that there is only a single factor to account for the variance. The introduction of 14 correlated traits and a single method factor (model 2) represents a better fit than the model with 3 correlated methods and a single trait factor (model 3).

In group 3 this assumption again receives further support. The introduction of 14 traits (correlated, uncorrelated; model 4, model 4′) yields a much better fit than the introduction of only 3 correlated methods.

In the comparisons of members from different groups the assumptions about the relative insignificance of the method factors compared with the trait factors were corroborated. Particularly striking is a comparison of model 2 and model 11. The introduction of 1 method factor, as against 3 method factors, albeit independent, did not represent a substantial improvement in fit (chi-square: 33.74, $df = 14$). Furthermore, comparison of model 4 (14 correlated traits) with model 2 (14 correlated traits and 1 method) does not lead to such a significant improvement in the fit of the model.

Although there are many hypotheses that can be compared in this way, the main purpose is to give an example of the advantages of this particular strategy in analyzing an MTMM matrix.

Conclusions

It should be obvious from the discussion that there are inherent advantages in adopting this strategy in analyzing an MTMM matrix. If only the models 14–16 had been tested, the results would have indicated that the models do not fit the observed data. No further information could have been gained from this simpler strategy. The decomposition of the full model (model 1) into different submodels and alternative models yielded significantly more information than a single theoretical overall test.

The fact that all the specified models do not fit the data indicates that there is something wrong in the measurement model. In our model specification we did not change the measurement model in order to stay within the MTMM paradigm. We introduced the full model ($\xi = 17$) and the x-variables were only influenced by specific trait factors. It could also be assumed that each x-variable is also influenced by other trait factors (more than one). In fact, the Mokken scale analysis at the item level indicates a smaller number of traits (scales). Thus, further analysis at the item level is advisable. An alternative strategy to this proposal rests in defining second-order factors to accommodate for possible confounded measurement. However, neither of these strategies was followed in the present study, to avoid violating the basic MTMM model investigated here.

Summary

This paper present a practical demonstration of validating a personality questionnaire via the multitrait-multimethod approach in confirmatory factor analysis. The strategy is outlined in detail using Jackson's Personality Research Form (PRF), peer ratings and self-ratings. Furthermore, different modeling alternatives suggested by Schmitt (1978) were applied to gain more information on the obtained data. Although none of the proposed models fit the data, the specified analysis strategy yields information on the methods and traits that is not evident prima facie.

Acknowledgements. The authors are indebted to Prof. A. Angleitner of the University of Bielefeld for providing the data analyzed.

References

Campbell, D.T., & Fiske, D.W. (1959). Convergent and discriminant validation by the multitrait-multimethod matrix. *Psychological Bulletin, 56*, 81–105.

Fiske, D.W. (1973). Can a personality construct be validated empirically? *Psychological Bulletin, 80*, 89–92.

Fiske, D.W. (1976). Can a personality construct have a singular validational pattern? Rejoinder to Huba and Hamilton. *Psychological Bulletin, 83*, 877–879.

Hubert, L.J., & Baker, F.B. (1978). Analyzing the multitrait-multimethod matrix. *Multivariate Behavioral Research, 13*, 163–179.

Jackson, D.N. (1975). Multimethod factor analysis: A reformulation. *Multivariate Behavioral Research, 10*, 253–276.

Jackson, D.N., & Paunonon, S.V. (1980). Personality structure and assessment. *Annual Review of Psychology, 31*, 503–551.

Jöreskog, K.G., & Sörbom, D. (1981). *LISREL V: Analysis of linear structural relationships by maximum likelihood and least squares methods* (Research Rep. 81–8). Uppsala: University of Uppsala.

Rezmovic, E.L., & Rezmovic, V. (1980). Empirical validation of psychological constructs: A secondary analysis. *Psychological Bulletin, 87*, 66–71.

Rezmovic, E.L., & Rezmovic, V. (1981). A confirmatory factor analysis approach to construct validation. *Educational and Psychological Measurement, 41*, 61–72.

Schmitt, N. (1978). Path analysis of multitrait-multimethod matrices. *Applied Psychological Measurement, 2*, 157–173.

Schmitt, N., Coyle, B.W., & Saari, B.B. (1977). A review and critique of analyses of multitrait-multimethod matrices. *Multivariate Behavioral Research, 12*, 447–478.

Stumpf, H., Angleitner, A., Wieck, T., Jackson, D.N., Beloch-Till, H. (1985). Deutsche "Personality Research Form" (PRF). Göttingen, Hogrefe.

Tucker, L.R. (1958). An inter-battery method of factor analysis. *Psychometrika, 23*, 111–136.

Epilog

JERRY S. WIGGINS

It is clear from the preceding contributions that personality questionnaires are still alive, although prognostic judgments of their viability appear to range from "guarded" to "critical." Psychometricians and even test constructors are often their own worst critics, and the present contributors are no exception to this generalization; the tone of most of the chapters is critical, tough-minded, and only guardedly optimistic. These are writers who have lived through the dark period in personality assessment which followed Mischel's critique of the trait concept in personality theory and measurement. Their heads are bloody, but unbowed.

The Trait Concept and Personality Questionnaires

In reading Amelang and Borkenau's (this volume) incisive summary of new research directions that have opened up in response to criticisms of the trait concept, one is struck more by what we *have* learned about the assessment of traits, than by the familiar lament about what we have not. The extensive literature reviewed by Amelang and Borkenau gives little hope for an early resolution of fundamental issues relating to the theoretical concept of trait in personality study. But this literature, and especially the empirical work of Amelang and his group, has identified ways in which predictions from trait measures may be improved, for whatever theoretical reason. Thus, if asked to identify a prediction paradigm in which improvements in validity coefficients might be anticipated, one could respond, with some confidence: "Predict multiple-act criteria in relatively unstructured social situations using traits that are observable and relevant (to the subject), items with good characteristics (e.g., comprehensible, moderate endorsement), and subjects who score high on social desirability scales." These empirical facts are not very informative with respect to the nature of the construct of trait in personality theory. What they do suggest, however, is that a potentially valuable spin-off from the trait controversy has been the discovery of ways to improve prediction in applied settings, regardless of the theoretical status of the concept of trait.

This interpretation is compatible with some of the observations offered by Fiske (this volume). Although he emphasizes the inadequacies of questionnaire-based measures of traits for scientific work, Fiske recognizes the contributions of personality questionnaires to applied personnel selection, particularly in relation to other assessment procedures. Considering the utility of correct decisions for many personnel assignments, even the modest incremental validity afforded by questionnaire-based trait measures is of considerable social importance. Because of this, Fiske considers the possibility of "patching up" the traditional approach to questionnaire assessment and doing the best we can with it. This might involve the development of a "short list" of useful traits and the identification of situations where such traits are manifested. In this connection, Fiske calls our attention to the need for considering other indices of the distribution of trait manifestations, rather than simply examining central tendencies. The standard deviation of scale means across situations and indices of the general level of manifestations across situations are two such possible measures.

But Fiske's main argument is that a scientific theory of personality cannot be based on self-reports of the questionnaire variety. What is needed is a reexamination of our current rationale for measuring traits by questionnaires with an eye to developing operationalized measures that are scientifically respectable. In this connection, Fiske notes, as do many others (e.g., Blalock, 1982), the need for a theory of measurement that will inform our basic observational procedures. Jackson's information-processing account of questionnaire responding (this volume) is a step in this direction, but unless this step signals a forthcoming paradigm shift, the outlook for personality questionnaires is gloomy.

Item Generation and Scale Construction

Kastner's notion of "pragmatic validity" (this volume) emphasizes semantic, as opposed to syntactic, properties of questionnaire items. He makes clear that assessment via personality questionnaires is a diagnostic communication process involving several different persons and that various "misunderstandings" may take place: between test constructor and respondent, test constructor and psychologist, psychologist and respondent, among psychologists, among respondents, etc. When asked to judge the extent to which different items were manifestations of the construct of *"Gelassenheit,"* differences emerged among psychologists, students, and persons.

Loevinger's (1957) ideas about the role of facet analysis in the construction of questionnaire items have been more frequently cited than implemented. Kastner's study of stress tolerance while driving a car provides a notable exception to this trend. Items were constructed to represent combinations of the three facets of intensity, duration, and control possibilities and then carefully rated for clarity of meaning, conceivability, and adequacy. When this "pragmatically validated" questionnaire was compared with a questionnaire of the same, but not validated, content, a substantial increase in predictive validity was found for the former in the prediction of the objective criterion of pulse frequency. In a sense, Kastner's research represents a return to the "correspondence point of view" (Buchwald, 1961), at least insofar as it is a radical departure from the empirical point of view that was once the predominant philosophy of test construction. Viewing the assessment process as a series of communications opens up new agendas for research (Leary, 1957). After-the-fact assessments of "misunderstandings" associated with syntactic characteristics of questionnaire items are less pragmatically useful than item construction procedures which, to some degree, ensure common meanings among the various participants in the assessment process prior to assessment.

That equally little attention has been paid to the syntactic or "surface" qualities of items assembled for the construction of personality questionnaires is evident from Angleitner, John, and Löhr's extensive analysis of items from the MMPI, the 16 PF, and Eysenck's personality inventories (this volume). Angleitner et al. were able to demonstrate convincingly that syntactic characteristics are related to internal psychometric characteristics of items and scales and, hence, may be related to the processing of item information by subjects. Their results nicely parallel those of Amelang and Borkenau (this volume), who report the effects of syntactic characteristics on scale validities (self-report versus trait-ratings by significant others). It is clear from the two research programs that item comprehensibility, ambiguity, and self-reference affect both the reliability and validity of questionnaire scales. The results with respect to abstractness suggest that this is an undesirable property with respect to measures of internal consistency and reliability.

Angleitner et al. endorse the concrete act approach introduced by Buss and Craik, but it may be premature to close the door on trait research conducted at different levels of abstractness (Wiggins, 1984). The generalizability of a self-report questionnaire may be limited if only a few specific acts are presented. The issue of evaluative content is, as always, ambiguous. Amelang and Borkenau report higher validities for items of high as opposed to neutral, social desirability. Angleitner et al. appear to view this as a characteristic that should be controlled or eliminated from assessment. In contrast, Paulhus (this volume) makes what is, to me, a convincing argument for retaining this source of variance in certain circumstances.

As Burisch (this volume) notes, the issue of which strategy of test construction produces the most "valid" multiscale instrument has not received much critical attention in recent years, although clearly it is a nagging issue that will not simply go away. The problem here is that results of empirical comparisons, starting with the classic study of Hase and Goldberg (1967), have generally failed to establish the clear superiority of one scale construction strategy over another, leaving the central issue unresolved. As Burisch notes in his meticulous examination of a dozen empirical studies directed at this issue, methodological difficulties in comparative validity studies militate against firm conclusions. Nevertheless, with respect to considerations of "stray shots" (scales correlating as high or higher with "alien" criteria) and economy of construction and administration, deductive scale construction strategies appear to have the edge on external scale construction strategies.

Although stray shots may not be of great importance in applied prediction contexts, they are of considerable importance in establishing the substantive validity of theoretically derived personality scales. It seems likely that scales derived under the facet-analytic procedure for ensuring semantic clarity described by Kastner (this volume) would produce fewer stray shots in relation to clearly specified and relevant criterion measures. Unfortunately, because of the emphasis on prediction of global social criteria in such studies, the importance of substantive validity has been played down. Again, we encounter the issue of whether or not we should "patch things up" in the hopes of greater predictive validity in applied contexts or whether we should direct our attention to the more fundamental issue of what personality scales actually measure.

Models of Item Responding and Self-Presentation

Jackson's summary (this volume) of the development of his threshold model for item responding provides an occasion for evaluating where we have been and where we might be going with respect to the study of item responding. The original context of this work is found in the spirited controversy that began more than 25 years ago regarding the roles of "acquiescence" and social desirability response styles in the MMPI. Although much of this work now appears to be misguided windmill tilting, it is true that it revolved around some basic psychological processes that must figure prominently in any scientific account of the meaning of responses to personality questionnaires. There is, of course, an applied issue having to do with self-deception and impression management in psychodiagnostic and personnel selection contexts. This issue is treated in detail by Paulhus (this volume). But the more basic issue is, and perhaps always has been, that of rendering a convincing account of the information processing that takes place when a subject responds to a personality questionnaire item. Jackson and his coworkers have made impressive first steps in this direction.

When we conduct a personality "assessment" or a personality "evaluation," or engage in personality "testing," it is not surprising that there is an *evaluation* component involved. What is surprising is that this major dimension of affective meaning should be viewed as vitiating the results of self-report questionnaires. It now seems clear that instead of debating whether or not evaluation is a legitimate parameter of item responding we should have studied *how* evaluation affects the process of responding. And that is exactly what Jackson and his coworkers have been doing for a number of years. Using only the two parameters of desirability responding threshold and salience of desirability for an individual, Jackson provides us with a highly convincing account of the process of item responding in personality assessment. In so doing he has reaffirmed the centrality of evaluation in personality assessment and, secondarily, laid to rest earlier concepts of acquiescence as a basic process. Jackson and Helmes' (1979) basic structure content scaling procedure is a significant conceptual and methodological advance in the measurement of item content. The focus on the subject as the basic unit of measurement, rather than the items to which he or she responds, restores a balance in a field that has too often seemed more concerned with items than people. Individual differences in threshold and sensitivity to both content and desirability dimensions seem to be a useful focus for a science of personality assessment.

One of the side benefits of the care with which the PRF was constructed is that it has provided an item pool whose psychometric properties are sound enough to permit application of the fine-grained scaling procedures of Jackson and Helmes. This opens up the possibility of a very productive cycle of basic and applied research. Analyses of the process of item responding should have implications for the construction of better items, which in turn could provide more clear-cut stimuli for further studies of the item response process, etc. This exciting work not only expands our field of study, but also helps restore our scientific respectability.

In reading Paulhus' fascinating chapter (this volume) on the "new look" in social desirability responding (SDR), I experienced feelings of both déjà vu and pride. I must confess that I had all but forgotten my own contributions to the response style literature some 25 years ago. (Is this self-deception or impression management?) The feeling of déjà vu was inspired by a reconsideration of a distinction I made between two kinds of social desirability scales: the *SD* scale of Edwards (factor alpha) and the *Sd* measure of social desirability role playing (factor gamma). The feeling of pride accompanied the recognition that this distinction might have been an important one after all, and this was gratifying because reprints of my response style work have been gathering dust for many years. For younger workers such as Paulhus, the era of the great response style controversy is history and, as history, it can be approached with an objectivity and a detachment that would have been hard to achieve at that time.

When viewed in the philosophical and psychological context in which Paulhus places it, the distinction between self-deception and impression management provides a framework for studying basic psychological processes that are fundamental to the science of personality assessment. Hopefully, this new look will replace two older views of the nature of response styles which I find particularly unproductive. The first is a view of response styles as "tics" in which more or less uncontrollable neural firings cause subjects to answer "true" or to cling to one portion of a Likert rating scale. The second and perhaps even more dehumanizing view of response styles is expressed in the paranoid conviction that virtually all test respondents are motivated to deceive us, mislead us, and otherwise make our lives difficult. From an interpersonal perspective, a person's attempts to maintain self-esteem and ward off anxiety are not viewed as "nuisance variables."

With respect to the major factor of psychopathology first identified in the MMPI (alpha), I strongly agree with Paulhus that rather than trying to "control" it, we should study it and identify the psychological processes that give rise to it. We have known for a long time that, with the exception of a few diagnostic groups, psychiatric patients say bad things about themselves on instruments such as the MMPI. Again, with the exception of a few diagnostic groups, the bad things psychiatric patients say about themselves correspond to bad things said about them by significant others and by clinicians (Payne & Wiggins, 1972). This fact enables us to sort patients into diagnostic categories and to distinguish them from more healthy individuals who tend not to say bad things about themselves. But it is clearly time that we moved beyond empirical fact and explored the reasons for this state of affairs. Paulhus' review emphasizes the adaptive value of self-deception in the maintenance of self-esteem and in the avoidance of anxiety and depression. From this perspective, an *absence* of self-deceptive tendencies represents a breakdown of normal coping mechanisms and may reflect an exaggerated and inflexible tendency to maintain poor self-concepts at the cost of psychiatric symptoms. The kind of "control" we need here is therapeutic rather than psychometric.

The impression management perspective comes to us from sociology and it must now be considered a major perspective in personality theory. Although this perspective was applied to the personality testing situation many years ago, it has recently resurfaced with considerable vigor. Proponents of the impression management position (e.g., Hogan, 1983), although presenting a well-articulated and convincing case, may have overstated it. Paulhus' review suggests that there are at least two kinds of social desirability responding and that they are conceptually and psychometrically quite distinct from one another. The topic of impression management is currently being actively explored in social psychology (Jones and Pittman, 1982), as are related concepts of self-monitoring (Snyder, 1974) and Machiavellianism (Christie & Geis, 1970). As Paulhus suggests, we need to distinguish among strategic, motivational, and skill components in impression management via selective endorsement of personality questionnaire items. Such investigations are likely to enrich our understanding of personality dynamics in general. From an applied perspective, it might be desirable to attempt to control for impression management tendencies psychometrically, but again, I would prefer to know a great deal more about what it is we are controlling before routinely excluding variance that may be critical to our understanding of dyadic transactions.

Ideally, the choice of a measurement model for combining questionnaire items into a total scale score should be dictated by theoretical considerations. In practice, almost all test authors recommend an unweighted cumulative measurement model in which responses are simply added up. Although the empirical evidence available on this topic appears to provide strong justification for this procedure, hope springs eternal that an alternative measurement model might produce scales of greater validity.

These hopes have once again been dashed by Hofstee and Smid (this volume) in a chapter that emphasizes the psychometric problems associated with more complex measurement models and the lack of available evidence for their utility. Thus, whether one uses differential item weighting, suppressor, moderator, or higher order functions, or even the person parameters inspired by Jackson's threshold model, it is unlikely that improvements in validity will be found over the unweighted cumulative scoring model. There may be very specialized circumstances in which alternative item combination models result in incremental validity, but these are often situations in which very high validity exists to begin with; a phenomenon I have elsewhere referred to as the "rich-get-richer-effect" (Wiggins, 1981). Until we develop personality scales of greater predictive validity, it is unlikely that we can anticipate improvements from alternative scoring models.

Itemmetric studies of personality questionnaires have examined syntactic properties of items (negation, passive voice) in relation to other item characteristics and in relation to the reliability and validity of personality scales. Angleitner, John, and Löhr (this volume) have tallied the proportion of items with such syntactic characteristics in several major personality questionnaires. Since such characteristics as negations and passive constructions are thought to make items more difficult to process, it was assumed that they ought to be avoided. In a highly informative essay, Helfrich (this volume) illustrates, with examples, that the case grammar approach and empirical findings from psycholinguistic research lead to predictions of processing difficulty that are different from those of a purely syntactic model. According to Helfrich, the distinction between item form and item content represents roughly the linguistic distinction between surface and deep structure. On this view, items should be constructed to minimize the length of processing from surface to deep structure. Recommendations for how one should do this are, at least in the examples given, different from the perspectives of linguistic theory and syntactic considerations, respectively. Although such a revelation is informative, it cannot help but add to the burden of the already beleaguered constructor of personality questionnaires, who must now add psycholinguistics to the already large number of technical specialties that must be mastered in order to construct a sophisticated personality questionnaire. Nevertheless, advances in cognate areas cannot be ignored when they have obvious relevance to the construction of personality questionnaires, and some type of interdisciplinary collaboration is clearly indicated.

It may be that mundane syntatic characteristics such as negation and passive voice can explain only a small portion of the variance of item comprehensibility. But, as seems to be true in so many areas of personality assessment, *direct global ratings* of such properties as "ambiguity," "comprehensibility," and "intelligibility" (Amelang & Borkenau; Angleitner, John, & Löhr, this volume) may provide reasonably satisfactory indices of the ease with which a questionnaire item may be processed. In this respect, the appropriate comparison may be between predictions of processing difficulty from contemporary psycholinguistic theory and from global ratings, rather than between predictions from simple syntactic properties and from psycholinguistic predictions. As noted by several of the contributors to the present volume, there is much to be said for keeping things simple.

The Assessment of Convergent and Discriminant Validity

If one were asked to identify enduring methodological contributions to personality assessment, Campbell and Fiske's (1959) design for analyzing convergent and discriminant validity within a multitrait-multimethod matrix would have to be placed high on the list. The conceptual appeal of this approach was so great that it gained immediate acceptance as a standard paradigm, particularly with respect to the estimation of trait and method variance in personality questionnaires. Nevertheless, despite its conceptual appeal, the early "eyeballing" method of analysis was felt by many to be unsatisfactory. In the ensuing years, a number of suggestions were offered for making the method more analytic. These methods have culminated in the structural equations approach of Jöreskog, which now appears to be the standard method for analyzing multitrait-multimethod matrices. Schwarzer (this volume) describes this method and applies it to personality and attitude data. His chapter illustrates the degree of specificity of hypothesis testing that is possible with this method and the depth of understanding that can be achieved when results are relatively clear-cut. Rudinger and Dommel (this volume) analyze the German version of Jackson's Personality Research Form and illustrate the range of hypotheses regarding latent variables that can be tested in a single data set. Their analyses also illustrate the fact that the method does not always result in clearly interpretable findings.

As various versions of LISREL become more widely available to users, the latent structure of existing personality questionnaires will almost certainly be examined in great detail. In the long run, the availability of this powerful multivariate tool will undoubtedly have a salutary effect on the field of personality assessment. The program demands that the user specify the nature and interrelations among latent variables with a degree of specificity that is unprecedented. We have come a long way from the old eyeballing days. But in this transition period, we must also realize some potential dangers in the widespread application of this program.

In a paper that should be read by everyone contemplating causal modeling, Cliff (1983) expresses concern that the availability of such programs may encourage us to suspend our normal critical faculties and forget very basic principles of scientific inference:

> The first principle is that the data do not confirm a model, they only fail to disconfirm it, together with the corollary that when the data do not disconfirm a model, there are many other models that are not disconfirmed either. The second principle is that ... if *a* and *b* are related, and *a* followed *b* in time, it is not necessarily true that *b* caused *a*. The third principle is that just because we name something does not mean that we are understanding it, or even that we have named it correctly. And the fourth principle is that *ex post facto* explanations are untrustworthy.

These shortcomings are, of course, not shortcomings of the method, they are shortcomings of the investigator. We must recognize that we now have software capabilities that vastly exceed the quality of our data and the levels at which we can conceptualize our data. Recognition of this state of affairs would serve to minimize possible abuses of a powerful analytic tool.

Summary

The state of the art of personality assessment via questionnaires reflects enduring problems associated with this method of measurement. We like to think we are measuring "traits," but many remain convinced that this concept is too amorphous for scientific work. We are coming to recognize that the testing process involves "communication," but we are only beginning to discover the linguistic and psycholinguistic implications of this fact. Just exactly what our subjects do when they respond to questionnaire items has never been known with certainty, although we are now studying this process in a more rigorous fashion. We still harbor the belief that subjects' responses can be combined in a more meaningful way than simply adding them up, but this does not seem to be the case. We are also convinced that more substantively oriented strategies of scale construction should result in more valid assessment, but the evidence for this remains thin. Response styles appear to be eternally with us, although we now view them in a more friendly fashion. The concepts of convergent and discriminant validity are every bit as appealing as they were 25 years ago, but our current space age technologies for investigating them only serve to underscore the fragility of our basic data.

Just how much progress has been made in attacking the enduring problems of our field? Let us stretch our imaginations a bit and pretend that the pioneer of personality questionnaires, Robert Woodworth, came to us today asking for guidance in the construction of a neuroticism questionnaire. What would we tell him? Obviously, we would have a great deal to tell him, and the vantage provided by this broader historical perspective illuminates the substantial and cumulative progress that has been made in relation to our humble beginnings. The theoretical and psychometric issues addressed in the present volume are so complex and highly specialized that they would be incomprehensible to the pioneers of questionnaire measurement. It is difficult to say with confidence where we are going, but it is reassuring to reflect on where we are relative to where we once were.

References

Blalock, H.M. (1982). *Conceptualization and measurement in the social siences*. Beverly Hills: Sage.

Buchwald, A.M. (1961). Verbal utterances as data. In Feigl, H., & Maxwell, G. (Eds.), *Current issues in the philosophy of science* (pp. 461–468). New York: Holt.

Campbell, D.T., & Fiske, D.W. (1959). Convergent and discriminant validation by the multitrait-multimethod matrix. *Psychological Bulletin, 56*, 81–105.

Christie, R., & Geis, F.L. (1970). *Studies in Machiavellianism*. New York: Academic.

Cliff, N. (1983). Some cautions concerning the application of causal modeling methods. *Multivariate Behavioral Research, 18*, 115–126.
Hase, H.D., & Goldberg, L.R. (1967). Comparative validity of different strategies of constructing personality inventory scales. *Psychological Bulletin, 67*, 231–248.
Hogan, R. (1983). A socioanalytic theory of personality. In Page, M.M. (Ed.), *Nebraska symposium on motivation, 1982*. Lincoln: University of Nebraska Press.
Jackson, D.N., & Helmes, E. (1979). Basic structure content scaling. *Applied Psychological Measurement, 3*, 313–325.
Jones, E.E., & Pittmann, T.S. (1982). Towards a general theory of strategic self-presentation. In Suls, J. (Ed.) *Psychological perspectives on the self* (Vol. 1). Hillsdale: Erlbaum.
Leary, T. (1957). *Interpersonal diagnosis of personality*. New York: Ronald.
Loevinger, J. (1957). Objective tests as instruments of psychological theory. *Psychological Reports, 3*, 635–694.
Payne, F.D., & Wiggins, J.S. (1972). MMPI profile types and the self-report of psychiatric patients. *Journal of Abnormal Psychology, 78*, 1–8.
Snyder, M. (1974). Self-monitoring of expressive behavior. *Journal of Personality and Social Psychology, 30*, 526–537.
Wiggins, J.S. (1981). Clinical and statistical prediction: Where are we and where do we go from here? *Clinical Psychology Review, 1*, 3–18.
Wiggins, J.S. (1984, May). The "mere" semantics of social perception. In Hampson, S.E. (Chair), *The social construction of personality*. Symposium conducted at the Second European Congress on Personality, Bielefeld.

References

Alexander, C.N., & Knight, G.W. (1971). Situated identities and social psychological experimentation. *Sociometry, 34,* 65–82.

Alker, H.A. (1972). Is personality situationally specific or intrapsychically consistent? *Journal of Personality, 40,* 1–16.

Alloy, L.B., & Abrahamson, L.Y. (1979). Judgement of contingency in depressed and nondepressed students: sadder but wiser? *Journal of Experimental Psychology: General, 108, 4,* 441–485.

Allport, F.H. (1937). Teleonomic description in the study of personality. *Character and Personality, 6,* 202–214.

Allport, G.W. (1921). Personality and character. *Psychological Bulletin, 18,* 441–455.

Allport, G.W., & Odbert, H.S. (1936). Trait-names: A psycholexical study. *Psychological Monographs, 47,* (1, Whole No. 211).

Alwin, D.F. (1974). Approaches to the interpretation of relationships in the multimethod matrix. In Costner, H.L. (Ed.), *Sociological methodology 1973–1974* (pp. 79–105). San Francisco: Jossey-Bass.

Amelang, M., & Bartussek, D. (1970). Untersuchungen zur Validität einer neuen Lügenskala [An investigation of the validity of a new lie-scale]. *Diagnostica, 16,* 103–122.

Amelang, M., & Borkenau, P. (1981). Vorhersagen für einige Personen und viele Merkmale. Oder: Konsistenz über Merkmale und Kontextbedingungen als Eigenschaft. In Michaelis, W. (Ed.), *Bericht über den 32. Kongress der Deutschen Gesellschaft für Psychologie in Zürich, 1980* (Vol. 2). Göttingen: Hogrefe.

Amelang, M., & Borkenau, P. (1982). Über die faktorielle Struktur und externe Validität einiger Fragebogen-Skalen zur Erfassung von Dimensionen der Extraversion und emotionalen Stabilität. *Zeitschrift für Differentielle und Diagnostische Psychologie, 3,* 119–146.

Amelang, M., & Borkenau, P. (1984a). Versuche einer Differenzierung des Eigenschaftskonzepts: Aspekte intradindividueller Variabilität und differentieller Vorhersagbarkeit. In Amelang, M., & Ahrens, H.J. (Eds.), *Brennpunkte der Persönlichkeitsforschung.* Göttingen: Hogrefe.

Amelang, M., & Borkenau, P. (1984b). Constructing cross-situational consistency in behavior: Some tests on Bem's thoughts on social desirability as a moderator variable. In Bonarius, H., van Heck, G., & Smid, H. (Eds.), *Personality psychology in Europe: Theoretical and empirical developments.* Lisse: Swets & Zeitlinger.

Amelang, M., & Löhr, F.J. (1983). *Formale und inhaltliche Gesichtspunkte der Item-Formulierung (Soziale Erwünschtheit, Verständlichkeit und Abstraktheit) als Einflußfaktoren der Validität* (Unpublished manuscript).

Amelang, M., Sommer, E., & Bartussek, D. (1971). Persönlichkeitsstruktur und Studienrichtung. *Psychologische Beiträge, 13,* 7–25.

Amelang, M., Kobelt, C., & Frasch, A. (1985). Auf der Suche nach Personen mit Eigenschaften: Untersuchungen zur Restriktion des Eigenschaftsmodells auf Untergruppen von Personen, Verhaltensweisen und Situationen. In Albert, D. (Ed.), *Bericht über den 34. Kongreß der Deutschen Gesellschaft für Psychologie in Wien,* 1984 (Vol. 1). Göttingen: Hogrefe.

Angleitner, A. (1976). *Methodische und theoretische Probleme bei Persönlichkeitsfragebogen unter besonderer Berücksichtigung neuerer deutschsprachiger Fragebogen.* Bonn: Habilitationsschrift, Psychologisches Institut der Universität Bonn.

Angleitner, A. (1981 a). *Teststatistische Kennwerte der Items aus 10 deutschsprachigen Persönlichkeitsfragebogen*. Bielefeld: Arbeitsberichte aus dem Projekt Persönlichkeitsfragebogen (No. 2), Universität Bielefeld.

Angleitner, A. (1981 b). *Teststatistische Kennwerte der Items aus 8 deutschsprachigen Persönlichkeitsfragebogen* für Kinder und Jugendliche. Bielefeld: Arbeitsberichte aus dem Projekt Persönlichkeitsfragebogen (No. 3), Universität Bielefeld.

Angleitner, A., & Löhr, F.J. (1980). Itemüberlappung zwischen Persönlichkeitsfragebogen als Problem für Validitätsschätzungen. *Zeitschrift für Differentielle und Diagnostische Psychologie, 1*, 127–136.

Argyle, M. (1977). Predicted and generated rules model of P × S interaction. In Magnusson, D., & Endler, N.S. (Eds.), *Personality at the cross-roads: Current issues in interactional psychology*. Hillsdale: Erlbaum.

Aries, E.J., Gold, C., & Weigel, R.H. (1983). Dispositional and situational influences on dominance behavior in small groups. *Journal of Personality and Social Psychology, 44*, 779–786.

Arkin, R.M. (1981). Self-presentation styles. In Tedeschi, J.T. (Ed.), *Impression management theory and social psychological research*. New York: Academic.

Arkin, R.M., Gabrenya, W.K., Appelman, A.S., & Cochrane, S.T. (1979). Self-presentation, self-monitoring, and the self-serving bias in causal attributions. *Personality and Social Psychology Bulletin, 5*, 73–76.

Ashton, S.G., & Goldberg, L.R. (1973). In response to Jackson's challenge: The comparative validity of personality scales constructed by the external (empirical) strategy and scales developed intuitively by experts, novices, and laymen. *Journal of Research in Personality, 7*, 1–20.

Bach, K. (1981). An analysis of self-deception. *Philosophy and Phenomenological Research, 41*, 351–370.

Bartussek, D., Weise, G., & Heinze, B. (1972). Reliabilität und faktorielle Validität des deutschen 16 PF-Tests von Cattell. *Arbeiten aus dem psychologischen Institut der Universität Hamburg, 19*.

Bass, B.M., & Berg, I.A. (Eds.), (1959). *Objective approaches to personality assessment*. Princeton: Van Nostrand.

Baumeister, R.F. (1982). A self-presentation view of social phenomena. *Psychological Bulletin, 91*, 3–26.

Beck, A., Weissman, A., Lester, D., & Trexler, L. (1974). The measurement of pessimisn: The Hopelessness scale. *Journal of Consulting and Clinical Psychology, 42*, 861–865.

Beckmann, D., & Richter, H.E. (1972). *Giessen-Test (GT). Ein Test für Individual- und Gruppendiagnostik. Handbuch*. Bern: Huber.

Bellezza, F.S. (1984). Reliability of retrieval from semantic memory: Noun meanings. *Bulletin of the Psychonomc Society, 22*, 377–380.

Belson, W.A. (1968). Respondent understanding of survey questions. *Polls, 3*, 1–13.

Bem, D.J. (1972). Constructing cross-situational consistency in behavior: Some thoughts on Alker's critique of Mischel. *Journal of Personality, 40*, 17–26.

Bem, D.J., & Allen, A. (1974). On predicting some of the people some of the time: The search for cross-situational consistencies in behavior. *Psychological Review, 81*, 506–520.

Bentler, P.M. (1980). Multivariate analysis with latent variables: Causal modeling. *Annual Review of Psychology, 31*, 419–456.

Bentler, P.M., & Bonnett, D.G. (1980). Significance tests and goodness of fit in the analysis of covariance structures. *Psychological Bulletin, 88*, 588–606.

Bentler, P.M., & Weeks, D.G. (1980). Linear structural equations with latent variables. *Psychometrika, 45*, 289–308.

Berman, J.S., & Kenny, D.A. (1976). Correlational bias in observer ratings. *Journal of Personality and Social Psychology, 34*, 263–273.

Bernreuter, R.G. (1933). Validity of the personality inventory. *Personality Journal, 11*, 383–386.

Berscheid, E., Graziano, W.G., Monson, T., & Dermer, M. (1976). Outcome dependency: Attention, attribution and attraction. *Journal of Personality and Social Psychology, 34*, 978–989.

Blalock, H.M. (1982). *Conceptualization and measurement in the social sciences*. Beverly Hills: Sage.

Block, J. (1965). *The challenge of response sets*. New York: Appleton-Century-Crofts.

Block, J. (1977). Advancing the psychology of personality: Paradigmatic shift or improving the quality of research. In Magnusson, D., & Endler, N.S. (Eds.), *Personality at the crossroads: Current issues in interactional psychology*. Hillsdale: Erlbaum.

Borg, I. (1981) *Anwendungsorientierte multidimensionale Skalierung*. Berlin Heidelberg New York: Springer.

Borgen, F.H. (1972). Predicting career choices of able college men from occupational and basic interest scales of the Strong Vocational Interest Blank. *Journal of Counseling Psychology, 19*, 202–211.

Borkenau, P. (1981). *Intraindividuelle Variabilität und differentielle Vorhersagbarkeit*. Unpublished doctoral dissertation, University of Heidelberg.

Borkenau, P., & Amelang, M. (1985a). The control of social desirability in personality inventories: A study using the principal-factor technique. *Journal of Research in Personality, 19*, 44–53.

Borkenau, P., & Amelang, M. (1985b). Individuelle Angemessenheit von Eigenschaftskonstrukten als Moderatorvariable für die Übereinstimmung zwischen Selbst- und Bekanntenratings. *Diagnostica, 31*, 105–118.

Borkenau, P., & Angleitner, A. (1985). Systematische Verzerrungen in der Beurteilung von Personen: Faktum oder Fiktion? In Albert, D. (Ed.), *Bericht über den 34. Kongreß der Deutschen Gesellschaft für Psychologie in Wien*, 1984, (Vol. 1). Göttingen: Hogrefe.

Bowers, K.S. (1973). Situationism in psychology: An analysis and a critique. *Psychological Review, 80*, 307–330.

Boysson-Bardies, B. de (1970). Syntax and semantics in memorization of negation. In Flores d'Arcais, G.G.J., & Levelt, W.J.M. (Eds.), *Advances in psycholinguistics* (pp. 237–245). Amsterdam: North-Holland.

Breznitz, S. (Ed.). (1983). *The denial of stress*. New York: International Universities Press.

Briggs, S.R., Cheek, J., & Buss, A.H. (1980). An analysis of the self-monitoring scale. *Journal of Personality and Social Psychology, 38*, 679–686.

Brokken, F.B. (1978). *The language of personality*. Groningen: Doctoral dissertation, University of Groningen.

Broughton, R. (1984). A prototype strategy for construction of personality scales. *Journal of Personality and Social Psychology, 47*, 1334–1347.

Buchwald, A.M. (1961). Verbal utterances as data. In Feigl, H., & Maxwell, G. (Eds.), *Current issues in the philosophy of science* (pp. 461–468). New York: Holt.

Burisch, M. (1978). Construction strategies for multi-scale personality inventories. *Applied Psychological Measurement, 2*, 97–111.

Burisch, M. (1984a). Approaches to personality inventory construction: A comparison of merits. *American Psychologist, 39*, 214–227.

Burisch, M. (1984b). You don't always get what you pay for: Measuring depression with short and simple versus long and sophisticated scales. *Journal of Research in Personality, 18*, 81–98.

Burke, P.A., Kraut, R.E., & Dworkin, R.H. (1984). Traits, consistency, and self-schemata: What do our methods measure? *Journal of Personality and Social Psychology, 47*, 568–579.

Buse, L. (1980). Intraindividuelle Merkmalsvariation und Validität eines Extraversionsfragebogens. Eine Untersuchung zur Gültigkeit des Eigenschaftsbegriffs. *Zeitschrift für Differentielle und Diagnostische Psychologie, 1*, 35–42.

Buss, D.M., & Craik, K.H. (1980). The frequency concept of disposition: Dominance and prototypically dominant acts. *Journal of Personality, 48*, 379–392.

Buss, D.M., & Craik, K.H. (1981). The act frequency analysis of interpersonal dispositions: Aloofness, gregariousness, dominance, and submission. *Journal of Personality, 49*, 175–192.

Buss, D.M., & Craik, K.H. (1983). The act frequency approach to personality. *Psychological Review, 90*, 105–126.

Butcher, J.N., & Tellegen, A. (1966). Objections to MMPI items. *Journal of Consulting Psychology, 30*, 527–534.

Butt, D.S., & Fiske, D.W. (1968). Comparison of strategies in developing scales for dominance. *Psychological Bulletin, 70*, 505–519.

Byrne, D. (1964). Repression-sensitization as a dimension of personality. In Maher, B. (Ed.), *Progress in experimental personality research* (Vol. 1). New York: Academic.

Campbell, D.T., & Fiske, D.W. (1959). Convergent and discriminant validation by the multitrait-multimethod matrix. *Psychological Bulletin, 56*, 81–105.

Campbell, N.R. (1952). *What is science*. New York: Dover. (Originally published in 1921).

Campus, N. (1974). Transsituational consistency as a dimension of personality. *Journal of Personality and Social Psychology, 29*, 593–600.

Cantor, N. (1981). Perceptions of situations: Situation prototypes and person-situation prototypes. In Magnusson, D. (Ed.), *Toward a psychology of situations: An interactional perspective*. Hillsdale: Erlbaum.

Cantor, N., Mischel, W., & Schwartz, J.C. (1982a). Social knowledge: Structure, content, use and abuse. In Hastorf, A., & Isen, A. (Eds.), *Cognitive social psychology*. New York: Elsevier/North Holland.

Cantor, N., Mischel, W., & Schwartz, J.C. (1982b). A prototype analysis of psychological situations. *Cognitive Psychology, 14*, 45–77.

Cattell, R.B. (1943). The description of personality. 2. Basic traits resolved into clusters. *Journal of Abnormal and Social Psychology, 38*, 476–507.

Cattell, R.B. (1957). *Personality and motivation structure and measurement*. New York: World Book.

Cattell, R.B. (1965). *The scientific analysis of personality*. Harmondsworth: Penguin.

Cattell, R.B. (1973). *Personality and mood by questionnaire*. San Francisco: Jossey-Bass.

Cattell, R.B., & Eber, H.W. (1962). *Specimen set for the Sixteen Personality Factor Questionnaire "16 PF", experimental edition der deutschen Form A und B*. Champaign: Institute for Personality and Ability Testing.

Cattell, R.B., & Eber, H.W. (1964). *The Sixteen Personality Factor Questionnaire*. Champaign: Institute for Personality and Ability Testing.

Cattell, R.B., & Tsujioka, B. (1964). The importance of factor-trueness and validity, versus homogeneity and orthogonality, in test scales. *Educational and Psychological Measurement, 24*, 3–30.

Cattell, R.B., Horn, J.L., Sweney, A.B., & Radcliffe, J.A. (1964). *The motivation analysis test, MAT*. Champaign: Institute of Personality and Ability Testing.

Chaplin, W.F., & Goldberg, L.R. (1984). A failure to replicate the Bem & Allen study of individual differences in cross-situational consistency. *Journal of Personality and Social. Psychology, 47*, 1074–1090.

Cheek, J.M. (1982). Aggregation, moderator variables, and the validity of personality tests: A peer rating study. *Journal of Personality and Social Psychology, 43*, 1254–1269.

Cheek, J., & Hogan, R. (1984). Self-concepts, self-presentations and moral judgments. In Suls, J., & Greenwald, A. (Eds.), *Psychological perspectives on the self* (Vol. 2). Hillsdale: Erlbaum.

Chomsky, N. (1957). *Syntactic structures*. The Hague: Mouton.

Chomsky, N. (1965). *Aspects of the theory of syntax*. Cambridge, MA: M.I.T. Press.

Christie, R., & Geis, F.L. (1970). *Studies in Machiavellianism*. New York: Academic.

Cliff, N. (1968). Adjective check list and individual differences in perceived meaning. *Educational and Psychological Measurement, 28*, 1063–1077.

Cliff, N. (1983). Some cautions concerning the application of causal modeling methods. *Multivariate Behavioral Research, 18*, 115–126.

Cliff, N., Bradley, P., & Girard, R. (1973). The investigation of cognitive models for inventory response. *Multivariate Behavioral Research, 8*, 407–425.

Cofer, C.N., Chance, J., & Judson, A.J. (1949). A study of malingering on the MMPI. *Journal of Psychology, 27*, 491–499.

Coleman, J.S. (1969). The methods of sociology. In Bierstadt, R. (Ed.), *A design for sociology: Scope, objectives, and methods* (Monograph 9). Philadelphia: American Academy of Political and Social Science.

Collins, J.E., Paulhus, D.L., & Graziano, W.G. (1983, August). Is self-monitoring a skill or a motive? *Meeting of the American Psychological Association,* Anaheim.

Comrey, A.L. (1980). *Handbook of interpretation for the Comrey Personality Scales*. San Diego: EdITS.

Crewe, N.M. (1967). Comparison of factor analytic and empirical scales. *Proceedings of the 75th Annual Convention of the American Psychological Association,* (pp. 367–368).

Cronbach, L.J. (1970). *Essentials of psychological testing* (3rd ed.). New York: Harper & Row.

Cronbach, L.J., & Gleser, G.C. (1965). *Psychological tests and personnel decisions*. Urbana: University of Illinois Press.

Crowne, D.P., & Marlowe, D. (1964). *The approval motive: Studies in evaluative dependence*. New York: Wiley.

Dahlstrom, W.G., & Welsh, G.S. (1960). *An MMPI handbook*. Minneapolis: University of Minnesota Press.

Dahlstrom, G.W., Welsh, G.S., & Dahlstrom, L.E. (1972). *An MMPI handbook. Vol. 1: Clinical interpretation* (rev. ed.). Minneapolis: University of Minnesota Press.

Dahlstrom, W.G., Welsh, G.S., & Dahlstrom, L.E. (1975). *An MMPI handbook. Vol. 2: Research applications* (rev. ed.). Minneapolis: University of Minnesota Press.

Damarin, F., & Messick, S. (1965). *Response styles as personality variables: A theoretical integration of multivariate research* (Research Bulletin 65-10). Princeton: Educational Testing Service.

D'Andrade, R.G. (1974). Memory and the assessment of behavior. In Blalock, H. (Ed.), *Measurement in the social sciences*. Chicago: Aldine.

Danheiser, P., & Paulhus, D.L. (1981, March). Self-monitoring and need for approval as impression management styles: Skill versus need. *Meeting of the Southeastern Psychological Association,* Atlanta.

Demos, R. (1960). Lying to oneself. *Journal of Philosophy, 57*, 588–595.

Dickes, P., & Steiwer, L. (1977). Ausarbeitung von Lesbarkeitsformeln für die deutsche Sprache. *Zeitschrift für Entwicklungspsychologie und Pädagogische Psychologie, 9*, 20–28.

Diener, E., Larsen, R.J., & Emmons, R.A. (1984). Person x situation interactions: Choice of situations and congruence response models. *Journal of Personality and Social Psychology, 47*, 580–592.

Dubois, B., & Burne, J.A. (1975). An analysis of the meaning of the question mark response-category in attitude scales. *Educational and Psychological Measurement, 35*, 869–884.

Duncan, O.D. (1975). *Introduction to structural equation methods*. New York: Academic.

Edwards, A.L. (1957a). *Techniques of attitude scale construction*. New York: Appleton-Century-Crofts.

Edwards, A.L. (1957b). *The social desirability variable in personality assessment and research*. New York: Dryden.

Edwards, A.L. (1970). *The measurement of personality traits by scales and inventories*. New York: Holt, Rinehart, & Winston.

Edwards, A.L., & Walsh, J.A. (1964). Response sets in standard and experimental personality scales. *American Educational Research Journal, 1*, 52–61.

Eggert, D. (1974). *Eysenck-Persönlichkeits-Inventar (EPI). Handanweisung für die Durchführung und Auswertung*. Göttingen: Hogrefe.

Ellis, A. (1946). The validity of personality questionnaires. *Psychological Bulletin, 43*, 385–440.

Endler, N.S., Hunt, J.McV., Rosenstein, A.J. (1962). An S-R-inventory of anxiousness. *Psychological Monographs, 76* (No. 17).

Engelkamp, J. (1974). *Psycholinguistik*. Munich: Fink.

Epstein, S. (1979). The stability of behavior: On predicting most of the people much of the time. *Journal of Personality and Social Psychology, 37*, 1097–1126.

Ericsson, K.A., & Simon, H.A. (1980). Verbal reports as data. *Psychological Review, 87*, 215–251.

Ertel, S. (1974). Satzsubjekt und Ich-Perspektive. In Eckensberger, L.H., & Eckensberger, U.S. (Eds.). *Bericht über den 28. Kongress der Deutschen Gesellschaft für Psychologie in Saarbrücken 1972* (Vol. 1, pp. 129–139). Göttingen: Hogrefe.

Ertel, S. (1977). Where do the subjects of sentences come from? In Rosenberg, S. (Ed.), *Sentence production. Developments in research and theory* (pp. 141–167). Hillsdale: Erlbaum.

Eysenck, H.J. (1947). *Dimensions of personality*. London: Routledge & Kegan Paul.

Eysenck, H.J. (1953). Fragebogen als Meßmittel der Persönlichkeit: Eine experimentelle Untersuchung. *Zeitschrift für experimentelle und angewandte Psychologie, 1*, 291–335.

Eysenck, H.J. (1959 a). *Das "Maudsley Personality Inventory" (MPI)*. Göttingen: Hogrefe.

Eysenck, H.J. (1959 b). Der Maudsley Personality Inventory als Bestimmer der neurotischen Tendenz und Extraversion. *Zeitschrift für experimentelle und angewandte Psychologie, 6*, 167–190.

Eysenck, H.J. (1962). *The Maudsley Personality Inventory* (Manual prepared by R.R. Knapp). San Diego: Educational and Industrial Testing Service.

Eysenck, H.J. (1964). *MMQ*. Göttingen: Hogrefe.

Eysenck, H.J., & Eysenck, S.B.G. (1964). *Manual of the Eysenck Personality Inventory*. London: University of London Press.

Eysenck, M., & Eysenck, H.J. (1980). Mischel and the concept of personality. *British Journal of Psychology, 71*, 191–204.

Fahrenberg, J., & Selg, H. (1970). *Das Freiburger Persönlichkeitsinventar (FPI) – Handanweisung*. Göttingen: Hogrefe.

Fahrenberg, J., & Selg, H. (1974). *Das Freiburger Persönlichkeitsinventar FPI* (2nd ed.). Göttingen: Hogrefe.

Fahrenberg, J., Selg, H., & Hampel, R. (1973). *Das Freiburger Persönlichkeitsinventar (FPI)*. Göttingen: Hogrefe.

Farr, J.N., Jenkins, J.J., & Paterson, D.G. (1951). Simplification of Flesch's reading ease formular. *Journal of Applied Psychology, 35*, 333–337.

Fekken, C. (1983). *Comparison of 4 models for predicting person reliability*. London/Ontario: *Doctoral dissertation, University of Ontario*.

Feather, N.T. (1983). Some correlates of attributional style: Depressive symptoms, self-esteem, and Protestant Ethic values. *Personality and Social Psychology Bulletin, 9*, 125–135.

Fillmore, C.J. (1968). The case for case. In Bach, E., & Harms, R. (Eds.), *Universals in linguistic theory* (pp. 1–88). New York: Holt, Rinehart, & Winston.

Fillmore, C.J. (1977). The case for case reopened. In Cole, P., & Sadock, J. (Eds.), *Grammatical relations* (pp. 59–81). New York: Academic.

Fingarette, H. (1969). *Self-deception*. New York: Humanities.

Fischer, G. (1974). *Einführung in die Theorie psychologischer Tests*. Bern: Huber.

Fishbein, M., & Ajzen, I. (1974). Attitudes towards objects as predictors of single and multiple behavioral criteria. *Psychological Review, 81*, 59–74.

Fiske, D.W. (1949). Consistency of the factorial structures of personality ratings from different sources. *Journal of Abnormal and Social Psychology, 44*, 329–344.

Fiske, D.W. (1966). Some hypotheses concerning test adequacy. *Educational and Psychological Measurement, 26*, 69–88.
Fiske, D.W. (1971). *Measuring the concepts of personality*. Chicago: Aldine.
Fiske, D.W. (1973). Can a personality construct be validated empirically? *Psychological Bulletin, 80*, 89–92.
Fiske, D.W. (1976). Can a personality construct have a singular validational pattern? Rejoinder to Huba and Hamilton. *Psychological Bulletin, 83*, 877–879.
Fiske, D.W. (1978). *Strategies for personality research: The observation versus interpretation of behavior*. San Francisco: Jossey-Bass.
Fiske, D.W. (1980). When are verbal reports veridical? In Shweder, R. (Ed.), *New directions for methodology of social and behavioral science: Fallible judgments in behavioral research* (No. 4). San Francisco: Jossey-Bass.
Fiske, D.W. (1981). *New directions for methodology of social and behavioral science: Problems with language imprecision* (No. 9). San Francisco: Jossey-Bass.
Fiske, D.W. (1982a, June). What can we do with personality questionnaires? *Bielefeld Symposium on Personality Questionnaires*, Bielefeld.
Fiske, D.W. (1982b). Convergent-discriminant validation in measurements and research strategies. In Brinberg, D., & Kidder, L. (Eds.), *New directions for methodology of social and behavioral science: Forms of validity in research* (No. 12, pp. 77–92). San Francisco: Jossey-Bass.
Fiske, D.W. (in press). Measuring to understand and understanding measuring.
Fiske, D.W., & Butler, J.M. (1963). The experimental conditions for measuring individual differences. *Educational and Psychological Measurement, 23*, 249–266.
Fiske, S.T., & Cox, M.G. (1979). Describing others: there's more to person perception than trait lists. *Journal of Personality; 47*, 136–161.
Flesch, R. (1948). A new readability yardstick. *Journal of Applied Psychology, 32*, 321–323.
Forgas, J.P. (1982). Episode cognition: Internal representations of interaction routines. In Berkowitz, L. (Ed.)., *Advances in experimental social psychology* (Vol. 15). New York: Academic.
Foss, D.J., Hakes, D.J., & Hakes, D.T. (1978). *Psycholinguistics*. Englewood Cliffs, NJ: Prentice Hall.
Franks, J.J., & Bransford, J.D. (1974). Memory for syntactic form as a function of semantic context. *Journal of Experimental Psychology, 103*, 1037–1039.
Frederiksen, N., & Melville, S.D. (1954). Differential predictability in the use of test scores. *Educational and Psychological Measurement, 14*, 647–656.
Frenkel-Brunswik, E. (1939). Mechanisms of self-deception. *Journal of Social Psychology, 10*, 409–420.
Gael, S., Grant, D.L., & Ritchie, R.J. (1975a). Employment test validation for minority and nonminority telephone operators. *Journal of Applied Psychology, 60*, 411–419.
Gael, S., Grant, D.L., & Ritchie, R.J. (1975b). Employment test validation for minority and nonminority clerks with work sample criteria. *Journal of Applied Psychology, 60*, 420–426.
Gergen, K.J. (1965). Interaction goals and personalistic feedback as factors affecting the presentation of self. *Journal of Personality and Social Psychology, 1*, 413–424.
Ghiselli, E.E. (1956). Differentiation of individuals in terms of their predictability. *Journal of Applied Psychology, 40*, 374–377.
Gifford, R. (1982). Affiliativeness: A trait-measure in relation to single-act and multi-act behavior criteria. *Journal of Research in Personality, 16*, 128–134.
Gifi, A. (1984). *Nonlinear multivariate analysis*. Leiden: DSWO.
Givon, T. (1979). *Syntax and semantics 12: Discourse and syntax*. New York: Academic.
Goldberg, L.R. (1963). A model of item ambiguity in personality assessment. *Educational and Psychological Measurement, 23*, 467–492.
Goldberg, L.R. (1968). The interrelationships among item characteristics in an adjective checklist: The convergence of different indices of item ambiguity. *Educational and Psychological Measurement, 28*, 273–296.

Goldberg, L.R. (1971). A historical survey of personality scales and inventories. In McReynolds, P. (Ed.), *Advances in psychological assessment* (Vol. 2, pp. 293–336). Palo Alto: Science and Behavior.

Goldberg, L.R. (1972a). Some recent trends in personality assessment. *Journal of Personality Assessment, 36*, 547–560.

Goldberg, L.R. (1972b). Parameters of personality inventory construction and utilization: A comparison of prediction strategies and tactics. *Multivariate Behavioral Research Monographs, 72* (2).

Goldberg, L.R. (1974). Objective diagnostic tests and measures. *Annual Review of Psychology, 25*, 343–366.

Goldberg, L.R. (1978). Differential attribution of trait-descriptive terms to oneself as compared to well-liked, neutral, and disliked others: A psychometric analysis. *Journal of Personality and Social Psychology, 36*, 1012–1028.

Goldberg, L.R. (1980, May). Some ruminations about the structure of individual differences: Developing a common lexicon for the major characteristics of human personality. *Meetings of the Western Psychological Association*, Honolulu, Hawaii.

Goldberg, L.R. (1981a). Developing a taxonomy of trait-descriptive terms. In Fiske, D. (Ed.), *New directions for methodology of social and behavioral science. Problems with language imprecision* (No. 9). San Francisco: Jossey-Bass.

Goldberg, L.R. (1981b). Language and individual differences. The search for universals in personality lexicons. *Review of Personality and Social Psychology, 41*(2), 141–165.

Goldberg, L.R. (1981c). Unconfounding situational attributions from uncertain, neutral and ambiguous ones: A psychometric analysis of description of oneself and various types of others. *Journal of Personality and Social Psychology, 41*(3), 517–552.

Goldberg, L.R. (1981d). Language and personality: Developing a taxonomy of trait-descriptive terms. In Fiske, D. (Ed.), *New directions for methodology of social and behavioral science. Problems with language imprecision* (No. 9). San Francisco: Jossey-Bass.

Goldberg, L.R. (1982). From Ace to Zombie: Some explorations in the language of personality. In Spielberger, L.D., & Butcher, J.N. (Eds.), *Advances in personality assessment* (Vol. 1). Hillsdale: Erlbaum.

Goldberg, L.R. (1983). *Out of the closet: An admission*. Unpublished manuscript.

Goldberg, L.R., & Slovic, P. (1967). Importance of test item content: An analysis of a corolary of the deviation hypothesis. *Journal of Counseling Psychology, 14*, 462–472.

Golding, S.L. (1975). Flies in the ointment: Methodological problems in the analysis of the percentage of variance due to person and situation. *Psychological Bulletin, 82*, 278–288.

Golin, S., Terrell, F., & Johnson, B. (1977). Depression and the illusion of control. *Journal of Abnormal Psychology, 86*, 440–442.

Gormly, J. (1983). Predicting behavior from personality trait-scores. *Personality and Social Psychology Bulletin, 9*, 267–270.

Gorsuch, R.G., & Cattell, R.B. (1967). Second stratum personality factors defined in the questionnaire realm by the 16PF. *Multivariate Behavioral Research, 2*, 211–224.

Gough, H.G. (1956). *California Psychological Inventory (CPI)*. Palo Alto: Consulting Psychologists.

Gough, H.G. (1957). *Manual for the California Psychological Inventory*. Palo Alto: Consulting Psychologists.

Gough, H.G. (1965a). Conceptual analysis of psychological test scores and other diagnostic variables. *Journal of Abnormal Psychology, 70*, 294–302.

Gough, H.G. (1965b). Avalidational study of the Chapin Social Insight Test. *Psychological Reports, 17*, 355–368.

Gough, H.G., & Heilbrun, A.B. (1965). *The adjective check list manual*. Palo Alto: Consulting Psychologists.

Gough, P.B. (1965). Grammatical transformation and speed of understanding. *Journal of Verbal Learning and Verbal Behavior, 4*, 107–111.

Green, B.F., Jr. (1978). In defense of measurement. *American Psychologist, 33*, 664–670.

Greenwald, A.G. (1980). The totalitarian ego: Fabrication and revision of personal history. *American Psychologist, 35*, 603–618.

Greenwald, A.G. (1982). Is anyone in charge? Personalysis versus the principle of personal unity. In Suls, J. (Ed.), *Psychological perspectives on the self* (Vol. 1). Hillsdale: Erlbaum.

Gulliksen, H. (1950). Theory of mental tests. New York: Wiley.

Gur, R.C., & Sackeim, H.A. (1979). Self-deception: A concept in search of a phenomenon. *Journal of Personality and Social Psychology, 37*, 147–169.

Guttman, L. (1941). The quantification of a class of attributes: A theory and method of scale construction. In Horst, P. (Ed.), *The prediction of personal adjustment* (pp. 319–348). New York: Social Science Research Council.

Gynther, M.D., & Brilliant, P.J. (1968). The MMPI K⁺ profile: A reexamination. *Journal of Consulting and Clinical Psychology, 32*, 616–617.

Gynther, M.D., & Green, S.B. (1982). Methodological problems in research with self-report inventories. In Kendall, P.C., & Butcher, J.N. (Eds.), *A handbook of research methods in clinical psychology* (pp. 355–386). New York: Wiley.

Hampshire, S. (1953). Dispositions. *Analysis, 14*, 5–11.

Hampson, S.E. (1982). Person memory: A semantic category model of personality traits. *British Journal of Psychology, 73*, 1–11.

Hase, H.D., & Goldberg, L.R. (1967). Comparative validity of different strategies of constructing personality inventory scales. *Psychological Bulletin, 67*, 231–248.

Hathaway, S.R., & McKinley, J.C. (1940). A multiphasic personality schedule (Minnesota). 1. Construction of the schedule. *Journal of Psychology, 10*, 249–254.

Hathaway, S.R., & McKinley, J.C. (1943). *Manual for the Minnesota Multiphasic Personality Inventory*. New York: Psychological Corporation.

Hedlund, J.L., Cho, D.W., & Wood, J.B. (1977). Comparative validity of MMPI-168 factor and clinical scales. *Journal of Multivariate Behavioral Research, 12*, 327–330.

Heilbrun, A.B. (1962). A comparison of empirical derivation and rational derivation of an affiliation scale. *Journal of Clinical Psychology, 18*, 101–102.

Heilbrun, A.B. (1964). Social learning theory, social desirability an the MMPI. *Psychological Bulletin, 61*, 377–387.

Heise, D.R. (1975). *Causal analysis*. New York: Wiley.

Helmes, E. (1978). *A multidimensional approach to personality inventory responding*. London/Ontario: Doctoral dissertation, University of Western Ontario.

Helmstader, G.C. (1957) Procedure for obtaining separate set and content components of a test score. Psychometrika, *22*, 381–393.

Helson, H., Blake, E.E., Mouton, J.S., & Olmstead, J.A. (1965). Attitudes as adjustments to stimulus, background, and residual factors. *Journal of Abnormal and Social Psychology, 52*, 314–322.

Hermans, H.J.M. (1969). The validity of different strategies of scale construction in predicting academic achievement. *Educational and Psychological Measurement, 29*, 877–883.

Herriot, P. (1969). The comprehension of active and passive sentences as a function of pragmatic expectations. *Journal of Verbal Learning and Verbal Behavior, 8*, 166–169.

Herrmann, T. (1973). *Persönlichkeitsmerkmale*. Stuttgart: Kohlhammer.

Hewitt, J.K. (1984). Normal components of personality variation. *Journal of Personality and Social Psychology, 47*, 671–675.

Hilgard, E.R. (1949). Human motives and the concepts of self. *American Psychologist, 4*, 374–382.

Hofstee, W.K.B. (1963). Enkele notities over G.J.S. Wilde's "Neurotische labiliteit, gemeten volgens de vragenlijstmethode." *Nederlands Tijdschrift voor de Psychologie, 18*, 481–499.

Hofstee, W.K.B. (1984). What's in a trait: Reflections about the inevitability of traits, their measurement, and taxonomy. In Bonarius, H., van Heck, G., & Smid, N. (Eds.), *Personality psychology in Europe: Theoretical and empirical developments* (pp. 75–81). Lisse: Swets & Zeitlinger.

Hofstee, W.K.B., Brokken, F.B., & Land, H. (1981). Constructie van standaard-persoonlijkheids-eigenschappen-lijst (SPEL). *Nederlands Tijdschrift voor de Psychologie, 36*, 443–452.
Hogan, R. (1983). A socioanalytic theory of personality: In Page, M.M. (Ed.), *Nebraska symposium on motivation, 1982*. Lincoln: University of Nebraska Press.
Hogan, R., & Briggs, S. (1983). Noncognitive measures of social intelligence. *Meeting of the American Psychological Association*, Anaheim.
Holden, R.R., & Jackson, D.N. (1979). Item subtlety and face validity in personality assessment. *Journal of Consulting and Clinical Psychology, 47*, 459–468.
Hörmann, H. (1971). Semantic factors in negation. *Psychologische Forschung, 35*, 1–16.
Hörmann, H. (1978). *Meinen und Verstehen*. Frankfurt/M: Suhrkamp.
Hörmann, H. (1981). *Einführung in die Psycholinguistik*. Darmstadt: Wissenschaftliche Buchgesellschaft.
Hörmann, H. (1982). Hidden determinants of understanding. In LeNy, J.-F., & Kintsch, W. (Eds.), *Language and comprehension* (pp. 251–260). Amsterdam: North Holland.
Hörmann, H., Pieper, U., & Engelkamp, J. (1976). Zur psychologischen Problematik sog. Altersdialekte. *Psychologische Rundschau, 27*, 12–27.
Hormuth, S.E. (1982). Self-focused attention and the adherence to personal standards. In Kosakowsky, A., & Obuchowski, K. (Eds.), *Progress in psychology and personality*. Berlin: VEB Deutscher Verlag der Wissenschaften.
Hornick, C.W., James, L.R., & Jones, A.P. (1977). Empirical item keying versus a rational approach to analyzing a psychological climate questionnaire. *Applied Psychological Measurement, 1*, 489–500.
Hubert, L.J., & Baker, F.G. (1978). Analyzing the multitrait-multimethod matrix. *Multivariate Behavioral Research, 13*, 163–179.
Hull, Y.G., & Levy, A.S. (1979). The organizational functions of the self: An alternative to the Duval and Wicklund model of self-awareness. *Journal of Personality and Social Psychology, 37*, 756–768.
Jaccard, J.J. (1974). Predicting social behavior from personality traits. *Journal of Research in Personality, 7*, 358–367.
Jaccard, J., Weber, I., & Lundmark, J.A. (1975). A multitrait-multimethod analysis of four attitude assessment procedures. *Journal of experimental Social Psychology, 12*, 149–154.
Jackendoff, R.S. (1969). An interpretive theory of negation. *Foundations of Language, 5*, 218–241.
Jackson, D.N. (1967). *Personality research form. Manual*. Goshen: Research Psychologists.
Jackson, D.N. (1969). Multimethod factor analysis in the evaluation of convergent and discriminant validity. *Psychological Bulletin, 72*, 30–49.
Jackson, D.N. (1970). A sequential system for personality scale development. In Spielberger, C.D. (Ed.), *Current topics in clinical community psychology* (Vol. 2, pp. 61–96). New York: Academic.
Jackson, D.N. (1971). The dynamics of structured personality tests: 1971. *Psychological Review, 78*, 229–248.
Jackson, D.N. (1975a). Multimethod factor analysis: A reformulation. *Multivariate Behavioral Research, 10*, 253–276.
Jackson, D.N. (1975b). The relative validity of scales prepared by naive item writers and those based on empirical methods of personality scale construction. *Educational and Psychological Measurement, 35*, 361–370.
Jackson, D.N. (1984). *Personality research form (3rd ed.)*. Port Huron: Research Psychologists.
Jackson, D.N., & Helmes, E. (1979). Basic structure content scaling. *Applied Psychological Measurement, 3*(3), 313–325.
Jackson, D.N., & Messick, S. (1961). Acquiescence and desirability as response determinants on the MMPI. *Educational and Psychological Measurement, 21*, 771–790.

Jackson, D.N., & Messicks (1962a). Response styles on the MMPI: Comparison of clinical and normal samples. *Journal of Abnormal and Social Psychology, 65,* 285–299.

Jackson, D.N., & Messick, S. (1962b). Response styles and the assessment of psychopathology. In Messick, S., & Ross, J. (Eds.), *Measurement in personality and cognition.* New York: Wiley.

Jackson, D.N., & Messick, S. (1976). *Differential Personality Inventory.* Department of Psychology, The University of Western Ontario: London (Canada).

Jackson, D.N., & Paunonen, S.V. (1980). Personality structure and assessment. *Annual Review of Psychology, 31,* 503–551.

Jackson, D.N., & Stricker, L.J. (1982). Is implicit personality theory illusory? Armchair criticism vs. replicated empirical research. *Journal of Personality, 50,* 240–244.

Jackson, D.N., Chan, D.W., & Stricker, L.J. (1979). Implicit personality theory: Is it illusory? *Journal of Personality, 47,* 1–10.

Janke, W. (1973a). Über die Konstruktion von Fragebögen. Bericht über ein Symposium: Das Dilemma von Persönlichkeitsfragebogen. In Reinert, G. (Ed.), *Bericht über den 27. Kongress der Deutschen Gesellschaft für Psychologie in Kiel 1970* (pp. 41–48). Göttingen: Hogrefe.

Janke, W. (1973b). Das Dilemma von Persönlichkeitsfragebogen. Einleitung des Symposiums über Konstruktion von Fragebogen. In Reinert, G. (Ed.), *Bericht über den 27. Kongress der Deutschen Gesellschaft für Psychologie in Kiel 1970.* Göttingen: Hogrefe.

Jansen, P.G.W. (1983). *Rasch analysis of attitudinal data.* Nijmegen: Doctoral dissertation, University of Nijmegen.

Janssen, J.P. (1978). *Zur Validität von SD-verfälschten Persönlichkeitsfragebogen in Extremsituationen und beim Rollenspiel.* Cologne: TÜV-Rheinland.

John, O.P., Goldberg, L.R., & Angleitner, A. (1984). Better than the alphabet: Taxonomies of personality descriptive terms in English, Dutch, and German. In Bonarius, H.M., van Heck, G., & Smid, N. (Eds.), *Personality psychology in Europe: Theoretical and empirical developments.* Lisse: Swets & Zeitlinger.

Jones, E.E., & Baumeister, R.F. (1976). The self-monitor looks at the ingratiator. *Journal of Personality, 44,* 541–559.

Jones, E.E., & Pittman, T.S. (1982). Toward a general theory of strategic self-presentation. In Suls, J. (Ed.), *Psychological perspectives on the self* (Vol. 1). Hillsdale: Erlbaum.

Jones, E.E., & Wortman, C. (1973). *Ingratiation: An attributional approach.* Morriston, N.J.: General Learning Press.

Jones, E.E., Gergen, K.J., & Davis, K.E. (1962). Some determinants of reactions to being approved or disapproved as a person. *Psychological Monographs, 76* (2, Whole No. 521).

Jones, R.R. (1965). The relationships between item properties and scale reliability. *Oregon Research. Institute Research Monograph, 5* (No. 1).

Jones, R.R. (1968, August). Differences in response consistency and subjects' preferences for three personality inventory formats. *Proceedings of the 76th Annual Convention of the American Psychological Association,* San Francisco.

Jöreskog, K.G. (1971a). Simultaneous factor analysis in several populations. *Psychometrika, 36,* 409–426.

Jöreskog, K.G. (1971b). Statistical analysis of sets of congeneric tests. *Psychometrika, 36,* 109–133.

Jöreskog, K.G., & Sörbom, D. (1978). *Lisrel: Analysis of linear structural relationships by the method of maximum likelihood (Version IV).* Chicago: NER.

Jöreskog, K.G., & Sörbom, D. (1979). *Advances in factor analysis and structural equation models.* Cambridge, MA: Abt. Books.

Jöreskog, K.G., & Sörbom, D. (1981). *LISREL V: Analysis of linear structural relationships by maximum likelihood and least squares methods* (Research report 81-8). Uppsala: University of Uppsala.

Kastner, M. (1982). *Ein Konzept zur internen Validierung psychologischer Fragebogenverfahren. Wuppertal: Habilitationsschrift. Bergische Univerität, Wuppertal.*

Kaufmann, W. (1956). *Existentialism from Dostoevsky to Sartre*. Cleveland: World publishing.

Kiecolt-Glaser, J., & Murray, J.A. (1980). Social desirability bias in self-monitoring data. *Journal of Behavioral Assessment, 2*, 239–247.

Kelley, H.H., & Michela, G.L. (1980). Attribution theory and research. *Annual Review of Psychology, 34*, 457–504.

Kenny, D. (1976). An empirical application of confirmatory factor analysis to the multitrait-multimethod matrix. *Journal of Experimental Social Psychology, 12*, 247–252.

Kenny, D.A. (1979). *Correlation and causality*. New York: Wiley.

Kenrick, D.T., & Stringfield, D.O. (1980). Personality traits and the eye of the beholder: Crossing some traditional philosophical boundaries in the search for consistency in all of the people. *Psychological Review, 87*, 88–104.

Keren, A. (1979). *Inhaltlich-semantische Analyse der Items aus fünf deutschsprachigen Persönlichkeitsfragebogen*. Bonn: Diplomarbeit, Psychologisches Institut der Universität Bonn.

Kierkegaard, S. (1959). *Either/Or* (Vol. 2, H. Lowrie, Trans.). New York: Anchor. (Original work published 1843).

Klingler, D.E., Johnson, J.H., Giannetti, R.A., & Williams, T.A. (1977). Comparison of the clinical utility of the MMPI basic scales and specific MMPI state-trait scales: A test of Dahlstrom's hypothesis. *Journal of Consulting and Clinical Psychology, 45*, 1086–1092.

Knudson, R.M., & Golding, S.L. (1974). Comparative validity of traditional versus S-R format inventories of interpersonal behavior. *Journal of Research in Personality, 8*, 111–127.

Krauss, R., Geller, V., & Olson, C. (1976). Modalities and cues in the detection of deception. *Meeting of the American Psychological Association*, Washington.

Krippendorff, K. (1970). Estimating the reliability, systematic error, and random error of interval data. *Educational and Psychological Measurement, 30*, 61–70.

Kuhn, T.S. (1961). The function of measurement in modern physical science. In Woolf, H. (Ed.), *Quantification: A history of the meaning of measurement in the natural and social sciences* (pp. 31–63). New York: Bobbs-Merrill.

Kuiper, N.A. (1978). Depression and causal attributions for success and failure. *Journal of Personality and Social Psychology, 36*, 236–246.

Kuncel, R.B. (1973). Response processes and relative location of subject and item. *Educational and Psychological Measurement, 33*, 545–563.

Kuncel, R.B., & Fiske, D.W. (1974). Stability of response process and response. *Educational and Psychological Measurement, 34*, 743–755.

Kusyszyn, I., & Jackson, D.N. (1968). A multimethod factor analytic appraisal of endorsement and judgement methods in personality assessment. *Educational and Psychological Measurement, 28*, 1047–1061.

Langer, I., & Schulz von Thun, F. (1974). *Messung komplexer Merkmale in Psychologie und Pädagogik – Ratingverfahren*. Munich: Reinhardt.

Lay, C.H., & Jackson, D.N. (1969). Analysis of the generality of trait inferential relationships. *Journal of Personality and Social Psychology, 12*, 12–21.

Lay, C.H., Burron, B.F., & Jackson, D.N. (1973). Base rates and information value in impression formation: *Journal of Personality and Social Psychology, 28*, 390–395.

Layton, P., & Simpson, A.J. (1975). Surface and deep structure in sentence comprehension. *Journal of Verbal Learning and Verbal Behavior, 14*, 658–664.

Lazarsfeld, P.F. (1959). Latent structur analysis. In Koch, S. (Ed.), *Psychology: A study of a science* (Vol. 3, pp. 476–543). New York: McGraw-Hill.

Lazarus, R.S. (1983). Costs and benefits of denial. In Breznitz, S. (Ed.), *The denial of stress*. New York: International Universities.

Leary, T. (1957). *Interpersonal diagnosis of personality*. New York: Ronald Press.

Lennertz, E. (1973). Thesen zur Itemsammlung bei Persönlichkeitsfragebögen. In Reinert, G. (Ed.), *Bericht über den 27. Kongress der Deutschen Gesellschaft für Psychologie in Kiel 1973*. Göttingen: Hogrefe.

Lennox, R., & Wolfe, R. (1984). Revision of the Self-Monitoring scale. *Journal of Personality and Social Psychology, 46*, 1349–1364.

Lewinsohn, P.M., Mischel, W., Chaplain, W., & Barton, R. (1980). Social competence and depression: The role of illusory self-perceptions? *Journal of Abnormal Psychology, 89*, 203–212.

Lewis, M. (1967). The meaning of a response, or why researchers in infant-behavior should be oriental metaphysicians. *Merrill Palmer Quarterly, 13*, 7–18.

Liberty, P.G., Lunneborg, C.E., & Atkinson, G.C. (1964). Perceptual defense, dissimulation, and response styles. *Journal of Consulting Psychology, 28*, 529–537.

Lienert, G.A. (1969). *Testaufbau und Testanalyse* (3 rd ed.). Weinheim: Beltz.

Linden, W., Paulhus, D.L., & Dobson, K.E. (in press). The effect of response styles on the report of psychological and somatic distress. *Journal of Consulting and Clinical Psychology*.

Linehan, M.M., & Nielsen, S.L. (1981). Assessment of suicidal ideation and parasuicide: Hopelessness and social desirability. *Journal of Consulting and Clinical Psychology, 49*, 773–775.

Lingoes, J.C., & Roskam, E. (1973). Mathematical and empirical analysis of two multidimensional algorithms. *Psychometrica Monograph, 38*(4, Pt. 2).

Lockard, J.S., & Paulhus, D.L. (in press). *Self-deception: An adaptive mechanism?* New York, Prentice-Hall.

Löhr, F.J. (1977). *Formale und inhaltliche Merkmale von Fragebogen-items – Zum Einfluß von Itemeigenschaften auf den Beantwortungsprozess bei deutschen Persönlichkeitsfragebogen* (Vols. 1, 2). Bonn: Master's Thesis.

Löhr, F.J. (1983 a). *Häufigkeits- und Intensitätsadverbien in den Items von Persönlichkeitsfragebogen*. Bielefeld: Arbeitsberichte aus dem Projekt Persönlichkeitsfragebogen (No. 5), Universität Bielefeld.

Löhr, F.J. (1983 b). *Sprachlogische und empirische Beziehung in Persönlichkeitsfragebogen für Kinder. Eine empirische Untersuchung zur Bezugsebene der Items*. Arbeitsberichte aus dem Projekt Persönlichkeitsfragebogen, No. 6, Universität Bielefeld.

Löhr, F.J. (In preparation). *Die Bedeutung von Itemeigenschaften für den Prozess und das Ergebnis der Beantwortung von Persönlichkeitsfragebogen*. Bielefeld: Dissertation, Fakultät für Psychologie und Sportwissenschaft der Universität Bielefeld.

Löhr, F.J., & Angleitner, A. (1980). Eine Untersuchung zu sprachlichen Formulierungen der Items in deutschen Persönlichkeitsfragebogen. *Zeitschrift für Differentielle und Diagnostische Psychologie, 1*, 217–235.

Löhr, F.J., & Schütte, W. (1982). *Zur lingustischen Analyse von Fragebogenitems – eine Pilot-Studie*. Bielefeld: Arbeitsberichte aus dem Projekt Persönlichkeitsfragebogen (No. 1), Universität Bielefeld.

Loevinger, J. (1957). Objective tests as instruments of psychological theory. *Psychological Reports, 3*, 635–694.

Lord, F.M. (1952) The relation of the reliability of multiple-choice tests to the distribution of item difficulties. *Psychometrika, 17*, 181–194.

Lord, F.M. (1980). *Applications of item response theory to practical testing problems*. Hillsdale: Erlbaum.

Lumsden, J. (1977). Personal reliability. *Applied Psychological Measurement, 1*, 477–482.

Luteijn, F. (1974). *De konstruktie van een persoonlijkheidsvragenlijst (de N.P.V.)*. Groningen: Doctoral dissertation, University of Groningen.

Magnusson, D. (1980). Personality in an interactional paradigm of research. *Zeitschrift für Differentielle und Diagnostische Psychologie, 1*, 17–34.

Magnusson, D. (1981). *Toward a psychology of situations: An interactional perspective*. Hillsdale: Erlbaum.

Magnusson, D. (1982, May). Persons in situations: Some comments on a current issue. *European Conference on Personality,* Tilburg.
Magnusson, D. (1984). Persons in situations: Some comments on a current issue: In Bonarius, H.M., van Heck, G., & Smid, N. (Eds.), *Personality psychology in Europe: Theoretical and empirical developments.* Lisse: Swets & Zeitlinger.
Magnusson, D., & Endler, N.S. (1977). Interactional psychology: Present status and future prospects. In Magnusson, D., & Endler, N.S. (Eds.), *Personality at the cross-roads: Current issues in interactional psychology.* Hillsdale: Erlbaum.
McCann, D.D., Zanna, M.P., & Higgins, E.T. (1980): Attitude change following induced compliance: An individual difference perspective. *Meeting of the Canadian Psychological Association,* Calgary, June 1980.
McCrae, R.R. (1982). Consensual validation of personality traits: Evidence from self-reports and ratings. *Journal of Personality and Social Psychology, 43,* 293–303.
McCrae, R.R., & Costa, P.T. (1983). Social desirability scales: More substance than style. *Journal of Consulting and Clinical Psychology, 51,* 882–888.
McGowan, J., & Gormly, J. (1976). Validation of personality traits: A multicriteria approach. *Journal of Personality and Social Psychology, 34,* 791–795.
McGuire, W.J. (1960). A syllogistic analysis of cognitive relationships. In Rosenberg, M.J., Hovland, E.I., McGuire, W.J., Abelson, R.P., & Brehm, J.W. (Eds.), *Attitude organization and change.* New Haven: Yale University Press.
Meehl, P.E. (1945). The dynamics of "structured" personality tests. *Journal of Clinical Psychology, 1,* 296–303.
Meehl, P. (1970). Nuisance variables and the ex post facto design. In Radner, M., & Winokur, S. (Eds.), *Minnesota studies in the philosophy of science* (Vol. 4). Minneapolis: University of Minnesota Press.
Meehl, P.E. (1972). Reactions, reflections, projections. In Butcher, J.N. (Ed.), *Objective personality assessment: Changing perspectives* (pp. 131–189). New York: Academic.
Meehl, P.E., & Hathaway, S.R. (1946). The K-factor as a suppressor variable in the MMPI. *Journal of Applied Psychology, 30,* 525–564.
Mehler, J. (1963). Some effects of grammatical transformations on the recall of English sentences. *Journal of Verbal Learning and Verbal Behavior, 2,* 346–351.
Mellenbergh, G.J., & Pannekoek, J. (1979). *The moderator effect reconsidered.* Amsterdam: Report of the Psychological Laboratory, University of Amsterdam.
Mervis, C.B., & Rosch, E. (1981). Categorization of natural objects. *Annual Review of Psychology, 32,* 89–115.
Messick, S. (1960). Dimensions of social desirability. *Journal of Consulting Psychology, 24,* 279–287.
Messick, S. (1967). The psychology of acquiescence. In Berg, I.A. (Ed.), *Response set in personality assessment.* Chicago: Aldine.
Messick, S., & Jackson, D.N. (1961). Desirability scale values and dispersions for MMPI items. *Psychological Reports, 8,* 409–414.
Mezzich, J.E., Damarin, F.L., & Erickson, J.R. (1974). Comparative validity of strategies and indices for differential diagnosis of depressive states from other psychiatric conditions using the MMPI. *Journal of Consulting and Clinical Psychology, 42,* 691–698.
Micklin, M., & Durbin, M. (1969). Syntactic dimensions of attitude scaling techniques: Sources of variation and bias. *Sociometry, 32,* 194–206.
Miller, G.A. (1962). Some psychological studies of grammar. *American Psychologist, 17,* 748–762.
Millham, J. (1974). Two components of need for approval score and their relationship to cheating following success and failure. *Journal of Research in Personality, 8,* 378–392.
Millham, J., & Jacobson, L.I. (1978). The need for approval. In Kondon, H., & Exner, J.E. (Eds.). *Dimensions of personality.* New York: Wiley.
Millham, J., & Kellogg, R.W. (1980). Need for social approval: Impression management or self-deception? *Journal of Research in Personality, 14,* 445–457.

Mills, C., & Hogan, R. (1978). A role theoretical interpretation of personality scale item responses. *Journal of Personality, 46*, 778–785.
Mirels, H.L. (1976). Implicit personality theory and inferential illusions. *Journal of Personality, 44*, 467–487.
Mirels, H.L. (1982a). The illusory nature of implicit personality theory. Logical and empirical considerations. *Journal of Personality, 50*, 203–222.
Mirels, H.L. (1982b). Tenacious inferential illusions: Experimental facts vs. critical fancy. *Journal of Personality, 50*, 245–250.
Mischel, T. (1974). Understanding neurotic behavior: From "Mechanism" to "Intentionality". In Mischel, T. (Ed.), *Understanding other persons* (pp. 216–259). Oxford: Blackwell.
Mischel, W. (1968). *Personality and assessment*. New York: Wiley.
Mischel, W. (1972). Direct vs indirect personality assessment: Evidence and implications. *Journal of Consulting and Clinical Psychology, 38*, 319–324.
Mischel, W. (1977). The interaction of persons and situation. In Magnusson, D., & Endler, N.S. (Eds.), *Personality at the cross-roads: Current issues in interactional psychology*. Hillsdale: Erlbaum.
Mischel, W., & Peake, P.K. (1982). Beyond deja vu in the search for cross-situational consistency. *Psychological Review, 89*, 730–755.
Mittenecker, E., & Toman, W. (1951). Der P.I.-Test. *Beihefte zur Wiener Zeitschrift für Philosophie, Psychologie, Pädagogik, 1*.
Monson, T.C., Hesley, J.W., & Chernick, L. (1982). Specifying when personality traits can and cannot predict behavior: An alternative to abandoning the attempt to predict single-act criteria. *Journal of Personality and Social Psychology, 43*, 385–399.
Morf, M.E., & Jackson, D.N. (1972). An analysis of two response styles: True responding and item endorsement. *Educational and Psychological Measurement, 32*, 329–353.
Moskowitz, D.S. (1982). Coherence and cross-situational generality in personality: A new analysis of old problems. *Journal of Personality and Social Psychology, 43*, 754–768.
Mulaik, S.A. (1964). Are personality factors raters' conceptual factors? *Journal of Consulting Psychology, 28*, 506–511.
Murphy, G. (1975). *Outgrowing self-deception*. New York: Basic Books.
Nelson, R.E., & Craighead, W.E. (1977). Selective recall of positive and negative feedback, self-control behaviors and depression. *Journal of Abnormal Psychology, 86*, 397–388.
Nisbett, R.E. (1980). The trait construct in lay and professional psychology. In Festinger, L. (Ed.), *Retrospections on social psychology*. New York: Oxford University Press.
Nisbett, R.E., & Ross, L. (1980). *Human inference: Strategies and shortcomings*. Englewood Cliffs: Prentice-Hall.
Nisbett, R.E., & Wilson, T.D. (1977). Telling more than we can know: Verbal reports on mental processes. *Psychological Review, 84*, 231–259.
Norman, W.T. (1967). On estimating psychological relationships: Social desirability and self report. *Psychological Bulletin, 67*, 273–293.
Norman, W.T. (1969). "To see ourselves as others see us!": Relations among self-perceptions, peer-perceptions, and expected peer-perceptions of personality attributes. *Multivariate Behavioral Research, 4*, 417–443.
Norman, W.T., & Goldberg, L.R. (1966). Raters, ratees and randomness in personality structure. *Journal of Personality and Social Psychology, 4*, 681–691.
Nowakowska, M. (1970). A model of answering to a questionnaire item. *Acta Psychologica, 34*, 420–439.
Nunnally, J.C. (1978). *Psychometric theory* (2nd ed.). New York: McGraw-Hill.
Olweus, D.A. (1977). A critical analysis of the "modern" interactionist position. In Magnusson, D., & Endler, N.S. (Eds.), *Personality at the cross-roads: Current issues in interactional psychology*. Hillsdale: Erlbaum.
Overall, J.E. (1974). Validity of the Psychological Screening Inventory for psychiatric screening. *Journal of Consulting and Clinical Psychology, 42*, 717–719.

Palmer, W.H. (1970). *Actuarial MMPI Interpretation: A replication and extension.* Doctoral dissertation, University of Alabama, Birmingham, AL.

Passini, F.T., & Norman, W.T. (1966). A universal conception of personality structure. *Journal of Personality and Social Psychology, 4*, 44–49.

Paulhus, D.L. (1981). Control of social desirability in personality inventories: Principal-factor deletion. *Journal of Research in Personality, 15*, 383–388.

Paulhus, D.L. (1982). Individual differences, self-presentation, and cognitive dissonance: Their concurrent operation in forced compliance. *Journal of Personality and Social Psychology, 43*, 838–852.

Paulhus, D.L. (1983). Sphere-specific measures of perceived control. *Journal of Personality and Social Psychology, 44*, 1253–1265.

Paulhus, D.L. (1984a). Two-component models of socially desirable responding. *Journal of Personality Assessment, 46*, 598–609.

Paulhus, D.L. (1984b). Self-deception: An information-processing model. *Meeting of the American Psychological Association,* Toronto.

Paunonen, S.V., & Jackson, D.N. (1979). Nonverbal trait inference. *Journal of Personality and Social Psychology, 37*, 1645–1659.

Pawlik, K. (1973). Right answers to wrong questions? A re-examination of factor analytic personality research and its contribution to personality theory. In Royce, J.R. (Ed.), *Multivariate analysis and psychological theory.* London: Academic.

Pawlik, K. (1979). Der „Interaktionismus" aus verhaltenswissenschaftlicher Sicht. In Eckensberger, H. (Ed.), *Bericht über den 31. Kongress der Deutschen Gesellschaft für Psychologie in Mannheim,* 1978, (Vol. 1). Göttingen: Hogrefe.

Payne, F.D. (1970). *Structured personality inventory items: Test-retest response consistency and item properties.* Urbana-Champaign: Ph. D. Thesis, University of Illinois.

Payne, F.D., Wiggins, J.S. (1972). MMPI profile types and the self-report of psychiatric patients. *Journal of Abnormal Psychology, 78*, 1–8.

Pepper, S. (1981). Problems in the quantification of frequency expressions. In Fiske, D.W. (Ed.), *New directions for methodology of social and behavioral science: problems with language imprecision* (No. 9). San Francisco: Jossey-Bass.

Peterson, C.C., & Peterson, J.L. (1976). Linguistic determinants of the difficulty of true-false test items. *Educational and Psychological Measurement, 36*, 161–169.

Peterson, D.R. (1965). Scope and generality of verbally defined personality factors. *Psychological Review, 72*, 48–59.

Phares, E.J., & Lamiell, J.T. (1974). Relationship of internal-external control to defensive preferences. *Journal of Consulting and Clinical Psychology, 42*, 872–878.

Phares, E.J., Ritchie, D.E., & Davis, W.L. (1968). Internal-external control and reaction to threat. *Journal of Personality and Social Psychology, 10*, 402–405.

Price, R.H., & Bouffard, D.L. (1974). Behavioral appropriateness and situational constraint as dimensions of social behavior. *Journal of Personality and Social Psychology, 30*, 579–586.

Pryor, J.B., Gibbons, F.X., Wicklund, R.A., Fazio, R.H., & Hood, R. (1977). Self-focussed attention and self-report validity. *Journal of Personality, 45*, 513–527.

Reilly, R.R., & Echternacht, G.J. (1979). Validation and comparison of homogeneous and occupational interest scales. *Applied Psychological Measurement, 3*, 177–185.

Rezmovic, E.L., & Rezmovic, V. (1980). Empirical validation of psychological constructs: A secondary analysis. *Psychological Bulletin, 87*, 66–71.

Rezmovic, E.L., & Rezmovic, V. (1981). A confirmatory factor analysis approach to construct validation. *Educational and Psychological Measurement, 41*, 61–72.

Rock, D.L. (1981). The confounding of two self-report assertiveness measures with the tendency to give socially desirable responses in self-description. *Journal of Consulting and Clinical Psychology, 49*, 743–744.

Roe, R.A. (1983). *Grondslagen der personeelsselektie.* Assen: Van Grocum.

Rogers, C.R. (1959). A theory of therapy, personality and interpersonal relationships as developed in the client-centered framework. In Koch, S. (Ed.), *Psychology: A study of a science* (Vol. 3). New York: McGraw-Hill.
Rogers, T.B. (1971). The process of responding to personality items: Some issues, a theory and some research. *Multivariate Behavioral Research Monographs, 6*(2).
Rogers, T.B. (1973). Ratings of content as a means of assessing personality items. *Educational and Psychological Measurement, 33,* 845–858.
Rogers, T.B. (1974a). An analysis of two central stages underlying responding to personality items: The self-referent decision and response selection. *Journal of Research in Personality, 8,* 128–138.
Rogers, T.B. (1974b). An analysis of the stages underlying the process of responding to personality items. *Acta Psychologica, 38,* 205–213.
Rogers, T.B. (1977). Self-reference in memory: Recognition of personality items. *Journal of Research in Personality, 11,* 295–305.
Rorer, L.G. (1965). The great response style myth. *Psychological Bulletin, 63,* 129–156.
Rorer, L.G., & Goldberg, L.R. (1965). Acquiescence in the MMPI? *Educational and Psychological Measurement, 25,* 801–817.
Ross, L. (1977). The intuitive psychologist and his shortcomings: Distortion in the attribution process. In Berkowitz, L. (Ed.). *Advances in experimental social psychology* (Vol. 10). New York: Academic.
Roth, D.L., & Ingram, R.E. (1985). Factors in the Self-Deception Questionnaire: Associations with depression. *Journal of Personality and Social Psychology, 48,* 243–251.
Rotter, J.B. (1966). Generalized expectancies for internal vs external control of reinforcement. *Psychological Monographs, 80,* No. 1 (Whole No. 609).
Rowe, D.C. (1982). Monozygotic twin cross-correlations as validation of personality structure: A test of the semantic bias hypothesis. *Journal of Personality and Social Psychology, 43,* 1072–1079.
Ruch, F.L. (1941). A technique for detecting attempts to fake performance on a self-inventory type of personality test. In McNemar, Q., & Merrill, M.A. (Eds.), *Studies in personality* (pp. 229–234). New York: McGraw-Hill.
Rushton, J.P., Jackson, D.N., & Paunonen, S.V. (1981). Personality: Nomothetic or idiographic? A response to Kenrick & Stringfield. *Psychological Review, 88,* 582–589.
Sachs, J.S. (1967). Recognition memory for syntactic and semantic aspects of connected discourse. *Perception and Psychophysics, 2,* 437–442.
Sackeim, H.A. (1983). Self-deception, self-esteem, and depression: The adaptive value lying to oneself. In Masling, J. (Ed.), *Empirical studies of psychoanalytic theories.* Hillsdale: Erlbaum.
Sackeim, H.A., & Gur, R.C. (1978). Self-deception, self-confrontation and consciousness. In Schwartz, G.E., & Shapiro, D. (Eds.), *Consciousness and self-regulation: Advances in research* (Vol. 2, pp. 139–197). New York: Plenum.
Sackeim, H.A., & Gur, R.C. (1979). Self-deception, other-deception, and self-reported psychopathology. *Journal of Consulting and Clinical Psychology, 47,* 213–215.
Sarason, I.G., Levine, H.M., Basham, R.B., & Sarason, B. (1983). Assessing social support: The social support questionnaire. *Journal of Personality and Social Psychology, 44,* 127–139.
Sarbin, T.R. (1981). On self-deception. *Annals of the New York Academy of Sciences, 364,* 206–235.
Sartre, J.P. (1966). *Being and nothingness* (H. Barnes, Trans.). New York: Washington Square (Original work published 1943).
Saunders, D.R. (1956). Moderator variables in prediction. *Educational and Psychological Measurement, 16,* 209–222.
Schanberger, W.J. (1967). A motivational distortion scale for the Sixteen Personality Factor Questionnaire. *Meeting of the Western Psychological Association,* San Francisco.
Schank, R.C. (1975). *Conceptual information processing.* Amsterdam: North-Holland.

Schmitt, N. (1978). Path analysis of multitrait-multimethod matrices. *Applied Psychological Measurement, 2*, 157–173.
Schmitt, N., Coyle, B.W., Saari, B.B. (1977). A review and critique of analyses of multitrait-multimethod matrices. *Multivariate Behavioral Research, 12*, 447–478.
Schneider, D.J. (1973). Implicit personality theory: A review. *Psychological Bulletin, 79*, 294–309.
Schneider-Düker, M., & Schneider, J.F. (1977). Untersuchung zum Beantwortungsprozess bei psycho-diagnostischen Fragebogen. *Zeitschrift für experimentelle und angewandte Psychologie, 24*, 282–302.
Schwarzer, R. (1982, June). Convergent and discriminant validity in personality assessment: Techniques for distinguishing trait and method variance. *Bielefeld Symposium on Personality Questionnaires,* Bielefeld.
Schwarzer, R. (1984). Worry and emotionality as separate components in test anxiety. *International Review of Applied Psychology, 33*, 205–220.
Schwarzer, R., & Schwarzer, C. (1982). Achievement anxiety with respect to reference groups in school. *Journal of Educational Research, 75*, 305–308.
Schwarzer, R., Jerusalem, M., & Lange, B. (1982). A longitudinal study of worry and emotionality. In Schwarzer, R., van der Ploeg, H., & Spielberger, C.D. (Eds.), *Advances in test anxiety research* (Vol. 1). Lisse: Swets & Zeitlinger.
Shaffner, D.R., Smith, J.E., & Tomarelli, M. (1982). Self-monitoring as a determinant of self-disclosure reciprocity during the acquaintances process. *Journal of Personality and Social Psychology, 43,* 163–175.
Sherman, M.A. (1976). Adjectival negation and the comprehension of multiply negated sentences. *Journal of Verbal Learning and Verbal Behavior, 5*, 219–227.
Shrauger, J.S., & Osberg, T.M. (1981). The relative accuracy of self-prediction and judgements by others in psychological assessment. *Psychological Bulletin, 90*, 322–351.
Shweder, R.A. (1975). How relevant is an individual difference theory of personality? *Journal of Personality, 43*, 455–484.
Shweder, R.A. (1977a). Illusory correlation and the MMPI controversy (Commentaries by Jack Block and Allan Edwards). *Journal of Consulting and Clinical Psychology, 45*, 917–924.
Shweder, R.A. (1977b). Illusory correlation and the MMPI controvercy: Author's reply to some of the allusions and illusions in Block's and Edward's commentaries. *Journal of Consulting and Clinical Psychology, 45*, 936–940.
Shweder, R.A. (1982). Fact and artifact in trait-perception: The systematic distortion hypothesis. *Progress in Experimental Personality Research, 11*, 65–100.
Shweder, R.A., & D'Andrade, R.G. (1979). Accurate reflection or systematic distortion? A reply to Block, Weiss, and Thorne. *Journal of Personality and Social Psychology, 37*, 1075–1084.
Shweder, R.A., & D'Andrade, R.G. (1980). The systematic distortion hypothesis. In Shweder, R.A. (Ed.), *Fallible judgement in behavioral research.* New directions for methodology of social and behavioral science (Vol. 4). San Francisco: Jossey-Bass.
Slobin, D.J. (1966). Grammatical transformations and sentence comprehension in childhood and adulthood. *Journal of Verbal and Learning and Verbal Behavior, 5*, 219–227.
Slobin, D.J. (1968). Recall of full and truncated passive sentences in connected discourse. *Journal of Verbal Learning and Verbal Behavior, 7*, 876–881.
Smith, E.R., & Miller, F.D. (1978). Limits on perceptions of cognitive processes: A reply to Nisbett and Wilson. *Psychological Review, 85*, 355–362.
Snyder, M. (1974). Self-monitoring of expressive behavior. *Journal of Personality and Social Psychology, 30*, 526–537.
Snyder, M. (1979). Self-monitoring processes. *Advances in Experimental Social Psychology, 12*, 85–128.
Snyder, M., & Gangestad, S. (1982). Choosing social situations: Two investigations of self-monitoring processes. *Journal of Personality and Social Psychology, 43*, 123–135.

Snyder, M., & Monson, T.C. (1975). Persons, situations, and the control of social behavior. *Journal of Personality and Social Psychology, 32*, 637–644.

Snyder, M., & Tanke, E.D. (1976). Behavior and attitude: Some people are more consistent than others. *Journal of Personality, 44*, 501–517.

Sockloff, A.L. (1976). The analysis of non-linearity via linear regression with polynomial and product variables: An examination. *Review of Educational Research, 46*, 267–291.

Spielberger, C.D. (1979). *State-trait personality inventory*. Preliminary professional manual. University of South Florida, Tampa, FL.

Spreen, O. (1963). *MMPI: Saarbrücken. Handbuch zur deutschen Ausgabe des Minnesota Multiphasic Personality Inventory*. Bern: Huber.

Stagner, R. (1977). On the reality and relevance of traits. *Journal of General Psychology, 96*, 185–207.

Stern, G.G. (1970). *People in context: Measuring person-environment congruence in education and industry*. New York: Wiley.

Sternberg, R.J. (1979). The nature of mental abilities. *American Psychologist, 34*, 214–230.

Sternberg, R.J. (1981). Testing and cognitive psychology. *American Psychologist, 36*, 1181–1189.

Stones, M.J., & Burt, D. (1978). Quasi-statistical inference in rating behavior. *Journal of Research in Personality, 12*, 381–389.

Stricker, L.J., Jacobs, P.I., & Kogan, N. (1974). Trait interrelations and implicit personality theories and questionnaire data. *Journal of Personality and Social Psychology, 30*, 198–207.

Strosahl, K.D., Linehan, M.M., & Chiles, J.A. (1984). Will the real social desirability scale please stand up? Hopelessness, depression, social desirability, and the prediction of suicidal behavior. *Journal of Consulting and Clinical Psychology, 52*, 449–457.

Stumpf, H., Angleitner, A., Wieck, T., Jackson, D.N., & Beloch-Till, H. (1985). *Deutsche "Personality Research Form" (PRF)*. Göttingen: Hogrefe.

Sudman, S., & Bradburn, N.M. (1982). *Asking questions: A practical guide to questionnaire design*. San Francisco: Jossey-Bass.

Tabachnik, N., Crocker, J., & Alloy, L. (1983). Depression, social comparison and the consensus effect. *Journal of Personality and Social Psychology, 45*, 688–699.

Taylor, J.B., Carithers, M., & Coyne, L. (1976). MMPI performance, response set, and the „self-concept" hypothesis. *Journal of Consulting and Clinical Psychology, 44*, 351–362.

Taylor, S.E. (1983). Adjustment to threatening events: A theory of cognitive adaptation. *American Psychologist, 38*, 1161–1173.

Tesser, A., & Paulus, D.L. (1976). Toward a causal model of love. *Journal of Personality and Social Psychology, 34*, 1095–1105.

Tesser, A., & Paulhus, D.L. (1983). The definition of self: private and public self-evaluation maintenance strategies. *Journal of Personality and Social Psychology, 44*, 672–682.

Tesser, A., & Rosen, S. (1974). The reluctance to transmit bad news. In Berkowitz, L. (Ed.), *Advances in experimental social psychology* (Vol. 8). New York: Academic.

Thurstone, L.L. (1928). The measurement of opinion. *Journal of Abnormal and Social Psychology, 22*, 415–430.

Timm, U. (1968). Reliabilität und Faktorenstruktur von Cattells 16 PF-Test bei einer deutschen Stichprobe. *Zeitschrift für experimentelle und angewandte Psychologie, 15*, 354–373.

Tränkle, U. (1982). Über Zusammenhänge zwischen der sprachlichen Schwierigkeit von Fragebogen-Items, teststatistischen Gütekriterien und Beantwortungsverhalten. *Diagnostica, 28*, 289–306.

Tucker, L.R. (1958). An inter-battery method of factor analysis. *Psychometrika, 23*, 111–136.

Tucker, L.R., & Lewis, C. (1973). A reliability coefficient for maximum likelihood factor analysis. *Psychometrika, 38*, 1–10.

Turner, C., & Fiske, D.W. (1968). Item quality and appropriateness of response processes. *Educational and Psychological Measurement, 28*, 297–315.

Turner, C., & Krauss, E. (1978). Fallible indicators of the subjective state of the nation. *American Psychologist, 33*, 456–470.

Turner, R.G. (1978). Consistency, self-consciousness, and the predictive validity of typical and maximal personality measures. *Journal of Research in Personality, 12*, 117–132.

Turner, R.G. (1981). Using subject generated descriptors. In Fiske, D. (Ed.), *New directions for methodology of social and behavioral science: problems with language imprecision* (No. 9). San Francisco: Jossey-Bass.

Turner, R.G., & Gilliland, L. (1979). The comparative relevance and predictive validity of subject generated trait descriptions. *Journal of Personality, 47*, 230–244.

Tyler, L.E. (1973). *Response stability, person-item distance and homogeneity*. Chicago: Doctoral dissertation, University of Chicago.

Tzeng, O.C.S. (1982). The artificial dispute over implicit personality theory: An answer to Jackson, Stricker, and Mirels. *Journal of Personality, 50*, 251–260.

Tzeng, O.C.S., & Tzeng, C.-H. (1982). Implicit personality theory: Myth or fact? An illustration of how empirical research can miss. *Journal of Personality, 50*, 223–239.

Van Heck, J. (1984). The construction of a general taxonomy of situations. In Bonarius, H.M., & Smid, N. (Eds.), *Personality psychology in Europe: Theoretical and empirical developments*. Lisse: Swets & Zeitlinger.

Voyce, C.D., & Jackson, D.N. (1977). An evaluation of a threshold theory for personality assessment. *Educational and Psychological Measurement, 37*, 383–408.

Wachtel, P.L. (1973). Psychodynamics, behavior therapy and the implacable experimenter: An inquiry into the consistency of personality. *Journal of Psychology, 82*, 324–334.

Wainer, H. (1976). Estimating coefficients in linear models: It don't make no nevermind. *Psychological Bulletin, 83*, 213–217.

Wason, P.C., & Johnson-Laird, P.N. (1972). *Psychology of reasoning. Structure and content*. London: Batsford.

Watson, G.B. (1933). New steps in personality measurement. *Character and Personality, 2*, 66–73.

Weigel, R.H., & Newman, L.S. (1976). Increasing attitude-behavior correspondence by broadening the scope of the behavioral measure. *Journal of Personality and Social Psychology, 33*, 793–802.

Weiner, B. (1978). Achievement strivings. In H. London & Exner J.E. (Eds.), *Dimensions of personality*. New York: Academic Press.

Weinert, A.B. (1982). *Deutscher CPI: Testanweisung und Test*. Bern: Huber.

Welsh, G.S. (1956). Factor dimensions A and R. In Welsh, G.S., & Dahlstrom, W.G. (Eds.), *Basic readings on the MMPT in psychology and medicine*. Minneapolis: University of Minnesota Press.

Wiggins, J.S. (1959). Interrelationships among MMPI measures of dissimulation under standard and social desirability instructions. *Journal of Consulting Psychology, 23*, 419–427.

Wiggins, J.S. (1964). Convergences among stylistic measures from objective personality tests. *Educational and Psychological Measurement, 24*, 551–562.

Wiggins, J.S. (1966). Substantive dimensions of self-report in the MMPI item pool. *Psychological Monographs, 80* (22, Whole No. 630).

Wiggins, J.S. (1973). *Personality and prediction: Principles of personality assessment*. Reading: Addison-Wesley.

Wiggins, J.S. (1979). A psychological taxonomy of trait descriptive terms: The interpersonal domain. *Journal of Personality and Social Psychology, 37*, 395–412.

Wiggins, J.S. (1980). Circumplex models of interpersonal behavior. In Wheeler, L. (Ed.), *Review of personality and social psychology* (Vol. 1). Beverly Hills: Sage.

Wiggins, J.S. (1981). Clinical and statistical prediction: Where are we and where do we go from here? *Clinical Psychology Review, 1*, 3–18.

Wiggins, J.S. (1984). The "mere" semantics of social perception. In Hampson, S.E. (Chair), *The social construction of personality*. Symposium on the Social Construction of Personality held at the Second European Conference on Personality, Bielefeld.

Wiggins, J.S., & Broughton, R. (1985). The interpersonal circle: A structural model for the integration of personality research. In Hogan, R., & Jones, W.H. (Eds.), *Perspectives in personality: Theory, measurement and interpersonal dynamics* (Vol. 1). Greenwich: JAI.

Wiggins, J.S., & Goldberg, L.R. (1965). Interrelationship among MMPI item characteristics. *Educational and Psychological Measurement, 25*, 381–397.

Wilde, G.J.S. (1962). *Neurotische labiliteit gemeten volgens de vragenlijstmethode*. Amsterdam: Doctoral dissertation, University of Amsterdam.

Willerman, L., Turner, R.P., & Peterson, M. (1976). A comparison of the predictive validity of typical and maximal personality measure. *Journal of Research in Personality, 10*, 482–492.

Winder, P., O-Dell, J., & Karson, S. (1975). New motivational distortion scales for the 16-PF. *Journal of Personality Assessment, 39*, 532–537.

Winne, P.H., & Marx, R.W. (1981). Convergent and discriminant validity in self-concept measurement. Annual Meeting of the *AERA*, Los Angeles.

Zanna, M.P., Olson, J.M., & Fazio, R.H. (1980). Attitude-behavior consistency – An individual difference perspective. *Journal of Personality and Social Psychology, 38*, 432–440.

Zedeck, S. (1971). Problems with the use of "moderator"-variables. *Psychological Bulletin, 76*, 295–310.

Zerbe, W., & Paulhus, D.L. (1984). Social desirability effects in organizational research: A review and extension. (Manuscript under review).

Author Index

Page numbers in *italics* refer to the bibliography

Subject Index

MIX
Papier aus verantwortungsvollen Quellen
Paper from responsible sources
FSC® C105338

If you have any concerns about our products,
you can contact us on
ProductSafety@springernature.com

In case Publisher is established outside the EU,
the EU authorized representative is:
Springer Nature Customer Service Center GmbH
Europaplatz 3, 69115 Heidelberg, Germany

Printed by Libri Plureos GmbH
in Hamburg, Germany